Rainer Maria Rilke

CREATIVE ANGUISH OF A MODERN POET

RAINER MARIA
RILKE

Creative Anguish of a Modern Poet

BY

W. L. GRAFF

PRINCETON, NEW JERSEY
PRINCETON UNIVERSITY PRESS

1956

Printed in the United States of America
by Princeton University Press at Princeton, N.J.

◇◇

PREFACE

◇◇

RILKE is sometimes called a phenomenon—which means, I suppose, that he simply happened like a phenomenon of nature, that his manner of being was beyond the control of human devices and calculation, including his own. We also speak of a phenomenon with reference to something unique and outstanding, a sort of freak of nature which can come about only through the simultaneous action of many forces in a remarkable coincidence of circumstances. On both counts Rilke qualifies for the denotation.

He is also often described as a paradox, and this designation, too, is fitting. His personality, his mode of experiencing and of expressing himself, belie and contradict much that we are accustomed to deeming reasonable, probable, or even possible. He never occupied a salaried or wage-earning position, had very few possessions, yet he never starved and always had a roof over his head; he travelled extensively in Europe and Northern Africa, was welcomed in the homes of the noble and rich, became the friend of some of the greatest writers and artists of Europe and the counsellor of hundreds of people in their moments of joy and distress. Rilke's sole function in life was that of being a lyrical poet, pure and simple, in a world dominated by economic and technical skills. And his great poetic genius seems to have sprung out of arid soil, lacking those fertile ingredients with which a cultural tradition of family and home enriches its heirs.

Therefore, if we wish to appreciate what he was and what he achieved we must try to identify and interpret the forces and circumstances which combined to produce him, and we must do so with a mind open for the paradox. With reference to the *Sonnets to Orpheus* Katharina Kippenberg writes that more than others he was his own mysterious law, and that his art was still more so. We should certainly go astray if we were to rely merely on systematic conceptual patterns, on conventional or personal ideals, be they of a philosophical or psychological nature. Our categories of understanding must be evolved out of the paradoxical phenomenon which Rilke was.

{ v }

An attempt of this sort cannot ignore the dangers inherent in all interpretation; complete objectivity would not only be impossible but undesirable. Interpretation, however, is not synonymous with speculation; it has been the author's special concern to keep his eyes constantly focussed on the whole context of available facts and realities. My aim is not to criticize in the sense of finding fault but to understand and to help understand, without succumbing blindly to the engaging imagery and music of Rilke's word. If my approach has at times a disenchanting effect, I hope that it does not conceal my genuine appreciation, but will serve to emphasize my deep regard for what under all circumstances must constitute the basis of enlightened praise: perspective and truth. As Marcel Brion points out, it ought not to impair our ultimate praise of a beautiful carpet, that we stop now and then to examine its reverse side. Rilke has become a controversial figure, arousing feelings which range from unadulterated worship through love and appreciation to plain dislike. Nothing can be gained, either for him or for his audience, by too idealistic and hagiographic accounts. If his work cannot survive the truth it will not survive at all. And for the understanding of a poet who time and again insists on his creative achievements being rooted in his blood it would be fatal in the long run to ignore their intimate origin, no matter how disturbing its nature proves to be. The future will tell whether his genius, seen in true perspective, will continue to demand attention and admiration. I shall feel rewarded if my appraisal contributes in some small measure to elucidating the issue. Fortunately the broad implications of Rilke's moods and thoughts are no longer a matter of mere conjecture. Relationships which not many years ago could only be surmised because of insufficient evidence have now been openly disclosed and widely confirmed.

I have written this book in English in order to suit the increasing number of people whose interest in Rilke is not matched by a corresponding knowledge of German. At the same time there is little doubt that, seen from abroad and, especially, against the background of a tradition and a language which were notoriously foreign to him, the physiognomy of Rilke and his world emerges with a more or less different distribution of light and shadow. For these reasons I may be forgiven for refraining from quoting in German, although the references are, of course, to the German originals. With very few exceptions, clearly identified by the references, the translations are mine and, on the whole, no claim is made for them except that of adequate correspondence of meaning.

To the Rilke scholar I owe perhaps some explanation or even apology for quoting the poet's words so freely with an apparent disregard of chronology. It is hoped that my reason and justification for doing so will be understood to conform to my conception of Rilke's pervasively concentric growth. In retrospect his mature symbols very often present the best formulae for the characterization of moods which in their earlier stages lacked full articulation. Where chronology matters it has been given due consideration.

The basic pervasiveness of Rilke's motifs also accounts for the way in which the material in this book is arrayed and articulated: as a progressive thickening of substance which ultimately reveals the fruit to be contained in the seed. The method is bound to entail a certain redundance as the circle gradually widens and fills, displaying enmeshed relationships and parallelisms by which the end is linked to the beginning. It also explains the careful attention given to Rilke's childhood and adolescent years, a feature which will, I believe, be especially appreciated by readers with a limited experience of German, since little of the poet's earlier writings is available in translation.

In order to avoid the awkwardness of numerous footnotes, the references are given parenthetically in abbreviations within the text, and the key to the abbreviations may be found at the back of the book starting on page 337. Moreover, the references have been kept at a minimum, especially in the first part of the book where early cycles of poems are paraphrased. The bibliography, which is here combined with the key to abbreviations, has been limited to the items currently referred to and, in a separate bibliography, to selected translations in English from Rilke's works and to the small number of books in English on Rilke. The vast literature to which I am indebted in one way or another could hardly be included in detail; nor need it be, since Ritzer's bibliographical work and von Mises' *Rilke in English* are available to the scholar. Besides, while acknowledging my debt to many unmentioned studies of Rilke, I have relied for my interpretation on Rilke's own works and on those factual reports and epistolary publications whose authenticity is beyond question; they are accounted for in the references.

I take much pleasure in thanking all those who by their interest and their moral or material support have contributed to making the completion of this work not only possible but a joyful task: to my colleague in the Department of German, Professor B. Meyer, for her secretarial help and relevant suggestions; to the Committee on Research of McGill University for financial assistance; to Professors D. L. Thomson, Dean of the Faculty of Graduate Studies and Research, and H. Files, of the Department of English, for valuable comment with regard to both form and contents of the manuscript; to Professor M. Mladenovic, of the Department of History, for his scrutiny of the chapters on Rilke's experience of Russia; and to Professor D. O. Hebb, of the Department of Psychology, for advice on the introductory chapter on childhood. I am also grateful to Mr. Richard Pennington, McGill University Librarian, and to the staff of the Redpath Library for their generous cooperation at all times.

For permission to quote a few lengthy passages I thank the publishing firms of Methuen & Co., London, England, and J. Mader, Gmunden-Bad Ischl, Austria, while I owe a special debt of gratitude to the Insel Verlag, Wiesbaden, Germany, and to the poet's daughter, Mrs. Ruth Fritzsche-Rilke, for their kindness in allowing me to reproduce and translate so profusely from a large number of books relevant to my subject. Last but not least, I pay homage to Mr. Benjamin F. Houston of Princeton University Press for the painstaking care with which he has edited the difficult manuscript and for the unruffled composure with which he has met the author's recurrent spurts of impatience.

McGill University, Montreal
February 1956

W.L.G.

CONTENTS

CONTENTS

Rainer Maria Rilke

CREATIVE ANGUISH OF A
MODERN POET

PRELUDE

CHILDHOOD is of the greatest importance in Rilke's life and work. This fact emerges even from a casual acquaintance with his writings and is, in theory, recognized by all Rilke scholars. Yet too often his thoughts are taken out of their organic context and endowed with general validity or proposed as norms of life. Such a procedure easily results in misunderstandings and confusion. There is no doubt that Rilke meant his poetry to have existential significance for himself; poetry was his most genuine way of being. And since he was himself deeply involved in the basic problems of life and death and, at the same time, happened to be a great poet, his often visionary reflections acquire intensely challenging implications also from a general human point of view. But in assessing these views it is imperative to realize that they did not develop by rational analysis or philosophic contemplation, that they remain steeped in sensuous experience which is by many underground channels connected with childhood dreams and adolescent ambitions. As Edmond Jaloux points out, Rilke's "consciousness is not logical, dissociative and deductive, like that of Proust; on the contrary, it is intuitive . . . agglutinative" (*Rec.*, 132). And Madame Saint-Hubert remarks that he "risks the remotest and most complicated deductions, without taking the detour of the intellectual combination: he does not leave the precincts of his sensation" (*Rec.*, 131; Silvaire-Vigée, 148ff). The result is a peculiar mixture of alogical intuition and reflective awareness.

The available information about Rilke's early years is exasperatingly scant and difficult to come by. In his own work there are few references to concrete childhood experiences. Rudolf Kassner, a friend and a man of keen insight, was so thoroughly convinced of the decisive role which childhood played in the poet's creative processes that he urged him to put down the story of it in words (*Das Inselschiff*, 122-123). But Rilke never produced anything in the nature of *Dichtung und Wahrheit*. The specific incidents which he does mention may be significant enough, but they are offered more or less as indicators in a broad psychological context in which chronology is irrelevant. For Rilke childhood was something so uncanny, so full of obscure anxieties, yet so rich and powerful, so replete with "white" joys, that he never tired in his attempts to evoke it, while at the same time he shunned with the fears of a nightmare everything that might unfold it in rational clarity. Kassner rightly points out a strong tendency to psychoanalytical self-treatment in Rilke's character and work (*Br.MTT*, xxxivff), but that tendency unquestionably functioned in the service and within the limits of his creative art; it by no means demanded systematic or scientific analysis. As Rilke puts it, scientific psychoanalysis might perhaps banish the demons but would most certainly drive out the angels as well (*Br. 1907-14*, 193).

Rilke's poetic symbols are the end-products of a slow and largely subconscious absorption of originally concrete and sensuous experiences. He calls them lyrical totals which cannot be itemized, because the single components and their interpenetration are usually too remote and too numerous to be clearly identifiable (*Br. Muzot*, 230). Therefore, we must approach his work as we would a finished piece of lace-work or tapestry. Without neglecting whatever external evidence is at hand, we must try as best we can to trace the threads and patterns back to their source by a careful interpretation of his poetic motifs and of his own confessions. Writing about his *Stories of God* (*Br. Frühzeit*, 92), he says that they "contain much childhood (not in the form of action, but in the form of atmosphere, anguish, and charm)," and that applies in a large measure to his whole work. With these considerations in mind let us recall some of the chief characteristics of childhood in general and of its significance in the life of man.

The human organism from the earliest stages of its existence is at the same time creative and receptive. Vital energies, the source and nature of which are little known, activate the child's whole being and reveal a remarkable ability to give shape and form to everything that comes within their reach. The child's senses are wide open to an ever-widening world of forms and sounds, of movements and things in which it finds itself immersed. According to its needs and the laws of its organism it absorbs, reshapes and articulates the sensory experiences which come from within and without. In the process of this osmosis it experiences untold pleasures of satisfying union and fitting adaptation; these it cherishes, desires, and seeks. It also experiences feelings of discordance and unsuitability; these it registers, but rejects and avoids. Of the distinction between what comes from outside and what slowly builds up within, the child is not aware. For a time at least the world which it creates for itself is the only world in existence. No trace as yet of that disturbing consciousness of dualism of object and subject. The bifurcation of past and future is not yet perceived; only the broad open spaces of an ever-lasting present. In it the child feels itself endowed with magic powers: it transmutes everything with sovereign unconcern into a world all its own. It gives names and physiognomies, and assigns their respective places, to all things and feelings which it has recorded and assimilated. It is self-centered and entirely at one with all its attitudes and gestures. Self-consciousness, that problematic feeling of being mirrored and judged by others with standards at variance with one's own, does not in the least interfere with its natural behavior. It is the glorious age in which the human being is king and lord in a realm of imaginary, yet truly possessed, reality.

Of course, there are moments when the child's creative power is challenged. But as long as the recalcitrant elements allow themselves to be subdued, its kingdom is not seriously threatened. After all, the grown-ups are there to help; they are taken for granted as ready instruments in the removal of obstacles. It is only when these obstacles become insurmountable that the child anxiously begins to realize and fear the existence of a potentially hostile world. For a while it may feel sheltered under the protective roof of its home, among the familiar things of its surroundings and in the providing care of its parents. But this confidence, this feeling of security, being itself the result of some sort of awakened awareness, shares with all conscious states their core of anxiety and brittleness. Before long, even the child's faith in the omnipotence of father and mother will be shaken, because the obstacles seem to come from a peculiar denseness and weight of things or from natural forces which transcend all manner of control. And should they be allowed to interfere, not because the grown-ups are unable to remove them, but because for some reason unexplained the latter choose to ignore or even bring them about, then the shock to the child takes on particularly serious proportions. For here it faces a situation where an instrument which it knows to be capable of achieving what is desired and which it implicitly considers available, nevertheless refuses to serve. It is clear that this whole process of slipping out of infancy into childhood and thence into adolescence must be accompanied by emotions which range from revolt and rancor to melancholy and sadness. No doubt, the maturer stages of consciousness have their compensations, but these can never bring back to life that magic world of unrefracted happiness and creative warmth with which early childhood may be graced. And when to all these factors are added the profound biological changes of growth, characterized by a bewildering fermentation and progressive assertiveness of sex, it becomes evident that maturing is a very serious business. It is not made any easier by the further discovery that the roots of it all are by no means confined to individual childhood, but spread via the mother's womb into genealogical ramifications of an obscure past.

Fortunately for the growing child the repressed feelings of personal abdication are captured and snugly cushioned in the existing moulds of religious, social and rational patterns held ready by family and tradition. But while some of the wayward strangeness of these repressed feelings is thereby lost, they are not completely robbed of their power, nor are they completely covered by the inherited patterns. Residues crop up in the form of phantoms in dreams and nightmares, or bring about symptoms of restlessness, anguish and guilt. As the circle of experienced reality widens, the patterns themselves may be questioned and subjected to increasingly searching tests as to their validity. In the measure in which they are found wanting, they will leave the former uncertainties and yearnings exposed and homeless. New and more suitable patterns must be found in different surroundings or at different levels of reality, or else they must be freshly evolved and shaped through painful personal struggles. Sometimes the traditional moulds prove elastic enough to be made to cover somehow the remaining doubtful elements. In other cases increasing loneliness forces the individual to search for new and suitable answers.

Carl Sieber, Rilke's son-in-law, in his book entitled *René Rilke*, takes issue with those who find in the poet's allegedly sad childhood and adolescence the source of the despair of Malte and of Rilke's insistent concern with death. He claims that what Rilke in later years called the weight of childhood was largely imaginary and no more than the emotional impression which his childhood had left behind (Sieber, 68ff). But I am not sure that he has proved his point. As he himself remarks, what appears to the ordinary person as harmless may take on gigantic proportions in the eyes of the sensitive poet. Those who see in Rilke's early experiences nothing but sadness are obviously mistaken; in a sense his optimism survived all shocks. Nevertheless it remains true that the sad impressions loomed large, certainly so far as later childhood and adolescence are concerned. I confess that I am not greatly impressed by accounts concerning Rilke's exuberant participation in journalism, literary club activities, and publicity enterprises during his Prague years (Sieber, Demetz). Too much evidence tends to show that they were peripheral manifestations concealing an underground of frustration mixed with turbid ambition and gnawing uncertainty. From his infancy there seem to have emerged memories of a state of undiluted happiness and magic for which he later yearned and which he desperately wanted to recapture. Not, of course, by the impossible means of obliterating the effects of mature consciousness but by regaining the naïve creative state on a newly-found level.

PART I

EARLIEST ENVIRONMENT

Kde domov muj?

Where is my home?
(Czech Folksong)

1. CHILDHOOD

◇◇

Erst eine Kindheit, grenzenlos und ohne
Verzicht und Ziel, o unbewusste Lust.

(*AW* I,392)

First came childhood, boundless,
unresigning and aimless. Oh guileless joy.

◇◇

RILKE was born in Prague at midnight on the fourth of December 1875. His birth was premature by two months. Only one day before the event took place the expectant but unsuspecting mother had bought a little gold cross on a chain which she intended to be her first present to the young life stirring under her heart. Both she and her husband wanted a girl, to make up for the loss of a daughter, Ismene, who had died very young. However, when their wish was not fulfilled, they were happy to look into the blue eyes of their tiny, but splendidly formed son. The fourth of December was a Saturday, the day of Holy Mary. It was natural that the devoutly Catholic mother should see in this a happy omen and place her son under the protection of the Queen of Heaven. When he was christened, the name of Mary was added to his long list of Christian names, and the little gold cross around his neck meant for the mother that Jesus had singled him out for special protection (Sieber, 63-64).

Phia Rilke was a woman who used her devotion as a cloak wrapped around her shallow life of frustrated yearnings. Her buoyant imagination was strong and vivid enough partly to conceal from her the drab realities of a small and cramped existence. She was able to create for herself an atmosphere of unreality in which she could perform the empty gestures of a grand lady at ease in the world of aristocratic living. Before she was married she had enjoyed the comfort and distinction of a well-to-do home and her girlish dreams did not have to float in a vacuum. But now she was married to a salaried railroad employee, forced to live in a rented house which was filled with a medley of nondescript furniture. She was faced with the reality of a husband whom, after the abrupt ending of military service, frustration had turned into a strait-laced bourgeois. She no longer enjoyed the affluence of her girlhood years. Between Phia's dream of distinguished gentility and the sober circumstances of a petty environment there was a sad and disconcerting chasm. It is characteristic of her astounding resiliency that she was able in a large measure to fill that gap by a persistent display of affectation. Dressed in black like a dowager princess, she made herself believe that her outward appearance covered like a magic mantle the nakedness of her real position. Rilke explained later that when a great party was to be given at his home he had to relinquish his nursery-room in order that the visiting guests be impressed by the ample sweep of his parents' dwelling (Schmidt-Pauli, 29). Behind the black screen, with birds of embroidered gold, he would lie awake in his little bed, his heart beating with fear lest one of the dancing couples discover him. And when his mother served to her guests a cheap table wine out of bottles which she had provided with labels of distinction, she did in reality more than fool herself and others. She experienced and breathed, as if it were true, the fancied atmosphere of mundane glory. What feeling of privation and emptiness remained, found soothing refuge in equally external gestures of religious devotion.

It would, nevertheless, be wrong to conclude that Phia was not sincerely religious, just as it would be unjustified to think that she was a spurious lady. By instinct she was both a lady and religious, and her instinct was genuine. But it was such that it allowed her to live only by indulging in a sort of theatrical sentimentality which prevented her from being simple and unpretentious. At bottom it was a form of the instinct of preservation, which enabled her to survive many rude shocks and to cling to life with undiminished vitality into old age. Rilke himself, who relatively early chafed under the artificiality of his mother's airs, recognized in moments of calm reflection, not without awe and admiration, that in her case the placing of appearances above reality was a source of enormous strength (*Br. 1892-1904*, 333; *Phia*, 72-74, 85-88). Rudolf Kassner observes that Rilke's passion for truthfulness had its roots in his mother's tendency to make-believe, with the result that his spirituality was sublimated sensuality and his fancy the narcissistic product of sex (*Br.MTT*, xxxvii). But the ensuing fallacy and lopsidedness of his later attitudes as well as of his heterodox tenets became the stimulus and ground for magnificent poetry. Conversely, Phia's own warped affectation was the fibre of her undauntable spirit of self-preservation.[1]

In the meantime, Rilke's education was in the hands of his mother, such as she was. In keeping with her congenital disregard of reality she brought her boy up as if he were a girl. Until his fifth year he wore long curls and was dressed like a girl; his toys were dolls whose hair he combed and with which he liked to play at cooking; his petty chores were those of the fair sex and on his birthday girl friends were invited to celebrate and play with him. It was a game of simulation in which the boy himself seems to have taken some delight. According to a story told by his mother he once knocked at her door when he had been naughty and appeared with his hair braided into pigtails and his sleeves turned up, saying: "Ismene stays with her dear mother, René is a good-for-nothing, I have sent him away, girls are more affectionate, aren't they?" (Sieber, 71).

The mother's solicitude, though warm and in a sense true, was excessive. She was anxious at all times to protect her only child from every possible harm. The fact that René was susceptible to disease only served to increase the precautions with which he was surrounded. Draughts were scrupulously avoided; for days he had to gargle with salt water; his bed was as downy as a bird's nest; as many as twenty-four different nurses were engaged in the first year of his life; his association with playmates was rationed. No wonder that the child became an easy prey to contagious diseases. During his second school-year he was absent two hundred times, while in the third he missed the last two quarters altogether. The

---

[1] Rilke's statements concerning his mother are sometimes very blunt. In a letter of 1904, after she had visited him in Rome, he expressed to Lou his feelings of horror at the sight of this lady "who cannot grow old," who "is as empty as a garment, ghostlike and dreadful. And to think that I am her child . . ." (*Br.Lou*, 143). To which Lou replied that perhaps he might do well to consider his mother as a sort of bacillus, "a single fat bacillus," which had to be thrown out of his system after causing what was in him to ferment. "Many a most blessed, most ideal mother is *sterile* in so far as affecting her child is concerned (germ-free nutrition!)" (*Br.Lou*, 147). And on November 2, 1907, Rilke wrote to Clara: "I have seen my mother; once more I feel unjust toward her and I do not know how it could be otherwise. . . . I can't get near her even with the faintest side of my being; knowing her conception of me I feel, as she looks at me, such a hole, such a void in me, that for her nothing of me has any validity—Who can step into a doll-house with mere pictured doors and windows instead of real ones?" (Sieber, 49). Lastly, in a poem of October 1915 Rilke compares himself to a building which he has laboriously erected stone by stone and which his mother, whom "Christ comes to wash every day," insists on tearing down with selfish unconcern (*Gedichte 1906-26*, 270).

vague memory of nightmares and of days of convalescence, when his mother read poems at his bedside, was never effaced.

Phia's religiosity was, of course, imposed upon her son. Through holy pictures and statues, both at home and at church, he was put on a familiar footing with God, Jesus, Mary, and the Saints. With his mother he performed sentimental gestures of devotion, such as kissing a saint's feet or the Holy Virgin's statue. He was made to kneel in prayer until he lost all sensation of where his knees ended and the hard bench began. On All Saints' Day they went to the churchyard and wandered about the graves lit up with little candles and made fragrant with wreaths and flowers. And we can well imagine that the child was deeply impressed with all the warm and sensuous rites and imagery of the Catholic church. With growing anxiety and hope the arrival of Christmas was awaited for weeks, until at last the door was opened and the trembling boy saw the tree with its burning candles and shining glitter.

Little René was taught by both his mother and his father to behave like a well-bred child. He learned exactly what to say and how to act in the presence of visitors or guests. In the hands of his mother he became a delightful object of display, a glamorous show-child, in whom the conventional praise of grown-ups could not help arousing a keen sense of vanity.

The father, Josef Rilke, was a good deal less eccentric than the mother. Reared for the army, he had taken part in the campaign against Italy in 1850, after which he was made an instructor in the military school of his regiment. His great ambition had been to become an officer like his two brothers, but a recurring illness prevented his dream from coming true. When he was reduced to the acceptance of a civilian post in the service of the railroad, his pride was severely shaken. A belated attempt to escape from his narrow office life in the hope of becoming the manager of a large country estate ended in failure. But the disappointed official never lost his sense of social decorum. His gentlemanly carriage and gallant manners were striking and when, impeccably clad, he walked in the streets of Prague, he was greeted with respect by many. The opinion which he thought others had of him was something he had to live up to, but his self-delusion remained more nearly within the limits of socially-accepted norms.

For his son he had the tenderest feelings and the highest hopes.

If René could become an officer, his own disappointments might lose much of their sting. With that aim in mind, he made his boy receptive to the idea of being sent to a military academy when the time was ripe. Since the father had excelled in athletics when he was young, he was anxious that his son, too, should develop a liking for virile exercise. Instead of dolls he gave him dumbbells and lead soldiers as toys. And from his uncles René received a sabre, a portépée with helmet, and a rocking-horse, so that in the midst of his dolls the child's soul would swing between simulated girlhood and actual boyhood. Now he would put his dolls to bed, talking to them like a mother, now he fancied himself a general leading his men into battle and being decorated for bravery.

For a time the boy surrendered to the warm feeling of parental affection, although he revealed distinct signs of personal consciousness and determination at an early stage. His mother relates that he always insisted upon choosing himself the poses for the many photographs which were taken of him. These poses seem to betray a remarkable sense of style and effectiveness, even of vanity. He was enormously eager to excel by a unique distinction of performance, a tendency which was greatly enhanced by Phia's vainglorious exhibitionism. Very early young René was impelled by an inner urge to write verses and his ambition in this respect was high. The date of his earliest poem is not known but Sieber places it considerably before 1885. It is a poem entitled *Plaintive Mourning* (*Klage über Trauer*) (Sieber, 82ff), in which a general who has fallen on the battlefield is lying on the bier amid universal desolation. The contrast between his former fame and his present state of annihilation is worked out sharply. Among the mourners the general's bride is singled out, her thoughts going back to the time when she tore herself away from her parents' arms in order to find a new happiness and a new home. In her despair she dies in the arms of her beloved husband.

In this poem the following words are underlined: eternal night, mourning, sorrow, home, her parents' arms. Sieber considers it unjustified to infer from this that young Rilke was by nature inclined to see the sad side of life. He points to the vigorous tone which prevails in the letters which the boy wrote during the same period from various places where he spent his summer holidays. In these Rilke boasts of eating like a wolf, of driving a carriage like a prelate's coachman, of imagining himself a dashing major or a decorated knight. His courage even reached such heights as to embolden him to climb trees! But, characteristically, his friends were mainly girls.

However, it must be observed that Rilke may very well have mentioned these boyish activities because they were unusual with him and deserved proud emphasis. Moreover, in diagnosing early proclivities it is hardly fair to judge individual acts and words only in the light of seemingly contradictory ones of the same period, disregarding entirely later developments. At any rate, this early poem does not conflict with Rilke's characteristics such as they unfold in the course of time: an intuitive knowledge of the frailty of human achievements and a keen sense of the sheltered warmth radiating from the lost home.

Young Rilke not only wrote verses, he also painted. A knight on horseback, with red cloak and red helmet, dashing up a hill, suddenly meets a dragon which he makes ready to kill with his drawn lance. The background is a fantastic landscape—a young officer, mortally wounded in battle, is supported by a companion, while the infantry are gloriously attacking the enemy; over a dead hussar the horse mournfully bends its head and a tree in the distance bends its top in sympathy; three horses running in a row; houses stretching up a slope; a pump out of which water flows; many islands with castles mirrored in the moving waves of the sea; broad steps, large trees, and statues in parks (Sieber, 78ff). It would be easy to point out later poems in Rilke's work in which these themes recur, and similar childhood drawings are mentioned by Malte Laurids Brigge in his *Notebook* (*AW* II,82). But what is more remarkable is that, according to Sieber, in all these water colors space and movement are emphasized. Space and movement are functions of reality which are known to have occupied Rilke with increasing fascination.

There is still another type of painting in which the boy indulged, namely caricature (Sieber, 81-82). Sieber mentions six copies of a doctor's head characterizing the latter's moods at different moments in his practice. Another picture shows an elderly lady in fancy dress, with the words underneath: "Old Antique Shop." Then, there is a fop's face bearing the inscription "Empty Ornamental Plant." Caricature is a trend which Rilke developed into a great art. Indeed there is something verging on caricature in a large number of the profiles of persons, things, and situations created by him. *Ewald Tragy* and

Malte's *Notebook* contain many typical examples, not to mention the old drum-beater in the *Fifth Elegy*, "shrunk inside his wide skin that was big enough to cover two men, one of whom was lying in the churchyard; but he, surviving, remains in the large, bereaved skin, deaf and sometimes a bit bewildered." And in the same *Elegy* there is the young man "who looks as if he were the son of a nun and a bull-neck." Something of the kind was undoubtedly inherent in the whole personality of his mother. With Rilke it became a means of striking, unexpected characterization and had its source in his uncanny power to expose prima-facie reality to the deflecting mirror of his subconsciousness. He possessed a tendency to open up flashing vistas into the obscure ramifications of his sensual being out of which would emerge ghostlike shadows as strange and weird to conscious experience as the latter was to them. Sieber, commenting upon a photograph of the three-year-old boy, concludes by saying that the "open look of his eyes, which in the face of the animal is so deep," reveals a child that seems to know so much even before it learns what it already knows (Sieber, 70). In the same context we may call to our minds that childlike and bewildered stare with which Rilke at various moments of his life used to wonder at the words of his own poems which had welled up from unknown depths.

2. THE CADET

◇◇◇

Antreten! Abmarsch!
(Sieber, 157)
On parade! Quick march!

◇◇◇

UNTIL Rilke was nine years old he lived with his parents, basking in the tender affection of his father and exposed to the extravagances of his mother. But in 1884, eleven years after their wedding, father and mother separated. The break, which was a deep one, apparently originated in the early years of their married life (Demetz, 12) and Rilke, who was a precocious child, became acutely aware of it very soon. In 1903 he writes: "My parents' marriage was already wilting when I was born" (*Br. 1892-1904*, 332). The poet's early home-life was, therefore, not undisturbed. For the next two years, until he went to a military academy in September of 1886, he was left in the care of his mother while his father occupied a different dwelling.[2]

The four years that followed are those which Rilke later considered the most dreadful ones of his life. We may agree with Sieber that the military schools of St. Pölten and Mährisch-Weisskirchen were neither better nor worse than other institutions of the same kind (Sieber, 85-86). Their aim was to raise young lads for a soldier's life and the emphasis was on strict discipline. Bodily endurance, athletics, fencing, swimming, riding, occupied a large part of the day. From four o'clock in the morning when the bugle sounded until the evening when the lights went out in the dormitories, every moment was regulated and supervised. The instructors were soldiers, the pupils mostly strong, healthy boys, willing to rub shoulders with each other and to fall in line with the impersonal spirit of the place. It is well known that even in the ordinary school the tyranny of public opinion is all-pervading. If you excel in the fields of activity which are understood and appreciated by your fellow-pupils, you are liked and admired. In a military academy physical skill and prowess above all are likely to elicit respect. On no account must you show signs of downright clumsiness, weakness, fear, or cowardice. Still less will you be forgiven if you withdraw within yourself and remain aloof as if you looked down upon the rest. You

---

[2] Valéry Rhonfeld describes Rilke's mother as a "highly gifted and pleasure-seeking" woman, the father as "a man of rare beauty but hard-hearted and selfish." She claims that both parents looked upon their son as a nuisance and that they sent him to military school partly in order to give him an education in keeping with their social rank and partly to enable them to break up their home because of their unhappy marriage (Hirschfeld, 714-715).

Here are some of the aphorisms which Phia Rilke jotted down in her diary and which throw some light on her attitude in matters of love and marriage.

"Many a wedding is only the prayer before the battle—Egoism is the basis of modern marriages—Esteem demands no love, but love cannot exist without esteem —Separation is the most accurate scale of love—A woman who has not loved has not lived—The so-called *strong* sex consists for the most part of foibles—Repentance is of no concern to those who truly love—The greatest fortune in love is faithfulness —A spiritual misalliance is a thousand times worse than a social one—Habit is quite often the only bond that holds two persons together in a lasting way—When people talk about women, what becomes of *objectivity*?—Who truly loves gives all and sacrifices nothing—The kiss is worth no more than its ardor—It is often a serious mistake of the parents that they give their children an education according to social rank; it would be more proper to educate them according to financial resources—Our opinions are shaped by our own experiences." (Phia, *passim*)

must prove that you can take it, if need be, with a grin. From what we know about the soft upbringing of René, his susceptibility to disease, his lack of boy friends and boyish exercise, his strong yearning for love and affection, his urge to write poetry, his religious bent, we can well imagine what kind of life was in store for him. His father was very anxious that he should become strong and hardened. He knew that it would take time and was prepared to be patient. It would not be easy for him to acknowledge defeat and to swallow his pride, if he ever had to admit that his son was not cut out to be an officer. Phia, on the other hand, profoundly pitied her darling boy whose loving home had been cruelly exchanged for what she called a prison. She kept writing him hysterical letters which tended to heighten his sensitivity rather than to calm it (Sieber, 102). To her it seemed more exciting to visualize her son as a great poet than as an officer. It was she, too, who kept stirring in the poor cadet an unwholesome, morose religiosity.

It seems of little importance, therefore, that by comparative standards these military schools were no worse than others, and it is likewise futile to speculate as to how René would have fared, had his mother not pampered him so childishly. The fact is that Rilke was profoundly unhappy and suffered immense agonies. Later he may have exaggerated somewhat the harm which this drawn-out experience had done to him, but there is an early story by him, clearly autobiographical, entitled *Pierre Dumont*, in which he vividly describes the melancholy return trip to the academy at the end of his vacation. Little Pierre does his best to make his mother believe that all is well with him while furtively he counts the hours and minutes of freedom left. His thoughts keep going back to happy holiday moments which he would fain clasp and hold onto forever. But the clock is merciless; and it is pathetic how at last he tears himself away from his mother's embrace, begging her to write soon and not to forget to take good care of Belli, the little dog, and to give his love to Julie, his cousin. And finally he hears the hard voice of the sergeant shouting: "The deuce, Dumont, don't you know it's time to report!" (Sieber, 141ff)

Neither Rilke's body nor his soul had been conditioned for the rough and tough routine of a military institution. The mere fact that his gold cross, which he had worn around his neck since the day of his birth, got lost as he exchanged his civilian clothes for a military outfit, gave him a shock which he did not easily forget. The outdoor exercises knocked him out again and again so that he was forced to spend days on end in the infirmary with colds or pneumonia. Feverish dreams haunted him, whereas refreshing periods of convalescence brought him the quietest joys. He wanted so much to do as the others or, rather, better than they; but since his awkwardness and weakness did not measure up to the demands, he was soon singled out as a misfit. That he consequently sought refuge in aloofness was interpreted as conceit and served only to excite his companions to greater abuse. Even when he was kicked or beaten, he did not strike back but merely said in a quiet voice to his unjust assailant: "I suffer it because Christ suffered it, silently and without complaint, and while you were hitting me, I prayed my good God to forgive you" (*Letters 1892-1910*, 19-20).

That his letters of the period do not contain more complaints can only be accounted for by his boundless desire to persevere and make good, in which efforts he was aided by his increasingly morbid religiosity and by his inborn yearning for excellence. Nor must we attach too much importance to certain reports which contradict Rilke's later pessimistic memories. If the young poet-cadet was permitted by his teachers from time to time to read his poetic effusions to his class, the fact remains that his classmates had little understanding of his lyrical efforts and greeted them with staring silence (Demetz, 39). In a letter to his mother, dated October 27, 1889, he thanks God for being well, cheerful, and happy, and attributes this condition to his practicing the golden rules, namely that truth is to be sought in the middle and that the ideal is: neither too little nor too much. He eggs himself on with an energetic *En avant*! and, then, proceeds to make naïve pedantic observations about the meaning of life. He dishes out to his mother all sorts of random illustrations from history in which such names as Copernicus, Evangelista Torricelli, Goethe, Faust, Scipio, Plato, Cato, Socrates, Robespierre are curiously thrown together. The message of this display of learning fresh from the classroom is that man without faith in God, who holds everything in His hand, is lost (Sieber, 98-101).

This letter shows clearly that the fourteen-year-old boy was still too young to know what it all meant, and we can understand why he fancied himself wanting to become an officer, as his father expected. He even dreamt of achieving fame and distinction in the service of his fatherland. This self-delusion still lingers in letters which he wrote a year after he left the military school (Sieber, 103). Yet at the same time his insistent requests that his parents come and visit him, still more the letters, full of melancholy sadness, which he wrote from his sickbed, are eloquent proof of his homesick loneliness (Sieber, 97-98). No doubt, Rilke's conflicting moods at this time were sincere, but they reveal a perplexed and confused mind. We need not go far from home to discover that attitudes can be hopelessly warped by outside influences which are not understood. In view of Rilke's whole development, it is unmistakably clear that his military aspirations were spurious. The true Rilke at this time is revealed far more authentically in such poems as *The Grave, Resignation, The Churchyard, The Orphan, All Saints' Day*, in which death and the transitoriness of things are the outstanding themes. This is confirmed by his secret visits to the little churchyard of the military academy where he often found refuge from his rude environment.

This is not to say that Rilke's resolute optimism which characterizes his later work was completely absent even in this period of suffering. For Rilke found consolation and real contentment in his solitary aloofness, in his poetic endeavors, and in those substrata of true religious feeling which for the time were submerged in mystical exaggeration. Much later, on March 11, 1907, he wrote to his wife Clara: "I did experience the true life in the little corner of the Academy's churchyard, where I was safe from my companions and from the utterly unsocial effects of their ruthlessness which, scissors-like and with unequivocal precision, clipped you out of the whole picture of the environmental mass" (Sieber, 94). Already at this time the real nature of Rilke's optimism is adumbrated: an optimism which is not gained by shrinking from sorrow and sadness but by passing through them with open eyes and tasting them out to the last dregs. To be sure, we are a long way yet from the lofty exultation of the *Sonnets* which will emanate from Muzot some thirty years later, but its rudiments are clearly discernible.

In the spring of 1891 Rilke's father capitulated before his son's continuing unhappiness and periodic illnesses. A little later young Rilke declared to Valéry Rhonfeld that he was "dismissed" because of "an affair of morals" (Demetz, 41). Whatever the real cause of his departure, René left military school on June 3. All the time the father had been anxious to avoid everything that might encourage the youth's passion for writing poetry. He tried to convince himself that if René could perform more simply the little tasks of the day he might yet grow healthy enough to become, if not an officer, at least a respectable citizen. Young Rilke himself went through a period of uncertainty and vacillation. His prospects of a military career were not completely abandoned, but at the same time he talked about preparing for some kind of profession. While recuperating in Prague he still liked to wear his military uniform, because it gave him greater prestige.

But the feeling of liberation after four painful years seems to have been great. The year which he subsequently spent at the Commercial Academy at Linz developed peculiar symptoms of his reaction to long frustration. It is true, the surrounding atmosphere was radically different from that of St. Pölten and Mährisch-Weisskirchen, but that alone cannot account for his amazing *volte-face*. Looking back at this short interlude, Rilke wrote later that it was one in which he was the least himself (Sieber, 109). But for the time being he was exuberant, perhaps frivolously so. As a former cadet he was respected in this lay world and his relationship to teachers and fellow-students was normal, if not excellent. He went hunting through snow and ice, enjoyed dancing, celebrated Carnival, visited the theatre, listened enthusiastically to a lecture by Rosegger, was proud of his "most elegant sitting-room" in a "most elegant home," read Tolstoy, wrote poetry and a history of the Thirty Years' War, and ended by getting involved in a muddled love affair, which seems to have impelled him to return to Prague. In a letter which he wrote soon afterward from his sickbed to his mother in Vienna he confesses that he had been foolish enough to let a passing infatuation get the better of him. He repents—and registers with satisfaction the fact that he is able to repent. But after all, he felt that the fire which had been kindled in his breast was a holy flame, similar to that which the priestesses of Vesta used to entertain. That he had allowed his stormy passion to blow the flame into a destructive conflagration, that was his mistake. He apologizes for having surrendered to a silly flirtation instead of to a noble inspiration of knowledge and truth. But now, thanks to the Lord, he is free again, and he reads with sentimental indulgence Goethe's *Elective Affinities* and *Wil-*

helm Meister, both of which, in different ways, served to place in perspective and to sober down the effects of his experience (Sieber, 108-110).

3. YOUTHFUL RESTIVENESS

◇◇

> Trotz. Der Gebogene wird selber Bieger
> und rächt an anderen, dass er erlag.
> (*AW* I,392)

> Defiance. Humbled at first, he now does the humbling
> and avenges on others his recent defeats.

◇◇

THERE now follows a time, from 1892 to 1896, which was of the greatest importance in Rilke's poetic awakening. All the way back into his early childhood we have observed an instinctive desire on his part to excel and to assert himself, not without secretly dreaming of glorious leadership. That his skills were not of a nature to impress the youths in the military schools was not the least among the complex causes of his distress. In his fragmentary *History of the Thirty Years' War*, on which he continued to work, it seems that he was above all interested in glorifying the heroic characters (Sieber, 104-107); he also seems to have taken great pleasure in signing his name as "René Maria Caesar Rilke" (Zinn, 218), although Caesar was not among his six Christian names. At any rate, he now became rapidly conscious of his real destiny as a poet and felt driven with increasing inevitability to a decision, painful and irresistible, to listen only to his inner voice, regardless of his parents' ambitions or his relatives' and acquaintances' judgments.

His mother was in Vienna and his father's quarters were not large, so that once more he was deprived of a home. His aunt Gabriele, a widowed sister of his father's, offered him a little room in her house. On the whole, Gabriele seems to have been a motherly soul who did her best to fill the gap which the parental division had created in her nephew's life (Sieber, 113). Rilke's uncle Jaroslav, whose only son had died and who was anxious to have someone succeed him in his law practice, had decided to finance Rilke's education, first at the gymnasium and then at the university. But Rilke was already seventeen years old and could not be expected to rub shoulders at school with students three or four years his junior; still less could he afford to start from scratch and to proceed at the normal slow pace of instruction. He, therefore, was allowed to catch up the lost time by preparing for his final examination with the help of private tutors. It is a matter of record that he worked very hard, completing his pre-university studies with much success in three years, and matriculated in 1895. During the following winter semester he studied chiefly philosophy, history of art, and literature at the German university of his native city, but in the summer of 1896 he switched over to law. This sudden change may have been due to pressure from his father or from the heirs of his uncle Jaroslav who had died in the meantime. Or was it due to Rilke's own qualms of conscience, since the stipend he still received had been specifically intended to enable him to become a lawyer? At any rate, these two semesters represent the only regular university training which he ever received.

While his letters of the period seem to indicate that he liked his intellectual pursuits, his boundless ambition caused him much anxiety. With remarkable lack of appreciation he is said to have ignored his aunt's affection and kindnesses, an ingratitude which he later regretted. The little room in which he studied and wrote poetry became a symbol of solitary joys and social isolation. Rilke had become used to feeling alone in a world of people who did not sympathize with his ambitious dreams. As early as September 7, 1892 he writes to his mother that he can experience God only by communing with flowers, trees, springs, and birds, not with human beings (Sieber, 115-116).

The necessity of having to skip man in his search of what he needed (be it called God or the creation of valid, enduring work) will lie like a curse upon his conscience all his life. Among his family and relatives he moved like a ghost, unfathomed and estranged. In a poem entitled *Old Story* he depicts an enthusiastic young poet, proud of his talent and striving for the highest goal. But his aunt and cousins call him conceited and warn him that he is doomed to loneliness; they withdraw from him with the smugly threatening words "We told you so!" on their lips (*BVP 1896*, 69). A few years after he left Prague, Rilke reviewed this period of groping self-discovery and described the painful experiences of his last days with his family: his father's attitude had become a source of suffering to him; he loved him with the melancholy affection of an orphaned son, yet felt utterly incapable of sharing the bourgeois ideals and constraint which marked in its every gesture the life of the punctilious parent. The knowledge that his father, even at this critical stage, stubbornly refused to understand the deep yearnings of his soul and to endorse his desire to escape from family bondage into a life of his own imparted to his decision to leave the gravity of tragic destiny.

There is reason to believe that Rilke's sentiments for his mother did not color nearly so deeply the anguish of his last days in Prague. In her vanity she was less perturbed than her husband by the yet dubious prospect of her son's becoming a famous poet. Rilke had an overwhelming need of that motherly affection of which he had a vague memory from early childhood. But by now Phia had revealed herself as so utterly shallow a woman that he had long ago familiarized himself with the feeling of being orphaned. His distress at being deprived of motherly love finds expression in many poems throughout his work. To Valéry Rhonfeld he writes: "You know that for the greater part of the day I was entrusted to a serving-girl, immoral and of few scruples and that the woman whose first and immediate care I should have been loved me only when it came to bringing me out in a new little dress before a few marvelling acquaintances" (*Letters 1892-1910*, 18). In the concluding pages of his autobiographical *Ewald Tragy* he relates how, on recovering from a sickness in which he is horribly shaken by feverish night-mares, Ewald hankers for company and warm friendship. When no one appears to still his longing, he pours out his soul in a letter to his mother: "Come, give me what belongs to me. It is still time; I am still soft and can be as wax in your hands." But his cry finds no echo, least of all in his mother, that slender, nervous lady, who is so proud when some stranger calls her "Miss." It is a cry of despair which rises to the heavens in search of an ideal beyond reach. Ewald throws his letter into the fire and watches it burn slowly in the small, wavering flames (*ET*, 62). The motif of the Prodigal Son in its travestied interpretation of the later Malte-mood is foreshadowed.

The ties which linked Rilke to his uncle and aunts were even more easily disposed of. Inasmuch as they emphasized his general feeling of isolation, they naturally contributed to the atmosphere of tenseness which enveloped him in the days of decision. But the satire and caricature with which Rilke depicts in the first part of *Ewald Tragy* the boring meals at the house of his aunt suggest an anticipation of profound relief (*ET*, 13ff).

4. EROS

Masken! Masken! dass man Eros blende.
Wer erträgt sein strahlendes Gesicht?

(*AW* I,390)

Masks! Masks! Let Eros be blinded.
Who can withstand his radiant countenance?

RILKE biographers usually brush aside as unimportant a love affair which the young poet had for three years in Prague. The object of his love, Valéry David-Rhonfeld (Vally), considerably older than himself, was the daughter of an officer whom he had met through one of his girl cousins. She helped him in his studies and encouraged him in his poetic endeavors. She is described as a somewhat eccentric woman who dabbled in things artistic and literary and who took pleasure in distinguishing herself by unconventional manners. After Rilke's death she sold his letters and poems addressed to her and commented that at first she had not really been in love with poor ugly René: she had only taken pity on him (Hirschfeld, 716). Though she admitted having come to love him later, her eccentric nature seems to have made her quite incapable of deep affection. And from the one hundred and thirty known letters which Rilke wrote to her the inference is drawn that for him, too, the relationship lacked depth and real significance. Indeed, judging by the sundry samples quoted by several authors, it appears to have been on the whole one of those trivial flirtations of adolescence. When it ended, Rilke did not express any great emotion in his farewell letter (Sieber, 127), and no mention of the affair is made in his subsequent writings.

Yet it is difficult to believe that a relationship which lasted for three years, at a time when Rilke was passing through one of the most decisive periods of his life, should not carry with it symptoms of typical Rilkean peculiarities. Sieber diagnoses his attitude at the time as that of an unavowed rebel who, not being able to satisfy his publicized ambition to become an officer, was anxious to show to the world that he was "different," since as a "poet" he was fit to associate with a girl like Vally (Sieber, 122-123). It is quite true that there was at the time something of the rebel in Rilke. Every fibre of his being revolted against the bourgeois values to which he was tacitly or openly expected to conform. There are even in his diaries and early writings expressions of Promethean challenge. The anti-bourgeois orientation of his character, which Rudolf Kassner calls one of his most distinguishing features, is most outspoken in these years. His boastful claim to kinship with one Count Jenison Wa(l)l-worth (*Br.vonOe.*, 39, 68f) and his lifelong insistence that he was of noble descent show that he had inherited more of his mother's vanity than he would care to admit. However, with him the desire to shine was accompanied by a growing dislike of sham and super-ficiality. If he was to excel, it was not by pouring cheap wine into bottles with spurious labels.

Without presuming to fathom the meaning of Rilke's early ex-periments in love, we may reasonably expect his later attitudes and conceptions to throw some light upon it. If Vally was not capable of real love and of assuming the full responsibility imposed by it, Rilke was hardly more so. The reasons were different, but the ex-perience with Vally certainly tended to make him aware of his own deficiency. If the passage quoted by Sieber from an unpublished diary of 1899 is legitimately thought to refer to the Vally affair, it would confirm such an interpretation. That quotation is as fol-lows: "That sensuality [sexuality?] is not a secret flame which al-ways flares up at the same place, let that be our pride and strength. We intend that it become a joy-bearing torch, which we hold laugh-ingly behind all the transparences of our being" (Sieber, 127). I am even tempted to quote in this connection the lines of the *Fourth Elegy*: "To us, however, where we mean one thing, the display of the other is already apparent. Enmity is closest to us. Are not lovers forever facing precipices one in the other, who promised each other open spaces, hunting, and a home?" And further: "And you, am I not right, who loved me for the poor beginning of love I bore you, which I always forgot because the space within your countenance, as I loved it, merged into cosmic space within which you no longer were. . . ." It may be considered preposterous to suggest the slightest connection between the profound reflections of the *Elegies* and the "poor beginning of love" of Rilke's high school years. But we must remember that the poet's mature symbols are "lyrical sums," the individual items of which are hidden in remote corners of the past. In a different context he implores the undefinable powers in him to guide his hand, tired from the day's involvements, in the creation of wonderful symbols and of "words whose last syllable I cover mysteriously with my life." They are to grant him "states of silence" which give him the right to "submerge so deeply under the waves of quiet waters that nobody even notices his movements beneath" (*Br.Frühzeit*, 231).

To be sure, there appears to have been something highly unrealistic and childishly sentimental in Rilke's relationship to Vally, with whom he is said to have had repeated meetings in cemeteries (Demetz, 125). Anybody who at the age of eighteen calls his girl "my dear, sweet, infinitely loved heart, my beautiful, divine Vally," and who signs himself "Your Hidigeigei," or "Your little grey tom-cat" (Sieber, 125), may be said to fancy himself in a world of fairies. But if we compare these effusions with those found years later in Rilke's letters to Benvenuta,[3] we are struck by a remarkable affinity. "Dear, dear soul," "sister dear," he writes; "good-bye, dear friend of my heart"—"my fairy-tale, fairy-tale of my heart"—"mediatrix with my future"—"beautiful, cheerful heart"—"Oh darling"—"My heart shall feel your heart as little John in Elizabeth felt Jesus in Mary"— "Good-bye . . . if only I could write everything to you, my dear;

---

[3] "Benvenuta" was the name given by Rilke to Mrs. Magda Graedener von Hattingberg, a talented pianist, who shortly before Christmas 1913 had chanced upon the *Stories of God*. Soon afterward she wrote to him from Vienna to express her admiration. The remarkable correspondence followed. In 1943 Benvenuta wrote her book *Rilke und Benvenuta, Ein Buch des Dankes*, and in 1949 some of Rilke's letters were published by Rudolf von Jouanne under the title *Rainer Maria Rilke . . . so lass ich mich zu träumen gehen*. Both these books are now available in English translation. Moreover, Benvenuta has now made public a more complete, though still unsatisfying, edition of her correspondence with Rilke, entitled *Rainer Maria Rilke. Briefwechsel mit Benvenuta* (see Key to Abbreviations under *Br.Benvenuta*).

every time I stop I feel like the woman who comes out of church thinking that she has finished praying—but at the next corner turns back, impelled to enter the church and kneel down again" (*So lass, passim*). True, here the outpourings come at the beginning or conclusion of letters which evidently bear the stamp of sincerity and overwhelming emotion. Or do they? Rilke had never seen Benvenuta, he only knew her through her letters to him. One is tempted to wonder how it was possible that Rilke who is known to have been afraid of the diffusive effects of music could suddenly find words of sublime eulogy for an uncannily feared art merely because a never-seen and never-heard woman was an enthusiastic musician. There is much that is unrealistic in both the Vally and the Benvenuta episodes. When Rilke actually met Benvenuta, the relationship dissolved soon afterward, leaving nothing but the dregs of reality sublimated by the radiation of a beautiful dream.

There remains the difference that Rilke knew Vally in person when he wrote his "insincere" letters to her. But can we be so sure that his inflated words of endearment were not inspired more by an imaginary ideal than by the living woman to whom they were addressed? Without such an ideal in the background his association with Vally could hardly have lasted as long as it did, although it admittedly outlasted its term by the sheer momentum of its existence. When it did come to an end, the realization of discrepancy between ideal and reality had become so unequivocal, that no deep feeling of regret was entailed.

That Rilke knew of such encysted tangles of ideal and reality in matters of love may be inferred from a passage in *King Bohusch*, one of his *Two Prague Stories* written a few years later. Poor Bohusch, the ugly hunchback with a beautiful soul, fancies that he is loved by Frantischka, the former flame of his late father. In reality Frantischka only took pity on the orphaned cripple. In a dream Bohusch sees himself at the altar at the side of the girl, when all of a sudden her younger, more beautiful sister appears from nowhere, demanding the bridegroom for herself because she has been secretly in love with him. Bohusch, who remembers having known her only fleetingly, is indignant at the disturbance caused. But it is clear that subconsciously he had sensed Frantischka's unauthentic affection, and that his dream brought forward another girl who would answer his intense longing for true love. And that is not yet the whole story of the subconscious web. The dream reveals the beautiful younger girl to be dressed as a nun. Poor Bohusch's infirmity had engendered in him a psychological complex which made him vaguely feel that no girl could ever love him, that the happy state of being loved on this earth was not for him. Spinning the web still further he dreams that his father had been the caretaker at Prince Schwarzenberg's castle in Prague, and as a child the little hunchback had often played with the Prince's beautiful daughter Aglaja. Of course, when she grew up, the caretaker's son saw her no more. But one day Aglaja became a cloistered nun. Only on White Thursday was the public allowed into the convent's chapel. And Bohusch, who never failed to be present on that day, was each time transfigured with joy as he picked out Aglaja's voice from among the singing nuns behind the wall. But one year the voice was there no more, and that was the same year when Frantischka, too, left him. From that time on Bohusch was a changed man (*ESF*, 159-167).

In Rilke's later work there are many mysterious elements which ultimately reach back to this period of adolescence or into the recesses of childhood. As a child he stayed for a while with his mother on the Adriatic coast in a country house not very far from Duino castle. There he played with a little girl called Amélie who used to leave some flowers in a secret place whenever she was prevented from meeting him. When at last the time to part had come, René presented his little girl friend with a ring. It turned out later that she entered a convent and became a nun and on the day that happened Rilke, who was at the military academy, had a dream in which, so he claimed, she returned the ring to him (*MTT*, 47f). There is a poem, written in 1907 on the island of Capri, in which the astonished poet wonders whether the rush of blood in his ears has suddenly become louder or whether he actually hears the voices of cloistered nuns rise from the latticed choir of a church. Here, too, a single voice detaches itself from the singing background, "a pale, a light, a small voice clinging to God's ear like the hollow of a shell" (*Gedichte, 1906-26*, 9f). Especially the mood which gave rise to Malte's *Notebook* is steeped in dark early memories; and, in the years following the close association with Rodin, Rilke's fancy is repeatedly haunted by lingering shadows of childhood dolls which keep fascinating him for years and hover over the entire *Fourth Elegy*. In the fall of 1920 and the spring of 1921 Rilke was staying in absolute seclusion at the castle Berg am Irchel in Switzerland. In two remarkable waves of productivity he wrote a number of poems which were allegedly "dictated" to him by a fictitious ancestor of the estate, Count C.W., and which are unequivocally fraught with dim memories. In one of them he addresses a girl who bears the same name as that which occurs in poor Bohusch's dream (*CW*, 33):

> Beautiful Aglaja, friend of my feelings,
> Our happiness rose with the lark's song
> High in the morning. Let us not fear the coolness
> At night after the summer's day.
>
> Curve of love, let us describe it. Its ascent
> Shall be ours in its infinite glory.
> But later, too, when it descends—how true.
> Like your delicate brow, so pure.

And the other poem, still more revealing, runs like this (*CW*, 10):

> That, sitting by the fire, I should think of you?
> No, you are mistaken, I read.—Ah, you weep?
> Can it be that you want me to serve again?
> For I loved not: I served.
>
> You subdued what in my youth
> Still defied and resisted.
> I deeded with letters of blood
> My own first year to you.
>
> Instead of riding, Olga, instead of hunting,
> I knelt by you; while others went off
> I knelt, something silky binding me
> Which flowed down from your grace.
>
> Did you sense all the while that I knelt?
> Or did you know: he looks away?
> Ah, I was the shell, Aphrodite,
> Which bore you, and *in* me was the sea.

"Olga" is also the name of a cousin whom Rilke mentions in a fiery and sensual poem of the early collection *Dreamcrowned* (*EG*, 93-

94). And later in 1914, when Benvenuta wrote to him that she had played the piano for a lady whose first name was "Olga," Rilke wrote this: "When I read: 'Olga,' something tugged at my heart-strings" (*So lass*, 63). It is a practice of Rilke's, observable everywhere in his work, to suggest a whole atmosphere of complex and typical mood by singling out one or several individual names, magically representative.

We cannot fail to discern in Rilke's experience with Vally a pattern which recurs again and again and which seems exceedingly symptomatic, not only of his whole attitude to women and love, but also of his peculiar kind of idealism. Did he not confess that he liked "to cover the last syllable of his word mysteriously with his life"? (*Br.Frühzeit*, 231). Rilke was thoroughly sensual, and his symbolism, even the most sublime, was rooted in red-blooded, sensual experience. The thick substance of life adheres even to those tropes and motifs which suggest an ineffable world of imagined yearnings. It is in this layer of inner sensual reality, not in any abstract ideal world, that we must eventually look for Rilke's Angel of the *Elegies*, for the maidens and women of his poems, for his Prodigal Son, for his *Weltinnenraum* (Inner Cosmic Space) (*AW* I,343), and last but not least, for his longed-for childhood (*AW* I,333).

5. EARLIEST PUBLICATIONS

◇◇

> Meine frühverliehnen
> Lieder oft in der Ruh
> überrankter Ruinen
> sang ich dem Abend sie zu.
> (FG)

> My songs of early years
> I often sang alone
> When Evening lulled my fears
> Midst ruins overgrown.

◇◇

IN THE letters to Vally there are over a hundred poems dedicated to her. A further collection, *Leben und Lieder*, published in 1894 and financed by Vally with the proceeds from the sale of a brooch (Demetz, 146), was also written in the course of their relationship. In spite of the fact that Rilke repudiated them later it is a pity that these early documents have not been made readily available. We can believe him when he says that he published only those poems which did not reveal his inner self. A proud and somewhat cultivated shyness in regard to his innermost personal feelings is a feature which can be observed all along, notwithstanding his desire, expressed in a letter to Baroness von Oestéren, to be read and understood by a sympathetic public (*Br.vonOe.*, 23). To such a desire he seems to have yielded only for a short time, and even then with the obvious awareness of the expediency of the extrovert endeavors. His correspondence with Baroness von Oestéren was confined to his last year in Prague, and while in it he indulges in all sorts of plans to found literary leagues along modernistic lines (*Br.vonOe.*, 30ff), he confesses at the same time that the only people in whom he cares to arouse interest are the few select who are able to understand, assent, and laud, not "the herd of philistines." He would rather be "endured by God than idolized by the mob" (*Br.vonOe.*, 38). With some of the sharp edges taken off this phraseology, the attitude here expressed remained much the same throughout his life.

In a letter to Ellen Key, Rilke rejects his earliest poems as if they had never existed (Key, 127). Elsewhere he claims that they were no more than an arbitrary pretext for inner concentration, adding that it would amount to star-gazing conceit if one were to see in these "most useless trifles" the germs of future developments (*Br.* I,212). In order to place these and similar statements in their proper perspective we must realize that Rilke's growth, unlike that of Hugo von Hofmannsthal, was spiral. The latter has been described, not without exaggeration, as a "dying Spring, which in a single night unfolds all its petals" (*Rec.*, 129). Rilke, at any rate, was inclined at each stage to look down upon the previous ones. "Believe me," he writes to Heygrodt in 1922, "I shall be glad, indeed it would suit me best to perform every new task under a new name" (*Br.Muzot*, 97). Even his *Book of Hours* had its turn of falling into disgrace, while at other moments he recognized its organic nexus with *Malte*, the *New Poems*, the *Elegies* and the *Sonnets*. As Rilke's mastery grew he tended to regard a work of art as a thing *sui generis*, which must be judged only by its inner laws. Not even the effect which it produces or its so-called beauty is relevant. "A work of art exists as such only in so far as it stands on its own feet, and the telling works of unknown artists that have been preserved, lose nothing of their significance and being because of our inability to link them to the events and dates of their author's lives" (*Br.Muzot*, 97-98).

Such views may have their legitimate place, but they cannot preclude other approaches at different levels. That Rilke himself considered the knowledge of certain biographical data as helpful in the understanding of a poet is evidenced by his desire to obtain information about Trakl's life, "not with a view to 'understand' in the literal sense of the word, but in order to be confirmed here and there in the secret instinct which guides us" (*Br. 1914-21*, 35). While Rilke's earliest poems do not reveal much more than the peripheral reverberations of hidden forces and deeper experiences, they can throw light upon psychological realities confirming later achievements, thus making them better understood. The mere titles and themes, such as *Morning Dew, Night Fancies, Spring Storm, In the Evening, Arrival of Spring, Spring Night* are revealing (Sieber, 117). Rilke was always much concerned with the phenomena of transformation, of slow creative change, of transition from day to night and from night to day, from winter to spring, from summer to autumn, from life to death, from childhood through adolescence to full consciousness. Eventually this concern will issue in the Orphic Metamorphosis of the *Sonnets*.

Several ballads contained in *Leben und Lieder* seem to disclose Rilke's sympathy with the poor, the miserable and oppressed, notably with the woeful life of the artist. The same feeling prompted him to circulate among the poor some of his poems printed at his own cost. He called them *Wegwarten* (Chicory), and in the foreword of the first issue he explained that the publication of cheap editions was not good enough because the really poor could not buy even these. It is reported that he sometimes dressed like a priest and distributed these pamphlets to the passersby at some important street corner in Prague (Demetz, 58). According to Paracelsus the chicory plant was believed to become human every hundred years and the hope was cherished that these gifts, too, might be so transformed in the souls of the poor. Only three issues materialized, the first two being published in 1895, the third in October 1896, when Rilke was already in Munich. The fact that this last one was no longer intended for the poor but for a few select members of a small literary group throws some light on Rilke's peculiarly short-lived philanthropic impulse. The second issue consisted of a dramatic sketch *Now and in the Hour of our Death* in which the situation is this: A poor woman is dying. She has two daughters, one grown-up, the other still a child. Her landlord threatens her with eviction unless the elder daughter, Helen, surrenders to his whims. When she refuses, the threat is about to be carried out. Helen yields, but the dying mother discloses the fact that the landlord is Helen's father (Sieber, 133-134). To Rilke's commiseration for the abandoned and helpless is added a sense of the horrid and gruesome. Both these Rilkean features will undergo important changes as time goes on, but in one form or another they are met with at all stages of his growth.

In 1895 Rilke also wrote the psychodrama *Murillo* which appeared in a quarterly published in Bremen and which reveals still another Rilkean characteristic.[4] Murillo, during a walk, suddenly takes ill and is taken to a farmer's house. A priest is called and, in order to prove his identity, the dying painter takes a charcoal from the priest's censer and draws an *Ecce Homo* on the wall. Sieber discovers nothing worthwhile in this (Sieber, 133). Yet here we have an artist whose authenticity is questioned. Unknown and anonymous he has only one means by which he can prove his genius: the production of a masterpiece. What better symbol than this could Rilke have chosen for himself? It is true, his own masterpiece was still wanting, but the feeling that some day he must create one in order to justify himself in the eyes of his father and relatives, in the eyes of the world, and above all in his own eyes was strong in Rilke, not only in his youth but in his later life as well.

[4] About the psychodrama in general and the Rilkean variety in particular see: Howard E. Roman, "Rilke's Psychodramas" in the *Journal of English and Germanic Philology*, vol. 43, no. 4 (October 1944), 402-410. However, I do not think it necessary to assume that Rilke had been inspired by an original Murillo painting which he might have seen in some art gallery either at Dresden or elsewhere. Cheap reproductions of Murillo's *Ecce Homo* were to be found in Europe among the religious pictures in almost every Catholic home. And surely, the simple plot of Rilke's play, as well as its personal relevance, was not beyond his inventive power.

6. OFFERINGS TO THE LARES

◇◇

Denn dann nur sind die Stimmen gut,

....

Wenn hinter dem Gespräch der Saiten
Geräusche bleiben wie von Blut.

(FG)

Our spoken word is only good,

....

When back of the conversing chords
are lingering noises as of blood.

◇◇

THE productivity of Rilke in the years immediately preceding his departure from Prague, September 29, 1896, was great. As his son-in-law puts it, Rilke was already then possessed with the demon of creativity, and he remained so all his life (Sieber, 132). Besides writing for various journals and editing one himself, he reviewed books and published at the end of 1895 a collection of poems with the title *Offerings to the Lares.* A copy of another collection entitled *Dream-crowned* is extant with a dedication dated as early as December 1896 (*ET*, 70-71). These poems, therefore, were also written mainly in Prague.

As the title indicates the *Larenopfer* are offerings to the household gods. In these poems Rilke roams about his native city of Prague, with its houses and bridges, its churches, monasteries and statues of saints, its tenements and industrial quarter. On the whole his dependence on poetic tradition is proof that he has not yet found the rhythm of his own soul. But he is groping his way toward that goal, avoiding blind subservience to established patterns. A few years later Stefan George will chide him for publishing unripe verses and for succumbing too readily to the music of his own word. Liliencron, too, blamed him for the same reason (Demetz, 85) and Rilke himself, in the *Book of Images* of 1899,[5] warns against this tempting

[5] Of the *Book of Images* Rilke prepared two widely divergent editions. The first was published in 1902 and contained 45 poems, all written before he went to Paris; the second appeared in 1906 and contained 66 poems, most of which were written in Paris, some in Italy and Sweden. Cf. G. Craig Houston, *Modern Language Review*, vol. 29 (July 1934), 333-336.

desire to sing too soon: "What play you, boy? Behold, your soul was caught between the pipe-stems of syringa's bush" (*AW* I,114).

Of course, if the high standard which Malte Laurids Brigge demands of the poet were to be rigorously applied, much of Rilke's poetry would have to be scrapped:

"Verses written early are not worth much. One should wait and gather meaning and sweetness all one's life, and a long one if possible, and then, at the very end one might perhaps write ten lines which are good. For poetry is not, as people think, feelings (these come early enough)—it is experiences. For the sake of one line one ought to see many cities, people, and things; one must understand the animals, the flight of the birds, and the movement of the little flowers as they open in the morning. One must let memory go back over the paths of unknown regions, to unexpected meetings and to long anticipated departures—to days of childhood . . . to parents . . . to mornings at the sea-shore . . . to nights of travel. One must have memories of many nights of love, no two alike, of the screams of women in childbed. . . . One must have . . . sat by the dead in rooms with open windows and fitful noises. And it is not enough to have memories. One must be able to forget them . . . and wait with much patience until they come again. . . . Not until they become blood in us, glance and gesture, nameless and indistinguishable from ourselves, not until then may it happen in a very rare hour that the first word of a verse rises and issues forth from their midst." (*AW* II,20-21)

Actually, while striving relentlessly for ever greater self-discipline and perfection Rilke knew very well where to draw the line between theory and practice. And certainly at the time of his groping adolescence other considerations prevailed. Reviewing a volume of lyrical poems in April 1896, he declares that the "lyrical poem is the most personal artistic expression, and the more personal it is, the more it means to us. Because that which is innermost and most intimate actually comes nearer to that which is universally human: Les extrêmes se touchent" (*BTK*, 73). More characteristically still, in a letter of December 1897 to the publisher Bonz, he admits that "poems which accompany every stage of my soul's yearning are experiences through which I ripen" and that he cannot write "poems of epic or lyrical style which can stand five or ten years of desk-air without their becoming deathly sick" (*Br. 1892-1904,* 48-49). They must be published during the period in which they were written, otherwise they will be superseded and no longer representative of the period of growth. It is with considerations such as these in mind that Rilke consented later to have the *Offerings to the Lares* and *Dreamcrowned* republished in a volume entitled *First Poems.* The pressure of growing pains which call for the liberating word was exceedingly imperative in him. "Growing" strikes a keynote of his work.

Rilke's poetry must be understood against the background of its birth and growth, if it is to be understood at all. It is of more than superficial interest that only a year before he died the thought of the household gods intruded again when he tried to explain to Hulewicz, his Polish translator, the implications of Malte's *Notebook* and the *Elegies:*

"For our grandparents a home, a fountain, a familiar tower, or even their clothes, their coat, were still infinitely more meaningful, infinitely more intimate [than those things are for us to-day]; almost everything a vessel in which they found and to which they added something human. Now there are urged upon us from America empty, indifferent things, things which are so only in appearance, gadgets for trapping life . . . a house, in the American sense, an American apple or vine, has nothing in common with the house, the fruit, the grape into which has filtered the hope and thoughtfulness of our forefathers. The soulful, lived things, those which are aware of us, disappear and cannot be replaced. We are perhaps the last ones who have still known such things. On us rests the responsibility of preserving not only their memory (that would be little and unreliable), but their human and 'laric' worth ('Laric' understood in the sense of the household gods)" (*Br.Muzot,* 374-375).

These words, in which the reference to "American things" must not be understood too literally, were written in an attempt to explain what was meant in the *Elegies* by that peculiarly Rilkean transformation of the outer world into "Inner Cosmic Space." In the *Offerings to the Lares* that transformation has not even been initiated, let alone achieved, but the foundation for it is being laid, the raw material in the form of memories and feelings is being gathered. On the whole, the things singled out are still fixed in their

intangible concreteness; they have not yet acquired that magic suggestiveness of inter-planetary and inner-worldly relationship with
which they progressively become fraught. But the atmosphere which
surrounds them is already heavy with fertile, promising warmth.

This environmental warmth oozes out of a series of seven poems
entitled *The Building* (*EG*, 7-11). In contrast with modern mass-
production buildings the interior of this old house, with its clock,
its old family silhouettes, its spinning-wheel, its spinet, its postil,
and its Madonna, palpitates with the life of generations. The wind
sings in the chimney as parents and children say their prayers together. The grown-up boy and girl bring home their mates, whom
they woo and marry with the blessings of the father. Grandchildren
romp about in the midst of lovingly communing things. Father dies
under the eyes of the silhouettes and the Madonna, and the clock
ticks on as one generation makes room for another.

The same fragrance envelops the churches and bridges and chapels,
the old Hradschin filled to the brim with fateful history, the saints
in dim candle-light, the St. Annas, St. Catherines, St. Wenceslases,
and St. Nepomucks in the niches of houses and bridges, the children
in rags before angels in gold tinsel, the vaulted rooms and quaint
balconies of age-worn dwellings, the village fountain, and even those
hybrid buildings where the heavy Baroque rubs shoulders with the
frivolous Rococo, the *Abbé* with the *Roi Soleil*.

Already here, as later in his letter to Hulewicz and in several
passages of the *Elegies*, the poet bemoans with melancholy wrath
the barbarianism which destroys these lovable human things and
replaces them with ugly barracks, tenements and smokestacks. The
gossip-filled murmur of the public fountain is silenced by the intruding forwardness of modern plumbing and the tap upstairs.
What this profanation does to man is reflected in the stupefied faces
and weary looks of men and women returning from Smichov, the
industrialized section of Prague. On the other hand, the effect of a
rich childhood in the midst of things and gestures filled with intimacy and warmth may be temporarily neutralized by a noisy world
but eventually it will break through in crucial moments of life. In
the fourth poem of a group entitled *Vigils*, a girl, lost in a night of
lust and sin, suddenly remembers another night in which she kept
vigil at her mother's deathbed (*EG*, 43).

The things dealt with in the *Offerings to the Lares* differ less from those occurring in the later poems than is admitted. Inconspicuous and patient, they share silently our moments of joy and sorrow, our everyday and Sunday moods; here and there they even create quietly about themselves an air of timeless knowledge and cosmic space. The old woman selling roasted chestnuts year in and year out in her never-changing, tidy stand at the street corner (*EG*, 25) is related to the blind beggar of the *Book of Images* standing on the *Pont du Carrousel* in Paris, "colorless like the landmark of nameless realms, like the immovable center of the stars" (*AW* I,119). She is akin to the Sybil of the *New Poems* who from time immemorial has been known as an old woman, yet "remains and walks the same street daily," whose age must "be counted like that of forests, in centuries" (*NG*, 137). Rilke's desire to penetrate into the core of things was as old as his native inclination to pour out his feelings, although it was to require much practice in self-discipline before it could be translated into artistic achievement. In Prague he had friendly relations with the painter Emil Orlik, whose work he admired because in it "the essence [der Extrakt] of things" seemed to have been caught with remarkable precision (Demetz, 72).

In the *Offerings to the Lares*, too, there are poems in which Rilke's lifelong concern with death is expressed. Already here the feeling prevails that this concern cannot be allowed to stifle the joy of living. The little boy who visits his mother's grave with his father need not be deprived of his gingerbread from the nearby fair. From the lips of a kneeling angel in the graveyard flutters a butterfly, and out of the earth-covered skull grows a forget-me-not. In the ballad-like poem *Rabbi Löw* the ties which bind the living to the dead are inescapable. When the grown-ups sin, innocence and childhood are murdered. When the death of childhood emerges from the consciousness of the adolescent, he is torn by nightmares and anguish (*EG*, 55-58). This mysteriously compensatory interrelation of all beings is likewise expressed in the poem *Dreams*. Night, richly adorned, brings with the gracefully giving hands of a Madonna a golden dream to a child; but as the price of that gift she must visit another child whose sick soul she carries off (*EG*, 23). Rilke's faith in life in spite of his awareness of death has its roots in his youthful vital urge inherited from his mother. Even Schopenhauer's pessimism is unable to overwhelm him. In a poem *And Yet* he admits reading "my"

Schopenhauer, whose view of the world as a prison full of woe he does not try to refute. But precisely in the solitude of that prison he strikes chords in his soul which sound happiness as pure as that which flowed from the violin of the entombed knight Dalibor (*EG*, 29).[6]

It is true that even at this time Rilke was not unaware of the fragility of his faith in life. In a sketch of January 1896 entitled *A Dead Girl* a girl is depicted who suffers from a strange mental disease. She is convinced that she died in her childhood, "a thousand years ago," when she saw one of her playmates, a boy, hold a little bird in his hands, stick his thumb cold-bloodedly into its mouth and choke the defenseless creature to death. Since that time the girl, who among her dolls had been sheltered from the coarser aspects of human nature, has walked through the days like a ghost from the other world. What brings her back to reality and life is the acquaintance she makes of a young man whose human kindness somehow reestablishes her faith. While observing him throw bread crumbs to a little bird in the woods she is reborn, and the two become engaged. Alas, soon afterward the young man contracts an incurable disease and must go away, leaving their short-lived dream of happiness unfulfilled. The girl wanders off to a pond and dies her second death (*BVP 1896*, 80-92). With a lyrical poet like Rilke even stories like this one, which lack all outward signs of personal involvement, may legitimately be interpreted as expressions of personal moods. At any rate, the disconcerting precariousness of the girl's regained faith in life was fundamentally the same as that to which Rilke knew himself to be exposed. It reached its climax some ten years later when during the "Malte period" his survival seemed seriously menaced. Yet owing to the amazing resiliency of his vital instinct, this supreme crisis, too, was weathered and ultimately left the poet steeled for new tasks.

In the nature poems of the *Offerings to the Lares* we find Rilke listening with equal intentness to the stillness in May when the earth is covered with hecatombs of blossoms, to the approaching evening when night prepares to scatter its diamonds in the blueness of space, to the autumn when the air is mouldy with the scent of

---

[6] In the second of his *Two Prague Stories* entitled *Brother and Sister*, Rilke refers to the knight Dalibor who had been entombed in a Hunger Tower and was said to have learned to play the violin through sheer longing (*ESF*, 233).

decaying leaves, to the summer night weary from the fever of a hot day, or to the morning in winter when the crisp cold reddens the ears and the sun kisses a dreamy new day. Knowingly the adolescent poet enters into the season of expectant dreaming, in which he will be crowned a king whom beggars and children may call brother (*EG*, 67). The beggars and the children are already appearing in such poems as *The Poor Child, Sphinx, The Mother, Behind Smichov, At the Ursulines' Convent, In the Suburb.* And King Evening, like one of the three kings of Bethlehem, follows the star which leads Him to Mother Night holding Her babe, the Dream, in Her arms, to whom He brings from the Orient His treasures of gold (*EG*, 24). Thus dreaming, the dreamer waits and listens. Rilke knows that in so doing he becomes oblivious of the world and its realities and that a moment of luck may pass him by. For dreams are like orchids, colorful and rich. They suck their vital sap from the roots of life and glory in their spurious blood. For a fleeting moment they create bliss, only to pale and die in the next. Yet, their fragrance keeps hovering over the waking world, which the dreamer knows to be moving softly above (*EG*, 30-31).

7. HOMELESS

Ich habe kein Vaterhaus
und habe auch keines verloren.
(*BB*)

I am without paternal roof,
nor have I ever had one.

THERE are a few poems of a strictly autobiographical nature in the *Larenopfer*. The one entitled *The House of My Birth* contains distinct memories of early childhood. It discloses clearly that Rilke did experience all the warm happiness which a true home can give. He remembers the blue silk drawing-room and the picture books. Great joy was derived from a doll's dress with strands of thick silver, but his arithmetic elicited many tears. On the window sill he played tramway or ship; already then he had a great liking for poems. The poem ends with the melancholy charm of a fairy tale: opposite his home in a palace lived a blond girl, a young countess, who beckoned to him and smiled when he threw her kisses. But now the palace has lost its charm as the girl is gone where she can smile no more (*EG*, 35).

I do not know whether some measure of reality is hidden behind the concluding lines of this poem, but keeping in mind that Rilke reminisces we may safely assume that a situation such as is described, imaginary though it may be, serves to identify a significant mood. Rilke yearned for female company and love. In his childhood years the happiness inherent in that yearning was hale and pure, not vitiated by the desire of possession or the fear of possible loss. The object of love is there, inviting and responding, but actual contact does not occur. It is like one of those dreams which are like orchids, beautiful in their sensual experience as long as they last. Seen in retrospect they pale and die, as indeed the object of yearning loses its real or imagined existence. But the fragrance of the dream floats on, and it is that fragrance which Rilke evokes in his poem. The time for such hale and pure experiences is childhood, the age of innocence, when the eyes still open restfully into the round sphere of life without yet being turned back upon themselves. Whether intentionally or not the situation depicted provides the pattern and outline of countless later ones in Rilke's life and work.

From his work let me quote only Abelone's song in Malte's *Notebook* (*AW* II,209):

> Thou whom I tell not that in the night
> I lie weeping,
> Whose soul maketh me languid
> As doth a cradle a child;
> Thou who tellest me not when thou liest awake
> For my sake;
> What if this feast
> Without fulfilment
> Be endured within us?
> Look at the lovers,
> When first they confessed
> How soon the lie leapeth to their lips.

Thou makest me alone. Thee alone can I exchange.
For a while it is thou, then again the rustling wind,
Or it is a fragrance without a rest.
Alas, in my arms I have lost them all,
Thou alone, only thou art forever born anew!
Because I never claimed thee I hold thee fast.

And from Rilke's life let me recall again his fantastic love of Benvenuta. Here is a woman whom he had never seen in body, who beckons invitingly from afar. The ardor of the kisses which the poet throws to her across space can only be gauged if his marvelous letters are read. How he clings to the dream in its childlike sensuality and hallowed purity! How he yearns, yet hesitates to cross the dividing space! And the dream, like the orchid, fades and dies upon awakening fulfilment, leaving only its melancholy fragrance in its wake.

When I entered the University is the title of another autobiographical poem. Rilke records with satisfaction that at last, at the end of wearisome years of retardment and frustration, he is what he longed to be, "ein Skolar," a university student. Originally he was to study law but he soon veered away from this arid pursuit. Medicine was tabooed by his girl, Vally, and so he contents himself, gladly enough, with the splendid liberal arts course which his university offered. The ambition to graduate does not seem to be overwhelming, as long as he can enjoy the feeling of being "ein Skolar" (*EG*, 27).

That a certain amount of adolescent bravado is manifest here cannot be denied. But the truth is that Rilke was never impressed by academic lore as such. He often thought that he might have found more enduring contentment in a medical career, but apart from that vague and intermittent hope of escape, neither degrees, nor professions, nor, indeed, any kind of conventional learning had the least attraction for him. He is a roving dreamer, homeless in the world of stereotyped knowledge, homesick for the artistic realization of a world of his own making. As early as 1892 he wrote that he strove for a firm, beautiful, and shining goal, not along the road where ordinary people trudge, not on the broad-trodden highway of the millions—no, his aim was "to press upward on paths of his own making for the cloudless light on high!" (*Br. 1892-1904*, 5).

Rilke's feeling of homelessness, of not belonging, was basically constitutional, but it was greatly strengthened by the circumstances of his life. His early education as a girl, his mother's hysterical pretense, his humiliation at the military schools, his father's bourgeois ideals, the separation of the parents, the general lack of sympathy with his ideals, and finally his lonely room at the home of an aunt —all these conditions produced a cumulative effect upon his daily existence and sentiments. The sensation of being an orphan was deep-seated and genuine, judging by the various poems evoking the delicate nostalgia of the isolated soul (*Br.Frühzeit*, 229-230, 235ff).

But the circumstances of isolation were not confined to his family surroundings. The double-faced city of Prague and the position of Czechoslovakia within a heterogeneous empire contributed their share. Prague was an outpost of German-Austrian culture in Czech territory. There was not much room left for understanding between the smug, but imperiled, feeling of superiority on the part of the German minority and the patriotic pride of the Czech people. It is true that outside of the political sphere the Austrian régime was liberal and respectful of freedom, but that did not prevent the cultural schism from being real. Rilke, whose heritage and upbringing were German, was deprived of the sustaining communion with the people among whom he grew up. There was a certain amount of literary activity among the German population, in which Rilke took part, but everywhere it was confronted with a foreign, though really native, world. If Rilke was to realize his great ambition as a poet, it became increasingly clear to him that he must part not only with his family but with his native city as well.

Even Austria as a whole, with its mixture of nationalities and languages, did not seem to Rilke the atmosphere in which he could thrive. He never learned to speak the Czech language, although he had warm sympathy for the people, the Bohemian landscape, and Czech folklore. But folksong, landscape, and the soul of the simple, suffering people were for Rilke akin to childhood, a state in which nationality is irrelevant. It matters little that the Czech people were not the sort of naïve folk whom Rilke, stung by the condescendent attitude of his German relatives and acquaintances, saw in them (Demetz, 160); what matters is the impression they made on him. Everything connected with childhood cast a spell over his soul, and the poems in the *Offerings to the Lares* which deal with the Czech land and folk are among the best of the collection.

For politics Rilke had a constitutional dislike. Its relative predominance in Prague only served to accentuate his sense of home-lessness. In a poem entitled *In Dubiis* he considered that man the greatest who pledges himself to no flag and, because he has detached himself from the part, now belongs to the whole. It ends with the thought that in that whole, which is his real home, his fatherland is no more than the house in which he was born into the world (*EG*, 36-37). In a poem of *Dreamcrowned* he dreams that the loud sick world has suddenly been reduced to dust; only the great idea of the cosmos remains in his heart. And that cosmic world proves to be what he thought it was: free of conflict, with nothing but the wings of the golden sun spread over the peaceful green forests (*EG*, 75). In a letter of December 1895 he expressed the desire to turn away from the earth, "that tiny clod in the Universe," and to surrender to the Universe, against whose background the earthly hardships almost dwindle to nothingness (*Br. 1892-1904*, 7).

PART II

FAREWELL TO PRAGUE

◇◇◇

Hab ich nicht recht . . . Vater?
(Fourth Elegy)

Am I not right . . . Father?

◇◇◇

8. PATIENCE OR SPEED?

◇◆

> Alles das Eilende
> wird schon vorüber sein . . .
> (*Son.* I,22)
>
> All that which hurries
> soon passes, is gone . . .

◇◆

IN THESE years Rilke is clearly undoing the knots which have held him bound to empiric contingencies; he is groping for that ideal realm where human discriminations are resolved, if not denied and obliterated. More and more he distrusts the pragmatic rationalization with which modern man moves away from fundamentals. In a poem addressed to the Czech writer Julius Zeyer, Vally's uncle, he applauds the latter's endeavors to keep alive in his people the love of their lore while not letting their patriotic ideals stray off to the stars through sterile self-glorification (*EG*, 30). Again, Rilke seems to have been slightly biased in favor of his sweetheart's uncle who in reality was not particularly interested in simple people. In Rilke's time there were among the Czech writers a cosmopolitan *avant garde* who were chiefly interested in streamlining Czech literature on the neo-romantic and symbolist patterns of Western Europe. They considered Zeyer as their inspired forerunner (Demetz, 149-150). In his two retrospective Prague stories (1899), *King Bohusch* and *Brother and Sister*, Rilke defines what is wrong with these writers and artists: between their art and their people there was an unbridged chasm. In their chase after up-to-dateness they swarmed abroad, to Paris and elsewhere, to garner substance and symbols, only to return home with a superiority complex and a *fin-de-siècle* attitude. They had ripened too fast in hothouse air on exotic food, so that their starving people did not know what to make of the fruit. Because of their impatience they had reached the end while still at the beginning (*ESF*, 225). There is a charming little poem in *Offerings to the Lares* which, whatever else it may mean, would seem to characterize the situation. It is called *The Fairytale of the Cloud*. A little cloud is attracted by the yellow-gold moon as the day draws to a close. Avidly it would like to filch and wrap around itself a bit of that glittering gold. Passing by, it lingers long enough to chew its cheeks full of the enchanting light. But soon the night picks up the brilliant lining, and the cloud, black again, disappears in the dark (*EG*, 39).

There would seem to be an inconsistency between Rilke's admonition to the Czech writers to be more patient and allow time for natural growth, and his envious praise of the fig tree in the *Sixth Elegy*:

> Fig tree, for long have I marveled how
> you all but forget to blossom
> and pour your purest secret, unpraised,
> into your timely, determined fruit.
> Like the spout of the fountain your curved boughs
> drive downwards and thither the sap: and, hardly awake,
> it leaps from its sleep into its happiest fulfilment.
> Lo, as God into swan.
>   . . . But we demur,
> alas, we are proud of blooming: too late do we enter,
> betrayed, into the core of our final fruit.

On close examination, however, the contradiction is more apparent than real. What the poet contemplates with envious eyes is that the fig tree is able to leap unretarded into the sweetest fulfilment *without thereby cheating the laws of organic and natural growth*. If man's maturing is to remain sound, it is a tragic necessity for him to grow slowly. At the same time his impatient reason and yearning heart may burn the stages and race ahead. Our natural growth, both individually and socially, is out of tempo with our rational and scientific accomplishments as well as with our dreams, and thus with the kind of world in which we exist. When we do reach ripeness, we are too late. The Czech artists have recklessly atrophied their organs of growth by severing the sap-bearing connections with their roots, their people. The fruit which they bear is anemic and brittle. That Rilke himself left the city and country of his birth without ever returning to stay is obviously a different matter. The physical and social surroundings in which he was born and grew up lacked the life-giving substance needed, and so he was driven both by inner necessity and by circumstantial pressure to seek and eventually create for himself a new home, nowhere and everywhere, near the very roots of birth and death alike.

Both the experience of coming too late and that of leaping ahead were causes of discontent in Rilke; in fact, they were correlated, the one occasioned by the other. The feeling that he had lost precious years in his childhood and youth never left him. His envious praise of the fig tree in the *Sixth Elegy* is its poetic expression, and in his famous letter to his former teacher of St. Pölten, General von Sedlakowitz, he declares bitterly: "At that time, when I left military school, I was confronted with the enormous tasks of my life, exhausted, abused in body and spirit, retarded at the age of sixteen. I had been cheated out of the most innocent part of my strength and consequently out of that irretrievable preparation, which would have laid down smooth steps for the ascent which now I was forced to begin enfeebled and impaired, with the steepest walls in front of me" (*Br. 1914-21*, 352). However, it would be wrong to assume that this early retardment was the only one, or that it alone accounted for his elegiac plaints. Coming too late, feeling betrayed through lingering growth caused humiliating anxieties at all stages of his life, while at the same time he kept demanding obedient submission to the laws of growth. As he puts it in one of his *Sonnets*, only then are we just when, in spite of all, we praise, because, alas, we are only "the sweetness of ripening peril" (*AW* I,313). And several months later, in December 1922, he exhorts us to become like flowers rooted in the soil, to follow our inner paths at the ordained spot (*AW* I,376-377). During and after his trip to Russia Rilke complains of being unable—that is, insufficiently ripe—to assimilate the overwhelming impressions and to find for them the liberating transforming symbols. And it is symptomatic that when the Russian experience eventually did crystallize in his first *Book of Hours*, the main motif which emerged was that of obscure, patient growth. Even the Russian God was never finished but kept ripening in the depths of the people's souls behind the impersonal features of their icons.

Throughout his life Rilke was waiting for the happy constellation which would concentrate all the disparate elements into the focal creative moment. In doing so he developed an extremely delicate sense of divination which enabled him to register the most subliminal pulsation of life. His waiting and hearkening was patient and impatient at the same time; patient because deep down in his soul he knew, and his experience confirmed, that the hour of the plastic word would come. "The hour bows down and touches me with a clear, metallic stroke: my senses are trembling" (*AW* I,9). It was impatient, because waiting is painful and the human mind and body are not always equal to the strain. In the same *Book of Hours* in which he exalts the unfinished God of the Russian people he impugns the Italian Renaissance paintings for their brilliant light and color and their undoubting finality of contour and expression. They impress him as too loud and forward, as having prematurely written *finis* under the processes of life. They paint Madonnas like fair mothers. "The branch of the tree god, which spreads over Italy, *has* already bloomed. Perhaps it would fain have filled the fruit before its time, had it not tired in the midst of growing; it will bear no fruit" (*AW* I,25). Likewise the Italian springs with their sudden burst of lavish flowering, the Swiss Alps with their ostentatious concentration of grandeur brought about by impatient Nature, are phenomena of haste which prevent mellow fruition. "All that which hurries soon passes, is gone" (*AW* I,295).

9. RILKE AND MRS. GRUNDY

⟡⟡⟡

> Lieber im Freien verrecken
> Als sich im Winkel verstecken
> Lauernd und lugend!
> *(BVP 1896)*
>
> Rather croak in freedom
> than hide in a corner
> waiting and lurking!

⟡⟡⟡

WE MUST return to Rilke, the youth. The realization that his true destiny was to be a poet took sharper form toward the end of his Prague years. His confidence and faith were great, although he could not foresee what the future held in store for him. However, he did have a premonition of the sacrifices involved; as he puts it later in his *Requiem* for Paula Modersohn-Becker, he knew that "somewhere

there is an old hostility between our human life and greatest work"
(*AW* I,219). Evident among other things is a poem in the *Larenopfer* bearing the title *The Young Sculptor*. An inner voice tells the
budding artist that he must leave his girl for Rome where he expects to produce a masterpiece. He promises her to be back in a year.
As he is carried off on the waves of his quest his sense of guilt drives
him back home, only to find his girl dead. And it is his dead girl
whom he sculptures for his masterpiece (*EG*, 15). The stark implications of this sad little story are impressive if we look at Rilke's
homeless wanderings, at the frightful solitude with which he was
to pay for the glory of his work.

There is an aspect to Rilke's personality which in its usual manifestations is distinctive enough but which at times takes on especially
sharp form. It does so with unexpected vehemence in the years of
his growing determination to sever his home ties and may be described as a resolute stubbornness in seeking for himself conditions
which will enable him to be himself, to devote his entire life to the
prompting demon in him. In order to bring about these conditions
he must resist and ward off—if need be, ruthlessly—whatever hindrances the world may oppose. In his childhood that impulse had
operated quite instinctively, inasmuch as he kept writing verse in
spite of discouragement at home and humiliation at school. Later it
became a conscious struggle, accompanied by much suffering to
himself and others. The hindrances were greatest and his resistance
most tenacious in his youth, when his writings were still groping
efforts, when in the eyes of the world his future was still uncertain
and his dependence on his family inescapable. He still had to find
his way out of a maze of conventions and adopted attitudes. In a
letter of April 1897 to Ludwig Ganghofer he says that a very dark
childhood had made him diffident, that he had to force his way out
of the military schools, that his relatives held the frightful view that
art was a mere pastime, to be indulged in when the day's work was
done. "Whoever does not consecrate himself wholly to art with all
his wishes and his worth can never reach the highest goal. Art is
not a martyrdom, but a battle for life" (*Br. 1892-1904*, 40). Elsewhere
he versifies (*Br. 1892-1904*, 5):

> A genius, so noble observers of men suppose,
> Is often doomed to ruin—

No!—If the period creates no great men for itself
Then the man will create himself a great period!

How deeply he resented the tyranny of public opinion is revealed
in a sketch dated February 1896 and entitled *A Character*. In it is
depicted the career of a businessman, who as a child was exhibited
as the pride of the family. Every Sunday he was called into the cold
parlor to be shown off and to be admired for his resemblance to
one or the other relative, for his cleverness, and for God knows what.
The little boy learned very quickly how "the others" wanted him to
be and act. When his father died, the youth took over the business,
and the rumors started at once: there were to be great innovations
and new enterprises. And true enough, they presently took place
and were crowned with success. Then it was being whispered that
the young man was engaged, and the name of the lucky girl was not
omitted. In due time, that engagement also came about and was
followed by the wedding. Some people had heard that the pros-
perous man was going to contribute a large sum toward a new
theatre. How could he refuse without hurting his business? It was
further gossiped that the young wife was with child. On this occasion the wind was very nearly taken out of rumor's sails for the
expected event did not happen. It was then discreetly suggested that
a water cure at a nearby spa might bring about the desired result, and
this stratagem was crowned with success. Next, well-wishing friends
had it on good authority that the prominent man was going to be
decorated. What else could he do but to satisfy rumor in this respect
as well? Finally, the poor fellow took ill. Out of feverish dreams
he was awakened by crowds of people gathered outside. On enquiry
he was told that a false rumor had spread that he was dead. Obediently the feeble man surrendered to his fever and died (*BVP 1896*,
75-80).

It is plain that in this little sketch Rilke did not intend to give a
realistic picture, but to cast ridicule on a type of attitude and to express his contempt for it. Lacking all redeeming features, the picture contains unconcealed signs of caricature. Or it might be dubbed
a parable. It opens up perspectives typical of peculiarly Rilkean motifs. Here is a man who lives, loves, and dies according to the pattern
devised by other people. It is usually claimed that the idea of the "authentic death" (der eigene Tod) was suggested to Rilke by the writ-

ings of Jens Peter Jacobsen. It is clearly foreshadowed in Rilke's sketch. The death of this businessman is of the same kind as those of the Hôtel-Dieu in Paris, where deaths are manufactured on the principles of the assembly line and disposed of as finished goods by means of classification and labelling (*AW* II,11-12). His death is akin to that of Paula Modersohn who, instead of living and dying in obedience to her own law of the creative artist, returned to her husband's world "where saps will have their way" (*AW* I,214) and died "like women long ago, died in the warm house, in the old fashion, the death of those in child-bed" (*AW* I,217-218).

> Too long this suffering has lasted,
> and none is equal to it; it's too hard for us,
> this tortuous suffering from spurious love,
> which, building on prescription like a habit,
> calls itself legitimate, feasting on injustice.
>
> ....
>
> For this is guilt, if anything be guilt,
> not to augment the freedom of a love
> with all the freedom in one's power.

Not much later, in June 1909, Rilke writes to Hugo Heller, the Viennese bookdealer, whose first wife, like Paula Modersohn, was a painter and died in child-birth: "The fate which I attempted to relate and to lament in *Requiem* (the inexorable fate which you too experienced at painful proximity) is perhaps the real conflict of the artist: the opposition and contradiction between objective experience and personal enjoyment of the world" (*Letters 1892-1910*, 345). And the life of the businessman sketched is manifestly as spurious as his death. It is one of those countless lives which, after their fortuitous owners have left them, lie about in the "museums of history like so many coats of mail, sedan chairs, and cradles which have never been occupied by genuine human beings," or "like those garments which are unable to stand alone and fold up against the walls, craving their support" (*AW* I,65).

In order to safeguard the independence and solitude needed for his work, Rilke was never at a loss to find the appropriate formula which often enough concealed a fair dose of sophistry. On April 29, 1901, he married Clara Westhoff, a close friend of Paula Becker, who in turn married Otto Modersohn a few weeks later, on Whitsunday, May 22. Paula was much disappointed and saddened when she found that marriage seemed to have made Clara forget their former friendship, and she complained to her in a letter of November or December 1901, at the same time accusing Rilke of having completely overpowered his wife's personality and obliterated her independence. "I have watched you with melancholy feelings," she writes Clara. "Rilke speaks too strongly through your words. Can it be that love demands of us that we become indistinguishable from our partner? No, a thousand times no. Is not the bond between two strong people so rich and full of blessings precisely because each reigns and serves in simplicity and peace, in joy and quiet happiness? . . . You have taken off much from yourself and spread it out as a carpet before your King. Dear Rainer Maria Rilke, I set the dogs at you. And I believe, it is necessary that I do so" (Modersohn-Becker, 165).

The interesting feature of this letter is that Paula blames Rilke for having seriously interfered with Clara's personal autonomy, for having violated her right to freedom in individual solitude. She accuses him of the very kind of male possessiveness which he will castigate so pathetically later. And it is significant that it was Rilke, not Clara, who answered Paula's letter in February 1902, shrewdly turning the gist of Paula's complaint to his own advantage and against her —an early and illuminating example of how Rilke could rationalize his own shortcomings to suit his own needs. With deep-felt wrath he wrote back from Bremen (*Br.Frühzeit*, 167):

"Does it surprise you that the centres of gravity have shifted, and is your love and friendship so distrustful that it wants constantly to see and grasp what it possesses? . . . I, too, am standing quietly and full of deep trust before the gates of this solitude, because I hold this to be the highest function of a bond between two people, that each should stand guard over the solitude of the other. For, if it lies in the nature of the indifferent and of the crowd to recognize no solitude, then love and friendship are there for the purpose of providing at all times the opportunity for solitude. Only those are true moments of communion which rhythmically interrupt periods of deep isolation."

It is true that when Paula wrote her letter, Clara was pregnant, and when Rilke answered he had already become a father and was faced with grave worries as to his and his family's future. But Paula's accusation refers to the whole period since Clara's wedding, and it is difficult to believe that she was entirely mistaken when she felt that Rilke put "his beautiful and colorful seals not only on his calligraphic letters" but on his wife as well (Modersohn-Becker, 165). When in 1906 Rilke was staying on the Island of Capri while Clara was in Germany, Lou Andreas-Salomé, in a letter to Clara, blamed Rilke for shirking his duty as a father and a husband. The poet's answer was one of the most stirring and most revealing confessions to his wife, a self-justification as much as it was an explanation and apology (*Br.* I,148-153).

Rilke's dogged determination to secure and safeguard his autonomy and freedom in a world of his own choice reached at times the pitch of outspoken rebellion. In the Nietzsche-inspired little poem of 1896 entitled *Flames,* he exclaims rudely: "Rather croak in freedom than hide in a corner waiting and lurking! Ever on to light, heedless of contempt and sneers! Far worse it is to label one's impotence virtue. Virtue is squalid! I am for the blazing fire of youth. Who shall condemn the flame? It is the heat of fever that engenders works and worlds!" (*BVP 1896*, 59). But a far more outspoken outburst of Nietzschean intransigence is the story entitled *The Apostle,* also of 1896. Most biographers do not know what to make of this defiant fit of insurrection or where to place it in the whole of Rilke's work. Nora Wydenbruck calls it a "puerile gospel of Hate" whose tenor she is willing to derive from the kind of manufactured "ideology" which Ewald Tragy (Rilke) concocts in Munich under the pressure of his snobbish acquaintances (Wydenbruck, 49). With its help Ewald, who until then had been a stray and lonely sheep, at once became a most popular member of the clique (*ET*, 48). I do not know on what grounds Mrs. Wydenbruck bases her view, but even if it were correct it would only mitigate somewhat the intensity of the mood expressed. The mood itself is entirely in keeping with Rilke's state of mind.[1]

In the large, brilliantly-lit diningroom of a hotel are gathered the men and women of wealthy society, displaying their effete wit and rich jewels and indulging in the finest wines and most sophisticated foods. They have been gathered thus for days. At one end of the

---

[1] Werner Neuse, too, in "Hauptmanns und Rilkes 'Der Apostel,'" *Germanic Review,* vol. 18 (October 1943), 196-201, sees no connection between Rilke's *The Apostle* and the rest of his work.

table sits a stranger, a pale, austere individual, dressed in outmoded fashion. A young widowed baroness who takes him to be an artist makes desperate efforts to attract his attention by conspicuously shooting the flashing reflections of her diamonds towards him. When these wiles fail she turns the conversation to a reported tragic fire in a nearby village which has made many people homeless. She proposes the formation of a charity committee for the purpose of alleviating the sufferings of the victims, singling the stranger out with a special invitation to join. Everybody agrees with the exception of the latter who replies in a brutal tone: "No!" In the midst of the general consternation he then proceeds to preach his gospel of callous hardness toward all human grief:

"You do a work of love, I go into the world to kill love. Wherever I find it I shall murder it. And I find it often enough in hovels as well as in castles, in churches and in free nature. I pursue it and give it no quarter. . . . People were green and gullible when the Nazarene came and brought them Love. He in His childish magnanimity thought He was doing them good!—For a race of giants Love could be a beautiful pillow, in whose voluptuous manner of response they might dream new dreams. But for the weak Love means ruin. . . . I do not speak of sexual love, but of charity, of pity and sympathy, of grace and leniency. There are no worse poisons in our souls! . . . He whom they glorify as the Messiah has turned the whole world into a hospital. The feeble, miserable, and decrepit He calls His children. And the strong are only there to protect them, to care for them and to serve the emaciated brood. And when I feel within me the flaming desire for Light, red-hot, deep, and heavenly, when I climb with firm step the steep, stony path of achievement, and when I see the bright heavenly goal shine, am I to stoop to the cripple who crouches by the wayside, am I to praise him, lift him, and drag him along while my burning strength cools off in the grasp of his marrowless corpse?—How are we to get to the top if we loan our strength to the weak? Never can the dull-witted, many-headed crowd be the bearer of progress; only the "One," the great one, whom the rabble hates in the dark instinct of its own smallness, can walk with divine power and a triumphant smile the road of the intransigent Will" (*ESF*, 347-357).

That is strong language, coming from a poet who is universally, and in a sense rightly, loved for his feelings of understanding; whom a sensitive and enthusiastic lady, Marie von Thurn und Taxis, could call the "Seraphico"; whose work seems replete with deep sympathy for the poor and disinherited. Regardless of how they may be interpreted, these words of *The Apostle* are there to remind us that there was something hard and ruthless in Rilke's make-up which we must face and try to understand. It is not enough to point out that they were meant vicariously, or that they were mere vaporizings of a restive youth chewing at his chains. Similar expressions of revolt occur too often. Rilke had read Schopenhauer and, no doubt, Nietzsche. Speaking of the Swedish writer Hans Larsson in a letter of July 9, 1904 he says: "Nietzsche, who acted as an opiate on many of our men at home, is for him a medicine which has made him healthier" (*Br. 1902-06*, 195).

It is difficult to estimate the extent of publicity which Rilke allowed these and similar unorthodox expressions to receive at the time. His diaries, his sketches, *The Apostle, A Character*, and others, his autobiographic *Ewald Tragy*, were not published until after his death, while his letters had, of course, very definite destinations. Though he could not entirely conceal his rebellious attitudes, he certainly did not proclaim them from the house-tops; he was still too dependent, financially and emotionally, on the good-will and understanding of his parents, his relatives and acquaintances, and he was exceedingly anxious to vindicate his genius in their eyes. Therefore, he was impelled to resort to all sorts of lies and concealments in order not to shock and alienate them too much (see below, p. 305).

10. RILKE AND CHRIST

<><><><><><><><><><><><><><><><><><><><><><><><><><><><><><><><><><><><><><><><><>

Ich kann mir nicht vorstellen, dass das *Kreuz bleiben* sollte, das doch nur ein Kreuzweg war. . . . Welcher Wahnsinn, uns nach einem Jenseits abzulenken, wo wir hier von Aufgaben und Erwartungen und Zukünften umstellt sind.

(AW II,306,308)

I cannot imagine that the *Cross*, which never was more than a Crossroads, should *remain*. . . . How foolish to sidetrack us towards a Beyond, when we are here surrounded by tasks and expectations and futures!

(Rilke, *Workman's Letter*)

<><><><><><><><><><><><><><><><><><><><><><><><><><><><><><><><><><><><><><><><><>

RILKE's attitude to Christianity underwent profound changes in his adolescent years. They were mixed with feelings of resentment against his mother and the kind of overwrought piety in which she had brought him up—of resentment, too, against the shackles which dependence upon mediating saints put on the freedom and autonomy of inspiration. He shook off the yoke of the Guardian Angel as is evidenced by his early Angel poems, one of which approaches Promethean daring *(FG,* 26):

> Stern Angel of Ebony,
> Giant unconcerned,
> Thy silence never yet
> melted in the heat
> of penitent hands.
> Thou, wrapt in burning prayers,
> Thy suppliants
> are proud:
> like Thee.
>
> Thou who turnest to stone,
> and above staring eyes becomest
> King, choose
> a race to whom
> Thou appearest just,

Giant of
seamy thought.

Thou who instillest fear
in all who are weary,
there's one greater
than Thou, Thy shadow.

Correspondingly Christ as a Mediator and Saviour was in Rilke's way, just as He was in the way of the "Apostle." Already in a poem of 1893 (unpublished, State Library, Berlin) the divinity of Christ is emphatically denied (Sievers, 79). That Christ allowed Himself to be worshipped as God was an expression of pride. Rather than recognize that He was human and mortal like the rest of us, He preferred to die on the cross and to gratify thereby His immense vanity. And in a series of seven poems of 1897 entitled *Visions of Christ* (Sievers, 80-85), the same theme is developed. Christ, as the father of a child born to Mary Magdalen, is thoroughly stripped of the supernatural. Only children have the right to call Him God, as only children are entitled to a Guardian Angel. Christ's death on the cross is a concession to the masses. Unable to understand His unique and strange greatness, they first thought Him a fool and then deified Him on Calvary and resurrected Him afterward. In reality, by so doing they degraded His eminent humanity. Other poems of the same period, such as *The Last Judgment* (BB, 80-87; NG, 147), *The Crucifixion* (NG, 157) and *The Last Supper* (NG, 176), of which other versions appear later, reveal Rilke's concern for the secularization of Christ, whose love for Mary Magdalen, though exemplary in the poet's eyes, was purely human. His death on the cross was not a sacrificial martyrdom, it was the confirmation of His obedient submission to the laws of life. His Last Supper merely underlined His unique solitude in the midst of misunderstanding and, therefore, betraying disciples.

There is a passage of blasphemous virulence from Ronda, Spain, dated December 17, 1912, and addressed to Princess Marie von Thurn und Taxis:

"Since Cordoba I have felt most rabidly anti-Christian, I read the Koran. . . . Truly, one ought not to sit down any longer at this depleted table and to pass off as food the finger-bowls which still stand about. The fruit has been sucked out,—to put it bluntly, there remains only to spit out the skin. And to think that Protestants and American Christians keep making new effusions with this tea-dust which has drawn two thousand years,—surely Mahomet was the next-best refuge. Like a river which tore its bed through primeval rock he breaks forth to the one God with whom it is grand to converse every morning without the use of the telephone 'Christ,' into which people keep calling 'hello, who is speaking?' and which gives no answer." (*Br. 1907-14*, 269-270)

It may be granted that this ill-humored boutade issued from his pen in a moment of general malaise, of physical suffering and spiritual dejection, at the sickening sight of deserted churches and chapels in Catholic-Moorish Spain. But there are scattered throughout his work plenty of other instances of the same character, of which his beautiful poem *The Garden of Olives* is a notable one. In it Christ is made to utter this cry of faithless despair (*NG*, 26-27):

> I am alone with men who grieve,
> Whom I through Thee would fain relieve,
> Through Thee who art not. O nameless shame. . . .
> ....
> For Angels shun the ones so praying,
> And nights for such do not wax great.
> Who lose themselves, in vain must wait,
> Disclaimed by fathers in wrath unswaying,
> Debarred from mothers' wombs by fate.

As late as 1922, simultaneously with his *Sonnets to Orpheus*, Rilke wrote the fictitious *Workman's Letter*, in which Christ as the Redeemer and Mediator is repudiated and His cross reduced to a mere roadmarker which is to be left behind and forgotten once the road shown has been chosen (*AW* II,305ff). In a similar vein elsewhere he defines religion as a mere direction of the heart, with the emphasis upon the direction, not upon any outline of aim. Everywhere Rilke shies away from bonds other than those which originate within him and resolve themselves in the inspired and longed-for poem. In this sense Rilke's god is the poetic name for the creative spirit of John 3:8, "the wind that bloweth where it listeth."

However, unlike Nietzsche Rilke was not consumed by a pugnacious zeal for the revaluation of values; in fact he admits that while he does not care for the Christian conceptions of a Beyond, he has no intention of attacking them. According to Lou Albert-Lasard, he later declined emphatically to read Nietzsche with her (Albert-Lasard, 79). His resentment was primarily aesthetic, caused by his intense craving for unhampered suzerainty in his poetic kingdom.

11. RILKE AND THE "NEIGHBOR"

◇◇

Fremde Geige, gehst du mir nach?
(BB)
Strange fiddle, do you follow me?

◇◇

BESIDES the uncompromising determination with which Rilke guarded his creative freedom, another ingredient helps explain his egocentric implacability. It may be identified as a tendency to unconditional abandonment. It is one of his greatest accomplishments to have channeled it into the supreme and unqualified surrender to poetic inspiration. In order to convey an idea of how completely enraptured he could be, it is enough to quote the stammering words which he wrote when he had completed his *Elegies*. "At last, at last, the blessèd hour, blessèd day, when the termination—as far as I can see—of the Elegies can be announced. TEN!—At last the Elegies are here. I have groaned these days and nights as I did that time at Duino,—but even then, after that travail, I did not know that such storms could sweep over one from heart and spirit. And that they could be survived! Enough, it is here. I went into the cold moonlight and stroked my little Muzot, like a big animal—those ancient walls which gave me *this*" (*Br.* II,308). Rilke was always in danger of surrendering, either to his poetic demon or to worldly enticements, to the point of losing his identity so that he was often compelled to wrap himself in an armor of hardness. There was an abysmal dread at the bottom of his solitude as well as behind his gestures of challenge and revolt. To convince oneself one needs only to read some passages from Malte's *Notebook*, for example Malte's weird encounter with the man afflicted with St. Vitus' dance in the streets of Paris (*AW* II,60-65). "Strange fiddle, do you always follow me?" the poet sings in the *Book of Images*; "why am I always the neighbor of those who anxiously make your strings complain that life is heavier than the vast burden of all things?" (*BB*, 42). Generalizing his own idiosyncrasy, he lets the monk of the *Book of Hours* pray (*AW* I,41)

> To the Kings be cruelty.
> It is the Angel before Love,
> And without this arch I would
> Have no bridge into Time.

Rilke came to adhere to the mildly Nietzschean view that pity must not seek to eliminate social misery, but rather to alleviate it by explaining its lawful function in the universal order of things. In a letter of 1924 to Professor Pongs he puts it this way (*Br.Muzot*, 330):

"I must confess that, whenever I have been compelled to share in the destiny of someone, what, above all, seemed important and urgent to me was this: to help the afflicted one to recognize the peculiar and special condition of his distress,—an act which, every time, is not so much one of consolation as of (at first inconspicuous) enrichment. It seems to me that nothing but disorder will be established if the general endeavor (which is a delusion) presumes to attempt a schematic mitigation or removal of suffering,—an attempt which encroaches on a person's freedom far more disastrously than suffering itself which, with indescribable accommodation and, as it were, tenderness, imparts to those who confide in it directions for deliverance from it, if not externally, at least internally."

Likewise, in a conversation with Benvenuta in 1914 Rilke points out that atavism has great power over man, whose cruelty and instinct to kill are deeply rooted in human origin. "Under the influence of civilization many people have combatted that instinct and allowed it to become atrophied, out of fear, for convenience' sake or God knows for what other obvious or remote reasons" (Hattingberg, 67-68). Even hunters, whose delight it is to kill, often profess to be genuinely fond of animals. Rilke feels that these subterfuges merely prove that man has no longer the courage to recognize the truth, to admit cruelty, or at least to think every kind of thought, even the most frightful and humiliating. And Rilke does not mean to state a mere fact; as is evident from one of his *Sonnets to Orpheus*, he means to approve and to bless the hunter's cruelty. In certain regions of the Karst,[2] so the poet himself explains in a note, a peculiar species of pale-colored grotto pigeons are lured out of their shelters by means of pieces of white cloth carefully suspended in the caves and waved back and forth. As the frightened birds swarm into sight they are shot down by their treacherous hunters—and "far be from the on-looker every expression of sadness" (*AW* I,305).

By the same token that Rilke demanded unimpeded freedom in his life and work he also insisted on a corresponding respect for the autonomy of others; and this, too, to the point of inexorability. His biassed and opinionated generalization of marriage as a meeting and match of "two solitudes," besides being fraught with sad implications of moral insensibility, would, if put into practice, easily result in the kind of drab coexistence in which, as Christopher Fry describes it in his *Venus Observed*, "the song is quiet and quiet is the song." Year after year Rilke's wife and later his daughter and granddaughter were left to shift for themselves in their respective solitudes, notwithstanding his occasional declarations and tokens of uxorial or paternal solicitude. It is quite true that Rilke was so constituted that his great work could never have been accomplished under conditions of normal social responsibility. Somewhere there certainly was "an old hostility between [his] human life and greatest work" (*AW* I,219). But only if that is duly recognized shall we be able to be just in our appraisal of his personal struggles as well as of his poetry.

[2] The Karst is the name of the limestone plateau on the Eastern coast of the Adriatic where Duino Castle was situated.

12. RILKE DREAMCROWNED

<><><><><><><><><><><><><><><><><><><><><><><><><><><><><><><><><><><><><>

Bettler können dir Bruder sagen,
und du kannst doch ein König sein.
(*EG*)

Though beggars call you brother
You still may be a king.

<><><><><><><><><><><><><><><><><><><><><><><><><><><><><><><><><><><><><>

EVEN before he went to Munich Rilke withdrew more and more into a world all his own in which he could spin the filigree of his dreams. Desperately anxious to prove to his family that, since he was already irrevocably involved, no other choice was left him but that of the "highly absurd vocation of a poet" (*Br.Muzot*, 430), he attempted feverishly to achieve success with his dramatic undertakings and to play a leading role in the literary circles of Prague. But much of this restless activity was as unrealistic as his dreams. The transformation of everyday reality into inner values of cosmic scope was still beyond his powers, but the ground in which they could germinate and mature was being prepared. It was the time when he fell in love with Maeterlinck's gossamery dramas of the soul. "Only souls experience," he writes in May 1896. "In Maeterlinck's drama the most eloquent language is silence and the catastrophe is 'crying stillness' " (*Br.vonOe.*, 33). It is for this kind of drama that he would like to found a "Free Theatre" in Prague (*Br.vonOe.*, 32). His own dramatic work of the period was still naturalistic, but he dreamt of something far more delicate, far more ethereal. In his vainglorious mood he fancied himself the author of a new kind of play which would be performed on the famous stages of Europe's capitals and, incidentally, bring in enough money to make him financially independent (*Br.vonOe.*, 38). A few years later he will write his *White Princess*,[3] a lyrico-dramatic sketch of incorporeal fragility, and his unrealistic *Daily Life*, whose performance in Berlin in 1902 was hissed by an unsympathetic audience. A similar attempt in that

[3] The first version of *The White Princess* was printed in the Journal *Pan* in 1899. A complete revised edition was written in Sweden in the fall of 1904, and it is this version which is to be found at the end of *Early Poems*.

{ 66 }

direction is a sketch in the form of a dialogue, entitled *The Blind Girl* (*AW* I,147-151), which he wrote in the fall of 1900. It was intended to go even beyond the mystical drama of Maeterlinck—to be a drama of yearning, pure and simple, only the touching, slender figure of a young blind girl whose feeling has slipped entirely to the surface of her body, "like a bloom spreading infinite fragrance. On her young breasts her feeling blossoms as with roses, firm, full roses—her groping fingers end in unseen lilies. No love, nothing but pure yearning, like a thing made of pure silk" (*Br.Frühzeit*, 392).

In the introductory poem of *Dreamcrowned*, also written before Munich, the poet crowns himself king of children and of dreamers, and wraps himself in purple and ermine woven by the sun (*EG*, 67). For the first time there appears in Rilke's work an attempt at covering a wider field of experience by a series of poems cyclically grouped. With the exception of an introductory one, *Royal Song*, the poems of this collection have no titles. The two collective headings "Dreaming" and "Loving" are still distinguished rather vaguely, since the poems which they contain merely share a fairly undifferentiated mood. But the tendency to cyclical production will become more pronounced and gradually result in more compact arrangements. It is a tendency toward greater concentration and coherence, designed to counteract the danger of overwhelming effusiveness to which Rilke was exposed. He says mournfully in a poem of a little later date that he would like to have strung his earlier poems together in wreaths, but that in his loneliness he dropped them one by one, and they rolled like loose corals deep into the night (*FG*, 5). The temptation to spend the momentum of his lyrical impulse in trickles was great, and to the fact that he succumbed so often we owe many beautiful poems and many beautiful letters. Those who knew him personally are unanimous in their praise of him as a fascinating conversationalist in intimate circles. But Rilke himself complains throughout his life of spreading himself out in epistolary or verbal communion, so that his energies were dissipated and spent when he needed them most. He struggled continually for unrelaxed concentration, built up slowly by painfully patient waiting. If the dam broke prematurely, precious potentialities for great work were lost, and long periods of suffering ensued.

On the whole the undertone of *Dreamcrowned* is one of melancholy loneliness, of homeless yearning. These sentiments are wrapped in a great variety of symbols: the deep colors of the setting day, the pale greyness of the dying year, the heavy weariness of the ripened grape, the emptiness of forgotten chapels through which the wind howls, the vanishing of childhood and love, the heady scent of the night, the stillness of the atmosphere broken only by the wings of a lonely butterfly or the thud of a falling apple. What he yearns for is the whiteness of fallen blossoms in the moonshine, the idyllic peace of a village with a Sunday mien, a little house with a mossy roof and lead-encased windows behind purple branches, the clear laughter of blond maidens, the cloud which is able to obscure even the sun. Together with the melancholy remembrance of the Christmas tree and the fairy tales of childhood there emerges the nostalgia for the symbols of his now churchless faith, for the miracle-performing Madonna, for the folded wings of the Angel, for the Sunday bells and the mysterious chapels saturated with the desires of those who pray. Among the love poems there are some which evoke the magic revelation of the budding heart, others tell of the anguish of parting and dying love, a few reveal the voluptuousness of the consuming flame of passion.

It is impossible to identify any specific experiences which may have inspired these love poems. The general impression created seems to be that Rilke is in love with love rather than with any person in particular. But that impression is, I believe, deceiving. Not only does Rilke mention one girl by name, a cousin Olga (*EG*, 93), but more than one suggestive passage points to an underground of reality. Besides, the more intimate one grows with his work, the more reluctant one is to admit that any part of it owes its origin to mere fanciful play.

There is a letter to Benvenuta which, in spite of its stylization, leaves no doubt that the girls who kindled his youthful imagination were many and were made of flesh and blood. It also confirms our repeated observation that his amorous feelings described the same curve in his childhood and youth as in later life—ascending as long as they remained yearning, descending from the moment they were caught in the web of entanglements. In the letter Rilke writes: "Girl-friends of my childhood—what has become of them? ... they would come along on the street, recognizable from afar in all the metamorphic forms of their loveliness; one could feel them in one's whole body even before they emerged round the corner, accompanied by their French nurse. Did ever any one of them suspect that I loved her?" Well may he ask, for this is what happened on one occasion as he was strolling along the promenade of some spa. Rilke reminiscingly admits that he no longer remembers exactly how she looked. "Something svelte, something blond, half turned away," is all that now flits back and forth in his memory. What he does remember clearly is that he must have betrayed somehow his secret rapture. For all of a sudden he was grasped under his arms by an unknown person, pushed through the crowd and placed right in front of the girl to whom the whole story of his intimate feelings was revealed. "I do not understand," he writes, "how all the blood that flushed to my face with shame had any strength left for any other function." The event had, of course, its own momentum, but the peak had been reached. What followed was in the nature of a disconcerting decrescendo:

"Not that we did not touch each other, not that we lacked endearing names for each other or that we failed to find deeply-felt words of hope that we might meet again—all this was there (I should think: only too much so), but it did not spring quite unmixed from inner fullness and generosity. Somehow we could have done without it, had not a certain distrust of life wrested it from us. Like many dogs that eat only if someone makes a gesture as if wanting to remove their dish, we snatched at each other, because somewhere there existed sickness and unforeseeable dangers, because at each moment somebody was dying, and so it was possible that we might be separated again by some such strange reality—What united us must have been mainly a sort of fear, yes that was it, we were afraid of each other and for our mutual bond, a frightful fear of life and death, which we breathed out and breathed back in, slightly diluted with a little real air. Besides, it was clear, that before me lay a completely uncertain future, and somehow we tried to bring that future under our control as long as it was still very young. In this way it might perhaps grow up as our prisoner and never discover its own wildness" (*So lass*, 39-41).

PART III

EMANCIPATION AND FESTIVE EXPECTANCY

◇◇◇

Er ging noch als ein Kind von Hause fort,
Früh stiegen seine Hände aus dem Spiel,
und seine Eltern redeten so viel,
und er verliess sie wie ein dunkles Wort.
und ward ein Wanderer.

(Br.Frühzeit)

He left his home, his childhood not outgrown,
His hands found purposes above all play,
And, oh, his parents talked and talked away,
He left them as one leaves a word unknown.
Became a wanderer.

◇◇◇

13. ALONE AND FREE

◇◇◇

Und jetzt kann es beginnen—das Leben.

(ET)

And now, Life can begin.

◇◇◇

ON SEPTEMBER 29, 1896 Rilke cut loose from the moorings of family and native city. He would never return to stay, except for a few short visits now and then. When he arrived at Munich at the age of nearly twenty-two years, he had left behind all the protected sanctuaries which a native society offers and in which a child and adolescent find shelter. He had done so of his own free choice, like the Prodigal Son, and was without a home, without a church, without a familiar god, without any kind of warm human attachment. He yearned for all these things with the full ardor of his lonely heart, but his yearnings by-passed the human world and strayed off into a rarefied atmosphere where they could find no living objects, only memories and future possibilities in a world with no bonds. He had the frustrated feeling that his childhood, like his mother, had been untrue and his adolescence shamelessly thwarted. He loved childhood as one loves a lie or a dream in which one is king. He loved "those soft, noiseless ways round about life toward God" (*ESF*, 110). Piety and the warm feeling of parental love were marvelous lies which made him happy as long as they were not discovered to be lies. And the discovery made him both sad and angry, for now he had to undo it all, retrace his steps, and start all over again.

His God, his Madonnas, his Angels and his saints, his home, his dolls, and his mother kept casting a spell over his imagination and held it firmly in their grip. But because now they were only shells which had lost their warm and precious substance, they became a source of growing nostalgia. He had thrown himself into a vacuum which, unattached and unbound, he was determined to fill with new life. And that life was to have no other law, no other binding obligation than those imposed by his creative demon. Every time he forgets himself from now on, every time he yields to his need for human involvement, for the warm feeling of "belonging," the result is spiritual disaster, not only for himself but for the others as well. The world which he will create for himself is one for which he must find a new pivot, a new anchor. In it there will be no room, not an inch of room, for authoritative mediation from outside, for finished knowledge, for stereotyped dogma, for final answers. No room either for lingering love which insists on continued proof and demonstration (*Letters to Merline*, 84). With infallible instinct Rilke will learn to recognize the moment at which enraptured embrace threatens to spread out and engulf. "Woe to the caress that is against the stars" (*Letters to Merline*, 86), he writes in February 1921 to Merline when that moment in their relations has come.[1] "I never live anywhere but in the world, that of the stars and the great wind" (*Letters to Merline*, 100). In that world, "somewhere on islands of space on which the ordinary laws of gravity do not prevail" (*Letters to Merline*, 83), all women who have crossed or will cross his path can safely be transmuted into his one "inner girl." "How can estrangements be possible there?" he asks with tantalizing naïveté (*Letters to Merline*, 100).

Rilke is justly admired and loved for the beautiful letters which he wrote to men and women, young and old, sharing with them the fruits of wisdom that grow on the tree of experience. But Rilke's wisdom and humane sympathy are true and valid on a singularly transcendent plane; they are characterized by an exasperating detachment and non-committal sereneness. In a sense many of his letters are monologues, psychological self-analyses, soothing to himself no less than to the addressees. They are "a sort of transition from oral communication to work-in-writing which is directed to nobody in particular" (Salis, 52); "I am talking to myself in front of you" (*Letters to Merline*, 66); "I am speaking as much *for myself* as for

---

[1] "Merline" was the name given to Elisabeth Dorothée (Baladine) Klossowska, the wife of the East-Prussian (Polish) painter and art-critic Erich Klossowski. The name "Merline" is the feminine form of "Merlin," the legendary son of a demon and a virgin princess, and means something like "sorceress." Rilke had met Baladine once or twice in Paris before the war. When in Switzerland after the war, he called on her at Geneva in the summer of 1919. But it was not until the following summer that the relationship became close. An extensive, though not complete, edition of their correspondence, prepared by Dieter Bassermann, has recently been published (see Key to Abbreviations under *Rilke et Merline*). A painter herself, Merline has drawn several portraits of Rilke and has illustrated his volume of French poems *Les Fenêtres*. It was she who sent him a copy of Ovid's *Metamorphoses* in December 1920. Both her sons, Pierre and Baltusz, live in Paris, the former as a writer, the latter as a painter. Rilke took a special fancy to Baltusz.

you" (*Letters to Merline*, 70)—these are confessions explicitly made to Merline, but implicit in much of his correspondence. As early as October 1900 he admits the same to Clara Westhoff (*Br.Frühzeit*, 50). Undoubtedly such a personal feature is germane to letter-writing and adds warmth and conviction to one's words. But Rilke's own existential problems were so uniquely interwoven with his creative anxieties, his solutions were conditioned by such an intense need of solitude and utter reduction, that his wisdom is apt to remain abstract and academic, except so far as he himself is concerned.

In this connection the following incident may be worth mentioning. In the winter of 1922 Eva Cassirer, the wife of the owner of the Odenwaldschule, had written to Rilke on behalf of an American-born lady, Alwine von Keller, who was employed at the school. Mrs. Cassirer had enquired whether Rilke would be willing to let this lady's twenty-year-old son, who suffered from melancholia, stay at Muzot for a while as his guest. Rilke's reaction was quick and unequivocal: he would like to think the matter over, but he added at once that the upshot of his considerations would be "No." The reasons given were not only that practical difficulties were against it, but that he could under no circumstances sacrifice his solitude which he needed for his work. And that, of course, was true, the more so as he was just conditioning his soul for the inner "hurricane" of the *Elegies* and *Sonnets*, and as he knew very well his inclination to absolute involvement.

Far be it from me to criticize Rilke's attitude. My sole concern is to identify and place in its proper perspective the nature of his understanding wisdom. His reply reveals it clearly as noncommittal and self-analytical. The advice which he does offer for the benefit of the boy's mother limps awkwardly in its impractical abstractness, after the peremptory refusal to act (*Br.* II,302-304): "Weariness of life in his years," he writes, "is after all only the negative of a great assessment of life, which has been so constantly disappointed that the attention ends by clinging to the hollow side of the mould, because the forces were checked with which the casting of the positive could have been attempted." This is the same simile which he uses repeatedly to characterize his own crises and those of Malte. "Besides," he continues, "one is never nearer a turning than when one's existence poses as 'unbearable,' even in its smallest and dailiest aspects —at such a moment, to wait a little while longer would be a challenge, at least of one's curiosity. How much beauty this young man must have experienced, in order that his condition could become so intense that he did not measure up to it, i.e. that he 'wrecked' it." And this, too, Rilke said to himself as much as to others.

When he came to Munich, Rilke had to his credit a completed secondary school and a truncated university education, a few small volumes of poetry, some dramatic sketches and literary reviews, and his *Dreamcrowned* which was on the point of being published. He had made some connections of small account in literary circles, but was unknown in the wider world. But he had brought with him a boundless ambition, the highest hopes, and a quietly unshakable faith in his poetic future.

A few years after leaving Munich, Rilke described retrospectively in his *Ewald Tragy* the moods and main experiences of that first year of separation from home. In looking for a place to live he wanders through the streets of the strange city from one prospect to another, in turn attracted and repelled by smells, people, and environment, half obeying a somnambulist instinct, half reflecting sharply upon every step of his exploration. In the end he chooses the first place he had looked at, because with all its drawbacks it had the advantage of supplying a tempting writing desk (*ET*. 32ff). In this description Rilke unwittingly outlines the pattern typical of his later journeys through Europe in search of the right place to settle and work. His dependence on the proper surroundings and climate was amazing. During long stretches of his life he runs away from one place and country after another, now buoyant with expectation, now despondent in utter despair. And more than once his elliptic peregrination lands him back in the place from which he started (see below, p. 288).

At the University of Munich he listened to lectures on art, especially that of the Italian Renaissance. He visited the art galleries, wrote for various journals, and frequented the Café Luitpold where he met other young aspirants to literary fame. Essentially he moved in his own orbit, shy of becoming a satellite to anyone. At one extreme was his recent aristocratic acquaintance, Wilhelm von Scholz, a young writer of Rilke's age from the Lake of Constance region, whose collection of poems entitled *Hohenklingen* (1897) was preceded by a dedication to his "faithful friend R. M. Rilke" (*BTK*, 278). The following year Rilke reviewed his friend's book with fair praise

(*BTK*, 98-102), but in his *Ewald Tragy*, a little later still, his attitude is considerably more critical. To Ewald his poet-friend appeared
as somewhat of a grandiloquent fourflusher, whose boastful icono-
clasm was no more than a thin veneer concealing the shallow vanity
of the conformist. No real understanding of his own impassioned
dreams could be expected from this talkative adolescent (*ET*, 43ff).
At the other extreme was Jakob Wassermann, the critical plebeian,
whose contempt for "idle dreams" and hollow phrases impressed
young Rilke as suggesting maturity and honesty (*ET*, 51-58). Some
five years later he also reviewed one of Wassermann's works, the
novel *Moloch*, stigmatizing the author's clever art of observation as
too consciously applied and elaborated, and not devoid of hatred and
irony (*BTK*, 58). The fact is that Wassermann had no understanding of Rilke's lyricism and coldly rebuffed the latter's pathetic appeal for help and encouragement.[2] Both these extremes, the immature neophyte and the illusionless realist, threw Rilke back onto
himself and accentuated his loneliness to the point of reminding
him of the days of the military academy. Other experiences with
people, and a short sickness accompanied by feverish dreams, seem
to have contributed their share. As at St. Pölten, Rilke withdrew
from the shallow as well as from the brutal realities of life, but now,
unlike then, his refuge was not religion, but art.

It is true that to the volume of poems which appeared at the end
of 1897 he gave the religious title of *Advent*, borrowed from the
Catholic liturgical year (*EG*, 101ff). But the spiritual hope and anticipation which that period before Christmas is intended to symbolize has been entirely secularized by the churchless poet. His soul
expects the birth of a Saviour, no doubt; it awaits the slow fruition
of the mystery of incarnation, but his yearned-for Saviour must be
conceived by the Holy Spirit of artistic creation; the incarnation
which he awaits must take place in the virginal womb of his ripening
Word. This is the meaning of Rilke's peculiar religiosity and here
is the key to his Catholic symbols from now on. Where the symbol
lends itself to such formalization that its tenor can be completely
transsubstantiated into purely metaphorical—that is, artistic—sig-

[2] Later Rilke acknowledged the service which Wassermann had rendered him
in Munich: "It is Wassermann to whom I owe the first, almost stern, reference to
these books [of Jens Peter Jacobsen and Turgeniev]; the lyrical indefiniteness in
which I was involved made him impatient. He had already learned to appreciate
the importance of labor in the practical exercise of art" (*Br.Muzot*, 307).

nificance, it becomes suffused with the nostalgic softness and resplendent iridescence of his word. Where too many of the dregs of childhood suffering keep clinging to the borrowed symbol, or where the latter, if transferred to the poet's plane, encroaches upon his jealously guarded creative sovereignty, it is often subjected to ugly distortion by inadequately controlled resentment.

More and more, art and existence tend to become interchangeable values for Rilke. In art nothing will be allowed to stand or mediate between the intuitively formative mind of the poet and the ever ripening substance of his soul. His fundamental *experience* is movement, time; his basic, but highly elusive *aim* is contour, space. Translated into the religious sphere, that means an endless struggle of creative man with the substance of God, and no interference on the part of divine creed or dictated finality of form is tolerated. Already during the poet's stay in Munich his God is on the way to becoming an artistic God, therefore, as far as Rilke is concerned, unfinished. For the time being these feelings are not yet consciously clear, but very soon, under the impact of Italy and Russia, they will blossom out.

14. ADVENT

Irgendwo muss es Paläste geben,

Dort wollen wir Feste geben—
märchenallein.

(Advent)

Somewhere there must be palaces

where we shall give festivals—
in fairy-tale solitude.

IN THE poems of Advent the process of creating a suitable God is still in the initial stage: the symbols are merely stripped of their supernatural connotations and contrasted with corresponding ones on the natural plane. The revealed God of Christianity is replaced by the God of metamorphic Nature, the soul is not that which timidly craves approval and dignity in life and then "dies a poor death in the incense smoke of Gothic chapels" (*EG*, 111); it is that which experiences a piece of eternity in the blue night of May when the earth is white with blossoms. The soul is a shrine from which all the praying ones have gone and in which dreamy pictures of saints merely wait and wait for Sunday, with its fullness of pews and its rolling organ tones (*EG*, 110-111).

The key mood of the poems is hopeful expectancy and cherished solitude. Clearly the young poet felt that the hour of fulfilment, the incarnation of the word would come. Like the shepherd who saw the star of Bethlehem, the wind drives its herd of snowflakes in the wintry forest, the fir trees listen expectantly in the cold air and stretch their branches along the white paths, in pious readiness for the one night of splendor on Christmas Eve (*EG*, 103). With amazing clairvoyance, the poet anticipates in a programmatic poem the future course of his growth. Dedicated to nostalgic longing, he roves through all the days; then, with a thousand roots, strong and broad, he intends to plunge deep into the reality of life, and finally through suffering, he hopes to ripen far out of life, far out of Time (*EG*, 107). In another poem, dedicated to Maeterlinck, his soul prays to "Blessed Solitude, as rich and pure and far as an awakening garden" that she may keep the golden door shut, before which its worldly wishes wait (*EG*, 107). Elsewhere he loves forgotten wallflowers, perplexed and waiting for someone to come; and blond maidens with flowers in their hair, who carry their dreams to lonely springs; and children, who have sung their songs to the sun and cast their big astonished eyes to the stars. The days he loves when they bring him songs, and the nights when they open up like flowers (*EG*, 108). His fancy evokes a white castle in white solitude, along whose white walls Nostalgia gropes with erring hands; all roads are snowed in, the clocks stand still, Time is dead. He yearns for palaces whose windows are blocked with white dust and into whose resounding halls reach days of the long dead past. In their haunted solitude he would like to give feasts, and he dreams of walking with the gentlest of women to the sacred pond of a familiar park lined with rows of old linden trees. Gleaming swans in pompous poses glide softly on the water whence roses rise like legends from a submersed city. The flowers standing about are like their children among whom they smile and listen and wait, not caring for whom (*EG*, 115-116).

The poems of *Advent* are again cyclically arranged, and the ones of "white solitude" belong to the first group, entitled *Gifts to Various Friends*. In the spring of 1897 Rilke met his mother on Lake Garda and from there proceeded to Venice as the guest of a young American chemist whose acquaintance he had made in Munich. He returned to Munich by way of Bolzano and the Lake of Constance. The second group of poems, entitled *Travels*, gives impressionistic glimpses of this trip and are a rather inorganic part of the cycle. The poems of *Findings*, the third group, exude the delicate fragrance of nascent love in springtime, which gradually grows into summer weariness and fades into autumn paleness and dies. The girl of his dreams was an unwanted child, excluded even from her mother's evening prayers. She had few wishes and only now and then yearned for the strange melody of a land with purple tents and white ways without dust. Then she would weave roses in her blond hair, but yet could not believe in love, even in the heart of spring (*EG*, 140). She was barely emerging from the age of innocence and looked with big, timidly wondering eyes into the day (*EG*, 138). Strange was her speech, strange her hair, strange her dress, strange her interrogating eyes which kept looking back into the land of childhood, where all her movements were still pure, quiet blossoming (*EG*, 130). When he first saw her beautiful face, shining like a dreamy land through the dark strands of her parted hair, it was like seeing through deep-colored pines into Spring lost in thought. A veiled smile played about the fringes of her lips, invisible to everyone but him, who saw the grace of Spring and was in a dream (*EG*, 129-130). With her he wants to steal from the loud circle of men and choose seldom trodden paths when the stars shine above the oak trees. At her side he feels at home and warm, the clocks strike faintly as from days gone by and nobody knows what they whisper and where (*EG*, 131). Through the curtain's fold Night fetches forgotten sunshine out of her golden hair, but he wants only to hold her hands and be quiet and good and full of peace. Her hands are such as are wont to give and must bloom with the happiness of others, they are as delicate as quivering birches in which a trembling rhythm lingers from their gestures of bestowal (*EG*, 132). Her fragrance floats like Spring through the pillows as she winds the torn fragments of his dreams into new wreaths (*EG*, 134). But the hour of awakening comes and the reality of day leaves him stranded again, lonely and listless and hearkening in breathless anguish. The lilies in the high glasses which her hands used to tend have died; the bliss, once so great and pure, is gone; to-morrow frosty winds will enter into their hearts—and then? (*EG*, 143)

As in the case of the love poems of *Dreamcrowned*, it is impossible to identify any particular love affair that would have inspired those of *Advent*. But there is no doubt that at this time especially the radiant charms of budding girlhood fascinated him powerfully, and we find that almost invariably his dream girls have golden blond hair.

In the poems of the fourth group, entitled *Mothers* Rilke glorifies motherhood. He dreams of a quiet woman with parted white hair in whose love he might bloom and render impotent the wild hatred in his soul. He remembers how mother would sing him to sleep and watch over his fear-filled dreams. He fancies his dream girl with child, sewing and singing into the whiteness of May, under the fragrant budding trees. And if the world casts shame on her painful and worried waiting, he tells her to smile and pray, for she stands on the threshold of a miracle, and the bashful swelling of her soul and body is caused by the waves of eternity. He evokes the grief of the mother whose daughter has gone astray, and he comforts the poor, destitute mother with the promise that when he grows up he will crown her Queen (*EG*, 147-151).

Rilke's veneration of the sanctity of motherhood was very deep and remained so throughout his life. But it, too, does not escape entirely the effects of his supreme concern for the inviolability of artistic creation. Where the two clash, or rather where Rilke thinks they clash, the primacy of artistic parenthood must prevail. In his *Requiem for Paula Modersohn-Becker* the poet leaves no doubt as to this (*AW* I,211-219).

15. LOU ANDREAS-SALOMÉ

◇◇

Reiche, Du, Träume gibst du meiner Nacht,
Lieder meinem Morgen. . . .

(Br.Lou, 24)

Thou who art so rich, to my nights thou givest
dreams, to my mornings songs. . . .

◇◇

IN THE spring of 1897 Rilke met two women, one of whom was to become of considerable importance for him. They were Frieda von Bülow, authoress and African explorer, and Lou Andreas-Salomé. Both were considerably older than himself, Frieda being forty and Lou thirty-six, and both were educated women. Their degree of maturity, their past experiences, as well as their intellectuality were of a nature to impress young, groping Rilke profoundly. If he attached himself to Lou rather than to her friend, there were reasons of personal idiosyncrasy on both sides.

When two years later, after Rilke's first Russian journey, Frieda expects him and Lou at the summer cottage of Bibersberg, near Meiningen, she refers to him, not without a sardonic grin, as the "Lou-man" and as "Lou's disciple" *(Br.Frühzeit,* 420). However, it must be said that despite Rilke's life-long naïveté and helplessness, he was always guided by an instinct of such unswerving sureness that never, not even in the case of Jens Peter Jacobsen or Rodin can there be any question of influence in the sense of complete ascendancy— capable of bringing about a reorientation which would not have taken place otherwise. "In the last analysis," he writes to Frieda with reference to his Russian experiences, "when one seeks something new, be it a new land or new things, one merely seeks a new expression which will help a personal confession to greater power and consciousness" *(Br.Frühzeit,* 17).

The above statement may be thought to contradict a much later one made in a letter of May 24, 1924 to Princess Marie von Thurn und Taxis: "You know that my friendship with Lou is thirty years old, and that without the influence of this extraordinary woman my whole development could not have taken the course which has led to a variety of things" (*Br.MTT*, 807-808). But when Rilke wrote that, he was anxious to defend Lou against certain apprehensions in the mind of the Princess. Rilke had recommended Lou as an outstanding psychoanalyst who might be able to help a young woman from the Princess' circle of acquaintances. The Princess, supported by Rudolf Kassner, had misgivings in regard to that recommendation, and Rilke seems to argue that if Lou's influence on himself was so beneficial there was reason to expect similar results in the case under consideration. It would be easy to show that whenever Rilke's development took a decisive turn under the aegis of some personality or experience, the change had already taken root in him and corresponded to an inner necessity which was determined to find suitable expression somehow.

Lou was the daughter of a Russian general and former Defense Minister under Czar Nikolai I. Under this Czar Russia's orientation to the West, carried out with such force by Peter the Great, was radically reversed and Russia was ordered once more to turn her eyes inward and to seek to express only her own soul. Lou's mother was of German descent and belonged to a family of clergymen of St. Petersburg. In the above-mentioned letter of 1924 Rilke states specifically that she was not Jewish, thus invalidating a rumor which had become widely accepted. During a visit to Avignon and vicinity in 1909 he found evidence indicating that among the Protestants who had been driven out of France in the seventeenth century there had been a family of Salomés who might be Lou's ancestors on her father's side (*Br. 1907-14*, 78).

Lou was perhaps not a blue-stocking, but she certainly had no inferiority complex, intellectually or otherwise, in relation to the male sex. In St. Petersburg, while still in her teens, she was madly smitten with a married man, the Dutch preacher Gillot, but her raving fervor underwent a sudden deflection when the much older clergyman mentioned the word "marriage" to her. At the age of twenty-one she met Nietzsche in Rome, through Malwida von Meysenburg, Wagner's friend, and Dr. Paul Rée, Nietzsche's companion. Lou became quite infatuated with Rée. But her intelligence, her blond beauty, and her keen interest in philosophy soon exercised a great charm on lonely Nietzsche who proposed to her after a short acquaintance. Her motives have often been suspected; the fact is that she turned the proposal down, although not without first leaving her answer in abeyance. Her relations with Rée, complicated by this turbid embroilment with Nietzsche, were unexpectedly caught in a web of ambiguity when she met her future husband, the tempestuous Java-born Andreas, an Orientalist who became a professor at the University of Berlin and later at the University of Göttingen. It is reported that a photograph taken in those days shows Rée and Nietzsche drawing a cart in which Lou stands cracking the whip (Albert-Lasard, 79). Her marital bond with Andreas, though never severed, was from the outset ill-starred—a sort of inexplicable and mutually-acknowledged vassalage from which consummation was excluded and which even proved to lack genuine community of mind and interest.

Lou's book on Nietzsche had already appeared in 1893, and we may be sure that through her Rilke's leanings toward certain Nietzschean attitudes were given fresh perspectives (Heller, 71-97). Later she became a keen student of Freud, partly by natural inclination, partly because her inquisitive mind and her intrigued heart became fascinated by progressive symptoms of morbidity in Rilke. But evidently even at the time of their first acquaintance in Munich she had a natural gift for analyzing complex psychological conditions, both for herself and for others (Simenauer, 120). Whenever Rilke refers to her in his letters, the aspect of her personality which stands out most is her amazing assuredness in the face of all problems of life. "She moves fearlessly midst the most burning mysteries, which do nothing to her. . . . She has life on her side, recognizing in harmless as well as in frightful matters the one force which disguises itself, yet always purports to be generous, even when it causes death" (Br. MTT, 303f). With her he experienced "the most significant moments, starting from which life became possible again" (Br.MTT, 317). He calls their first meeting, at a time when he did not know where to go or how to make a start, a unique event in his life, as unique as birth itself (Br. 1907-14, 168). "You can explain to me what I do not understand," he writes, "you can tell me what I should do; you know what I must, and what I need not fear" (Br.Lou, 48). "You were the right door through which I entered into the open" (Br.Lou, 250). "I am the individual ant that has lost its head; you, on the other hand, see the edifice and assure me that it is whole, and that I shall find my way back and make myself useful again" (Br. 1907-14, 166).

There is no doubt that Lou's psychological insight and analytical rationality interpreted for him many puzzling conditions of body and soul with which he had to cope. As her interest in Freud developed, these interpretations became more and more colored by sex and its subconscious complexes. Judging by Rilke's own confessions there is no doubt that his body caused him enormous defeats even to the very end of his life (*Br.Lou*, 498-505). Lou's diagnoses served to take much of the sting out of his physiological and mental troubles, with the result that he was able better to understand the delicate mechanism of his sensory as well as creative experiences. Such enlightenment was highly appreciated throughout his life, but particularly at this early stage of his poetic career. It was perhaps the most vital factor which made him seek Lou's company at this time, as it also kept the fire of their relationship burning in later years, giving it new food at each crisis. That is why Rilke's letters to her are on the whole fraught with such deep, body-and-soul-searching confessions, with such dark introspective self-analyses. At the end of such a confession of January 10, 1912, he writes: "There —your old mole has again dug up something for you and thrown nothing but dark earth across a good path. To you I say such intimate things, like the people of the Old Testament" (*Br. 1907-14*, 171). At the end of 1925, when the symptoms of his insidious disease became alarming and threw him into a state of frightful phobia, Lou admitted not having grasped sooner the real significance of his afflictions (*Br.Lou*, 503). She may have accentuated in Rilke the consciousness of his bodily functions within the framework of his creative processes, but if she did so, it was not in contradiction with his own needs and trends.

We have already pointed out that Rilke was extremely sensitive to climate and environment: now it was too hot, now too cold; now too dry, now too damp; now too stormy, now too quiet; now too cloudy, now too sunny. The effects of his body—and that includes sex —upon his creativity are among the most perplexing mysteries to him. Not only are they in considerable measure instrumental in opening the sluices of "inspiration," they also lend color and plasticity to the images and symbols which emerge—deep penetrating color and radiating plasticity. "It may be," he writes in 1912, "that the continuous distraction in which I live has in part bodily causes; perhaps it is the result of too thin blood" (*Br. 1907-14*, 167)—one of several remarkable premonitions of the cause of his death by leukemia. He sometimes feared that his body would make a caricature of his creative spirit. "A soul, whose function it is to harmonize itself in the immense hyperbolisms of Art, must be able to count on a body which apes it in nothing, which is precise and exaggerates nowhere" (*Br. 1907-14*, 183-184).

In a letter of February 13, 1924, Rilke complains that lately the state of his health has compelled him twice to seek a cure at various spas. "This getting mixed up with doctors is something indescribably confusing to me; it is comparable to the feeling of being suddenly forced to deal with my soul via the priest. For twenty-five years my dealings with my body have been so direct, and conditioned by such strictly mutual understanding, that I have a feeling that this medical interpreter penetrates like a wedge into our tacit agreement" (*Br.-Muzot*, 237). His relationship to his mother and to childhood, his concern with pre-natal existence, in the womb and beyond, his feeling, as it were, of blood-relationship with death, his wonderment at birth, bloom and decay, his anxieties and dreams, his creative throes, his sexual bi-polarity anchored by one pole in his dolls and by the other to his rocking-horse, his struggle with craftsmanship versus inspiration, his tension between the masculine world of action and his feminine productivity—these and similar matters were focal problems upon which Lou was able to throw much light. Some of the most characteristic passages of Malte's *Notebook*, and several significant ones of the *Elegies* are to be found as live experiences in Rilke's correspondence with Lou. The *Third Elegy* in its entirety delves with uncanny knowledge into the vortex of pre-natal origin.

Rilke's attitude to psychoanalysis was indeed of more than superficial significance. In the latter part of 1911 and in 1912, when his state of health and feeling of sterility reached a distinctly low level, he took the possibility of psychoanalytic treatment into serious consideration. After finishing his Malte *Notebook* he believed for a time, and confessed repeatedly, that he never could nor would write again. He called this work a "water-shed," but one in which all the waters had run back one way so that on the other side there was nothing but aridity (*Br.Lou*, 246). He even thought up the idea of finding some kind of occupation in civilian life which he would carry out mechanically, like an automaton. Lou apparently advised treatment only on condition that these intentions were meant seriously; otherwise, if renewed creativity were still to be hoped for, he had better let things take their course (*Br.Lou*, 262-263). She knew that Rilke's depression was only temporary and that a "disinfection of the soul" (the expression is Rilke's, *Br. 1907-14*, 182) through psychoanalysis would do more harm than good.

And Rilke himself agreed, though his wife Clara submitted to treatment in the spring of 1912 (*Br.Lou*, 269), because—as Rilke puts it—"in her case things are different, her work has never helped her" (*Br. 1907-14*, 183). He himself felt that his whole work was after all a kind of self-treatment, even though through long practice it had lost much of its therapeutic virtue and become more and more demanding (*Br. 1907-14*, 183). But to do away with the tension and conflict between body and soul would be to sap the very foundation of his creative work. When in 1914 his Munich doctor Stauffenberg tried again to persuade him to accept treatment, Rilke felt that "it would be atrocious and nauseating to scale off childhood in morsels, atrocious for one whose need was not to dissolve within himself the unmastered elements of childhood but rather to use them up in inventions and sentiments—in things, in animals, if need be . . . in monsters" (*Br. 1914-21*, 14).[3]

Rilke's intuitive doubts about the therapeutic value of psychoanalysis are confirmed by recent studies in anthropology. Margaret Mead in her book *Male and Female* points out that the veil which separates the subconscious must never be removed completely. "The primary experiences of childhood" must be transformed into the disciplined symbolism of adult life, and civilization depends on this. "Those who have not succeeded in making these transformations go mad and fill our insane asylums. Those who keep an easy access to their own early memories but who have also talent and skill become our artists and our actors; those who can combine these early basi-

---

[3] In Switzerland, shortly after the war, Rilke was struck by the importance which psychoanalysis played in that country, especially in Zürich: "nearly all these otherwise neat and angular young people are analyzed—just imagine: such a sterilized Swiss in whom all corners have been swept clean and polished—what sort of inner life can there be in his soul ("Gemüt") which is free of germs and lit with shadowless light like an operating-room" (*Br. 1914-21*, 272).

Lately the belief has been expressed that toward the end of his life Rilke did succumb to the promptings of friends and of his own sick body that he submit to psychoanalytical treatment (Holthusen, 53; Simenauer, 688). Of course, in view of the disturbing symptoms of ill health, it is not impossible that he was caught off his guard at a critical moment and did what was against his better judgment. However, a conjecture is no proof.

cally human experiences with vision and love of mankind become prophets. . . . If the veil is withdrawn the artistic imagination sickens and dies, the prophet looks in the mirror with a disillusioned and cynical sneer, the scientist goes fishing," and the public at large is irrevocably frustrated (Mead, 58-59).

Rilke's instinct in these matters was amazingly sure and dependable. As early as 1899 he had written in his diary: "I fear only those contradictions within me, which have a tendency to reconciliation. My contradictions must hear of each other only rarely and through rumors. Like two princes of distant lands, who all of a sudden find out that they hate each other because they both start out to woo the same maiden" (*Br.Frühzeit*, 203). And "the maiden," as becomes clear from what follows, is nothing else than the spirit of the creative moment.

In the light of these developments it is no wonder that when Rilke made the acquaintance of Lou in the spring of 1897, he realized that he had made a precious discovery. At her suggestion he changed his name from René to Rainer. Lou suspected in the French name a whim of his eccentric mother who could so easily substitute "Renée" for it. At any rate, "Rainer" sounded more masculine and more German, and it must be admitted that its clear ringing vowel and modified rhythm lend it greater distinction and charm. It was Lou who made the young poet more conscious of his achievements and potentialities, thus heightening his self-assurance and sense of responsibility. His handwriting, which until now had been rather sloppy, became painstakingly neat. And it was Lou who kindled in Rilke the desire and hope of going to Russia with her and her husband.

16. ITALIAN RENAISSANCE AND FLORENTINE JOURNAL

<><><><><><><><><><><><><><><><><><><><><><><><><><><><><><><>

> Das waren Tage Michelangelos,
> von denen ich in fremden Büchern las.
> (*Stundenbuch*)
>
> Those were the days of Michelangelo,
> Of which I've read in foreign books.

<><><><><><><><><><><><><><><><><><><><><><><><><><><><><><><>

ALREADY in Prague the contiguous Slavonic world had thrown broad shadows over Rilke's soul. In his nostalgic character cognate traits had developed which obscurely challenged those implanted by the experience of Western patterns. His religious bent had slowly been absorbed by his artistic dreams and longed for vast spaces in which a demolished god could begin a new birth and growth. At the Commercial School of Linz he had read Tolstoy, and in Munich Wassermann drew his attention to Dostoyevsky and Turgeniev. In Prague he had admired the Czech poet Julius Zeyer, the pseudo-aristocratic writer who in the course of his restless wanderings had visited Russia three times and who confessed that "Russia burned in his soul like a strange curse" (Demetz, 147). Rilke had also been in Italy and had studied Renaissance art at various times. The more he learned about things Russian under the impact of Lou's friendship the more the contrast between Russian and Western culture and history became a fascinating phenomenon. In Wolfratshausen near Munich, where he stayed for a while with her, he was still much concerned with the Italian Renaissance, but the profile of Russia cast its shadow over their conversations and studies with increasing insistence.

In the meantime, however, he went once more to Italy in the spring of 1898. He went at the end of March by way of Arco and Venice to Florence and nearby Viareggio and remained there for over a month. During that period and for a while afterward, when he stayed at Zoppot near Danzig before returning to Berlin, he wrote a diary for the avowed purpose of proving to Lou and to himself his progress in mature reflection and analysis. His indebtedness to Lou in this respect was gratefully acknowledged: "Oh marvellous woman," he wrote toward the end of his Florentine days, "who have loaned me so much space. For if the days of Italy have showered me with treasures, it is you who have made space in my soul where dreams and anxieties used to crowd. You have restored magnificence to me" (*JF*, 132-133). Rilke had prepared for this Italian journey with the greatest fervor. In August 1897 he had written to Frieda von Bülow from Munich that he and Lou were "reading in the most various books on Italian Renaissance Art. . . . From the early golden age of Florence we want to push forward by degrees to the Caraccis. . . . I am especially fascinated by one Florentine master of the Quattrocento—Sandro Botticelli. . . . His Madonnas with their weary sadness, their great eyes asking for release and ful-filment, those women who dread growing old without a holy youth, stand at the heart of the longing of our time" (*Letters 1892-1910*, 28-29). "Oh! the tender suffering of those who have come too early," Rilke writes in his diary with reference to Botticelli; "they are like children who have entered into the room of the Christmas tree be-fore the candles are lit and the toys shine in the light" (*JF*, 117). The other Renaissance painters were only interested in doing justice to the religious motifs of the Bible and holy legends, without want-ing anything for themselves—"save at most the solution of some problem of color technique or of pure form; along comes Sandro Botticelli and in his naïve longing for God perceives that the Ma-donna, in her deep sympathy ennobled and sanctified by her strange motherhood, can quite well become the herald of his own sadness and of his weariness. And in fact all his Madonnas look as if they were still under the spell of a melancholy story, quite bare of hope, that Sandro has been telling them" (*Letters 1892-1910*, 28-29).

Rilke's *Florentine Journal* devotes much space to comment on Renaissance art and artists: Rafael, Fra Bartolomeo, Botticelli, Gior-gione, Fra Angelico, della Robbia, Michelangelo. This splendid ef-florescence of religious art struck him as too luxuriant and easy blooming. He missed the anxieties of slow germination and growth into final mellow fruit. It was like a spring that would fain become summer but had exhausted all the resources of creative Nature by lavishness of color and final clarity of form. In so doing it had cheated the summer out of its toilsome ripening and the autumn out of its sweet fulfilment. Rafael he compares to the blossoming of June, bright and warm, but incapable of maturing. Michelangelo, that towering genius, possessed all the elements needed for patient deployment, at times he had even outstripped the summer, but because no precursors had created the vast space in which his genius could spread out, he, too, remained spring (*JF*, 128). Only Botticelli impressed Rilke as vaguely conscious of inchoate gestation. The sad and weary nostalgia of his Madonnas seemed to betray their author's awareness of bashful trepidation in the presence of life's unsolved mystery. They are weary from the feeling of not having been wounded; they cannot forget that they have borne without throes nor that they have conceived without ardor. Their motherhood is full of guilty yearning because it fell into their laps unearned (*JF*, 115).

Rilke's lyrical approach to Italian art is striking. His own congenital dependence on protracted parturition made him partial to Botticelli who seemed like a stray and distant brother of the Russians. But this partiality itself was not devoid of nostalgia for the opposite. If Rilke felt related to slow-maturing Russia, he also envied the Italian fig tree, whose sap, "hardly awake yet, straight from its sleep, leaps to its sweetest fulfilment" (*AW* I,264). Italy and Russia, the West and the East, are the two branches of the broad stream of the poet's creative consciousness which issues into the *Book of Hours*. Their beds were fully channeled, and their waters were flowing vigorously, even before he saw Russia eye to eye. It is a mistaken view which proclaims that the *Book of Hours*, even the first one, was inspired by Russia alone or that it reflects the Russian experience purely. Rilke liked to call Russia his real home, but what he meant was some imaginary land of which the kind of Russia he saw was the symbol. In reality the land existed nowhere. Had Rilke chosen Moscow instead of any of his Western haunts for his work-a-day activities, he would have fled from it with the same regularity if not with more determination. The fact is that after his second trip he never returned to Russia, although he had met enough people there who would have welcomed him warmly. Russia and the West were the two princes who found themselves at war with each other because they had started out to woo the same maiden. And if facts have any meaning, Rilke must have felt that he could better find his maiden, if not in the domains of the Western prince, at least from his grounds as base.

In Florence Rilke stayed in a *pension* among roses. But he avoided the city as much as possible in order to enjoy the Tuscan countryside and the wide spaces of the Ligurian Sea. The contours of golden-haired girls and weary women blended gloriously with the sunlight of Spring and the flowering brilliance of the landscape. What Rilke saw in them was the same as what he had found in Botticelli's Madonnas: the quivering expectation and languid anguish of budding girlhood—and the melancholy lassitude of motherhood in hopeless search for its lost dreams of youth. And that corresponded to what Rilke found in his own expectant soul, with the emphasis, however, on the mood of hopeful expectancy. There is a note of assured optimism running through his diary. He felt young and healthy; as he bathed in the ocean the gently recurring waves seemed full of promise. In the company of Lou at Wolfratshausen he had learned to walk barefooted in the green grass; here at the seashore he could combine the feeling of intimate contact with the Earth, the mother of male strength, with that of total envelopment in the womb of the sea, the mother of Venus, of that nostalgic Venus which Botticelli had painted (*JF*, 115-116).

Inspired by the sea, Rilke mused about the function of the artist, about his own poetic future, about his relation to childhood and God, about the meaning of birth and motherhood. It sometimes happened that against its background, under the blue sky, there appeared a Brother of Mercy in black cassock who had been called on a sad errand. And the shadow of death would appear to him (*JF*, 93-98; *Br.Muzot*, 333-341). But Rilke had already begun to prepare a permanent place for death in his optimistic pattern of life. At the sculptured tombs of bishops and princes in the churches of Tuscany he felt that death had willingly entered into friendly alliance with life, above all with art. It no longer meant destruction but timelessness. In the presence of these tombs as in the presence of the blue sea you lose all fear of death, which hands over its power to life in the person of the artist, saying: Here, since you build and create, use force where needed, like me. You must know what is worn and weary and brittle and, therefore, is ready to perish (*JF*, 149-151). Here we have again that expression of Nietzschean pitilessness which we have already mentioned, and it reveals itself clearly as of aesthetic origin. The sculptor must meet death not only by hewing it out in stone in order that it may peacefully communicate with the living, but in so doing he must also be inexorable in the disregard of all that is irrelevant or weak. Rilke's conception of the artist as here expressed bears a great resemblance to Nietzsche's. The artist's function is to create God, a god eternally in the making. With each work the artist creates space for some new force and it is the duty of each to add to the expanse of that space so that the last one, who will come at the end of many generations, will carry in him all that is energy and force in the universe. The individual artists are only precursors, John the Baptists, paving the way for Him, toward whom everything converges. Outside of Him there will be nothing. He no longer prays, He Is. Every gesture He makes is creation. All artists are ancestors of a God (*JF*, 160-161).

The *Florentine Journal* shows clearly that for Rilke there existed a distinct affinity not only of art and religion, but of art and God, of art and death, of art and life. Art was for him the supreme consummation of existence, the ultimate justification and goal of creation. Rilke could not conceive of religion otherwise than in terms of creation. In motherhood woman creates herself in the womb and realizes herself in the child, thus weaving for herself worlds of power and possibilities. Her religion is motherhood. The ordinary person becomes productive in prayer. To the extent to which his religion is inherited, his prayer is custom-made, but through it he, too, frees himself from the bondage of the accidental and rises to the order of universal law. Rilke rejects the supernatural in the current sense of the word. Mysticism as well as death has a place in life only on condition that it be understood as a natural force (*JF*, 98).

However, he was deeply concerned with the secret forces of soul and spirit, with that invisible world in which cause and effect may still prevail but extend in modified form beyond the realm of matter. He will call humility the force of gravity of the soul. In a letter of 1897 to an adept of hypnotism he admits that spiritualism exercises a great power of attraction on him, because in the recognition of many idle forces and in the subjugation of this power he sees the great liberation of our remote descendants. In particular the artist must struggle through the misty fumes of crass materialism to those spiritual intimations that build for him the golden bridge into shoreless eternities (*Br. 1892-1904*, 31-32). The atheist is "a barbarian" (*JF*, 40) not because he does not believe in a personal God, but because by definition he is godless through and through, which means uncreative, sterile. Rilke's religion is art, which everywhere and at all times creates the metamorphic contours of a future Godhead.

That is why he sings the praise of pantheistic periods in history: they come from a great love and true faith when man feels generous again and kind toward God, when he understands that God cannot find room in a distant heaven. The God of Heaven has a cramped and pitiful existence in small space. Only when the whole universe is open to receive Him can He stretch His limbs and dream in the thousands of things. The kind of God that is thought behind or above the things is an idle God, a self-sufficient God with idle hands. God is *in* the things, and that is where the artist must find Him (*BTK*, 227).

17. THE THINGS AND THEIR MELODY

◇◇

Die Dinge singen hör ich so gern.

(*FG*)

The things, I like so much to hear them sing.

◇◇

THE things become for Rilke the repositories of the most divine treasures. But they are held in bondage by man, who is only intent upon invading them and violating their innocence by ruthless exploitation. To him they remain closed and the God in them remains forever hidden. It is the artist's mission to liberate their riches from their prison, to let them unfold and sing their deep melody. Wood is allowed to be wood and iron iron, instead of raw materials. And the means which the poet among the artists has at his disposal to perform that miracle is the Word. But the Word, like the things, has been profaned by everyday use; it has been stripped of its virginal freshness, imprisoned by definitions or levelled out by talk. Words have become walls within which the soul has no room and is doomed to stunted growth. Often they are used to conceal the soul instead of revealing it. Words of this kind are poor, starving words, and can never shine over the high tops of life. They reveal neither God nor the Thing. But let one of these tired, anemic words be uttered by the lips of one in love, how unsoiled, how radiant with childhood is its ring, as on the first day of Creation! "Someone says 'The Light!' and it sounds as if he said 'Ten thousand suns!'; he says 'The day!' and you hear 'Eternity!' It is because his soul has spoken, his creative soul. The lover has spoken as an artist, and only the artist can use the word so lovingly that the thing touched by it opens like a flower and fills the world with its sweetness. The artist is a magician, whose life-giving word grows mysteriously beyond the ordinary range of his faculties. He is a lute within whose darkness maidenly beauties dream of liberation by the touch of the strings" (*BTK*, 174).

Rilke was lyrical through and through. When he sang to a thing his bewitching melody, with its rich assonantic and alliterative insistence, the thing answered back like bird to bird. And yet in his *Florentine Journal* (*JF*, 59) he admits having met music nowhere on his path. "In each work of any one of the Arts," he writes, "all the effects of 'Art' must be realized. . . . A poem does not need music" (*JF*, 60). And in a review which he wrote a year later he observes that the lyrical tone "has nothing in common with the melody in music. Its laws are different (instinctive and unwritten), and its effects are other than those of a sonata or symphony" (*BTK*, 106). Stimulated by various acquaintances and occasions, Rilke was often inspired by musical experiences, and already in Florence he was confident that the time would come when he would be able to speak of musical art, too. "For I shall go in search of music" (*JF*, 60). But his reflections on the subject both in his letters and in his poems show that he tended progressively to grant his whole-hearted appreciation to it only when it could somehow be transmuted into plastic or architectural form, into space. For the composer, who need not situate his sentiments in everyday life, "pours out dormant possibilities in his evasions, and only he who knows the magical word can awaken them and convert them into gay festivals" (*JF*, 60).

In Worpswede, only a short time after his *Florentine Journal*, he finds fault with Carl Hauptmann because his poetic inspiration comes from music, not from things (*Br.Frühzeit*, 289). He calls music the art which "puts order" into noises and lures "pearls onto strings" (*Br.Frühzeit*, 375). The function of music as he understood it was to liberate the "plastic images" ("Gestalten") which are waiting and hidden in the things and to make one "edifice out of many" (*Br. Frühzeit*, 376). In due time these early intimations gain greater clarity: in Egypt, in the spring of 1911, it was in the presence of the plastic grandeur of the Sphinx, and two years later, in Spain, in the contemplation of El Greco's *Crucifixion*, that the mystery of music revealed itself to him with the most spontaneous force (*Br. Benvenuta*, 25, 67). Still later, in 1918, he calls music the "breath of statues, which transforms feelings into audible landscape, into heart-space" (*AW* I,396), and in the *Sonnets to Orpheus* it erects its temple "with vibrating stone in unusable space" (*Son.* II, 10); Orpheus sings, and "a high tree" rises "in the ear" like "a temple" (*Son.* I, 1). In 1925, the effects of music are perceived not only by the ear, but somehow also by the eye, "like cupolas which arch in some ideal world." Somewhere music "stands" (*AW* I,397), like the stream of water in a fountain.

Rilke knew very well, also, the enrapturing power of music, as is evident from his early poem *Music* (*BB*, 22) and from scattered statements in his letters. With his natural inclination to complete, uncontrolled surrender, he instinctively steered shy of influences which might diffuse and disintegrate the plastic substance of the image on which he depended. That is what attracted him to the sensuous realism of Jens Peter Jacobsen, to the Worpswede painters and to the sculptor Rodin. Under the spell of Rodin's modelled and disciplined work he goes so far as to call music "the opposite of Art" (*Br.* I,56), accusing it of lack of concentration. Only Beethoven and Bach find grace before his judgment, because they loathed diffusion; Beethoven found his concentration in life, Bach in prayer.

It is true, in a poem of 1913 Rilke implores music to "overwhelm him with rhythmical wrath" (*AW* I,324) because his heart had been too long in the mood of husbanding its movements. But that poem arose at a time when the prolonged tension caused by Rodin's example of relentless devotion to impersonal observation and daily work had nearly congealed Rilke's lyrical spirit. A reaction was inevitable, which was greatly responsible for the weird ecstasy with which he plunged into worship of a woman, Benvenuta, whom he had never seen, and of her music which he had never heard. Yet even in this poem, what he expects of music is that it enable him to fill with the swell of his song the "vaulting" heights of his heart. And in a sister poem issuing out of the same experience (*AW* I,324), he tries in vain to divine the favorite music of her whom he loves but who never came and whom he had, as it were, lost in advance. The only way in which he can find her is in the form of "images of distant lands, of experienced cities and towers and bridges and unexpected turns of the road." For Rilke music was dangerous because it accentuated his expansive lyrical nature and threatened to dissipate its energies. He longed for ecstatic concentration, but out of it must issue forth a plastic world. That was the kind of ecstasy which he admired in the painter Cézanne.

The music of Rilke's poetry comes not solely from the melody and rhythm of his word but from the blend of these with the visual images of his transfigured experiences. "I am a picture," he says; "my life is the composed stillness of the shaped figure. I am beginning and end of the gesture" (*Br.Frühzeit*, 374). The substance which fills the space between the beginning and the end is not of decisive importance; it may consist of the most inconspicuous things or the most recondite inner happenings. They gain meaning only through the way in which they are outlined against their surroundings. What matters is that they be given form and contour, and these emanate from their soul. The soul of the thing is what matters, that which endows the most insignificant being with the beauty of a whole. Lyrical beauty so understood appeared to Rilke far superior to the current drama and the novel, in which matter predominates and which "are still subservient to the multitude and must, like the King's jester, try to guess what kind of a joke may best suit the momentary whim of His Majesty, The Public" (*BTK*, 99). The drama of which Rilke dreamt was one in which the word fraternized with silence in order to create soul-space rather than eventful complications; the kind of lyrical drama initiated by Maeterlinck (*BTK*, 181ff).

Lyrical poetry had the advantage of not being popular, thereby gaining the supreme freedom which comes from solitude. The real work of art can belong only to the solitary. Commenting on a performance of *Pelléas et Mélisande* at Das Neue Theater of Berlin in 1899, Rilke regrets that Maeterlinck, "the prophet of the few," was debased by the many into the curious eccentric, acclaimed for his oddities and condescendingly accepted for his vaporous whims. That is the crowd's way: by granting to the egregious ones its short-lived homage and the fame of the day, it guards itself against their distressing uniqueness (*BTK*, 176). The lyrical poet is not in such danger of becoming the victim of coarse stratagems of the crowd.

And Rilke proudly hopes to become like those utterly lonely ones who do not carry their thoughts on their foreheads but only unveil their yearning in rhymes and their burgeoning dreams in their eyes. For that is the way of the whole ones: to remain solitary, until the noisy multitude is forced to its knees as by shining lances; only then do they raise their hearts like monstrances with which they bless the kneeling throng (*FG*, 16).

18. BETWEEN DAY AND DREAM

◇◇

Ich bin zu Hause zwischen Tag und Traum.
(*FG*)

I am at home between Day and Dream.

◇◇

IT IS obvious that in these first years after Prague Rilke was busy gathering honey out of life and experience, and building cells in his soul to receive it. The themes and motifs which honeycomb his work are beginning to thicken. Many of them have been visibly shaping up in the developments described so far; they will be easily recognizable in the more mature work to follow.

The little volume of poems entitled *Mir zur Feier* appeared at the beginning of 1899. They arose chiefly in Florence and in the following year in Berlin. The influence of the Ligurian Sea, the Tuscan landscape, and the Florentine painters is clearly discernible in many. They were published under the signature of "Rainer Maria Rilke," thereby acknowledging Lou's stewardship. Their cyclical arrangement is more artistically articulated and they represent a distinct advance over his previous work, both in poetic craftsmanship and in the crystallization and symbolization of themes. Their general tone is one of confidence and cheerful youth and the awakening from dream to consciousness is manifest throughout. It is as if his knowing boyhood were consciously emerging out of his dreaming girlhood, with the vague premonitory feeling, however, that the latter was the wiser and would prevail in the end (*VPN*, 16).

Each of the three cyclical groups is introduced by a key poem, which spreads, as it were, its winged fragrance over the poems under it. The first group is ushered in by a poem of rich melody which characterizes life as growing out of pure, homeless yearning into wishes which are "soft-voiced dialogues of daily hours with eternity," and then into the silent hour of deep self-realization. The mood expressed in it extends to a sub-group of poems, entitled *Angel Songs*. The poet is by no means prepared to strip his dreams of their power. He merely allows them to well up like the stream of a fountain from their turbulent darkness in order to let them fall back, brightened and in intervals of songs, into the obscurity of the hollow from which they came. By this process they lose their terror so that childhood can become once more the land of innocent beginning, to be sought and recreated without dread. Only by hearkening with breathless and silent wonder into the depths of his being can the poet know what the wind wants of him even before the birches quiver. His soul must open wide and spread like a festive garment over the musing things if his life is to attain to fulfilment. But no attempt must be made to bare and understand life in its naked existence: that would ruin its festive lustre. Life must be embraced with naïve surrender, its flowering gifts accepted as the wind blows them one's way. The child never thinks of stopping to save and store them; it merely plucks them out of its hair and holds out its young years for new ones.

Anxiously the poet wonders if the white, silver-winged souls of children will not disappoint their dreams and tangle up their laughing songs as they move in ever wider circles into the awakening voices of life and the thousand noises of the day. He has silenced his own longings for the loud hustle and weaned himself from the strange doings of men, but young and bare, he offers his swelling breast to the coming wind which will carry him inland. Amidst the dusky pines he throws off his dark guise like a lie from shoulders and bosom and, naked and pale, shows himself to the sun and sea, proud of his youth and waiting for the surf in festive spirit. On the poor, sickly, and homely words of every day he will lavish the colors of his richest holidays and make them shine with new meaning and stride with holy awe in his songs. But he knows that he is only a forerunner, heralding the arrival of greater ones for whom the roses will unfold like red flags in the wind. He even has his sad days of doubt, when he kneels down and takes off his crown, wondering whether its jewels are genuine or made only of grief. Untoward memories of his mother's distorted devotion remind him of his childhood frustration. The poor saints of wood, whom she showered with gifts and flowers taken from her own son's life, remain mute and proud in cold ingratitude. And Christ, the true King of children, whom he used to praise in song and seek with all his heart, has lost His power as well as His charm. Lonely, the poet must open his arms to May and find room in them for its tarrying impatience and weary spirit.

The *Angel Songs* are a nostalgic farewell of the poet to the Guardian Angel, who used to watch over him with His folded wings. As a child Rilke would pray to Him in his dark moments of the night and the Angel would take pity and lay His bright heaven into his frightened hands. He would carry his prayers and tears, his thanks and sufferings into the home of the cherubs, where they grew into whispering groves. In the Angel's eyes was the splendor of the first day, and upon His cheeks the demureness of a bride throwing a purple veil over her soul's fright in the presence of the bridegroom. The child was so little in the nearness of the Angel's blessing hands, and the Angel so big! For a long time the growing boy could not let go of Him, even though he had slowly lost faith in the reality of Guardian Angels. For the Angel became poor and small in his arms, while he himself became big. Now it was the Angel's turn to beg for help and friendship, and the boy's to take pity on Him. And the Angel could spread His wings freely and soar to the stars, whereas the boy was to find his way in life, unaided and alone. To the Angel he gave back His heaven while he himself remained on earth. And slowly the two began to recognize each other and get accustomed to each other's changed position. But often the Angel would look back upon the lonely boy and long to perform His sweet duties again at his bedside. And the boy felt sorry for the forlorn Angel, who was like a bird in a sunless climate, at the mercy of a leafless, windy winter.

In the spring of 1900 Rilke wrote to Lou of some squirrels which he used to have when he stayed in Italy as a child. He bought very long ropes for them, in order that their freedom should come to an end only in the tops of the highest trees. "It was no doubt very wrong," he says, "that I kept intruding as an outside power into their light existence (namely, after they had grown up and needed me no longer); but in a way it was their intention, too, to go on taking cognizance of me, for often they came running after me, and it looked as if they asked for a chain" (*Br.Frühzeit*, 44). That is the way with Rilke's Angel. He never lost sight of Him, although the meaning given Him underwent profound changes.

The second group of the cycle is headed by a poem of a listening cloud over the woods, whose darkening shadow no longer causes gloom, but because of its promise of refreshing rain means hope for the dreaming harvest. Rilke's relative optimism finds expression in a small number of nature poems, followed by his delicate maiden songs. These, in turn, contain, besides the core of the *Maiden Songs* proper, the *Profiles of Maidens* and the *Prayers of the Maidens to Mary*. Over these poems spread the bright Italian sky and the melancholy charm of Botticelli's Madonnas. Flower-gathering girls wait dreamily for something mysterious and great to happen, and pray out of their awakening souls to the Virgin-Mother, over whose ripe and weary motherhood the suffusing rapture of the Annunciation keeps hovering like a golden dream. Their own mothers have no answers for their throbbing hearts, since the years of their cool blooming are forever gone.

19. THE ETERNAL GESTURES

Jede Türe
in mir gibt nach . . .
          (*Advent*)

Every door
in me gives way . . .

IN THE poems of the third group of *Mir zur Feier* Rilke strikes new chords as a prelude to the *Book of Hours*. The leading poem, originally addressed to Lou, separates the world of the dream from that of the word. Dreams are like "marble Hermes which we place in our temples and brighten with our wreaths and warm with our wishes." Words are "busts of gold with which we parade in our conscious days." Neither dream nor word can by itself reach to the "cool shores of the living gods," but through either "we throw radiant shadows which perform the eternal gestures." It is into the realm of the "eternal gestures" that the following poems lead us, far from the world with whose "evening glow the poet fringes his solitude." In the growing dusk of the streets tired walls exchange last window greetings, bright and hot, until objects whisper to each other: which of us is now I and which is you? And when inside the houses the clocks strike as near as if they struck in our very hearts, the poet, too, foregoes his name and identity and yields to the enveloping and unifying power of Night. His whole childhood wells up and he feels one with many who lived before. His dream tells him the truth: not one mother has made him, a thousand mothers lost their lives and left them to the sickly boy. Whatever we may have called things in our nights and dreams, it is not our name that makes them great but the quiet forces within them, concentric and effective. "Can someone tell me," the poet asks, "whither I reach with my life? Whether perhaps I float in the storm and dwell as a wave in the pond, and whether even I am the white birch shivering in the cold spring air?" The words of men are like "walls behind which glimmers their meaning as in distant blue mountains." Young Rilke shuns the shallow words with which man claims to define reality (*FG*, 91):

> I fear the word of men so much.
> Whatever they say they so clearly espouse,
> And this they call dog and that is a house,
> And here is beginning and the end is such.
>
> I fear their meanings, too, their ironic nod;
> What will be and was, they are sure of it all;
> No mountain so high it could ever enthrall,
> Their garden and goods just border on God.
>
> I fain would warn them and fend them away.
> I like the things, and to hear them sing.
> You touch them: they stiffen and lose their ring.
> You kill and destroy all the things of my day.

And the last poem is so much in the spirit of the *Book of Hours*
that it may be considered an anticipation of its God (*FG*, 102):

> You must not wait until God comes to you
> and says: I am.
> A God who admits His strength
> makes no sense.
> You must know that God has breathed through you
> from the beginning,
> and when your heart is aglow and does not reveal it,
> then God creates in you.

More and more Rilke will try to capture experiences which reach
far beyond anything that can be perceived with our senses. Paul
Valéry, in many respects the exact opposite of Rilke, whom Rilke,
in the latter years of his life, nevertheless admired and translated,
probably for the very reason that by his more rationally colored
sensibility he achieved poetic effects which the musically experiencing Rilke envied—Paul Valéry admits in an interview of 1927 that
for quite a time he was unable to appreciate the strange genius of
his German translator. But he ended by liking him, and "through
him such things as I would normally and directly not care for, that
mysterious and all but unknown depth-world of dreamy thought
to which I have given such names as mysticism or plain occultism,
a knowledge of omens, premonitions, inner religious voices, intimate confidences of far-away things—which at times seem like the
confidences of a woman. Rilke confronted me in a delightful way
with all those things of life which I did not know or which I decidedly scorned" (Salis, 115).

We have seen that Rilke had a dangerous tendency to surrender to
the many and sundry stimuli coming from outside, and that concentration in solitude was the one thing to be achieved. "I run out,
I run out, like sand running through fingers. I have all of a sudden
so many senses which all thirst differently. I feel myself swelling
in a hundred places, but most of all in the middle of my heart"
(*AW* I,21). These words which a young monk of the *Book of Hours*
is made to utter in great anguish, spring from the poet's own soul.
What disturbed Rilke all his life was that this visible and tangible
world was only one side of reality, and indeed the less important
one. In it ruled consciousness of time, and that meant consciousness

of "running out like sand running through fingers." To surrender to it as if it were the beginning and end of all true existence was the one sure way for him of rendering his creative work totally impossible. "My life is not this steep hour, in which you see me hurry so," he prays to God through the Russian monk's mouth; "I am a tree before my background, I am only one of my many mouths, and the one which closes first" (*AW* I,19).

Just as the unseen half is as truly a part of the moon as the visible half, there is a side of reality invisible to the eye of the body. In fact the mysterious forces which rule in the visible world have their source in the invisible one, just as the stem, the branches, and the top of the tree are fed through its unseen roots by unseen elements of life. But to gain consciousness of the invisible side of reality the ordinary organs of perception are inadequate. "Through senses not yet named, whose seat has not yet been identified, we have received yearnings and sensations which we shall never lose" (*Br.Frühzeit*, 397-398). Time, in this other world, is levelled out, and light is not its medium. It is perceived, as it were, with "the farther side of our eye-balls" looking inward (*Br.Reisegefährtin*, 77). In it we need not keep separate the thousands of things in their concrete individuality since we experience them in the forces which shape them, in the roots from which they stem. The present is embedded in the past, and the future lies dormant within both.

Rilke often complained of having a poor memory, that is, of not remembering details in their multiple singularity. The substance of his experiences became insensibly absorbed and entered, nameless, into his bloodstream (*Br.* I,372). Names are stuck like lights close to our foreheads, but they are temporal makeshifts from which we must free ourselves if we wish to come near to ourselves and to God. "The living all make the mistake of distinguishing too sharply" (*First Elegy*). They behave like "the wind which brushes the branches and says: *My* tree. . . . They say: *my* life, *my* wife, *my* dog, *my* child, and know very well that every thing: life, wife, dog, and child are strange organisms against which they stumble blindly with their outstretched arms. . . . They *own* their wife as little as they own the flower, which lives its life alone and strange" (*AW* I,83). "When my reason measures, I know how deep, how long, how far things are, but God simply *is*, and Time is no more than the atmosphere vibrating around Him" (*AW* I,48). Anxiously the poet asks himself in a lyrical part of his diary dated November 21, 1899: "Where am I, where? Perhaps in a room? . . . Perhaps in a name? And the name clings about me like an old frame which secretly fears that it may have lost its contents. Yet it holds the picture, but he whom it depicts in the very definite garb of passing moments has changed; his face has become wilderness and his hands are awake in the night. . . . Where am I, where? Perhaps in a body. And my limbs know of a woman in whom they sprouted, and the shrub, pointing to the earth, asks me: do you know it? But I know it not. I can only believe that I was long before I began" (*Br.Frühzeit*, 232).

The invisible world is experienced subconsciously, not in the form of a present continually shifting in a forward direction, leaving a growing mass of unrecoverable past behind and feeding on a future yet unrealized, but rather in the form of a sphere or circle in which there is neither beginning nor end (*AW* I,49). If we stand in its center, every point of its circumference as well as of its surface and volume is simultaneously within range. From such a point of vantage it is possible to view at each moment the whole in a fresh and total embrace, not at the end of a slow addition. "Our longings are nothing but memories coming out of the future," Rilke says (Albert-Lasard, 162); "sometimes I remember so clearly things and times which have never been," he writes elsewhere in his diary in December 1900; "I see every gesture of people who never lived and I feel the flowing intonation of their never uttered words. Never born ones die. Indeed, that which never was is that which comes, comes over us—that which is new. And I remember distant futures" (*Br.Frühzeit*, 408-409). Within this global reality everything is connected, however remotely, with everything else. Expressions such as these anticipate in a truly remarkable way the metamorphic world which we shall encounter in the *Sonnets to Orpheus*.

In a poem written before 1902 a lover imagines that his beloved must hear him when he raises or lowers his eyebrows. To every gesture of love, even the most inconspicuous one, there is a sympathetic response somewhere in the world. "The impression of my slightest movement remains visible in the silken stillness; indelibly the subtlest emotion leaves a trace in the stretched curtain of space. Upon my breath rise and fall the stars and to my lips sweet fragrances come to water; I can see the wrists of remote Angels" (*BB*,

21). "As old royal families are related to all the neighboring thrones, thus we are forever related to every force, even when we are tired, frightened and estranged. Infinitely much that happens far away and to others has a bearing upon us" (*Br.Frühzeit*, 396). "Whoever goes somewhere in the world, goes without reason in the world, comes toward me" (*Br.Frühzeit*, 372). "There comes a time when every past loses its weight, when spilled blood is like splendor and splendor like ebony to our feeling. . . . Every cruelty becomes some day glory in grandchildren" (*Br.Frühzeit*, 371-372). "A glass reveals what moved my ancestor, a book betrays what he secretly cherished, and this satin, which used to rustle around the bodies of bygone women, keeps falling back into its old accustomed folds" (*Br.Frühzeit*, 241). The little books of Paula Becker are bound in "the silk of soft bridal gowns of long ago" (*BB*, 108). A charming gesture, beautifully made by her, is the delicate distillation of whole periods of history. The poet is like "a flag surrounded by vast distances." He anticipates the coming winds and experiences them while the things below do not yet stir "and the dust is yet heavy" (*BB*, 58). In the concentration of his being, in the center of cosmic happening, he perceives the simplified gestures of the universe: the flight of the bird and the swaying of the tree. Nature, which God created transient, comes back to him eternal. "Lo, in the Madonna Lisa woman has long been ripe as wine; no other woman ever need be, for no other woman adds anything new" (*AW* I,83).

20. SEARCH FOR THE IMAGE

Ich ruhe nicht, bis ich das eine erreicht:
Bilder zu finden für meine Verwandlungen.
(*Br.Frühzeit*, 339)

I shall not rest until this has been achieved:
Till I've found images for my transformations.

"PEOPLE who would like to express themselves in Art before reaching the stage of concentration," Rilke writes in September 1900, "merely magnify single fragments of their nature into disproportion and remove themselves more and more from all harmony, the first cause of all Art" (*Br.Frühzeit*, 301). That which is manifold in the visible world the artist must absorb and bring back to its original unity and simplicity, in order that his eyes open in all directions like the eyes of the child. Calculation is characteristic of man at home in the light of passing day. "All those who seek Thee, tempt Thee," says the Monk of the *Book of Hours* (*AW* I,67). Rilke's creative experience was akin to that of the prophet and of the magician. Subconsciously embedded in the feeling of cosmic unity which comprises life and death, he found symbols and uttered words which seemed to come from somewhere beyond the range of his conscious faculties and to extend into a sphere of meaning which transcends rational comprehension. Much later, in 1924, when he had reached supreme mastery in the symbolization of such extraordinary experiences, he puts it in this way in a poem entitled *The Magician* (*AW* I,390):

> He calls it. It startles and stands.
> What stands? The other; all that he is not
> becomes being. And the whole being turns
> a swiftly wrought face, that is more, toward him.

For the time being, however, the symbols are less abbreviated, more rambling. In a poem of the *Book of Images*, dating from the Schmargendorf period, he says: "My room and this expanse, awake above dusky land, are one. I am a chord stretching over rustling, broad resonances. The things are like bodies of violins, full of murmuring darkness; in them dreams the weeping of women, and stirs in its sleep the wrath of whole generations" (*BB*, 55). In another poem of the same period he implores Night in a fervent prayer: "Night, still Night, into which are woven very white things, red, colored things, scattered colors which have been elevated into the one Darkness, the one Stillness—put me, too, into relationship with the multiple which you convert into yourself. Are my senses still too much involved in play with the light. . . . Judge by my hands: are they not lying there like tools, like things?" (*BB*, 56). For nights at a stretch he would like to fill pages with delicate symbols which are not from his tired hand, but which betray that he himself *is* hand—the hand of One who does wonderful things with him. Into the darkness dimensions and forces emerge which use him, if he is willing to serve (*Br.Frühzeit*, 231).

More and more often it happens to him that he cannot say: "I am," but that he must say: "It is." "A single poem which I succeed in making causes all my limitations to vanish. There is not a thing in which I do not find myself: not my voice alone does the singing: something sings within me" (*Br.Frühzeit*, 244). On the occasion of Paula Becker's engagement he blesses her in a poem in such words as these: "It is so strange to be young and to bless," but "you see, my hands are much more than I in this hour in which I bless. I raised them, they were both empty; I was ashamed and paralyzed with fear in the knowledge of their empty lightness. But directly in front of you someone laid such beautiful things in these poor hands that they have almost become too heavy for me." An unknown giver has made him the equal of the trees: "the winds become softer and rustle in me, and I bless you" (*Br.Frühzeit*, 75-77).

Rilke possessed an unearthly desire and ability to explore that which is on the other side of the apprehensible, to retrace his experience back into the womb, as it were, and to feel subconsciously the elemental forces of life and of death. Unlike most people he was thrilled when circumstances enabled him to stay in some old castle where he could commune with the ghosts of ancestors whose often agitated lives and tragic deaths he ferreted out with eager delight; where mysterious noises would drill holes into the silence of candle-lit evenings and weird shadows would flutter about the framed portraits of dead men and women (*Br. 1914-21*, 259-260). His inclination to merge into the occult or to vanish into solitude tended to make him a stranger among men; as he reappeared into everyday life his current familiar name took on a hollow, weird ring, as if it no longer could serve to identify and place him. It made him solitary in the midst of friends (*Br.Frühzeit*, 249-250).

The paradox of it is that normally such an addiction tends to threaten a person with wiping out all outlines, and merging all distinctions into vague, nebular movement. How could Rilke ever hope to put such a constitutional proneness for occult "realities" into the service of concentration and precision? For, as he says himself through Malte, the true poet hates the "approximate" (*AW* II,144). If the phenomenal world, conditioned by time and consciousness, impressed him as unreliable and shadowy, could he expect more light and clarity from the subconscious with its dark weaving forces?

This paradox touches the very core of Rilke's creative anxieties. Somehow its dangerous, contradictory implications had to be brought to terms, if he was to realize his great ambition of creating poetry at once sculpturally compact and radiantly suggestive. Rilke was quite aware of the dangers besetting his work. In 1903 he compares his early poetry to the formation and re-formation of clouds in flux, a comparison which could be applied with equal justice to his God of the *Book of Hours*. A few months earlier, as he was writing the *Book of Poverty and Death* in Viareggio, he conjured the spirit of St. Francis of Assisi, "the brown brother of God's nightingales," whose song caused even "the yesterday and the forgotten to come back." "As their bridegroom he touched the crying hearts of maidenly sisters, and the pollen of his song, gently falling from his red mouth, floated dreamily toward their open corollas and lay down in their interior which was replete with the promise of bloom. And they received him, the immaculate one, in their womb which was their soul. And their eyes closed like roses and their hair was filled with the nights of love. And when he died, as light as one without a name, he was dispersed and distributed: his seed flowed in the creeks and sang in the trees and, quieted, looked at him out of the flowers. He lay and sang" (*AW* I,108).

Rilke's art of embracing the diffused and fluid in images of concrete form is apparent here. To that which denotes pure dissemination, to that which is neither here nor there but, as amorphous force, everywhere, he weds his symbols of sensuous beauty and places them like petals of roses on a precious bowl for our wonder. And the erotic quality of his subconscious experience is as conspicuous here by its delicate charm as it is by its somber obsession in the *Third Elegy*. His problem was to rescue and tap its creative potentialities while controlling its diffusive and flooding pressure. And since he was a poet of extraordinary conjuring power, his means of control could only be the form-giving verbal symbol.

How liberating he could feel the word to be when faced by the experience of the indefinite is manifest from a peculiar piece of prose which he wrote in Spain in the early part of 1913 (*AW* II,264; *MTT*, 45f). Although expressed in the anonymous third person, it evidently describes his own inner happening. As he took his usual leisurely stroll in the garden of Duino castle which sloped fairly steeply toward the sea, he mused over a book. Suddenly the idea occurred to him to go and lean into "the shoulder-high fork of a shrublike tree." Immediately he felt so agreeably propped and richly embedded that he remained there, without reading, completely abandoned to Nature, in a state of semi-conscious contemplation. Slowly he became aware of a strange sensation, as if vibrations hardly perceptible passed over into him from the interior of the tree. They could not be caused by the gentle breeze moving down the slope, since the tree sheltered him. And more remarkable than the sensation itself were the effects which it produced: it seemed to him that he had never experienced more delicate movements; his body was treated as if it were a soul and enabled to register a measure of influence which, strictly speaking, in view of the usual distinctness of bodily reactions, could not have been felt. Anxious to account for what was happening to him, he at once found the expression which adequately described it: "he chanced to find himself on the other side of Nature." As in a dream this word gave him joy and it seemed to him almost unconditionally fitting. The containing word had immunized a weird sensation from its possible disturbing effects.

Rilke's ambivalence reveals itself everywhere with unmistakable clarity. His subconscious self, whose obscure complications caused him endless anguish, must be carefully cultivated as the fertile soil out of which the edifice of his art was to rise. And his conscious self, whose transient experiences made him equally unhappy, had to supply him with fitting symbols and radiant contours for the rich sap of the subconscious flow. There is no better illustration of this than his years in Paris at the side of Rodin. While on the one hand he was learning from his master the art of rising above lyrical effusiveness into the disciplined practice of the *modelé* and the obedient fingering of the sculptured surface, he descended with equal, if not with greater, abandon into the frightful depths of Malte's nightmares and anguish.

There seems to be little doubt that Rilke's association with Lou had brought about a greater awareness in him of his constitutional ambivalence, of which eventually Orpheus and the Angel will become glorified symbols. For the time being he was still groping, but, as we have suggested, even now he knew that if ever he was to come out on top of his dreams, he must do so through the cultivation of his visual sense, whose form-giving power would strip the dream of its unreality, yet retain its creative significance. "You must invent an image for your feeling," he says in a poem of 1899, "in children's words or in the summers of linden trees there must be something which compares with it" (*Br.Frühzeit*, 239).

His Worpswede diary contains a fictitious letter from a girl to her friend, Helene. It was allegedly written from Lake Garda in April 1900. Actually Rilke was at that time in Berlin-Schmargendorf and his first Russian journey was already over, but the experience described in the letter evidently goes back to a recent stay in the Arco region, perhaps in the early part of March 1899, a month and a half before he went to Russia. The writer of the letter recalls the days which she spent with her friend, dreaming the most glorious dreams. Even in the daytime Helene would remain shrouded in the cloud of her latest dream, "her eyes turned inward and her pale forehead lit, as it were, by a strange light. In her eyes was no room for the day and her slender hands lingered forlornly in her work like lonely orphans." But now, on the shores of the Italian lake, the girl has come to realize the dangers of such dreamy roaming in imaginary lands. "We have scarcely seen our mothers, and our fathers' tender care has remained unnoticed." She does not even remember the color of the walls in her own room at home; their dreams had made all walls transparent and the beauties of surrounding nature had been no more than the vague occasion for their somnambular wanderings. An experience which she has had among the vineyards of Arco has opened her eyes. Walking in the hot midday sun along a path hemmed in by the high stone wall which separates the wine-growing slopes, she is fascinated by the delicate grassy blades protruding out of the grooves of weather-eaten mortar and covering the wall as with a carpet. What causes her to marvel still more is the darkness of the grooves themselves. It is a darkness which seems to come and go like little waves and is produced by numerous small lizards which start moving when frightened by too much noise. And each of thousands of these little reptiles turns its black eyes toward the observing girl. That which at first appeared like mere darkness has revealed itself as consisting of countless astonished and imploring eyes. And that is, so the girl writes to Helene, how all walls, indeed, all things are: in them are eyes anxious to meet our eyes. If we fail to see them we are blind and go about with empty stare. "Tear your eyes from your dream's lips, Helene! Turn them to the things, to the sun and to good people, in order that they, in turn, may fill you with their looks. In my eyes are now a thousand eyes" (*Br.Frühzeit*, 258-262).

PART IV

RUSSIA AND THE RUSSIANS

◇◇

Nah is das Land,
das sie das Leben nennen.
(Stundenbuch)

Near is the land
that they call Life.

◇◇

21. RUSSIA, THE LAND OF THE FUTURE

◇◇

> Du bist die Zukunft, grosses Morgenrot,
> über den Ebenen der Ewigkeit.
> > (*Stundenbuch*)
>
> You are the future, great morning glow,
> over the plains of Eternity.

◇◇

RILKE's journeys to Russia fit naturally enough into his whole development, not only spiritually but also geographically, as it were. His proximity to the Slavonic world in Prague oriented his mind in the direction of the most influential exponent, Russia. In the Czech people he had found that simplicity and warmth of childhood which he had failed to enjoy for long in his home or to find at all in his bourgeois and overbearing German environment. In Linz his attention had been drawn to Tolstoy and in Munich Wassermann had introduced him to the work of Turgeniev and Dostoyevsky. The religious connotations of their writings, so closely akin to their art, answered his profoundest needs, as a compensation for the perfunctory shallowness of his mother's religiosity and for the disregard of his poetry on the part of his family and acquaintances. And last, but not least, his Russian friend Lou opened up for him fascinating vistas of the vast reality of a people and land that seemed to correspond to his longings for pristine truth and patient growth.

Rilke's ideal of the "eternal Russian" had fairly taken shape in his mind before he ever set foot on Russian soil. Angelloz quotes him as saying to Ellen Key: "When I arrived in Moscow for the first time, everything was known and had long been familiar to me. . . . It was the city of my oldest and deepest remembrances . . . it was my home" (Angelloz, 119). A few days before his departure Rilke wrote that he was anxious to celebrate Easter a second time under the fuller sound of the Kremlin bells, after the thin-voiced Easter which he had just witnessed at home (*Br.Frühzeit*, 8). And from St. Petersburg, toward the end of his first trip, he confessed to Frieda von Bülow: "All things have no other purpose than to become images in one way or another. And they lose nothing thereby, for in the measure in which they express us ever more clearly our soul descends over them in an enveloping embrace. And I feel in these days that Russian things will grant me names for those most timorous yearnings of my pious nature which ever since childhood had longed to enter into my Art" (*Br.Frühzeit*, 17). On his arrival in Moscow he spent only a short time in his hotel, despite his fatigue, and proceeded at once into the city. "I saw this—" he says, "in the dusk the gigantic outline of a church; at its sides, in the mist, two small silver chapels; on the steps, pilgrims waiting for the gates to open. This sight, so novel to me, moved me to the very core of my being; for the first time in my life I had an inexpressible feeling, something like a 'home-feeling'—the very strong feeling that I belonged somewhere, indeed somewhere in this world" (Brutzer, 103).

The two visits to Russia obviously belong together as two concentric rings of a single experience. The first one started on April 25 and ended in the middle of June 1899. The second extended from the beginning of May to August 20, 1900. Apparently the plan to see Russia was first conceived in Zoppot near Danzig, where Rilke spent a few weeks in the company of Lou, on his return from Viareggio in the spring of 1898. A great deal of preliminary information about Russia was gathered, even with the help of a Baedeker, but the poet did not progress far enough to be able to speak the language. Consequently his first trip was on the whole exploratory and beset with many handicaps. It seems that, in part at least, his intentions were journalistic, inasmuch as he hoped to use his new knowledge and experience for the furtherance of his career as a writer. He arrived in Moscow with Lou and her husband on the Russian Holy Thursday and stayed there for a week. The Easter celebration, with its thousands of people walking from church to church and extending to each other the accolade of peace, with its hundreds of church bells ringing their glorious message of "Christ has arisen!", made an overwhelming impression on Rilke. It filled his heart with longing for the rest of his life.

He hardly visited Moscow museums this time as he was too busy taking in the life of the people and making numerous new acquaintances. He even had the opportunity of paying a short visit to Tolstoy who happened to be in the city. The aged Russian writer cautioned Rilke and Lou against encouraging bigotry and superstition by joining the Russian peasants and pilgrims in their religious manifestations, a warning which was heartily ignored (*Br.-Lou*, 36). Rilke called Tolstoy "the first and most touching man" in the new land (*Br.Frühzeit*, 12), and in his kind old hands he laid a copy of his recently published *Two Prague Stories.*

The Russian people appear to Rilke full of reverence and piety; they and their land impress him as "new" in the sense of not having reached a definite stage of crystallization, of being full of future and dark womb-life. Their palaces and churches look as if they were just emerging out of the soil and would find completion some day much later. He complains that his experiences and impressions are still so chaotic that he does not know yet what they all mean. He finds himself in the position of the fisherman whose net is so heavy with catch that he must first return home before he can take stock (*Br.Frühzeit*, 16). He links Russia with Italy, calling it a remarkable complement of his earlier Florentine spring. Florence, with its great art of external and formal perfection, is felt as a preparation for Moscow, with its greater depth and finer simplicity. Rilke is glad to have seen Fra Angelico before the beggars and supplicants of the Iberian Madonna.[1] According to Dostoyevsky's daughter, Liubov, her famous father was also reminded of the Russian people when he saw the peasants of Northern Italy. "The Russians travelling in Italy," she writes, "are often surprised to find in the depths of Tuscany or Umbria peasantwomen of the same type as those they have seen at home. They have the same soft and patient look, the same endurance in work, the same sense of self-denial. The costume and the manner of knotting the handkerchief about the head are similar. Thus the Russians love Italy and look upon it as to some extent their second country" (Dostoyevsky, A., 159). Rilke also visited St. Petersburg, the city through which Western ideas, social life, and civilization kept filtering into the empire of the Czars. Here he made the rounds of museums and was able to catch a glimpse of the mundane brilliance of its social life. But on the whole he was less interested in the individuals he met than in

[1] The Iberian Madonna (or Virgin of Iberia) is the copy of an icon in the Iberian Chapel of Moscow. The original is in the Iberian Monastery on Mount Athos in Greece. The reproduction, solemnly executed in 1648 with prayers and feasting by the monks and presented to Czar Alexis Mikhailovich, was carried through the streets of Moscow almost every day until recent times in a carriage drawn by six horses, the people bowing low as it passed (*GG*, 72).

the Russian type, the patiently waiting being that is chiefly concerned with slow maturing: the symbol of his own organic development.

On July 1, 1899, Rilke was back in Schmargendorf-Berlin, ready to organize his Russian impressions, to expand them through further study and to try to make Russian literature more widely known through translations, articles, and theatrical undertakings. He even arranged a little Russian sanctuary in a corner of his apartment, wore the Russian smock and spoke German with a Russian accent. By now he was able to understand the language without difficulty and made steady progress in speaking and writing it. But although he made the most determined efforts, now and later, and even insisted from time to time on writing poems in Russian, he could never quite master the language. Miss Schill begs him in 1900: "If you want to write me in Russian for practice, I shall be pleased to receive further Russian letters from you—but to be quite frank: I am sorry that I shall no longer read your beautiful German, which you use to such perfection. . . . One can master thoroughly only one language, that is, feel the breath of its soul!" (Brutzer, 15). Of course Rilke was too much of a poet not to agree with this point of view, but, as he admits in 1907 to a Swedish friend, certain inner experiences often compelled him to use a foreign medium because they could be adequately expressed only in it (Br. 1906-07, 242).

His Russian studies reached their climax in the months of August and September 1899 when he stayed with Lou at the cottage of Bibersberg near Meiningen. When they had left, their host Frieda von Bülow wrote complainingly: "I got very little pleasure out of Lou's and Rainer's visit. . . . They threw themselves body and soul into the exploration of things Russian and studied with phenomenal zeal all day long . . . as if they were preparing for a terrible examination. And when we did come together at mealtime, they were so tired and exhausted that no stimulating conversation could develop" (Br. Frühzeit, 420). They studied the language, the literature, and the history of Russia in all its aspects: political, religious, cultural, and especially the history of art. The latter covered a wide field: pre-Christian art, the Kiev and Novgorod-Pskov church architecture, ancient fortifications, interior church structure and decoration, enamel and filigree work, iconography, miniatures, costumes, furniture, articles of household and daily use—especially those of the sixteenth and seventeenth centuries. They were interested in Russian folklore: old songs (pesni), and tales of fairies and of legendary heroes (byliny). All the time Rilke was keen to learn a great deal about the relationship between Italian and Russian painting, in order to be able to distinguish what seemed to be most specifically Russian. He trucked Roman (i.e. Italian) memories for Russian impressions (*Br.Frühzeit*, 11). What appeared to him to characterize the Renaissance people most was a lust for life so impetuous that they closed their ears against the dark rush of their blood and their eyes to the precipices gaping on the fringe of their ephemeral exuberance. "Is it to be wondered at that these people were overcome by a desire for haste, a tendency to pile the sum total of festive magnificence upon each passing day? And so we can understand the crowding of figures on the pictures of Florentine painters, who were anxious to bring together on one canvas all their princes and women and friends. . . ." (*GG*, 163).

With unconcealed approval Rilke followed the trend of many Russian painters of the nineteenth century away from Western patterns, motives and techniques, back to native contents and forms: Ivanov's (1806-58) tragic and solitary struggle for naïve realism against the rule-ridden "Academy"; Kramskoy's (1837-87) later leadership of that growing movement; Ilya Repin's incorruptible Russianism in spite of his extensive travels in Italy, France, and Germany. Among the writers it was especially Pushkin, Gogol, Turgeniev, Dostoyevsky, Tolstoy, Chekhov, Lermontov, and the rustic Droshin who became Rilke's favorites. Pushkin's fairytales fascinated him, and traces of his *Poltava* are found in some poems of the *Book of Images*. In the episode of Grisha Otropyev in Malte's *Notebook*, Rilke had in mind Pushkin's historical tragedy *Boris Godunov*. Gogol was for him the Little Russian deeply embedded in the tradition, history and religion of his people, Turgeniev the scrupulous and loving observer of nature, Dostoyevsky the soul of the poor and forsaken whose pure and humble love is as much a mere direction of the heart as their yearning for God. In Tolstoy, "the eternal Russian," Rilke saw the kind, grey-haired artist of Russian poverty, love and humility, who had made "a dragon out of life in order that he could become the hero fighting it" (*Br.Frühzeit*, 367). It was above all he and Gogol who elicited Rilke's statement that their great kindness prevented the Russians from remaining artists.

But even the *Resurrection,* which was written during the period of Tolstoy's resentment against art, was eloquent evidence of his irrepressibly artistic nature (*Br.Frühzeit,* 35). Of Chekhov Rilke translated the *Chaika* (Sea-Gull) and he considered the possibility of this as well as of *Uncle Vanya* being performed on the German stage. He loved Droshin as the plain, earth-bound son of the Russian land and people, behind whom he could hear the old byliny and pesni.

Everywhere Rilke sought that which confirmed his own movement of soul and could thus become an image of his yearning. More important than the works of the artists were often their human quality, their prophetic mediation between God and man, their humble brotherliness and closeness to origin and to God, their silent association with earth and thing, their patient suffering in the struggle for an eluding ideal of perfection. The intensity of their conflicts and tensions was to him a warrant of their God-creating power. Their gigantic aims and plans, which seemed to reckon with thousands of years, stamped them as the prophets and precursors of Eternity. Their "holy slowness," in sharp contrast with Western forwardness and pride, kept them humble and conscious of their shortcomings and imperfections. Rilke interpreted the tragic dissonances and painful self-criticism of so many Russian artists as positive features, promising a glorious, though remote future.

"The Russian people," he writes to Miss Schill on March 5, 1900, "seem to live fragments of infinitely long and mighty eras, and although they linger in them only for short moments, over these moments lie nevertheless the dimensions of gigantic intentions and hasteless growths" (*Br. Frühzeit,* 130). Russia is the land of God, with its winds and waters and forests rustling on the fringe of Christianity. Like God, it can neither be cleared nor lightened; it cannot be depicted with ordinary colors and light. It can only be named in its simple being, in its kings of yore and their deeds and battles (*AW* I,47). It is Earth in its indifferent waiting, for which all seasons are like summers and all crops are pure rhythm; which bears the walls of cities with no less patience than the fields and the churches and the monasteries (*AW* I,47). Its endless steppes and heaths are like a sleeping sea under whose congealed waves, the kurghans or grave-mounds, are buried ancient generations. In this country, in which the graves are the only hills, the people are chasms.

They are deep, dark, and silent, and their words are only feeble bridges over their true being. "Russia," he writes later, "was reality, and at the same time the profound daily realization that reality is something remote which comes infinitely slowly to those who have patience. Russia is the country where people are solitary, each with a world inside him, each full of darkness like a mountain, each abysmal in his loneliness, unafraid of humiliation and, therefore, religious. People full of distant space, uncertainty, and hope: people in the making. And above it all there is a never defined, eternally changing, growing God" (*Br.Frühzeit*, 419).

22. SECOND RUSSIAN JOURNEY

Alles wird wieder gross sein und gewaltig.
Die Lande einfach und die Wasser faltig,
die Bäume riesig und sehr klein die Mauern.
(Stundenbuch)

All will be vast and mighty once again,
the waves will fold more broadly, the land be plain,
and trees will rise like giants and walls will shrink.

THIS view of Russia as the land of the future, the typical symbol of his own deeply-felt need of endless, patient growth, remained Rilke's all his life. "Perhaps," he writes to Lou in 1903, "the Russian is made to let the history of the world pass by, in order to fall later into the harmony of things with his singing heart. All he need do is wait and, like the violin player who has not yet been given the signal, patiently sit in the orchestra, holding his instrument with care in order that nothing shall happen to it . . ." (*Br.Lou*, 105). After the first World War Rilke met many White Russian emigrants in Switzerland, Paris, and elsewhere and he consistently felt that the Russian Revolution was not a genuine expression of the people, especially not of the peasants. Russia, so he thought, had only gone underground into its roots, where it would slowly gather strength for a great future (Brutzer, 13). He even used the example of Russia's withdrawal from the West as a means of vindicating his own withdrawal from the responsibilities of family and home. In a remarkable letter of December 17, 1906, he writes to his wife, Clara: "I feel somewhat like the Russian people, of whom those who are far away have become distrustful and say that it is high time that they reverse the course of their development and fall in line with the normal process of civilization; that in order to get somewhere they must at last face realities. And, to be sure, they would get somewhere, just as the Westerners have got somewhere, to this and to that, from one thing to another. But would they get to the one Thing which alone is the object of their soul's yearning, over and beyond almost everything else?" (*Br. 1906-07*, 136-137). Much later still, in July 1920, commenting on Liubov Dostoyevsky's biography of her father, he is quite willing to agree with her that the Russian Revolution was in reality a kind of ruse on the part of the muzhik (whom Rilke calls the inexhaustibly enduring and constructive element of Russia), whose secret aim it was to withdraw more easily from Western influence and thus to become more truly himself (*Br. 1914-1921*, 306). The Russian was no more fit to act as a revolutionary than "a cambric handkerchief was suited for wiping inkspots" (*Br. 1906-07*, 253-254). In one of the *Stories of God* entitled *The Lay of Justice* Rilke glorifies the uprising of the peasants of Southern Russia in the seventeenth century. But he is careful to explain that it was not a revolt against the rule of the Czar but against foreign usurpers, the Polish Pans and greedy Jews, who exploited the land and its people ruthlessly. Visibly annoyed by the post-war propaganda which tended to make Russia the scapegoat for all ills he writes in 1920: "[Russia] has made me what I am, from there my nature issued forth, all that is home to my instinct, all my inner origin is there (*Br. 1914-21*, 292).

What has been said of the Russian artists also applies to their works: in them, too, Rilke sought above all that which echoed his lyrical moods. Miss Brutzer mentions Nicholas Gay's (1831-1894) painting entitled *What is Truth?*, in which Pilate, the transparent satiated Westerner, confronts Christ, the dark unfathomable Russian, the One "who does not laugh," the Stranger who, unrecognized and persecuted, wanders on earth, "eternally coming" (Brutzer, 23). And Kramskoy's first picture *Christ in the Desert* depicts Christ, as Rilke does in the poem *The Garden of Olives*, not as the Redeemer and the Son of God who triumphs over the temptation of the devil, but as the despairing human being who has lost his way. Especially Kramskoy's last, unfinished work *The Derision of Christ by Herodias*, with that horrible last laughter of the pagan woman, made a deep impression on Rilke who remembered the stinging effect of similar derision from his military school days.

It is worth while quoting at length Rilke's words concerning it from his Worpswede diary of 1900 (*Br. Frühzeit*, 271-272):

"Kramskoy had felt for years: there is laughter.—And he tried to paint this laughter. He painted it in distant and in ever closer figures. And the laughter grew, it became broad, broad, it hired a hundred faces, came over poor and rich, over kings and mercenaries. Before the laughter seized them they all remained alike; in their laughter they became individuals. . . . And all of a sudden it dawned on the artist: it must be that everybody laughs. The world laughs. Laughter is the voice of the world. And the painter can no longer counterbalance the overwhelming weight of this laughter. He must seek somebody who can restore the equilibrium, he must invoke, recognize, and create someone who does not laugh. And with infinite anxiety he seeks and waits. And from afar comes The One who is eternally coming. And he places Him, bound, among the unbound ones. There He stands. . . ."

When Carl Hauptmann, who was among those to whom these words were directed, objected and affirmed that the world was not laughter, that such a statement was the invention of misunderstood genius, Rilke replied: "True, the world is not laughter, but it is the great mean accident, whose loudest and readiest voice is laughter. And for the solitary one, the earnest one, this laughter which he hears can only be the expression of that hostility which the disturbing masses mean to him. He *does* hear laughter. It may very well be that that which is behind it does not look like laughter, it may be work or poverty—but away above it all there is laughter from a hundred mouths." Rilke, who felt that he had been cheated out of a happy childhood, puts similar views into the mouth of a child in his *Stories of God*. The grown-ups, who pride themselves on experience and education, in reality grow more and more stupid. "They take off their hats to each other, and when a bald head appears they laugh. Indeed, they do nothing but laugh. If we children were not intelligent enough to weep once in a while, there would be no equilibrium whatsoever in these matters" (*GG*, 116).

During his second Russian journey Rilke was able to see far more and better than he had the year before. He was more at home in the language, had an idea of the lie of the land, and had greatly widened his knowledge of Russia's historical and cultural background. He started out with Lou at the beginning of May 1900 and headed again straight for Moscow. Easter was already past, but the three weeks which he spent in the Russian capital were used most effectively in coming into closer contact with the people, in widening his circle of acquaintances, in visiting churches and monasteries and browsing through museums. They stayed in a hotel opposite the Kremlin. In the Tretyakov and other galleries he was able to see many of the paintings about which he had read in Schmargendorf and Bibersberg. He went to an Aramtzevo village where two years before there had been a colony of painters comparable to the Worpswede colony with which he was soon to become acquainted. He was impressed by the nearby Sergei Troitzki monastery, one of the four main monasteries of the Russian empire, a city by itself containing about twenty churches and cathedrals, surrounded by fortified walls, and to which a continuous flow of pilgrims would journey from all parts of the huge country. At the end of May, Rilke and Lou proceeded via Tula and Kiev to Saratov on the Volga. From Tula they took a sidetrip to Yasnaya-Polyana in order to call again on Tolstoy, whose whereabouts they had learned by chance on the train.

After this meeting, which reveals a rather unbridgeable gap of strangeness between Rilke and Tolstoy,[2] the journey was resumed for a two weeks' stop at the Holy City of Kiev, the chief city of Old Russia, which turns its back on all modernism. Here Saint Olga started her first conversions, here historic monuments, churches, cathedrals, and monasteries with their relics and icons supply mystery and food to the piety of thousands of simple folk. It was in Kiev that Rilke visited the Petershki subterranean monastery, of which he writes to his mother as follows (Brutzer, 104-105):

"For hours you can even today walk through the corridors (not higher than a middle-sized person and not wider than the span of his shoulders), past the cells, in which the saints and miracle-per-

---

[2] A critical estimate of Rilke's relationship to Tolstoy is given by E. M. Butler in an article, "Rilke and Tolstoy," *Modern Language Review,* vol. 35 (1940), 494-505.

forming, solitary monks in their holy frenzy used to live. Today there is in each cell a silver coffin, and the one who once lived here a thousand years ago lies uncorrupted in the precious shrine, clothed in rich damask. Uninterruptedly pilgrims from everywhere, from Siberia to the Caucasus, plough through the darkness and kiss the covered hands of the saints. This is the holiest monastery in the whole empire. Holding a burning candle in my hands I have walked through all these corridors, once by myself and once in the midst of the praying throngs. Of all this I have gained deep impressions and it is my intention to visit these strange catacombs again before I leave Kiev."

In the second *Book of Hours* this weird experience has given rise to a poem in which Rilke describes the mole-like existence of these monks "rolled up like embryos . . . in their mothers' wombs" (*AW* I,73). In the same book an equally weird experience, actual or vicarious but, at any rate, symbolically autobiographical, resulted in a vivid picture of the frenzied prostrations on the part of a god-seeking monk, whose monstrous demons of lust, vanity, and pride were driven out only when he had stripped off his garments and stood naked before God (*AW* I,80; Ockel).

On June 17, Rilke penetrated into the Ukraine, visited several villages in the surroundings of Poltava and, starting from Saratov, took a five days' trip northward on the Volga. The vast plains and forests on both sides of the mighty river, interrupted by sparsely scattered villages or cities, or by a steed racing across the steppes, meant for the poet the ideal and primeval landscape, in which everything was majestic—the land, the water and the sky. The expanses of vastness, with their far-flung kurghans or grave-hills, became a symbol of his soul yearning for boundlessness and anonymity. In Nizhni-Novgorod he visited again the churches and their icons and at the end of the Volga trip, at Yaroslavl, he spent three days with poor peasants in the surrounding country, sleeping without a bed and sharing their frugal meals. In one of the Volga villages a peasant woman expressed her feelings of sympathy with the strange and rare visitor by saying these farewell words to him: "I suppose, you, too, are only folk" (Lou, *Rilke*, 25).

23. CRISIS

◇◇

> Auch noch auf voneinander getrenntesten Schiffen
> ging es für uns desselbigen Weges stromaufwärts—
> weil unser dieselbe Quelle wartet.
>> (Lou, *Lebens.*, 179)

> Even on ships farthest apart we would go
> the same way upstream—because the same source
> awaits us.
>> (Rilke to Lou, before embarking
>> on their trip up the Volga)

◇◇

RILKE returned to Moscow on July 5 for another fortnight, and then proceeded to Zavidovo in the government of Tver to pay a week's visit to the poet Spiridon Dimitrich Droshin, whose house was placed amidst roses and fragrant meadows. "In this country," he writes to his mother, "there are still people so full of faith and piety that all the events in the family are somehow linked to miraculous, mysterious prayers and their secret fulfilments." "In this country there are still princes whose ancestors are saints" (Brutzer, 9). On July 25 he went to St. Petersburg where he spent three weeks visiting libraries and gathering more important information about Russian art from his new acquaintance, the painter and art critic Alexander Benois. For a while he was left alone here by Lou who had gone to visit her relatives in Finland. In those days Rilke passed through a period of emotional crisis, which on one hand tended to make him all the more dependent on Lou, on the other hand heightened his consciousness of dependence and, hence, weakened the very fabric of their relationship. He wrote her an "ugly" letter—which unfortunately is lost—in which, according to Lou's reminiscences (Lou, *Lebens.*, 182-183), he called himself "a near reprobate" on account of the "arrogance" of his prayers, that is of his poems in the manner of those of the *Book of Hours.* Evidently in the years prior to the *Book of Hours* Rilke wrote many poems of an erotic nature to Lou. He then destroyed them because the sensual substratum had been insufficiently transmuted into poetic substance. However, fragments were rescued by Lou and some of them appear to be scattered through the *Book of Hours*. Even one whole poem, which on the face of it and in its present context is a forceful expression of the search for God, was originally a sensual love poem. On Lou's insistence it was incorporated in somewhat attenuated form in the *Book of Pilgrimage* (Lou, *Lebens.*, 175):

> Put out my eyes: I yet can see you.
> Block to my ears all entrance: and I can hear you.
> Without my feet I can go to meet you.
> Without a mouth I still conjure you.
> Break off my arms: I shall embrace you
> with this my heart as with a hand.
> Tear out my heart: my brain will flood,
> and though you throw the flame into my brain
> I will uphold you on my blood.

Lou's answer to the above-mentioned "ugly" letter is also lost, but it must have been on the whole reassuring, for in a further letter Rilke profusely thanks her and begs her in terms of almost morbid supplication to come back to St. Petersburg as soon as possible (*Br. Lou*, 37-40). Lou characterized the mood of this letter as "another expression of that extravagance" which he himself had become used to calling smilingly "the pre-Wolfratshausen one" and which seemed like "an incomprehensible relapse" (Lou, *Lebens.*, 182-183).

It must be kept in mind that the origin of the *Book of Hours*, especially the *Book of Monkish Life* and the *Book of Pilgrimage*, whose poems Rilke often called "prayers," was closely connected with his Russian experiences, and these, of course, were intimately shared with Lou. While at Wolfratshausen in the summer of 1897, Rilke and Lou were part of the time in the company of Lou's husband and a few other acquaintances, but for several weeks they occupied part of a cottage by themselves. Afterward in Schmargendorf and on their Russian trips they clung together as if by a pre-natal and unbreakable union. Of this whole period Lou writes: "If for years I was your wife it was because you were for me the first true reality, body and person indistinguishably one, an incontestable fact of life itself. . . . It was not one half in each of us that sought the other half: one whole, astonished and thrilled, recognized itself in the other whole, elusive and incomprehensible. And so we were brother and sister—but as in primeval times, when the marriage of brother and sister had not yet become a sacrilege" (Lou, *Lebens.*, 173-174).

However, already the Tuscan diary contains entries revealing the brittleness of Rilke's human relationships in general, from which even this early attachment to Lou was not immune. After they had met in Zoppot on his return from Florence and Viareggio the poet felt like a child who, having been sent on an errand to get some urgently needed medicine for a sister who had suddenly taken ill, became so enchanted by the warm morning glow that he played on the way and forget all about the real purpose of his mission. He returned home without the expected remedy. Moreover, young Rilke resented Lou's superior wisdom and her imperturbability which made him so dependent on her. He felt that his recent experiences in Italy, the thought and poetry which they had inspired, and his heightened confidence in a future wrapt in vague dreams ought to have made such an impression on her that an exchange of roles was evidently in order. He now considered that it was his turn to dispense guidance and advice to a woman who had remained behind in a past of memories no longer valid. When he found that Lou's superior attitude of assuredness had remained unaltered, he was indignant and "hated her" because she was too great. Nevertheless, for the time being his restiveness yielded to her sober maturity, as she insistently confronted him with the question: where do you expect to go from here? (*JF*, 154-157)

Toward the end of the second Russian journey things began to happen which seriously loosened their bond of intimacy. Rilke seems to have shown the change through various symptoms of anxiety and even of hallucination (Lou, *Lebens.*, 180-183). His "ugly" letter from St. Petersburg was more than the manifestation of a passing whim; the fact is that on his return to Germany toward the end of August he lost no time in going to Worpswede, in answer to an invitation from the painter Heinrich Vogeler, whom he had met in Viareggio in 1898 and with whom he had kept up a friendly correspondence. Worpswede became an important station in Rilke's life: besides meeting the other painters of this colony on the heath, he was much taken by two young women, Paula Becker, a painter of extraordinary talent, and Clara Westhoff, a sculptress who had studied under Rodin. At the end of September he decided to settle among these people but suddenly changed his mind and returned to Berlin, allegedly to pursue his Russian studies. To what extent Rilke's desire to be near Lou influenced his unexpected departure, it is difficult to say. At any rate, his mind and heart remained much occupied with the personalities of the two girl artists of Worpswede, while thoughts of marriage intruded with increasing momentum and supplied food for critical conversations with Lou. At the end of February 1901 Rilke returned to Worpswede with the intention of staying, and on April 29 he married the young sculptress, Clara (*Br. Lou*, 523). They fixed up an old farmhouse as their home and lived together until the end of August 1902, when financial troubles forced them to separate. Meanwhile a daughter, Ruth, was born on December 12, 1901, presumably prematurely like Rilke himself twenty-six years earlier. Husband and wife went to Paris where they lived and worked independently in separate quarters, leaving Ruth in care of Clara's parents at Oberneuland near Bremen.

Obviously Lou did not relish the idea of Rilke's tying his future to the life of another woman. Already at St. Petersburg she had felt that it was high time for him to go out into the world and broaden his experience in other lands and among other people in order to overcome his neurotic condition and to achieve the spiritual detachment necessary for his creative work. Her own attitude, too, had slowly crystallized into a sort of non-committal fatalism expressed in the words: "I am forever faithful to memories; I shall never be so to human beings" (Lou, *Lebens.*, 184). When Rilke finally departed they made a mutual vow "not to indulge further through correspondence in their habit of confiding everything to each other, *except in the hour of greatest distress*" (Lou, *Lebens.*, 184). In "a last appeal" she warned him not to carry out his matrimonial plans and expressed the fear that his pathological condition might lead to suicide (*Br. Lou*, 41-43). That was the end of their intimate love relationship. It was not to be expected that Lou would be the first to reopen the interrupted communication. Indeed, in their whole subsequent friendship it was always Rilke who took the initiative in moments of crisis, and that happened for the first time on June 23, 1903, when he had finished writing his book on Rodin and was on the point of returning from France to Worpswede, depressed by recurrent sickness and the horrors of Paris. As time went on he relied more and more on Lou's diagnoses of his bodily and mental disturbances; one cannot help being profoundly touched by the tone of childlike helplessness of the letters which he wrote from the sanatorium of Valmont at the end of 1925 when he seemed to expect a cure from Lou rather than from his doctor (*Br. Lou*, 498-505).

One experience, insignificant in itself, of their second Russian trip, stands out as an example of Rilke's peculiar creative manner. I believe that it is somehow connected with another observation by Lou, according to which Rilke visibly suffered from a sense of retardment caused by crowding images that found inadequate release. One evening they saw a horse being led out to pasture for the night; it was a fiery horse, but a wooden block was attached to one of its front feet in order to check its course as it attempted to race across the plain. The impression which this made on Rilke precisely at this moment was so deep that years later, when he saw another horse in the countryside near Paris, he was so upset that his blood rushed to his face and he became plunged in deep contemplation (Kippenberg, 158-159). And in the spring of 1922 the Russian steed leapt again into his consciousness and entered, triumphantly transfigured, into the *Sonnets to Orpheus*, as a symbol of exuberant awareness of space, contained like a "legendary cycle" within (*Son.* I, 20).

24. RILKE'S RUSSIA AND REALITY

To the Russian it will be much easier to
rid himself of the bourgeois bureaucratic
system which has been imposed upon
him only from above, and then he will
be the freest man in all Europe.
(Alexander Herzen, quoted by Gitermann, III,137)

RILKE planned to return to Russia for a third visit; it appears that he even vaguely contemplated settling in the land which he consistently called his real home. But instinct taught him better. Only a few weeks after he had been back in Germany he wrote these revealing words to Paula Becker: "*My* environment is *not* placed around me. Far away on distant paths have I seen the cities which I inhabit and the gardens which whisper above me are separated from me by many rivers. Churches which stand on the shores of the Volga . . . ring their great rising bells to me morning and evening, and songs, which the blind and the children sing, hover about me like lost souls and touch my cheeks and hair" (*Br.Frühzeit*, 53). Rilke realized very soon and with increasing clarity that the kind of home he needed for his work was something intangible, which he could take with him wherever he went. It was not so much a house, a family, and a country which he might call his own, although that, too, haunted his imagination as a tantalizing mirage, but rather a kind of atmospheric space woven out of memory and divination, a home whose main virtue it would be to impart to him the feeling of belonging, of brotherliness, but which would not involve any bonds of narrowing responsibility or break down the safeguards of individual solitude. And that was what Russia meant for him, the Russia of the blue spaces stretching across two continents, with its instinctively religious people, insular in the solitude of their souls, yet brothers and equals before their obscure God and before death. Here was anonymity in great communal diffusion coupled with impenetrable and inviolate autonomy. "The Russian," Rilke writes in 1920 to his former teacher at St. Pölten, Sedlakowitz, "has shown me in so and so many examples, how an enslavement and affliction so overpowering that all forces of resistance are permanently swept away does not necessarily bring about the death of the soul. There is, at least for the Slavic soul, a degree of subjection so complete that even under the most grievous and oppressive burden there develops something like a mysterious space of free play, a fourth dimension in which a new, limitless and truly autonomous freedom begins, no matter how distressing future conditions may prove to be" (*Br. 1914-21*, 354).

In a letter of March 17, 1926 to a young lady-friend he evaluates retrospectively the relative meaning of Russia, Italy, and Paris for his poetic development. Italy "in its clearly variegated fullness of forms, was the primer, so to speak, of my mobile existence. . . . Russia . . . became in a sense the foundation of my mode of experiencing and aperceiving, while Paris was the basis of my will to shape and form" (*Br. Muzot*, 409). The question whether Rilke's characterization of Italy and Russia was objective and just becomes less perplexing if we remember that the same landscape viewed by different artists necessarily results in as many interpretations. Each of them is likely to have caught some essential aspect of reality, while it would be presumptuous to assert that any one could have captured the whole truth.

Rilke, the lyrical poet in need of suitable images and symbols, may be forgiven for disregarding those facets of the Russian soul which would have proved incompatible with his secret yearnings. The stinging consciousness of sin, for example, and the corresponding craving for redemption, these Dostoyevskyan features could yield nothing of value to Rilke the poet. It is also obvious enough that less indulgent interpretations can be given to the coarse superstition and abject existence of the muzhik, or to the savage and cruel features in the Russian character in contrast with the admired virtues of humility and brotherliness. Nor could Rilke have allowed the anarchical and nihilistic tendencies of nineteenth-century Russia to blur his view, although in the *Book of Hours* he does indulge in the utopian dream of a churchless and stateless world of shepherds and peasants (*AW* I,76). Likewise the numerous attempts at rebellion on the part of Russian peasantry against Czarist rule are consistently ignored. The entire picture of Russia and the Russian as delineated by Rilke is fragmentary and one-sided, but those who demand objective impartiality in this respect forget the differences of aim and approach in the artist and the scholar. Where is the artist who has not made use of his inalienable privilege of choice when poetical truth is concerned, a kind of truth which results mainly from the adequacy of image, symbol, mood, and thought?

For all its limited range, what Rilke found in Russia corresponded in some measure to true realities. Nicolas Berdyaev points out that according to Chaadaev the powers of the Russian people had not been given effect in history; they remained in a potential state, as it were. "In Russia there is a preeminent example of virgin soil. Its very backwardness provides a possibility of choice." About Russian orthodoxy Chaadaev is quoted as follows: "Concentrated upon itself, plunged deep in its own thoughts, locked in its own life, thus the human mind was built up in the East. On the other hand it developed in the West by scattering itself about, twisting itself in all directions and striving against all hindrances" (*Berdyaev*, 37). In this respect Rilke was very much in agreement with Chaadaev and the above views could have been written over his signature. In taking over from Byzantium the leadership in matters of art and religion,

Moscow's orientation toward independence from the West became a conscious trend. It is true that Byzantine penetration in the West has been great, especially in Italy where Rilke could observe it in Florence and Venice; but on the other hand the powerful influence of Rome, the Italian Renaissance and, later, Western civilization in general, constantly tended to drive a wedge into the basic isolationism of the East. It is a matter of historical record that these influences caused serious conflicts in Russia, not only during the reign of Peter the Great, but before and after as well, and that they threatened again and again to displace the center of gravity of her whole way of life and thought.

In view of the peculiar ambivalence of Rilke's personality and mode of experience it was natural that his intuitively creative bent should have found confirmation in Russia's mysticism of feeling, while his craving for architectural structure and pictorial clarity should have made him sensitive to the boldness of the Florentine masters, the realism of the Worpswede painters, the *modelé* of Rodin, and the passion for truth in Cézanne. We have already pointed out that he liked Botticelli because he saw in him some affinity with the Russians. It can also be said that the creative processes of Rodin and Cézanne, at least in so far as they became significant for Rilke, combined both Eastern and Western features in the sense of Rilke's distinction (*Br. 1902-06*, 125). The mere emphasis which Rilke put on natural growth, unimpaired by foreign meddling or mediation, tended to make him resent the contamination of Russian art and life by the West. And I believe that Lou's influence confirmed that trend.

Unlike the West, Russia never gave birth to a Renaissance which caused religion, art, and science to part ways and to seek independent aims. For centuries the icon painters were monks or saints, for whom anonymity, fasting, and praying were prerequisites. Not the hero, but the saint was the ideal of Russian art. The subordination of individual modes to a strict code of formal rules sanctioned by tradition was the result of the ritual origin and meaning of the icon. Rilke knew the "famous recipe book of all iconography, the painters' manual of Mount Athos" as well as the "so-called Kievski Paterik (an Old-Russian collection of hints and prescriptions for the representation of Biblical subjects)" (*Br. Sizzo*, 11-12). In the *Book of Monkish Life* the monk-artist pledges himself to tell and describe the Russian land—which has the attributes of God—not with "bolus and with gold, only with ink from the bark of the apple-tree" (*AW* I,47). The icon, with its two-dimensional simplicity reminiscent of its derivation from the fresco, was long confined to the churches, where, together with the iconostase—the wall of icons—separating the choir from the nave, it was essentially an object of cult. In the course of time it was covered with layers of shining metal, leaving only the head and hands free. And the frame, too, was often loaded with lavish metal ornamentation. In Rilke's poetry this appears as a symbol of God's concealment and remoteness; in reality it was decorative and could serve at the same time as a means of protecting the image from the effects of multitudinous kissing.

To Rilke Russian orthodoxy appeared less as a matter of creed than as an expression of national communal belonging. When the church loosened its monopolistic grip on the icon, every private home reserved its "red corner" for a Madonna or a Saint. In spite of the autocratic rule of the Czars the feeling of brotherliness was genuine and deep. Its ideal model was supplied by the national saints Glebb and Boris, brother-princes represented on numerous icons. Pilgrims were not deterred by distances of thousands of miles from travelling to Kiev and Moscow to worship at the great shrines. Bearded prophets and myth-tellers, sometimes assuming the attributes of God, would magnetize whole regions of the land.

Russian architecture, too, presented typical features whose symbolic significance confirmed Rilke in his deepest feelings. Part of the primitive wooden house was underground and its roof was steeply sloped. While no doubt climatic conditions had something to do with this arrangement, it also reflected a twofold Russian trait: close affinity with the Earth and a skyward *élan*. St. Basil's cathedral in Moscow, built on the order of Ivan the Terrible in the sixteenth century, makes the impression of being pushed out of the soil like a complicated asymmetric yet organic growth. Its onion-shaped and spirally-twisted cupolas suggest consuming flames rising like eternal prayers to Heaven. Rilke in studying Rodin's sculptures marveled likewise at the way they grew, as it were, out of the amorphous rock.

25. THE EARTH

◇◇

> Kein Jenseitswarten . . .
> Nur Sehnsucht . . . dienend sich am Irdischen
>   zu üben.   (*Stundenbuch*)
>
> No awaiting of a Beyond . . .
> only a longing to grow humbler in the service
>   of the Earth.

◇◇

MORE and more Rilke became conscious of being deeply related to
the Earth, where the God of creativeness spreads His "hundred roots
which drink in silence" (*AW* I,10). In the *Book of Hours* that feeling is very strong. It finds expression in his great liking for the tree
as a symbol of earthbound life that rises upward to fruition. Or the
poet feels himself go "through massive mountains, in their hard
arteries, like an ore, alone" (*AW* I,89). Soon after his first Russian
trip he wrote the beautiful poem *Annunciation. The Words of the
Angel* (*AW* I,122-123). In it the Angel enviously calls Mary a "tree,"
while He himself is no more than "the day," "the dew," "the beginning," or "a breath in the woods," all modes of being which are
confined to the periphery, the fringe, the mere surrounding atmosphere:

> Thou art not nearer God than we,
> from Him we all are far.
> But blessed oh, so splendidly
> Thine hands most surely are.
> Of woman's hands who ever knew
> such ones as shine from Thee?
> I am the day, I am the dew,
> Thou, Lady, art the tree.

The poem reminds one of a Biblical sketch by the painter Ivanov.
Rilke was much interested in Ivanov's work (Brutzer, 33) and he
probably saw the *Annunciation* at the Rumiantsov Museum in Moscow (Réau, I,177). The Angel, tall and broad, with spread wings,
in shining garment made entirely of light, His foot barely touching

the ground, looks down toward the Virgin, His right hand following His look. And Mary in her humble smallness, dressed in simple dark color, her white face in contemplation, her delicate hands in open readiness, stands firmly on the Earth, like a young tree radiating warmth and splendor, self-contained in its fullness and glory.

The Earth is for Rilke in many ways the antithesis of the World. "World" implies man, and that means willful, impatient pride, intent upon violating the secret intentions of the Earth; it means ambiguity and dualism, unauthenticity and mass conformity. For Rilke in particular it means fateful involvement, danger of surrender, with a resulting dilution of his creative potentialities. The Earth, on the other hand, means silent, unperturbed deployment of creative forces. Submission to its quietly operating laws is—at least so he feels in his proud humility—his inescapable duty. Again this singling out of specific features for purposes of suitable symbolization is partial, no doubt, but if it strikes an incontestable core of truth, the adequacy of the corresponding symbols is assured.

Rilke's vow of consecration to the Earth does not mean that he pledges himself to greater realism, at least not in the usual sense of that word. It only means that he rejects all suggestions of other-worldly transcendentalism. All the transitory things and processes of the Earth, instead of exchanging their earthly reality for a supernatural one in a radically different Beyond, are merely channeled into the inner space of the artist's soul where they are transformed into invisible realities capable of endlessly changing form. All the springs of the years become sublimated into pure Spring; all the women of the Earth, past, present, and future, come together in the one Madonna Lisa (*AW* I,64). But they remain within the global confines of a double-faced earthly reality, visible here, invisible there. Rilke's experience of the inner world, of the visible world transformed into the invisible is characteristically immanent—or rather narcissistic. It is active and dynamic, but its movement does not issue in extra-personal action and realization. In it "the inner man sees his inner ... never yet loved, maiden" (*AW* I,322-323). Only toward the end of his life did Rilke begin to delineate a conception and ideal of more virile engagement. In a poem of February 1924 he realizes that after his hitherto "winged enraptures" it is time for him to "build of the unfamiliar bridges the boldly calculable arch," that joining forces with others is no proud betrayal of the "indescribable relations" and that it is with active man that God desires to take counsel (*AW* I,399-400).

In Rilke's experience of Russia there are undoubtedly some remarkable oddities. We have seen that he had turned away with undisguised disgust from the kind of sentimental religiosity practised by his mother; that he considered the whole of Western Christianity as so outmoded that no more than a hollow shell was left; that even the art which grew out of it, the Renaissance paintings as well as the Gothic cathedrals, had ended in a blind alley and stopped short of final fruition; that God was not to be captured through communal worship but to be experienced only as a direction of the individual soul. He resented the "stern Angel of Ebony whose cold looks never melted in the heat of penitent hands" (*FG*, 26). Yet, when it comes to Russia, all these aversions not only vanish but are converted into enthusiastic approval. We see him mix with the streams of praying pilgrims, walk with a candle in his hand through the underground monastery of Kiev, grow enthusiastic over the churchbells of Moscow as they call the throngs to communal devotion. He is profoundly moved by the sight of faithful peasants kissing the hands of dead monks. For Tolstoy, the native Russian, all these manifestations carried implications of empty superstition not unlike that which Rilke saw in the piety of Western Christianity. Peter the Great, "a typical Russack, staged burlesque travesties of ecclesiastical processions" (Berdyaev, 15). But Rilke considered such expressions of Russian religiosity as laudable and beautiful. To Benvenuta he writes in 1914 that the Russian soul "knows of no boundary between divine and human harshness," that it experiences instinctively all suffering caused by men as "that which in the last analysis it is: a submersion of God in an experience of the divine" (*So lass*, 49-50). We may ask: is that feature of the Russian soul so different from that which Rilke himself revealed already in the Military School, when he quietly suffered rough treatment at the hands of his companions because "Christ suffered it silently and without complaint?" (*Letters 1892-1910*, 19-20). Was not here also "the boundary between divine and human harshness" ignored? Yet this fundamentally similar form of the religious Rilke later deprecated with bitterness (see above p. 20).

It is quite obvious that our poet's partiality in regard to Russia, while not without a measure of validity, is to be explained by the fact that in Russia Rilke did not see the awful gap between religion and behavior with which he had been faced to his consternation at the military school and at home. It is certain that it was not he who agreed with the Russian painters, but these agreed with him, when they depicted Christ neither as the Redeemer of fallen and sinful man nor as the Mediator between man and a finished, immutable God. To them, as to him, Christ was a profoundly disillusioned, though superior, human being, condemned to remain unrecognized and ununderstood, not unlike Ahasverus, indeed not unlike the artist who felt himself essentially his equal. Rilke, the artist, could not thrive in an atmosphere vitiated by the consciousness of original sin; it would have paralyzed his wings at the start; it would have challenged his unquestioned lordship in a jealously guarded realm. There is no trace of humility but only boundless pride in Rilke's rejection of mediation or redemption of any kind. For him the true and only mediator between man and God is the artist. Rilke's much vaunted humility lies elsewhere: in his recognized dependence on, and his consequent submission to, the inner laws of his art. In the spring of 1921 he penned a little poem in a copy of his translation of the *Sonnets from the Portuguese* by Elizabeth Barrett Browning, in which he shrewdly asked himself how it was possible that humility could easily turn into pride. "What becomes of proud humility? Does it become a lie? No: it becomes superabundance—and the most magnificent vessel for the satiety resulting from surfeit" (*Gedichte, 1906-26*, 382). In other words, when humility becomes so plentiful that it overflows, it is magically transformed into pride—a pride which is really nothing but an overdose of humility! The above poem was dedicated to a Protestant minister, who may well have raised the question of Christian humility in his communications with Rilke.

Rilke's God was wrapped in the inner laws of creation, and it is about them that he circles in the *Book of Hours*. Unlike the Christian God, Rilke's cannot be reached by a mere act of faith (*Br. Muzot*, 75); to his God one cannot convert. He cannot be defined in the "light" of formula or of anthropomorphic outline, but must be communed with deep down in the roots of one's being. In one sense the immanent nearness of God inspires confidence and hope, in another His perplexing remoteness causes agonizing resignation. If the poet is dependent on Him, He in turn is dependent upon the poet, for only through the artist can God, the creative genius, operate. And this God is never completed but must be eternally rebuilt. A finished God would mean the end of the artist's growth, therefore of art, therefore of life as a worthwhile reality. Rightly or wrongly Rilke thought that he found all this in Russia and the Russian. He believed that Russian things could "grant him names for those most timorous yearnings of his pious nature which ever since childhood had longed to enter into his Art" (*Br. Frühzeit*, 17). In this sense, too, Russia becomes "the foundation for his mode of experiencing and aperceiving" (*Br. Muzot*, 409). The icon painters did not presume to individualize God or the Madonna or the Saints, as the Italians had done; behind their stereotyped colors and strictly normalized lines the Russian people were free to create each his own God and Saints in ever renewed and fresh movements of the soul. Likewise the choirs in the Russian churches and cathedrals hide the Holy of Holiest from the eyes of the faithful behind partitions made of icons, which are opened only on the rarest occasions.

The sort of Pantheism with which Rilke sympathized was like this: God is in the stone, in the clay, in the word, and calls on the artist or the poet to give Him glorious form in endless metamorphosis. God can no more be defined or understood than the forces of life or the laws of art; those who attempt to do so are doomed to failure. God ripens in the obscure depths of the artist's soul, whose duty it is to wait obediently for the throes of His birth. Rilke's considerations about, or dealings with, God are never purely religious. He cannot understand people who take, and try to feel, God as a given entity instead of using Him as the raw material of their creative endeavors (*Br. MTT*, 38). How close Rilke's God comes to art and creative inspiration can be inferred from this passage of a letter to Benvenuta: "The decisive element in art, that which people have long been accustomed to calling 'inspiration,' is, to be sure, not given into our power; but this much I have always known: that it could not be otherwise in view of our undependability. That this is so has never troubled me, I have never used the slightest artificial stimulus to bring 'inspiration' about. When faced with the divine our logical attitude is to be patient, for it measures with standards all its own" (*So lass*, 24).

Besides being characterized by metamorphic growth the Russian God as conceived by Rilke possesses still another feature that makes

Him acceptable. In 1921 he writes to Ilse Blumenthal-Weiss (*Br. Muzot*, 75):

"I have an indescribable trust in those people who did not arrive at their God through 'faith,' but who experienced God by virtue of their nationhood, within their own tribe. Like the Jews, the Arabs, and, in a measure, the Orthodox Russians. . . . To them God is origin and hence also future. To the others [viz. the Christians of the West] He is a derivative, something to which they are foreign or from which they have become estranged, something they can strive toward or away from—and so they constantly need the mediator, the link, the one who translates their blood, the idiom of their blood into the language of Godhead. . . . [For these] religion easily becomes synonymous with morality, whereas an 'originally' experienced God distinguishes between good and evil not with reference to man but with reference to Himself. . . . Religion does not mean duty, renunciation, restraint, but within the vastness of the Universe it is: a direction of the heart."

The Christian God of the West had come to mean for Rilke something arbitrarily extrinsic, which laid down the law to man from above. He meant duty, accountability not to oneself but to Him. Against this interference from outside the kind of artist that Rilke was rebelled with insistent pride, while he reserved his humble submission to the immanent God of his narcissistic yearning. Obviously, as he saw it, a God to whom one "belonged" by virtue of tribal origin was more compatible with his artistic ideal. The element of organic growth, so important in his conceptual and poetic development, could find easy confirmation here. When Rilke emphatically denies in the first *Book of Hours* that God is in communal experience ("im Verein") (*AW* I,77), he aims at communal worship by Western Christians, who have relegated their custom-made God to Heaven and have imprisoned Him in their churches in keeping with their bourgeois standards. The Russian peasant appears safeguarded against that sort of levelled-out God by the icons which allow his pious imagination free scope, and by the immensity of his land which makes for individual solitude in the midst of tribal communion. Communal worship under those conditions does not impair the solitude of the soul. The artist in Rilke rebels against every kind of communal endeavor purposely devised and organized by man (*GG*, 138ff). In 1914 he admits to Benvenuta that in the depth of his soul he felt related to the soul of the Slavs. This affinity, he thinks, is characterized by the shadow and light, reaching out from the religion of childhood over his ever startled conscious life. He identifies it with his kinship to the inner creative forces which, though undefinable, were to him indubitable in their effects. With them he was forced to contend for good and for evil; they were his Fate, his God, or his Angel, terrifyingly strange yet clingingly near. Around them he circled as "the lion circles around the fire in the dark desert." The precise metaphysical attributes which Western Christianism had bestowed upon its God made Him for Rilke unavailable as an intimate leavening power. The intended precision actually produced the opposite effect on him: imprecision of action, if not utter frigidity (*So lass*, 49).

Rilke's early conflicts in Prague and at the military academies, his mother's fantastic exhibitionism, and the shallow yet dictatorial patterns of belief and behavior of his environment, are clearly discernible in all these attitudes. On general grounds one would expect the catholicity of the New Testament, which superseded the national religion of the Jews, to agree better with Rilke's supra-national orientation. In reality, that catholicity appeared to him spurious and formalistic, conditioned by dogmatic definition rather than by intimate experience, predicated on the assumption of a Christ-God, supreme Mediator and Redeemer. And yet when his possessions were confiscated in Paris at the outbreak of the first World War in 1914, among the objects whose loss he regretted the most were a daguerreotype of his father and a picture of Christ, which ever since childhood he had cherished among his intimate possessions (*Br. 1914-21*, 25). Nor must we forget that Rilke loved St. Francis, the *poverello* of Assisi, of whom Catholicism boasts no less than of Innocent III. When all is said and granted, the fact still remains that his early Catholic upbringing had given him the names and symbols for many characteristic yearnings of his poetic nature, even though they became twisted in the process. Perhaps we may describe the situation by quoting the poet himself: "Children's Catholic impulses give them days of deep longing and bliss. After that there comes descent, downfall, relaxation, until for the first time they fall in love—only then, as that love begins, do they gently grope back for a recovery of those things lost in a dim past" (*Br. 1892-1904*, 287).

PART V
THE BOOK OF HOURS

Da neigt sich die Stunde. . . .
                (Stundenbuch)

The hour bows down. . . .

26. CONCENTRATION

◇◇◇

Und es kann sein: eine grosse Kraft
rührt sich in meiner Nachbarschaft.
                    (*Stundenbuch*)

And, it may be, a mighty force is astir
the while I stand about and demur.

◇◇◇

THE circumstances which mark the origin and publication of the *Book of Hours* reveal characteristic features of Rilke's creative manner and these, in turn, tend more and more to lend all themes of his poetry their peculiar Rilkean physiognomy.

Developments so far have shown that our poet was essentially dependent upon a gradual crystallization of subconscious yearnings and hidden motifs of which he became increasingly aware. They have also shown that he was greatly exposed to the danger of being carried away by the tides of inner and outer experience, by the teeming swell of images, and by the easy flow of his musical word. In order to counteract the diffusive effects and the vague patterning of his lyrical expansiveness he felt that he must strive for greater precision of symbol and for more enduring concentration.

One way of achieving concentration was by avoiding as much as possible the squandering of his inner movements through social involvements, epistolary analysis, or isolated poetic release. In so doing the pressure could build up to a high pitch so that a broad stream of cyclically coherent poems could well up from an intensely concentrated mood. The *Book of Hours* originated thus. The first book, entitled the *Book of Monkish Life*, was written, three and a half months after his first Russian trip, inside twenty-five days, between September 20 and October 14, 1899. And its poems came forth, in part at least, in thick sheaves: thirteen of them on September 22, eight on September 24, and eleven on September 26 (Mövius, 51-57). The second book, called *Book of Pilgrimage*, was penned in eleven days, between September 15 and 25, 1901; and the third one, the *Book of Poverty and Death*, between April 13 and 20, 1903. Only a month after the first book, the *Stories of God*, which are embedded in the same experience, came about in similar fashion, in eleven nights.

In one of the prose comments which accompany the original version of the *Book of Monkish Life* the monk admits that he was "almost" an artist because he allowed himself to be built by his verses instead of building them; that because he managed to bring his many feelings under control they became verses in spite of the fact that they leaped into words out of chaos and wilderness (Mövius, 178-179). In another such comment we read that the latter part of one poem occurred to him, all finished, as he stepped breathlessly out of the garden over the threshold of his softly lit cell. And the verses came over him with such serene harmony that he looked forward to a restful night of sleep. But "just in front of sleep there came trotting along another little poem which he smilingly recognized" (Mövius, 180). Elsewhere he joyfully notes that he strides upward over his verses as over steps without becoming tired (Mövius, 177).

In response to an inquiry about the origin of the *Book of Hours*, made by a girl student in the spring of 1911, Rilke writes from Paris (*Br.* I,303-304):

". . . I was occupied with other matters [Russian studies]. Then, on waking up in the morning, or in the evening when you could hear the silence, there arose in me—they had done so for some time—words which came out of me and seemed to be right, prayers, if you wish—at least that is what I took them to be, or rather not quite: I uttered them and I organized myself by means of them for the unknown things of the sleep or of the beginning day. But by and by I was struck with the intensity and the return of these inner dictates; one day I started writing down lines, this writing itself strengthened and encouraged the inspiration; to the instinctive joy of the inner movement was added the pleasure of what by now had become work, and while I thus responded to my inner acoustics there emerged in steady progression that which you know as the *Book of Monkish Life*. The other parts came about later: with them it was, of course, no longer possible to be mistaken about their genesis, they were work from the outset, but this work was never the kind that is foreseen and willed: it erupted from the distress of inner dislocations, from their very core, and could neither be called nor suppressed. To that extent this book is an honest one, with all the earmarks of something irrepressible, similar to the cry which one restrains and which yet breaks forth abruptly, regardless of whether there is room for it in the dense world. On the other hand, seen from the point of view of work, it involved the aimless joy characteristic of all art; in this sense it differs from prayer, and has a vanity which prayer lacks. But what is prayer—do we know?"

This passage describes in retrospect the "inspirational" mood out of which the *Book of Monkish Life* issued, on the whole spontaneously. As Rilke became aware of it he nurtured it, so that now "inspiration" was aided by "work." But he makes it quite clear that this kind of work was entirely different from that which Rodin taught him later in Paris: "it erupted unforeseen and unwilled." The *Book of Monkish Life* was something that "happened" to him and that he instinctively recognized as capable of being cherished and repeated. In October 1900 he writes from Schmargendorf to Clara Westhoff, excusing himself for having run away from Worpswede sooner than originally planned: "behind me in the vast sea of background, the work is already building up for me like a loving wave, which will soon seize me and envelop me—wholly, wholly. . . ." (*Br. Frühzeit*, 51).

In proportion as Rilke's whole existence came to depend upon his art, this manner of creative intuition became for him a cause of endless wonder; it was bound to become the supreme object of his wooing, the center around which his work gravitated, the mysterious core of all his imagery. Some twenty years later the *Sonnets to Orpheus* welled up in the same astonishing way, "often many in one day (the first part of the book came into being in about three days), entirely unexpectedly. I could do nothing but accept the dictate of this inner swelling, purely and obediently . . . (with the exception of few poems at the beginning of the second part, all *Sonnets* remained in the chronological order of their appearance)" (*Br. Sizzo*, 42).

The three waves which carried ashore the three books of the *Book of Hours* are separated from one another by a period of two, or nearly two, years each. Between the first book, written in Schmargendorf, and the second, written in Westerwede, Rilke remained for a while near Lou in Berlin, made his second voyage to Russia, paid a prolonged visit to Heinrich Vogeler, one of the Worpswede painters, returned to Schmargendorf for the winter to consolidate still further his crop of Russian impressions, and settled in Westerwede where he married Clara Westhoff in the spring of 1901. Between the second book and the third he spent another eight months in Westerwede, occupied a house on the heath, became a father, experienced Paris, made the acquaintance of Rodin, and took refuge in Viareggio, where the *Book of Poverty and Death* was written in the spring of 1903. Until nearly a year after this there are hardly any references in Rilke's work to the poems of the *Book of Hours*. The few times he does mention them in passing he calls them "prayers." Lou Andreas-Salomé states that he was extremely reluctant to having them published at all (Lou, *Rilke*, 57: Mövius, 11). Ruth Mövius doubts the correctness of that statement, and I am inclined to agree with her in so far as Rilke's reluctance must be understood as conditional and temporary. She quotes an unpublished letter of January 16, 1904, to the Insel-Verlag in which Rilke writes: "Besides, there is (as may already now be revealed) another manuscript for which I hope some time to gain acceptance by the Insel-Verlag; but this can come up for consideration only one or two years from now" (Mövius, 11).

Rilke's demurring attitude toward the publication of the *Book of Hours* no doubt had many causes and it would be difficult to identify them all. But some enlightening observations in this respect may be made here, while other relevant factors will be pointed out later (See below, p. 305). His desire for concentration through cyclical composition has already been noted; his Russian (and Italian) studies before, during, and for several months after his first Russian journey had yielded nothing enduring. All of a sudden, during three stormy weeks in the fall of 1899 the dam broke: besides many other poems and sketches there appeared in thick-coming waves a whole stream of poems, out of the same compact mood. They came to him on walks in the surrounding woods and in the dusk of his room with such spontaneity and fullness that when it was all over, he could only marvel at these gifts of Heaven. Even six years later, as he made the manuscript ready for publication, he let them stand in the order in which they had arisen, omitting only a few and making few corrections and additions (Mövius, 220ff, 250). Here at last was the fisherman's catch in lavish abundance, here was that longed-for concentration which held promise of future riches.

Though Rilke soon became aware of the frightening precariousness of such dependence on the pregnant moment, he felt that since

it had come in such triumphant glory once it must surely come
again, provided that he keep his soul in chaste readiness so as not
to prostitute it through promiscuous sharing. "Only a thin wall is
between us, by chance; for it might be: a call from your mouth or
mine—and it vanishes ever so noiselessly" (*AW* I,11). The poet
must be like Ruth the Moabitess, who performed her task as Boaz'
handmaid during the day and did not follow the young men,
whether poor or rich; but in the evening she made her soul ready,
washed and anointed herself, put on her raiment and went to where
Boaz lay on the threshing-floor, uncovered his feet and lay down
by him saying: "Spread thy skirt over thine handmaid." In the expectation of a recurrence of the creative moment Rilke threw a veil
over his soul in order to save it from contamination as life went on
and plunged him into new worlds, in Worpswede and Paris. "And
in your presence my soul is a woman, and is like Naomi's daughter-
in-law, like Ruth" (*AW* I,62).

At the end of this first great outburst of luxuriant poetry Rilke
uttered no exclamations of enraptured surprise, no moans of utter
exhaustion as he did later on completion of his *Elegies* and *Sonnets*.
At least, if he did, his letters do not record it. But in the *Book of
Monkish Life* there are signs that these feelings were not absent:
"The hour bows down and touches me . . . my senses tremble" (*AW*
I,9). In circling around God, "the age-old tower," the poet still
wonders whether he does so as a young falcon, which during his period of training is jerked back by the hunter's line every time it tries
to fly upward, or as a storm sweeping by in short-lived fury, or as a
great, enduring song (*AW* I,9). But this much he knows (*AW* I,12):

> If only there were stillness once, complete,
> if things which I by chance must meet
> were hushed, and if the sound
> of laughing neighbours and my senses found
> no echo in my heart on waking bound—
>
> Then could I in a thousandfold
> reflection think you through, and hold
> and own you (as long as lasts a smile)
> and lavish you on all that's young or old,
> as offerings of thanks.

His confidence in future realizations is unshakable (*AW* I,17):

> From this: that once you have been willed,
> I know that willing you's allowed.
> Though all that's deep we disavowed:
> when in the mountain there is gold,
> and though to mine it no one cared,
> some day by streams it will be bared
> which wrest, from what the hard rocks hold,
> the best.
>
> Though not at our behest:
> *God does unfold.*

The young poet knows that he is only the interval between the extreme tones of birth and death, but that these two tones become reconciled in the dark interval and that the resulting "song remains beautiful" (*AW* I,19). In his life he saw to it that the contradictions within him did not merge into harmony: that would have destroyed the inner tension essential to his work. But in his poem, in "the interval of his song," reconciliation was his glorious aim. To harmonize life's many contradictions in a gratefully captured symbol, that meant community with God in festive solitude whence all noisy money changers were banished. In spite of his fear that "his right hand might part company with its left mate" he felt "vast spaces unfolding on his forehead," and as never before his "book" could begin (*AW* I,21-22).

27. THE CYCLE CONTINUED

Ich habe Hymnen, die ich schweige.
(*Stundenbuch*)

I have hymns which to myself I keep.

Whether Rilke intended, while writing the *Book of Monkish Life*, to expand it with further cycles is very doubtful. But once it was there it became a matter of vital importance for him to wait for, and to work toward, a renewal of the experienced inspiration. For he certainly felt that the mood out of which it had issued had not been exhausted and comprehensively articulated. He did not abandon his Russian studies, but they tapered off rather rapidly after his second voyage, as other experiences began to superimpose themselves. Lou Andreas-Salomé and Ruth Mövius are of the opinion that if the second and third books of the *Book of Hours* contain fewer specifically Russian poems it is because Russia had by then become so thoroughly bone of the poet's bone and flesh of his flesh that special reference to it was no longer called for (Mövius, 75). That view is only partly correct, and the correct portion of it must be still further qualified. Each of the succeeding books, while doubtless echoing Russia, puts into relief hitherto less articulate motifs and progressively dilutes the peculiarly Russian ingredients.

In the last analysis the Russian aspects in Rilke's work are not there in so far as they are Russian but in so far as they are Rilkean. And Rilke was essentially ambivalent; in him Western patterns and yearnings competed with Eastern, Slavonic ones, simultaneously always, though at times the former, at times the latter, prevailed, at times they both merged in beautiful harmony. What was "Russian" in him was there all along and will remain there as a co-original component of the Rilkean complex. For that reason, and for that reason alone, Ruth Mövius is justified in interpreting the *Book of Hours* backward, from the third book to the first (Mövius, 102). Under the impact of accumulating experience original Rilkean motifs became gradually more transparent; in the light of their clearer crystallization their former refractory substance could be more easily broken down. Indeed, the late *Elegies* and *Sonnets* are helpful in understanding the *Book of Hours*.

Rilke definitely meant the *Book of Pilgrimage* to be a continuation of the *Book of Monkish Life*, but when it was finished the original, though modified, mood still remained incompletely expressed. New patience had to be mustered, new experiences had to be awaited, in the hope that the circle would at last be closed, perhaps in a third attempt. But that hope, too, was frustrated. The *Book of Poverty and Death*, the fruit of a further two years of waiting, originally contained three additional poems which Rilke scrapped in the final version, thus tacitly acknowledging the disconcerting elusiveness of his aim (Mövius, 240-242).

These three poems contained no new thoughts, no new images; above all, they failed to yield anything that could serve as a clasp uniting the beginning and the end of the circle. Rilke seems to have been aware of this when he struck them out. He must have become fearful lest the end should never heave in sight. However, that even now he did not give up hope is evidenced by the above quoted letter to the Insel-Verlag in which he promises to enter into negotiations for publication at the end of one or two years. Obviously he expected a fourth and final inspirational experience. And indeed, in August of 1904, while in Sweden, the *Book-of-Hours* mood came over him again and resulted in the beginning of a fourth book, of which only two poems were written (Mövius 13-14, 243). But these, too, brought nothing that was not already to be found in the previous books. This fact, coupled with the realization that the complexion of the original mood had radically changed, is responsible for his putting a stop to the whole thing and for his growing readiness to start negotiations with the Insel-Verlag.

In a letter of April 13, 1905, in which these negotiations are initiated, Rilke writes: "The work in question is a great, well rounded-off cycle of poems—a series of elevations and prayers is to be grouped into a formal whole (in keeping with its natural growth), and in memory of the *Livre d'heures* the volume is to be entitled *Book of Hours*, with the subtitles: *First, Second, and Third Book of Prayers*" (Mövius, 9). What is interesting in this passage is that at this time the poet seems to have considered his *Book of Hours* "a well rounded-off cycle of poems, to be grouped into a formal whole." And surely, the arrangement is a good deal more richly articulated in its unifying tendency than in any of the previously attempted cycles. Each of the three books ends with a poem in which all the individual currents of mood and thought flow into the universal sea of a pantheistic Deity. In the first book this is symbolized by the mythical Russian *Kobzar* whose old songs have flowed into the thousand ears of Time and Wind and now return to him in fresh melodies from the mouth of the praying monk (*AW* I,51-52). In the second book the treasure-digging monk opens his bleeding fingers like branches of a tree into the wind, and through them sucks God out of space, where once, in a fit of impatience, He had shat-

tered Himself (*AW* I,85). And the third book ends with the dissemination of St. Francis' song throughout Nature and in the loving hearts of women (*AW* I,107-109).

Nevertheless, these symbols themselves are essentially open and
do not preclude the possibility of beginning all over again. The
words which Rilke puts in parentheses in the above quoted statement, "(in keeping with its natural growth)," sound very much
like an apology. In view of the whole development so far described,
we are entitled to wonder whether Rilke was trying to whistle in
the dark, the more so as there was some reason for doing so. He
was very anxious to produce a great work, "well rounded-off" and
organic "as a whole," and it was important at this stage that these
qualities be pointed out if the publisher was to be persuaded to accept the manuscript. After all, until now there was nothing in Rilke's
record that might raise unusually high hopes in a publisher's mind
(*Br. Verleger*, 6-7). *The Stories of God* were too unique to suggest
further elaboration of the theme. In 1902 a collection of poems with
the title *Book of Images* had appeared, but only in an edition of
five hundred copies. Rilke must have felt vaguely that unless he
had faith in the authentic virtue of his own work he could not expect to arouse it in his publisher. In fact he is quoted as having
admitted later to Franz Werfel that he considered his *Book of Hours*
formless, a mere inspiration. "I could have continued to write poems
in that way indefinitely, without beginning or end" (Mövius, 14-
15). And to Hans Carossa he is reported to have said words to the
same effect (Mövius, 249).

The part of the statement in the above quoted letter which does
not partake in the self-delusion apparent in the rest is that which
is between parentheses; there is no doubt that the poems of each of
the three books of the *Book of Hours* were the result of "natural
growth," if by this we mean the compact concentration of mood
out of which they emanated. But such a mood can still remain un-
disciplined; it can still result in fragmentary, unfinished work, no
matter how homogeneous otherwise. And that is what the *Book of
Hours* in the last analysis remains: an unfinished symphony. Its
unity is entirely wrapped up in its subjective origin. Its three suc-
cessive cores, related but not identical, are wonderfully radiant and
productive, but the emanating rays or poems shoot off into space,
uncontained by any denseness of object which would gather them

and give them outline. Admittedly the poet circles about God, but since he rejects all anthropomorphism his God cannot serve as a form-giving object. Besides, we have seen that Rilke's God is fundamentally his creative genius, an inner force which seeks manifold manifestations in a process of growth and ripening, a force which shakes down leaves and fruit as soon as they have achieved temporary fullness, in order to leave the field open again for new births and growths. The concept of "openness" in the sense of unbounded readiness for a new day, a new beginning, is one which becomes more meaningful for Rilke as time goes on. "What is as beautiful as beginning?" (*Br. Frühzeit*, 311)

The development suggested here in regard to the *Book of Hours* will be repeated years later in connection with the *Elegies*. When in January 1912 the first two *Elegies* arose at Duino, Rilke had the same feeling of not having given final form to the mood which had caused them. Then, as in the days of the *Book of Hours*, he refused to have the unfinished work published, although this time the publisher was anxious to do so (*Br. MTT*, 150).

28. MOULTING

◇◇◇

O Bäume Lebens, o wann winterlich?
(*Fifth Elegy*)
Oh trees of Life, when are your winters?

◇◇◇

THE problem which Rilke faced with increasing insistence was how to avoid diffusion at the ends of a creative mood which was concentrated at its source. By a process of slow realization, which passed through the stage of pictorial awareness among the painters of Worpswede and crystallized under the impact of Rodin's sculptural genius, he came to distrust and renounce altogether his instinctive urge of effusive productivity—to give up altogether his bold circling about God and to place himself squarely in front of individual things or events in order to experience and express more nearly their objective and true reality. It was a painful process of moulting, during which old growth continued for a time to scale off while new vital substance was forming. The critical point was reached in Rilke's first Paris years. *The Notebook of Malte Laurids Brigge*, in its somber contents, reflects the depths and the dangers of the crisis, but the new manner is expressed in the method of its composition: the intrepid and detached self-observation, with which a decisive change of creative manner is objectively and patiently realized, in guarded prose, over a period of years.

In this connection it may be noted that the *New Poems*, which represent the clear victory of the New over the Old, were written during the same period as Malte's *Notebook*. What is more interesting still is that even while the third book of the *Book of Hours* was in the making, in 1903, the *New Poems* were already putting in an appearance; and by the time the fourth book was contemplated in 1904 they had made an impressive start. On the other hand, the *Book of Poverty and Death* itself already expresses moods and thoughts essentially the same, though not so warped, as those of the *Notebook*, but in the latter they are boldly articulated in a prose which has been disciplined and chastened after the example of Rodin. Rilke's two-pronged artistic consciousness at this stage, oriented on one hand toward inspiration and on the other toward quietly "fragrant" penetration of the object, is implicit in many parts of the *Book of Poverty and Death*; at times it becomes quite explicit, for example in such a passage as this: "My word shall be so sweet as to arouse desire, and yet not intoxicating like wine. . . . For my voice has grown in two directions and has become a fragrance and a cry" (*AW* I,96).

This manner of shedding skin while new growth is being formed is put into still sharper relief if we remember that the *First Part* of the *New Poems* was published in 1907 and the *Second Part* in 1908, whereas the work of crisis, the *Notebook of Malte*, was completed and published only in 1910. A number of letters of this period reveal that in proportion as the new, "sculptural" manner of the *New Poems* triumphed, Rilke had to make increasingly determined efforts to sustain the Malte-mood, which in reality was being overtaken and left behind. The whole tangle reminds one of the encysted overlapping in matters of love which we have noted earlier.

In due time, however, the kind of concentration that had given birth to the *Book of Hours* was replaced by another kind, which consisted in a more systematic localization and a deeper penetration of individual experiences and things, giving them clearer outline and more adequately sustained symbolization in a sort of cosmic soul-space. What this means can perhaps best be illustrated by quoting the leading poem of the *Second Part* of the *New Poems* entitled *Archaic Torso of Apollo* (*AW* I,155). The object which Rilke had in mind was a torso which he may have observed and studied in the Louvre (Hausmann, 21ff). The poem deals not with a thing of nature but with a thing of art—and creative art, if authentic, proceeds in a manner comparable to that of the Divine Creator Himself. The thing to which life and form are to be given must be experienced from the innermost core from which its soul spreads into every part of its body on whose surface it shines in a contained glow. The torso is that of a God-Artist, more particularly the god of poetry and of orderly, disciplined music, in contrast with Dionysos, the god of ecstatic, intoxicating music. Hence the poem emphasizes precisely the kind of concentration which Rilke craved at this time, so that the somewhat unexpected turn at the end, that laconic admonition "You must remould your ways," is truly an integral and organic constituent of the poem. The basic motif is that of artistic creation which, as we have seen, was also that of the *Book of Hours*, and which in one form or another is Rilke's life-long concern. But whereas in the *Book of Hours* it was embedded in the symbol of an undefinable, diffused God and, therefore, could not be fitted in a plastic mould, in the *New Poems* it is experienced in the form-giving soul of concrete objects or events.

ARCHAIC TORSO OF APOLLO

We've never known his quite unheard-of head
in which the eyeballs once grew ripe. But, lo,
his torso, candelabrum-like, aglow!
and in its glance, not out- but inward spread,

there's radiant life. Else could its vaulted chest
not stun and daze, and in the gentle twist
of waist no smile could go and seek a tryst
with seeds which in the fertile middle rest.

Else would this faceless stone abruptly stop
under the shoulders' transpicuous prop,
nor glisten so like to a wild beast's hide,

and would not send from everywhere the rays,
as does a star. There's neither spot nor side
that sees you not. You must remould your ways.

For about a decade Rilke practised this manner of willed de-tachment, of alleged self-effacement with intense passion, until his intuitively inspirational nature rebelled. The anxiety which accom-panied his self-imposed containment under the massive weight of sculptural technique is easily recognizable in numerous passages of his letters and poems; it even slipped treacherously into the very application of his new style. As early as 1903 he wrote the remark-able poem *The Panther*, often cited as a striking example of his ob-jective poetry (*AW* I,189). The vague memory of glorious freedom which still lingers in the soul and body of the encaged animal is in a real sense Rilke's own nostalgic memory of his now subdued lyricism. In the first two *Duino Elegies*, written in 1912, the irre-pressible lyrical impulse asserted itself again with elemental force, but not until June 1914 did the smouldering revolt break out into the open, and bring about a new determination. In a poem entitled *Wendung*, which may perhaps be translated as *Turning*, if not as *Crisis*, the poet has become distressingly aware that his disciplined observation had gradually degenerated into implicit renunciation, and carried in its core an imploring sigh (*AW* I,321-323).

He had long achieved it through looking.
Stars broke down and knelt
under the pressing, insistent gaze.

....

Gazing how long?
How long a time intensely wanting,
imploring deep down in his look?

....

For, behold, to seeing there is a limit.
And the better seen world
wants to thrive in love.

Work of the eye is done,
do now heart-work
to the images in you, the imprisoned ones: for you
have overpowered them: and in the end you know them not.

Behold, inner man, your inner maiden
gained out of a thousand
natures, gained only now,
that creature, never yet loved.

With this clear realization Rilke starts a new ascent on his spiral
path to perfection: without undoing what he had accomplished
by way of plastic and sculptural composition he now is ready to
return to the warmer climate of creative inspiration. At the height
of this new ascent stand the *Duino Elegies* and the *Sonnets to Orpheus*. Especially in the latter, inspiration blends in supreme harmony with sculpturally finished form. Rilke's "inspirational" manner of writing has been contrasted with Trakl's tortured lyrical
composition. In a letter of 1931 by André Gide to Wolfgang Schneditz, the French author expressed his astonishment at the fact "that
Rilke, sitting on a bench in the Jardin du Luxembourg, would pen
the longest poems in a notebook, as by an inner dictate, without
correcting or crossing out a word" (Trakl, 96). The striking feature
of this declaration is that it suggests Rilke's basic dependence on
some sort of inspiration even at the time of his *New Poems*. In December 1909 Princess Marie von Thurn und Taxis was in Paris
where she met Rilke for the first time on the occasion of a tea to
which she had invited him and the Comtesse de Noailles. The
latter lady had expressed the wish to meet the strange German poet
who had been writing her "quite unusual letters." During their
conversation, the French poetess complained of the difficulty which
she often experienced in trying to give final form to a single verse.
When Rilke stared at her with big incredulous eyes she insisted:
"Well, don't you find that it can be frightfully difficult?" But Rilke
did not seem to understand. "No, not at all. . . . " he said with
serenely disarming conviction (*MTT*, 6-8).

Needless to say, in this whole context the word "inspiration" must
never be understood too literally, above all not in any supernatural
or mystical sense, as if Rilke's words had been revealed to him

prophetically by a god or spirit. Nor must it be thought that in his creations there was no work involved; on the contrary, they were the fruit of much labor, in part subconscious, in part highly deliberate and progressively more disciplined. "They were work from the outset, but this work was never the kind that is foreseen and willed: it erupted from the distress of inner dislocations . . . and could neither be called nor suppressed" (*Br.* I,303). In other words, Rilke was forced to yield to inner tensions which were accompanied by images and rhythms of great intensity, but what erupted through them and could neither be called nor suppressed was "work." No doubt the forces at play were mysterious in so far as their roots were deeply embedded in the substrata of consciousness, for which reason Rilke often used the word "grace" or *bénédiction* to describe their operation; but he knew very well that the whole process was a natural one and that all its elements, however obscure in some of their aspects, were latent in his blood. It is precisely because of his acute awareness of these conscious and subconscious interactions that the creative function as such could become his main concern.[1]

Roughly speaking, Rilke's spiral development may be summed up as follows: somehow he was forced to evolve ways and means by which he could control the centrifugal forces inherent in his richly creative, but vulnerable, genius. In order to do so he came to set up a barrier of contrasting theory and practice which curtailed exuberant inspiration and resulted in dense, restrained poetry

[1] An interesting illustration of how inspiration and work went hand in hand can be found in Hans Jaeger, *"Die Entstehung der fünften Elegie Rilkes," DuV*, vol. 40 (1939), 213-236. See also H. Pongs' discussion of the *Tenth Elegy* in *DuV*, vol. 37 (1936), 97-99. Also in the recently published volume of poems, *Gedichte 1906-26*, a number of truncated and revised versions of poems reveal the interdependence of inspiration and work.

In this connection a study by H. W. Hagen ("Rilkes Umarbeitungen. Ein Beitrag zur Psychologie seines dichterischen Schaffens," *Form und Geist*, Bd. 24, 1931; Leipzig) shows conclusively that Rilke's revisions of poems written earlier are chiefly the effect of Rodin's lesson "toujours travailler" and of Cézanne's example of obstinate penetration into the "motif." The forces at work were the same as those which produced the *New Poems*: in both cases Rilke consciously practised creative empathy, entering into the core of things in order to recreate their inner rhythm and style. The "things" of the *New Poems* were such as belonged to the outside world, those of the revisions were such as belonged to the poet himself, but both kinds had in common that they were already endowed with organic form before the poet attempted to recreate them. It will be found that in regard to his authentically original, "inspirational" poetry Rilke's instinct was so sure and infallible that he seldom had to cross out or substitute.

of a decidedly antithetic and self-willed nature. When that was done he could reach back into his basic endowment and put all its magic riches into the service of discipline, thus achieving mastery and balance on a higher plane. In itself that kind of development is nothing unusual; it shows the natural curve of all growth. But, as has been pointed out above, what is fascinating in the case of Rilke is that the process itself became the fundamental theme and object of his poetry, and that it was metamorphosed into imagery and verbal suggestiveness of iridescent beauty.

29. SEASONS AND CLIMATE

◇◇◇

O, wind,
If Winter comes, can Spring be far behind?

(Shelley, *Ode to the West Wind*)

◇◇◇

THE genesis and complexion of the *Book of Hours* also illustrate the close connection of Rilke's creative work with climate and landscape. Except in his letters, the seasons and the land do not, as a rule, supply the substance of his poetic motifs, although a certain number of poems can be cited in which they do. On the whole their function is catalytic, inasmuch as they elicit and quicken creative expression; or it is symbolic, in that they grant him a wealth of images and a deep, earthy background for his poetry. Rilke often points out that the autumn was his most propitious season, but a cursory examination would tend to show that spring was equally effective. Of the summer he says that it is "never and nowhere his high season. Always and everywhere it is something that has to be endured" (*Br. 1902-06*, 201). The summer is only "an anticipation and a simile of what is to come" (*Br. 1902-06*, 238). It deceives you and makes you believe that because you hold the fruits of the year in your hand, you are secure in the knowledge and control of Nature's forces (*AW* I,55). As to winter, that is the season of Nature's pause and recapitulation, when the ripe seeds which had fallen into Earth's lap invisibly swell in secret preparation of a new birth. It goes without saying that Rilke's seasons are not to be understood astronomically, but typically and symptomatically.

Since the *New Poems* and Malte's *Notebook* originated from a determination inspired by Rodin's motto "toujours travailler," they may be expected to cut across all periods of the year. But in his "inspirational" work the spring and the fall certainly played a predominating role. The first two books of the *Book of Hours* and the abortive fourth one, the *Cornet*, and the *Stories of God* were borne on the wings of autumn winds and storms. The *Book of Poverty and Death* was a child of spring, and so were the *Sonnets* and, by and large, the *Elegies*. Storm and winds are the counterparts in Nature of the poet's creative surges. They mean turmoil and uproar; they sweep away the torpor of winter and the vanity of summer. Under their whip the trees roar and the sea billows, as the blood pounds against heart and veins. They are the voice of a wrathful God who fans the dying flames of life when the conceit of summer has wilted and approaching barrenness strikes the faithless with prostration (*BB*, 65). But those who, like the poet, have faith and youth, are freed of a leaden weight and know that the time to celebrate is near (*BB*, 141-149). To them the storm is the great transformer that levels out the ages and, like a verse in the psalter, gives solemnity and force and eternity to the land (*BB*, 137). The storm evokes the majestic grandeur of Old Testament prophecy; it evokes the wide open spaces of the Russian steppes, through which Mazeppa, the Hetman, raced. Like him, the poet feels tied to the steaming back of the galloping steed, his eyes open like a pond, while all things vanish except the sky above (*BB*, 59). God does not like what stagnates, no more than the poet cares for stupor. "Art's struggles are like the storms that carry the seeds, and its victories resemble the Spring" (*JF*, 47-48). Like the wave of inspiration, the storm at night is the great gesture in which God gathers the multiple things in one mighty grasp (*Br.Frühzeit*, 239). Like the wind curling in eddies and whirling the fallen leaves into the air, the poet "lives his life in growing circles" (*AW* I,9), and with "his feelings which have wings he gravitates about God's face" (*AW* I,18). He feels the storm coming like the portentous sea, or like a hoisted flag (*BB*, 59).

From Ronda, Spain, Rilke wrote to Lou in December 1912 that he would like to find again a place like Schmargendorf, where the rain and the storm had proved so stimulating in the fall of 1899 (*Br. 1907-14*, 280). *The Book of Pilgrimage* begins with the lines: "The tempest's fury is no surprise to you since you have seen it grow" (*AW* I,55), and while the *Book of Poverty and Death* was being written in Viareggio, "the sea was tumultuous and raging" (*Br.Frühzeit*, 88). Commenting on the *Cornet* in 1924, Rilke writes that it "was the unexpected gift of an autumn night, written in one sweep in the light of two candles flickering in the wind; the clouds passing over the moon elicited it" (*Br. Muzot*, 308). To André Gide, who toyed with the idea of translating it, Rilke explains: "The chief quality of this poem of youth consists in the inner rhythm, the rhythm of the blood which passes through it, carries it by storm from end to end, without a single moment of hesitation or doubt" (*Br.* I,485; Silvaire-Vigée, 136ff). Rilke calls it "this . . . 'parable' of youthful agitation" (*Br. Muzot*, 318) and is astonished at "the dash of this adolescent ancestor who, with cheeks still warm from childhood, races through love to death, to the apotheosis of death—dazzled" (*Br.* I,485). It was in the January storms of 1912 at Duino that the *First Elegy* rang in his ears: "Who, if I cried, would hear me from the ranks of the Angels" (*AW* I,245). And when at last the *Elegies* and *Sonnets* were completed in the spring of 1922, he referred to the experience as to that of a "mental hurricane that caused everything in him to crack" (*Br. Muzot*, 114).

Besides their storms the spring and the autumn have another feature in common, which no doubt influenced Rilke's creative impulses: they both are seasons of transition. They are ambivalent, reaching simultaneously into the travail of winter and into the efflorescence of summer. Their restless struggle for equilibrium is due to the clash of extremes, just as Rilke's work is dependent on the strife of opposing forces. Both spring and autumn are pivots of time and space. They are made of memory and anticipation. The frustrated past insists upon being included in any future fulfilment. The result is a vortex of anguish and determination, a feverish nervousness, both feared and sought. Nature passes through its periodic moultings, shedding old skin and forming new vital matter.

That Rilke experienced these seasonal transitions thus is confirmed by many passages in his writings. "How tangled the seasons have become," he writes to Merline in February 1921 (*Letters to Merline*, 74). In the fall of 1899 the Rilkean monk notes at the end of his first poem: "In the evening of September twentieth, when after prolonged rain the sun passed through the woods and through me." At the end of the second poem we read: "On the same evening, when once again wind and clouds came" (Mövius, 167-168). A little further we find this: "On returning home, in the evening, as the tree-tops in the woods became silent, they held their breath and hearkened"; and then follows a poem of suspense as the last leaf of the old century turns (Mövius, 170):

> I live when at its end the century stands.
> You feel the wind that by a leaf is blown
> which God and you and I with words have sown
> and yet is held and turned by unknown hands.
>
> You know: another page holds forth its lustre
> to which still anything can come.
>
> Dark forces gather, their strength they muster:
> each other's eyes they darkly plumb.

It is interesting to note that Lou Andreas-Salomé not only shared with Rilke this way of experiencing the seasons but that she saw clearly its vital relationship to him (Lou, *Lebens.*, 173):

"April, *our* month, Rainer—the month preceding the one which brought us together. How it makes me think of you; and that is by no means accidental. For does it not contain all four seasons: with its moments of metallic atmosphere reminiscent of snow and winter, beside others with a glowing sun; and beside autumn-like storms which cover the damp earth with countless hulls of buds instead of with colourless leaves—and does not all the while Spring, of which one knows before seeing it, dwell in this earth? From all this stemmed that calm and natural directness with which we became linked together like something that had always been."

30. SPACE AND LANDSCAPE

◇◇

Wieviele von diesen Stellen der Räume
waren schon immer in mir. . . .

> (*Son.* II,1)

How many of these regions of space already
were in me. . . .

◇◇

WE HAVE repeatedly pointed out Rilke's tendency to translate existential experience into spatial form and we saw that tendency at work in his earliest attempts at painting. In the *Book of Hours* nature and landscape account for almost the whole gamut of metaphorical symbolization. When God gave form to amorphous movement he "rounded his warm, wise hands" (*AW* I,12) about it, and placed His voice, the Word, between Himself and Time, just as the artist does when he creates. Out of the storm of inspiration emerges the enduring poem, like Venus out of the tossed waters of the sea (*NG*, 107-109).

It was in the endless steppes of Russia, on the heath of Worpswede which had been wrested from the watery waste, in the open space around cathedrals, and in the sight of the billowing sea at Duino and Viareggio that Rilke felt the impact of fall and spring storms most powerfully. Their openness at both ends gave him a glorious sensation of breadth and spiritual mobility. And the sky was vastly available when the dense foliage had not yet formed or when the trees were being denuded.

What Rilke instinctively sought was some sort of valid symbol in which he could experience time and space so interlocked that the result was one indivisible reality. The open spaces, apparently boundless in all directions, served that purpose best at the time when lyrical expansiveness prevailed. The little village on the moor was only a "transition between two endless spaces"; its last house was "solitary like the last house of the world" (*AW* I,71). God is "the great morning-glow over the plains of eternity . . . the cock's crow after the night of Time" (*AW* I,74). It is clear that space, thus conceived in boundless openness, threatens to cancel what feeling of safety and security it promised, and so it was to be expected that later, during the Rodin period, Rilke sought the fitting symbol for his bi-polar experience in individual, self-contained things. But the result was very much the same, for in Rodin's sculptural objects he saw each time an inner universe, just as in each of his *New Poems* there is immanent movement in soul-space.

It is a fact that Rilke preferred the plain to the mountainous regions. But, as in the case of the seasons, that, too, must not be understood narrowly. For example, he loved the canton of Valais, the Rhône Valley, and the Provence in spite of their mountains. In a letter to Countess Sizzo he points out that in those regions the mountainous backgrounds did not impress him as massive: the whole landscape in front of them is woven, as it were, into the "melody of a Gobelin" (*Br. Sizzo*, 28). Even in Paris, in the rue de Varennes, he often admired the glimmering atmosphere in the distance which suggested "a beautiful face in spiritual transparence" (*Br. Sizzo*, 28). Paris was the only city which for Rilke could become a landscape of life and death (*Br.* II,470), like the city of sorrow in the *Tenth Elegy*.

And there was landscape on the faces and bodies of human beings as well. In the *Book of Hours* the Virgin Mary "blooms like a meadow about God's face" (*AW* I,44), and the monk asks God: "Does not my Maytime prayer ripen in your glance as on a tree" (*AW* I,19)? Elsewhere he says of the poor: "In their eyes is the solemn darkening of light streaks of meadow on which a sudden rain falls in summer" (*AW* I,102). "When they [i.e. the poor] sleep, their bodies lie floating like a stream," and "their sex is as strong as a dragon and waits in the valley of shame" (*AW* I,104). Referring to Clara Westhoff's modelling of her grandmother's face Rilke visualizes the eyes of the young sculptress going laboriously "with slow, hesitating, and attentive steps, over furrows and folds, on the many neglected paths of ageworn experiences, stopping with piety and devotion at every milestone" (*Br. Frühzeit*, 48). If you lay the mask of Rodin's *Man with the Broken Nose* down in front of you, "you have the impression that you are standing on a high tower and that you overlook a rugged land on whose entangled paths many peoples have traveled" (*Rodin*, 24). With bitter humor Rilke wrote from a Swiss sanatorium at which, in August 1923, he sought relief from insidious symptoms through massage: ". . . and so the grotesque situation has come about that every morning an old gentleman, lost in thought, walks on his hands over my body. A circus attraction" (Salis, 126-127). And from Muzot he praises to Merline the purity of the "features" of the Valais landscape: "Really, at times it seems to possess everything that constitutes the charm and the soul of a face one loves" (*Letters to Merline*, 148). Already in the *Book of Hours* the outer landscape is being transmuted into landscape of the soul: "Your whole sky listens into me" (*AW* I,18), says the monk to God, and to his soul: "Be heath and, heath, be wide. Have old, old kurghans, growing and scarcely recognized, when the moon rises over the broad, prehistoric land" (*AW* I,51).

In the *Book of Hours*, too, the landscape is woven into the whole as into the "melody of a Gobelin," and it is anything but adornment; it is warp and woof of its texture, the fundamental tone of its melody, the element of constancy in its rhythm. It is true that the degree of amalgamation of symbol, image, and content varies a great deal. Ruth Mövius analyzes one instance of symbolization in the *Book of Monkish Life* in order to show how the poet's fancy assimilates and transforms a piece of experienced landscape into suggestive imagery. On Rilke's walks through the Schmargendorf woods in the company of Lou Andreas-Salomé, it often happened that deer passed by so tame that they would stick their noses into the coat pockets of the walking couple. At the end of a poem which, according to the concurrent prose comment, was written "as the evening descended over autumn and hands," the monk prays to God in these words: "Often when I see you with my senses, your oneness becomes divided: you walk [i.e. through the woods] like many shining deer, and I am darkness, and I am forest." In other words, as the dusk settles over the woods and himself, the monk feels identified with the darkness of the forest, whereas God passes like shining deer through him. The terms of the metaphor can be equated like this: dark woods are to shining deer as the monk is to God. In another poem, written the following day, the monk says: "For what are churches and cloisters, as they emerge and rise, but harps, melodious consolers, through which the hands of half-redeemed people pass before kings and virgins." This poem came about "in the morning-woods, in the presence of deer that walked, golden, among the stems of the trees as musical tones move through the vibrations of sun-filled chords." Since this is a morning prayer, the woods appear now as clearly distinct tree stems, and the progressive chain of association has become: tree stems are to shining deer as chords of the harp are to musical tones as rising churches and cloisters are to praying hands (Mövius, 66-67).

Similar metaphorical abbreviations are met with everywhere in the *Book of Hours* and in Rilke's whole work. As his mastery grew their denseness tended to increase and their crispness to emit rays of meaning in all directions. This is one reason why his symbols are often so baffling. Moreover, in the *Book of Hours* they appear in such bewildering luxuriance as to leave you at first breathless and dazed. Almost without a pause you are shifted from one metaphorical pattern to another and are afforded little chance to let any one in particular sink in and spread out. What is still more confounding is that, all along, these patterns seem to contradict and cancel each other. Now God is identified with the roots extending underground, now with the cathedral which men build above, now with the ship that approaches the coast, now with the coast that awaits the ship. In the *Book of Monkish Life* the Italian Renaissance is blamed for not having matured God the Father, for having lavished all its luster on the Son (*AW* I,25); in the *Book of Pilgrimage* the Father is like a wilted word which one puts in old books that are never read (*AW* I,61), whereas the Son is the heir into whose lap fall all the riches of the past and all the promises of the future (*AW* I,60, 63). At one point the nomad life of the pilgrim is the symptom of poverty dear to God (*AW* I,44-45, 78), elsewhere "blessed are those who never went away and stood still in the rain without a roof" (*AW* I,104). In one breath God is called "the diver and the envy of the towers" (*AW* I,36) or: "the future, the great sunrise red, the cock-crow, the dew, the matin, the maid, the stranger, the mother, and death" (*AW* I,74). Yet, through it all there runs a fundamental and all-embracing unity, for God himself is "a forest of contradictions" (*AW* I,36), "the eternal metamorphosis of gold into sunlight" (*AW* I,101), "the quiet center of the solitary monologue" (*AW* I,18), the recurrent refrain in the poet's song (*AW* I,30, 39).

The spatial universe into which Rilke's inner experience reaches out is three dimensional, comprising vertical depth and growth as well as vast horizontal expanse. At the basis is Mother Earth, the womb of all life. That Rilke felt his creative genius to be a feminine endowment is not surprising (*Br.* I,107). He sometimes speaks of the voluptuous rapture caused by the exercise of his art. To a young poet he explains that "artistic experience is so close to sexual experience, to its pain and rapture, that the two phenomena are actually nothing but different forms of the same longing and bliss" (*Br. Dichter*, 20). "In one creative idea come to life a thousand forgotten nights of love and these fill it with nobility and elevation" (*Br. Dichter*, 25). The *Book of Hours* contains many similes giving substance to the erotic quality of his creativeness. The Virgin Mary is "like a vineyard bearing fruit" (*AW* I,26), the temptations of the young monk go "like rumors of God through his dark blood" (*AW* I,31). God is as poor "as the seed inside a maiden who would fain hide it and presses her loins in the hope of choking the first breathing of her pregnancy" (*AW* I,101). In the earth, as in the womb, life is yet anonymous, names are still irrelevant. The earth, like God, is open and equally receptive to all kinds of cultivation and fertilization: to the ploughing and seeding in spring and to the harvesting in autumn (*AW* I,47). Through its veins, as through God, runs the sap into roots, and sleep the ores of potential gems. And out of it God is born into trees and flowers, mountains and valleys, and into the bodies and souls of animals and men (*AW* I,89)—just as the memory of man's obscure origin lies dormant in the subconscious and rises through childhood into knowing life. Sometimes the sensual substance is only crudely assimilated so that the murky sensation of the physiological still clings to the image. In the *Book of Poverty and Death* the poet-monk asks God to build a beautiful womb for the great artist of the future, whose shame is to be erected like a gate in a blond grove of young hair, and who is to lead the way, through the ineffable one's organ, for a thousand seeds gathered as white hosts on horseback (*AW* I,94-95)—certainly a unique prayer in the mouth of a unique Rilkean monk.

The variety of landscape represented in the *Book of Hours* covers the whole range of Rilke's travels and experience, and stretches from the Ligurian Sea to the Volga. It comprises the plains and the mountains, the country and the city, their people, animals, birds, and plants, with suns setting and suns rising, in all seasons and all kinds of weather. While it is true that each of the three books has its own emphasis, it is also a fact that each draws upon the poet's whole memory of experienced lands and climates. And, as Rilke says of Marianne Alcoforado, the Portuguese nun, out of a soul filled with such landscape, it is inevitable that songs emanate, day and night. "For, transplanted into a heart, it all acquires a voice, and it talks and whispers and cries outward" (*Br. MTT*, 393). God, whom the poet-monk considers his own son, inherits his whole landscape: "the green of gone-by gardens and the still blue of torn skies. Dew from a thousand days, the many summers that proclaim the suns, and all the springs with their glory and plaints like so many letters of a young woman." He inherits "the autumns which, like costly garments, are scattered in the memory of poets, and all the winters, like orphaned lands . . . Venice and Kasan and Rome; Florence and the cathedral of Pisa, the Troitzka Lavra and the Monastir, which under the gardens of Kiev forms a labyrinth of corridors, dark and entwined; and Moscow with bells like memories" (*AW* I,63).

31. PSEUDONYMITY AND DON JUANISM

◇◇

> und manchmal . . . . .
> ging eine Neigung durch sein Angesicht
> zu einer, die vorüberkam.
>
> (*AW* I,184)
>
> and sometimes . . . . .
> his eyes bowed secretly
> to a woman passing by.

◇◇

THE so-called prayers of the *Book of Hours* are attributed to a Russian monk, who was at the same time a painter and a poet. He lived in a cell in a monastery, and it sometimes happened that a young novice would be entrusted to his wise care. The monastery was under the jurisdiction of the Metropolitan at Moscow, to whom the praying monk sometimes reported on the spiritual life at the monastery. One such report was contained in the original version, and later omitted (Mövius, 209-215).

All this, of course, is fiction, which is by no means carried through consistently. In the *Book of Poverty and Death* we learn that the monk has been placed in "the deep anguish of very large cities," particularly of Paris, which is "like a flight from flames" (*AW* I,91), where "the smiling of a gentle race becomes distorted in nameless nights" (*AW* I,92). Apart from that, Ruth Mövius has shown by an analysis of the original prose comments of the *Book of Monkish Life* that the fictitious monk is insensibly identified with the poet Rilke. This does not mean that the two can be equated without reservation, but it does point to a close kinship.

Rilke had resorted to similar "pseudonyms" before. The early sketch *Pierre Dumont* (Sieber, 144ff) and the later *Ewald Tragy* are two examples. The lame Ewald of the *Stories of God* belongs in the same category, and so does Malte Laurids Brigge as well as the "Workman" in the remarkable fictitious letter on God (*AW* II,305ff), which Rilke wrote at the time of the *Elegies* and *Sonnets*. In fact, I am convinced that a closer study of the *New Poems* will reveal many, if not all, of these supposedly objective poems to be in their essence oblique self-analyses. A desire for mystification was undoubtedly an active ingredient in Rilke's life and work. His attitude to psychoanalysis clearly suggests it, and his early statement that he wanted to "cover the last syllable of his word mysteriously with his life" would indicate that he was not unaware of it. Did he not claim "the right to submerge so deeply under the waves of quiet waters that nobody even noticed his movements beneath?" (*Br. Frühzeit*, 231) And Ewald Tragy confesses: "You must know: I lie very often. According to the need, sometimes upward, sometimes downward; in the middle ought to be I, but often I feel that there is nothing at all in between" (*ET*, 25).

In a sense, this sort of duplication of one's self may promote detachment and objectivity, but it may just as easily serve as a ruse for the preservation of the poet's non-committal "openness" and freedom. Rilke certainly used the device largely for the latter purpose. He shared with Kierkegaard a liking for the incognito as a key to unlimited possibilities; these two men had in common a fairly clear consciousness of ambivalence. What Rilke intimated by his simile of the two hostile princes who woo the same maiden, Kierkegaard formulated more directly by saying: "ambiguity is a constant incitement" (Kierkegaard, *Gegenwart*, 21). Just as Kierkegaard was, and at the same time was not, Victor Eremita, Frater Taciturnus, or Johannes de Silentio, Rilke, too, was and was not Ewald Tragy, the Russian monk, or Malte. Both men were seekers of God out of a conscious conflict between art and religious faith, although the centers of gravity and, therefore, the distribution of emphasis were different. With Kierkegaard it was religion, more particularly Christian religion and ethics, which waged war on art and emerged victorious, thereby undoing in the end much of his basic ambiguity. The pseudonym is essentially an aesthetic contrivance, a disguise which finds no recognition in the eyes of God. With Rilke, on the other hand, art very early absorbed religion, subdued and subordinated it by asserting its creative lordship over a God of its own making and a corresponding moral order. The religious Kierkegaard openly admitted that his decision not to marry Regina Olsen was not prompted by a desire to practise the counsel of Christian perfection (Rehm, *Kierkegaard*, 75-76), whereas Rilke the artist seemed extremely anxious to prove that by shunning ordinary entanglements and bonds he only obeyed the God of his art more perfectly. Rilke's existential ambiguity was never resolved; on the contrary, it became more pronounced as his fancy evolved more and more decisively his own symbolic myths. These were designed to embrace both life and death, God and man, art and reality, and he tried hard to give them real existential validity. But few who read the letters of his last days of suffering will be inclined to believe that his efforts were successful (see *Br. Lou* 498-505; *Br. MTT*, 884, 949ff).

While the goals and ultimate attainments of Rilke and Kierkegaard were diametrically opposed, the forces at work were very much the same, and the resulting tension produced cognate symptoms. The fascination of the possible, the fear of bonds imposed from outside, the adventurous toying with temptation, the scornful disregard of bourgeois conventions and ideals as well as of institutionalized Christianity—these are features conspicuously common to both. Of course, in view of the divergent goals and relative emphases, they present different facets, but the analogy remains striking. Kierkegaard's paradoxical attitude toward Regina Olsen has its counterpart in Rilke's relationship to women. We have seen that in Scandinavia in 1904 the *Book-of-Hours* mood caused a belated and abortive spurt of inspiration, and in those days Rilke translated Kierkegaard's letters to his fiancée. But, unlike Kierkegaard, Rilke seems to have succeeded fairly well in obliterating the sense of sin, although he liked to experiment with its inherent inclination to explore and yield. He admits that for many, sin is a legitimate roundabout way to God, but for those who, like himself, feel naturally embedded in "the whole" it would be an intolerable hindrance (*Br. Muzot*, 195). "Compared with the very old and justified claims of instinct, our will is far too new and young a force" (*Br. Muzot*, 140-144).

Rilke strips sin of its moral connotations and reduces it to a mere disturbance of equilibrium on the natural plane. He particularly refuses to acknowledge it in those vital areas where, in his opinion, Christian morality has put it with especial emphasis, namely in the sphere of sex. He would rather favor the frank return to a phallic deity (*Br. Muzot*, 140). Nevertheless, there is no doubt that he was often tormented by a sense of guilt, if by guilt we understand a kind of biological malaise or mental anguish; for example, when illness prevented his aching body from cooperating with his creative soul, or when inner restlessness caused him to seek social distractions which interfered with needed concentration. It was a sense of guilt and fear that made him blame a young poet for having become impatient with life and committing suicide (see below pp. 240ff), and a young woman painter for having betrayed her art by returning to her husband and becoming a mother (see below pp. 236ff). Rilke's peculiar resentment of man's selfishness in violating woman's solitude and freedom stems from the guilty feeling of not being able himself to assume the responsibilities of love and marriage.

Moreover, Rilke knew very well the peculiar anxieties of sensual and spiritual temptation. The old monk in the *Book of Hours* warns the young novice (*AW* I,30):

> The carnal lust takes also hold of you,
> and naked arms undo your thoughts divine;
> on holy pictures cheeks of ashen blue
> are strangely made with flames to shine,
> and all your senses lie like serpents prone
> enveloped by the reddish tone,
> and sprawl and stretch to the pipe's and tabor's drone.

In another poem the monk confesses that he had strayed off from the obscure depths of God into the conceit of light, where Lucifer, "the Prince of Light, the shining God of Time" reigns in the proximity of Angels (*AW* I,38-39). In a letter to Princess Marie von Thurn und Taxis, Rilke makes the strange statement that the taste of an apple, more than that of any other fruit, is translated in his mouth into essence of spirit (Geist). "Perhaps," he adds, "that explains the original sin (if it was one)" (*Br. MTT*, 96).

The difference between Kierkegaard and Rilke may be illustrated further by their different treatment of the Don Juan motif. Mozart's *Don Giovanni* was for the musically disposed Kierkegaard the *ne plus ultra* of diabolically enrapturing music. We need only read the *Diary of the Seducer* in *Either-Or* in order to understand why. Elsewhere in the same book the Danish writer pours out this hymnal song (Kierkegaard, *Werke*, 94):

"Hear Don Juan: Hear the music portray his life. Like the lightning that leaps out of the thundercloud he breaks forth from the unfathomable gravity of life, swifter than lightning, in a wilder zigzag but equally sure of aim; hear, how he rushes into the ever-changing flood of worldly appearances, rams the firm dams of life; hear the light, floating tones of the violins, the beadlike laughter of joy, the exultation of lust, the blissful feasts of delight; hear, how he races along, past himself, ever wilder, ever more fleeting, hear the passion in the word of unbridled desire, hear the surging of love, the whisper of temptation, the vortex of seduction, hear the silence of the moment, hear, hear, hear Mozart's Don Juan."

As far as Rilke is concerned, he undoubtedly was no stranger to the fascinating quality of seduction. In this connection the psycho-analytically-oriented Lou Andreas-Salomé would perhaps be inclined to use the word "masochism," which she actually does use in reference to a line from one of Rilke's French poems (Lou, *Lebens.*, 186). At any rate, in Rilke's letters to Merline as well as elsewhere in his correspondence with women there are passages which subtly remind one of Kierkegaard's diary as well as of Lou's remark. But on the whole, Rilke, who had blunted his sense of moral sin, had integrated the demonic peculiarities of this sort of experience into the general pattern of problematic love and creativity. While Kierkegaard called every poetic existence a sin, for Rilke art bordered on the "Terrible" and "Monstrous."

In a poem entitled *Don Juan's Choice* (AW I,185) the Angel enjoins the famous seducer to put his bewitching passion into the service of "true love," that is, to transform the women "committed" to him into other Héloïses, into women whose love passes through their unworthy lovers and issues beyond them in glorious, but renouncing solitude:

And the Angel came to him: be wholly
ready now. And here is my command.
For what I need is this: that somebody
surpass all those who at their side
make sweetest women bitter.
True, you, too, know hardly better how to love,
(interrupt me not: you are mistaken),
but you do glow, and it is written
that many will you lead
into the solitude which has
so deep an entrance. Let enter
those whom I've committed to you,
that, growing, they outlast
and outcry Héloïse.

Surely, there is not much difference between what Don Juan is here ordered to do and Rilke's own attitude in regard to some of Merline's early letters which expressed ardent desire, mixed with artificially generated resignation and stoically subdued revolt in the face of her lover's highly-conscious and self-sufficient decisions. On October 17, 1920, Rilke had suddenly made up his mind to spend the winter in the solitude of Castle Berg instead of, as previously planned, at the side of Merline in Geneva (*Rilke et Merline*, 77ff). He arrived at his retreat on November 12 and wrote six days later (*Letters to Merline*, 46):

"No, Merline, I am not at all surprised to find you so strong, what makes you valiant now is that same freedom that allowed you to penetrate into the sanctuary of our love and kneel down there, not as a mere adorer, but as a priestess-elect holding up to the god the final sacrifice, with arms straining under the delicious weight. . . . Reap your harvest, Merline, the first harvest of Love; labor to store in the granaries of the soul the innumerable crop that we have ripened by our constant warmth. A 'hunter of images,' I go up into my mountains, unsociable, taciturn; I lose myself. But you, my delicious valley, you, flute of my heart, you, vase of clay to which I, a humble artificer of love, have given the inspired curve that marks you for divine uses for ever—may you have the innate imperturbable patience of the landscape and the flute and the sacred vase."

Is it too far fetched to imagine for a moment that the Don Juan of the poem is a sort of pseudonym of Rilke, and that the Angel is a further duplication of the poet, so that the whole assumed dialogue of the poem turns out to be a self-admonishing monologue? It certainly would not be strange to hear Rilke say to himself: "True, you hardly know better how to love, (interrupt me not: you are mistaken), but you do glow, and it is written that many you will lead into the solitude, which has so deep an entrance."

Nor is there, from a Rilkean point of view, anything unusual in the circumstance that the Angel is pictured ordaining, as it were, Don Juan for a weird kind of priesthood in which chosen women are to be sacrificed on the altar of love . . . and expected to like their ensuing privation. If we give unbiassed thought to the circumstances surrounding, and the confessions made in regard to, such women as Vally, Lou, Paula Becker, Clara Westhoff, Marthe, Benvenuta, Lulu Albert-Lasard, Merline, Mimi Romanelli, Erika Mitterer, not to mention others, less prominent, or the "Olgas," "Aglajas," and "Abelones" shrouded in mystery—if, moreover, we read attentively the poetry concerned with such and similar experiences, we can somehow understand the process of sublimation, of poetic consecration which they are made to undergo in the poet's fancy.

In the autumn of 1914, when the effects of the Benvenuta crisis had tapered off, Rilke's Don Juanism got him involved once more, this time with the painter Lulu (Lou) Albert-Lasard, a married woman who, like Rilke, lived in Munich and was homesick for Paris where she had stayed for a while before the war. Judging by the poems which the affair elicited, the relationship was from the start highly ambiguous, with Rilke constantly aware of his own fickleness, yet tempted to excite feelings of desire and bondage in his partner. When Lulu's husband discovered that he was being made a cuckold, Lulu found herself faced with the threat of divorce and, in order to spare Rilke the ensuing unpleasantness, she suggested that he escape to Berlin. But no sooner was he there, than he lured her to join him and to spend Christmas with him, a Christmas which seems to have lacked the luster of childhood faith (*Gedichte, 1906-26,* 560-564). Quite unexpectedly and without a warning he left Berlin again in January 1915 for the Bavarian mountains. To Princess Marie, who suspected a renewed influence of Benvenuta, he replied (*Br. MTT,* 399f):

"It is not M.v.H[attingberg]'s fault (I saw her only rarely in Berlin and we hardly write each other at all), but . . . incorrigible as I am, I have since again experimented with not remaining alone. . . . What can be said of it is after all the same cruel thing: that I find myself under the weight of someone else's life, which again turns out to be a strange one and which, with its complications and embarrassments, proves to me once more that life is all but impossible, here and there and everywhere, especially in me. I should like to help, and expect to be helped myself; it is an unfathomable fallacy that people think that I can help them when in reality I literally lure them into the trap of my pseudo-help in order thus to gain help for myself. God knows what will come of it now . . . everything seemed more propitious this time, more capable of being lived, until outside circumstances interfered; what will happen nobody knows, once again I shall have to save myself, but I should like not to leave any ruins or evil consequences behind."

The Princess wrote back, irritated: "Why do you always insist on saving silly geese who want to save themselves—the devil take the geese—he will most surely bring them back. . . . It seems to me, Dottor Seraphico, that compared with you the blessed Don Juan was an orphan boy. And you always pick out such weeping willows who, believe me, are not so 'weeping' at all—it is you, only you who mirror yourself in all those eyes" (*Br. MTT*, 404). Perhaps the Princess took Rilke's proneness to entanglements too seriously. The role of the seducer had a secret fascination for him, and the resulting complications were part of it.

Early proof can easily be read into those parts of Rilke's Worpswede diary which deal with his relations with Paula Becker and Clara Westhoff (*Br. Frühzeit*, passim), and abundant evidence is scattered throughout his work. It is illuminating, for example, to read certain passages from his letters to Mimi Romanelli, his "amie vénitienne" in the years 1907-1912 (Simenauer, 265ff). To a young girl who was staying in the room below Rilke's at the sanatorium of Valmont, the sick fifty-year-old poet sent a strange Easter message suggesting that after the numbness of winter the apple trees in bloom will perhaps "rehabilitate Eve. With an air of innocence the earth will always bring forth apples, though for the most part without the serpent's knowledge of it" (Silvaire-Vigée, 208f). Don Juanism of a fairly undiluted and, at times, lascivious sort is manifest in his correspondence in poems with Erika Mitterer, a Viennese girl in her teens. Rilke was nearly fifty years old when it started, and his last poem to her dates from a few months before his death (*Br. Mitterer*, 56). He saw her only once, when she visited him at Muzot a year and a half after he received her first poem. Likewise the notes which Rilke sent to Natalie Clifford Barney, the enigmatic American-born authoress of the *Lettres d'une Amazone*, are characterized by what Lou Albert-Lasard calls "a tone of respectful insistence" (Albert-Lasard, 160). In the "Salon de l'Amazone" of Miss Barney—"cet aimable danger d'une grâce parfaite" (Barney, 176)—the celebrities of Paris and from abroad met for many years —artists, poets, scientists, the *haute volée* of society—and Rilke, too, during his last stay in Paris in the first half of 1925, exchanged letters with her, trying unsuccessfully to arrange a meeting (Barney, 75-87). To Mrs. Albert-Lasard, Rilke admitted "bashfully, as if confessing a blemish": "Yes, I know, I possess a great power of seduction" (Albert-Lasard, 141). It seems that few women sensitive to the spell of the word were able to resist Rilke when he made his words "rustle like tree-tops over their heads" or when he "lulled them to sleep with his heady silence" (*FG*, 3). Lou Albert-Lasard called him once "an adventurer of the soul," to which he replied: "Alas you are right, a thousand times right, unfortunately—but—perhaps—it is necessary that it be so" (Albert-Lasard, 144). And did not Rilke write in his monograph on Rodin: "In all depravities, in all lusts against nature, in all desperate and vain attempts to discover eternal meaning in life, one can detect something of that longing which makes the great poets" (*Rodin*, 38).

It may seem incongruous to evoke the figure of Christ in conjunction with that of Don Juan. Yet, if we read carefully such poems as *Pietà* (*NG*, 28) and *Christ resurrected* (*NG*, 159), especially if we do so in the light of the sermon *L'Amour de Madeleine*, which Rilke admired and translated in 1912, we cannot fail to see that in the poet's fancy these two, Christ and Don Juan, belong together like master and disciple. Mary Magdalen, like the women "committed" to Don Juan, like Merline in the hands of Rilke "the humble artificer of love," is to be "given the inspired curve that marks her for divine uses for ever." True, Christ did not yield of His body more than His head and feet to Magdalen's fragrant oils and flow of soft hair, but that only reveals His greater skill in the excitation of love. Granted, too, as Rilke points out in a letter of April 3, 1912, that unlike other lovers Christ did not just vanish in order to cast His charm over new victims, but that even in His death He was still present as a precious object of desire and love (*Br. 1907-14*, 232); that only proves His greater mastery in showing the way to eventual desireless bliss. For the Rilkean God, that ineffably vague and obscure power toward whom Christ's tantalizing withdrawal orients Magdalen's longing, is a God who does not return love, who only sees to it that love becomes an aimless passion, a simple and pure movement of the heart. Never did Christ "refuse or deny Magdalen the right to boast of her love ... but when, to anoint Him, she came to the grave, her face covered with tears, He had arisen for her sake: in order to tell her more joyfully: No. . . . In order to make of her a woman of love who no longer leaned out to her beloved one, because transported by enormous storms, she outreached His voice" (*NG*, 159). On reading attentively certain passages from the letters to Merline or to Mimi Romanelli (Simenauer, 267f) one cannot help feeling that Rilke's skill at this play of hide and seek with the hearts of women was every bit as astute as that which he attributes to Christ.

Rilke's translation of the sermon *L'Amour de Madeleine*, whose author was thought to be Bossuet, was not a mere stylistic exercise; it, too, was an expression of sympathetic approval (*Br. 1907-14*, 129). While the author's picture of the relationship between Christ and Magdalen remained in conformity with the intentions of the Bible and with Catholic faith, it contained many features capable of ambiguous interpretation and Rilkean adaptation. In order to show why it appealed to our poet and, at the same time, was related to his Don Juan motif, it suffices to quote a few passages. "What do you mean," the French preacher asks Christ, "when you pull so strongly at the hearts and draw them so firmly to you, and then go away when they do not in the least expect it? How cruel you are! What a strange game you play with the hearts that love you" (*Magdalena*, 27). When the poor abandoned women complain, "Jesus laughs at their plaints; He lets it happen that they exhaust and consume themselves in inexpressible desire. He even undertakes to kindle the flame of their passion and watches them from a distance, and it does not move Him; He makes fun, as it were, of their imagination and rage. That is how He treated Mary Magdalen also. At first nothing is too much for Him. She wants His feet, He gives them; she wants to kiss them, He lets her; she wants to anoint His head, He endures it; the Pharisees grumble, He defends her; Judas is scandalized, He praises her" (*Magdalena*, 28-29). But, "as soon as He has made the bond tight enough, He cautiously withdraws His hand." He not only stops giving, but "by and by takes away what He has given" (*Magdalena*, 29). When He arises from the grave and appears before her again, He has only one thing to say to her: Noli me tangere . . . (*Magdalena*, 31).

Merline read these passages, as well as Abelone's song and Bettina Brentano's letters, for the first time in the fall of 1920, when Rilke, fully aware that their relevance would not escape her keen sense of divination, sent her copies of his translation of the sermon, of Malte's *Notebook*, and of Bettina's letters. The impact on the woman passionately in love forced her to trim her feelings and to prepare her heart for future privations (*Rilke et Merline*, 45ff). And in a strange confusion of judgment blinded by love, on the threshold of their intimate relations, she could exclaim "He is a saint! he is a saint!" (*Rilke et Merline*, 69).

Referring to Rilke's admiration for such women as Gaspara Stampa, Marianne Alcoforado, Mary Magdalen, and others, Rudolf Kassner points out that his friend had always shown a special liking for what we are wont to call old maids. Not out of pity, Kassner insists, but because Rilke experienced women from within. Kassner, therefore, once remarked to him that he had found in real life a striking confirmation of the kind of world envisaged in his friend's poetry. For in actual life he had met so many wonderful old maids and so incredibly many foolish mothers that it really looked as if all the wise Virgins of the parable had become spinsters and all the foolish ones mothers (*Das Inselschiff*, 124). Merline, too, with her remarkable womanly instinct, sensed the significance of this parable when she once called herself apologetically "une vierge folle" (*Rilke et Merline*, 48).

PART VI

POET AND SAINT

◇◇◇

Stimme im Dornbusch. Streife, wem sie gilt,
die Schuhe ab und krümme sich und schlage
den ganzen Mantel vors Gesicht und sage
in seinen Mantel: Herr, ich bin gewillt.

(AW I,370)

Voice in the burning bush. Let him for whom it's meant
slip off his shoes, bow low, and throw
his cloak over his face and say
into his cloak: Lord, I am willing.

◇◇◇

32. TERRIBLE SOLITUDE

◇◇◇

Hast Du noch nie bemerkt, wie verachtete, geringe
Dinge sich erholen, wenn sie in die bereiten
zärtlichen Hände eines Einsamen geraten?

(Br.Frühzeit, 242)

Have you never noticed how little, neglected things
recover when they get into the willing, tender
hands of one who is solitary?

◇◇◇

IF RILKE could use the monk as a pseudonym, and if he could call his poems prayers, these devices must point to some kind of affinity. Monkhood is related to sainthood: if the monk is no saint, at least he strives to be one. Certainly the same cannot be said of Rilke. His admirer and friend, Princess von Thurn und Taxis, was quite right when she wrote in January 1913: "No, Dottor Seraphico, you are not a 'saint'—even though you may shuffle about on your knees day and night (on your spiritual knees, *bien entendu*). And that is as it should be. A saint could never have written the *Elegies*" (*Br.MTT*, 255). We might add: a monk, even a Russian monk, could never have written the *Book of Hours*. But the Princess was equally right in calling her poet "Dottor Seraphico," the name with which tradition has adorned Saint Bonaventure, the disciple of St. Francis of Assisi. If we are not too particular, we have no difficulty in finding in the circumstances of Rilke's life and work peculiarities which may lead to the impression that he was a kind of "modern saint." The *Book of Hours* alone, with its search of God, its insistence on humility, brotherly love and poverty, on anonymity and detachment from the world, with its wrath over godless cities and its intimacy with death, supplies ample food for such an assumption. And his life seems to confirm it in many ways: his periodic retreats into solitary confinement, his flight from human entanglements, his craving for unquestioned concentration, his flagrant disregard of private possessions, his scorn of all artificial stimulants, his unfulfilled longing for love and home, and with it all the magic charm that seemed to keep him provided for and to rescue him from critical situations.

Paul Valéry, after visiting Rilke at Muzot, was startled by the terrifying austerity of its ancient tower. "I considered such isolation hardly possible; endless winters in such lavish intimacy with stillness. . . . Dear Rilke, you seemed to me locked up in pure time and I feared for you the transparence of an all too uniform life which lets death shine too clearly through the sequence of externally identical days" (Salis, 104). While staying in Castle Berg am Irchel, Rilke saw no human being for months, with the exception of his unobtrusive housekeeper Leni and the pastor of nearby Flaach who often brought him his milk and mail. Looking back in sad memory to the pre-war years of Paris, he wrote in 1921 that during his long stay in the French capital he saw perhaps eight people, obviously meaning thereby such people as were allowed to enter into the intimacy of his life and thought (*Br.* II,265). Shortly before the first two *Elegies* were written, he spent Christmas of 1911 in complete, "undiluted" isolation in the large castle of Duino and was hoping for "walls so high that the stars would be visible in daytime" (*Br. 1907-14*, 164). Edmond Jaloux remarks that while the world of Proust is that in which we live, that of Rilke is one in which one meets more often the poets and the saints (Salis, 218). R. von Salis, Rilke's young Swiss friend, noticed monk-like features in the poet's face (Salis, 48), Romain Rolland referred to him as "the young monk of the rue Campagne-Première," the street in Paris where Rilke lived before the war (*Rilke-Gide*, 123), and Rilke himself would sometimes call his places of retreat cloisters or cells (*Br. 1914-21*, 280). On his return to Germany from Viareggio where he had written his *Book of Poverty and Death* he wrote to Lou in August 1903: "Oh if only I could have working days, if only my most secret heartchamber were a workshop, a cell and refuge for me; if all that is monkish in me could yield a monastic way of life, for the sake of my work and devotion" (*Br. 1892-1904*, 385). He knew very well that somehow life and art ought not to be incompatible, and he would have liked not to divorce them; but every time he surrendered to life he felt like a loiterer who lets golden opportunities slip by, like one who "in a dream can't manage to get his clothes on and on account of two recalcitrant shoe-buttons neglects much that never comes back" (*Br. 1892-1904*, 388).

The result was that Rilke sought and cherished strict solitude, to be sure, but only when he had reason to expect poetic inspiration, or when he put all his determination into the service of Rodin's "tou-jours travailler." Only then did he subject himself to a kind of monas-tic rule, chosen and defined by himself. At other times he deliberately sought distraction in social companionship or in travel. When soli-tude had outlasted its virtue, either because it had given him the longed-for poem or because it persistently refused to do so, it became a terrible burden, an unnatural imposition. When he was being treated at the sanatorium of Val-Mont in February 1926 he dreaded the prospect of returning to his Tower of Muzot because he was afraid that he would not "be a match for the austere laws of isola-tion. . . . With this superhuman Angel you can wrestle only when you feel the sap of work in your veins; otherwise His demoniac power overwhelms you, and turns into a constant and inescapable judgment" (*Br.* II,511).

When he wrote that, his sickness no doubt influenced his feelings, but it did not cause them. In times of health they found expression, too, both in his letters and in his poetry. In the summer of 1924 he complained to Clara, his wife, that at times his solitude made him suffer and had the effect of a drawing poultice which had been ap-plied too long (*Br. Muzot*, 296). Here is a passage from a letter which he wrote to Merline in November 1920 while he was nursing his solitude at Castle Berg in the hope of picking up again the loose ends of pre-war productivity (*Letters to Merline*, 48-49):

"O Dear, how many times in life—and never so much as now—have I told myself that Art, as I conceive it, is a movement contrary to Nature. No doubt, God never foresaw that anyone of us would turn inwards upon himself in this way, which can only be per-mitted to the saint because he seeks to besiege God by attacking Him from such an unexpected and poorly defended quarter. But for the rest of us, whom do we approach when we turn our back on events, even on our future, in order to throw ourselves into the abyss of our being, which would engulf us were it not for the sort of trustfulness that we bring to it, and which seems stronger even than the gravita-tion of our Nature? If the meaning of sacrifice is that the moment of greatest danger coincides with that when one is saved, then cer-tainly nothing resembles sacrifice more than this terrible will to Art. How tenacious it is, how insensate! All that the rest forget in order to make their life possible, we are always bent on discovering, on magnifying even; it is we who are the real awakeners of our own

monsters, to which we are not hostile enough to become their con-
querors; for in a certain sense we are at one with them; it is they,
the monsters, that hold the surplus strength which is indispensable to
those that must surpass themselves. Unless one assigns to the act of
victory a mysterious and far deeper meaning, it is not for us to consider ourselves the tamers of our internal lions. But suddenly we
feel ourselves walking beside them, as in a triumph, without being
able to remember the exact moment when this inconceivable reconciliation took place (bridge, barely curved, that connects the
terrible with the tender . . .)."

I have quoted this confession at length because it puts us right
into the midst of that world which is ruled by the Terrible Angel
of the *Elegies*. It also throws light on Rilke's tendency to toy with
temptation and danger. He refused to make his inner "monsters"
harmless, by means of psychoanalysis or otherwise, but was determined to face them and even to fraternize with them for the sake
of his art. Again, Lou's word "masochism," or Nietzsche's "amor
fati," comes to mind. To Princess Marie Rilke wrote in 1910 that "Art
is the most passionate inversion of the world, the return road from
the infinite on which all honest things come toward us" (*Br. MTT*,
27). In a poem of the *Book of Images* he exclaims: "How small is
that with which we wrestle, how big is that which wrestles with
us. . . . That is the Angel who appeared to the wrestlers of the Old
Testament: when the sinews of his opponents stretch, metallic, in the
contest, He feels them under His fingers as chords with deep melodies. He whom this Angel has conquered is not attracted by victories. His growth is this: to be profoundly vanquished by what is
ever greater than himself" (*BB*, 137-138). And so it is that "beauty
is nothing but the beginning of terror; we barely endure it, and we
admire it so because it serenely disdains to destroy us. Round every
Angel is terror" (*AW* I,245)—"And yet, woe is me, yet must I hymn
you, well-nigh deadly birds of the soul, knowing your power" (*AW*
I,249).

Art, as Rilke conceived it, forced him to turn his back on time and
to face squarely the abyss of his own being in frightful isolation. The
"monsters" of which he speaks, and which solitude conjured up,
were those which the subconscious threw across his path and of
which his Malte *Notebook* is so full. They were the ghosts of his
feverish nightmares of childhood and youth, of his anguished suf-

fering at St. Pölten, of his sexual bi-polarity, of his frustrations in love, religion, and home, of his sterile worldly distractions, and scores of similar phantoms which demanded recognition and shelter. Art was "a reversal of all his forces, a changed direction of soul which can never be accomplished without a number of crises" (*Letters to Merline*, 47). It was the result of "terrible tensions of inner experience, over which nobody has power," and yet it was able "to achieve such indescribable reality in the realm of the spiritual" (*Br. 1907-14*, 175-176). He marveled that his heart could survive such immeasurable extremes. In due time he resolved to practise the reserve of the ancients or of the troubadours, who knew where to draw the line of their human relations. Once, in Naples, in the presence of ancient tombstones, he suddenly realized that he "never ought to touch human beings with stronger gestures" than did these men and women hewn in stone (*Br. 1907-14*, 170, 188), an observation which found expression in several poems and in the *Second Elegy* (*AW* I,374, 249ff).

Therefore it is Rilke's refrain that true love ignores all specific bonds. "Love has given me everything only when it was able to remain on the wing, without even setting its foot on my heart" (*Letters to Merline*, 85). The true lover should follow the example of God, "that illustrious paramour [who] uses the ruse, the cautious wisdom never to show Himself." Hence love is nothing but aimless labor. Perhaps, he continues, that is why people who love each other, leave each other (*Br. 1907-14*, 84)—a neat rationalization of what happened to his marriage. Rudolf Kassner tells a delightful story which shows that Rilke, even in childhood, instinctively singled out those impressions which suited his artistic frame of mind. Kassner has it from the mouth of Rilke himself, whom he calls the most inimitable story-teller (Kassner, *Erinnerung*, 298f):

"There was in Prague an elderly uncle, a bachelor, who had only one passion, a tic of the soul: birds. A whole room was filled with them. One day a week the boy Rilke and a little girl cousin were invited to the uncle's house for dinner. The latter would come out of the birds' room which was adjacent to the dining-room, with feathers in his hair and beard and with his coat completely covered with them. Nobody was permitted to enter the birds' sanctuary. Whenever the uncle got up from table in order to take the birds a small chickenbone or a piece of fruit, there streamed through the open door the sounds of many, many singing, calling, shrieking birds. But one day it all came to an end. No more cages, no more singing or shrieking, no more feathers in uncle's beard and hair. In lieu of the birds: a red-haired, speckled, very gaily dressed person with a loud voice. All the many birds, of which nobody had ever been allowed to get a glimpse, had been changed into that woman, who, as was to be expected, never left the uncle, and at last buried him."

Unlike certain other artists Rilke could not divide himself between art and everyday pursuits. "Others," he writes, "have at their disposal large amounts of reserves for direct, concrete intercourse; indeed, far from living on their reserves, they use them to augment their resources and inner tension, which then, on the other side, prove themselves of benefit to their artistic performance. With me it has never been that way" (*Br. Muzot*, 59). He points out as a special example the case of Stéphane Mallarmé, "the most sublime, the 'densest' poet of our time," who could nevertheless live his daily life as a teacher of languages (*Br. Muzot*, 144).

Rilke was also hypersensitive to the crippling effects of reflection and deliberate planning. Not only would observation by others tend to paralyze him, but his own awareness and conscious enjoyment of what was going on had the same ruinous effect. "I am so inordinately sensitive," he writes, "and if somebody's eyes rest on me that is enough to paralyze me somewhere" (*Br. 1907-14*, 47). And the Russian monk prays: "Those who seek Thee, tempt Thee" (*AW* I,67). "To pray" means to him "to cover all kneeling and trusting with many gold and blue and colorful cupolas in order that the others may not observe it" (*AW* I,41). "Only on those who do not watch over themselves can Nature lavish its infinite play" (*Br. Muzot*, 42). Rilke remembers "experiencing the most astonishing embarrassment, when as a youth I had managed to steal an hour of solitude in my room by meeting the usual family curiosity with the explanation of why I needed this hour and what I planned to do with it: that alone sufficed to render worthless the limited isolation achieved. I had traded it, as it were. The sound which had fallen upon this hour destroyed its innocence, impounded it, made it sterile, empty. Even before I entered my room, my betrayal was already there ahead of me, and filled the room and every corner of it with something that had spent itself, that had lost its mystery and substance" (*Br. Muzot*,

60-61). For the same reason Rilke professed an instinctive reluctance to read all criticism or appraisal of his work. It would have endangered his naïve approach to it. When Merline questioned him about his unfinished *Elegies*, he solemnly implored her never to do so again. "I cannot play any trick, nor make any direct effort" (*Letters to Merline*, 47, 81). In his Worpswede diary he exhorts himself to "look out when you pray, in order to make sure that nobody listens" (*Br. Frühzeit*, 234). Elsewhere he writes: "Again and again I should like to be aware only of the stars above me which from their distance see everything at once, in the whole, and therefore do not bind anything, but leave all free in all . . ." (*Br. 1907-14*, 47).

Similarly Rilke avoided as much as possible commenting on the work of others, partly, no doubt, because he disliked controversy, but, partly too, because doing so might have made him too conscious of his creative processes. On the other hand he liked to praise what was worth praising. It is true, he did act as a sort of literary adviser to the Insel-Verlag, especially during the war years when Dr. Kippenberg was with the armed forces in Belgium. But he knew that in this case his function as a reader and critic of manuscripts would not boomerang and strike at his own creative consciousness whose delicate mechanism was fully appreciated and scrupulously respected by his publisher and by Katharina Kippenberg. It is also worth noting that Rilke's semi-professional advisory capacity was put forward by his publishers as the chief ground for a petition to the War Department in Vienna that he be released from military service, and for a later request that this exemption be continued. Accordingly he even felt it "his duty to ask for manuscripts" (*Br. Kippenberg*, 156, 216, 226).

Rilke's susceptibility in this respect was all the more paradoxical as on the other hand he was perpetually driven to self-mirroring reflection. What made things worse was that his fancy was so plastic, so objectively personalizing, that his mirrored self often took on an independent life as a ghostly double. It was a frightful complexity which he could make harmless only through his poetic work: his art had to help him solve his existential paradoxes. Malte records a ghastly childhood experience (*AW* II,91-96). One day he was ferreting through some closets in his father's house and discovered all sorts of masks and costume material. Driven by a spirit of adventure he wrapped some of this material around himself and tried on a mask, wondering what sort of effect it would make. As he looked in the mirror he was at first amused, but, as the result of a little accident, the strangeness of the reflected image suddenly overwhelmed him. Engrossed in his experiment he had failed to notice a table with all kinds of bric-a-brac and knocked it over. The rattling noise and the scattered bits of glass, spreading a pungent fluid on the floor, caused him to forget for a moment the rags around his body. In his desperate efforts to rub the greasy spots off the floor his costume got hopelessly into his way and he became more and more entangled. Another quick look in the mirror showed him his other self with horrible vividness and sent him into a fit of frenzy. Crying for help he ran wildly for the door, trying madly to tear off his garb, until at last he fell to the floor unconscious. Another instance of hallucination is related elsewhere. As a child Malte was kneeling on a chair in front of a table and drawing various things on paper, when an awkward movement caused him to lose his crayon. He crawled under the table in search of the lost object. Before long his hand, groping in the semi-darkness, appeared to him as something by itself which did not belong to him, and kept creeping back and forth like a menacing claw (*AW* II,83). We have already mentioned the experience which Rilke had in his lonely castle of Berg am Irchel. On two occasions in the evening he saw, sitting on a chair opposite him, a man who claimed to be one of the deceased owners of the castle, the fictitious Count C. W. And this person allegedly dictated to Rilke a number of strange poems, which were later published under the title of *Posthumous Poems of Count C. W.* (*CW*, 37-40).

This power of impersonation was also at the root of Rilke's tendency to abandonment and surrender. All things other than himself tended to stimulate and quicken his self-duplicating instinct. They thus tempted him not only to look at them through his own eyes but also to look at himself through theirs. The subjective-objective quality of his letters as well as of his poetry, especially of his *New Poems*, derives from this paradoxical situation. From this point of view it is easy to understand why Rilke went with such devotion and love to the things rather than to human beings. Lifeless things, and those among the living beings who shared in some measure their guileless simplicity, were able to mirror back to him those features which he needed for his work. They showed him what "openness" or, as he often called it, "pure being" meant; that it implied freedom and the possibility of virginal creation. On the other hand, rational, critical, self-willed, and self-conscious man threw back at him the image of his own ambiguity and bifurcation. To lose himself in the thing had its dangers, no doubt; but the thing was patient, obedient, humble; it was susceptible of assimilation and could be abandoned at will. To lose himself to a human being, or even to a dog, tore him asunder and made a caricature of himself—and a person or a dog was not so easily disposed of. When he was offered a dog for companionship in his lonely Tower of Muzot he declined, saying: "Even this would cause too much of a relation, in view of my proneness to enter into the life of such a companion. All living beings that make demands on me find in me an infinite readiness to grant them the right to do so, and out of the resulting complications I must painfully extricate myself, when I realize that they use me up completely" (*Br. Muzot*, 82-83). Again he writes: "I have no window on human beings, once and for all. They mean something to me only in so far as they become articulate within me" (*Br.* II,345). He admits that his many friends are incapable of giving him anything in return for his constant squandering of himself, "because I give and unload myself brutally, without consideration or concern for the other person" (Lou, *Rilke*, 63). When Rilke lavished his assent and praise on such human beings as the shepherd, the child, the Russian peasant, the maiden, the poor, or the blind, these were not meant to be real persons such as they are encountered in actual life. They were rather personifying symbols for certain functions of innocence and virginity, for the state of mind and soul akin to the "state of grace," which he craved and needed.

33. CONQUEST THROUGH ART

◇◇

> Auch die Kunst ist nur eine Art zu leben . . .
> *(Br.Dichter)*
> Art, too, is but a mode of living . . .

◇◇

RILKE uses the word "grace" only from time to time, but what is meant by it is spread all through his work in a great variety of symbols. Undoubtedly he had learned to appreciate the beauty of it in his Catholic childhood, but like all his religious categories it was reinterpreted as a function of art. Just as the Christian is incapable of doing any good deed without the grace of God, in the same way in art grace is always the decisive factor. For Rilke "grace" came to mean a primal state at the broadest base of the pyramid of consciousness, where differentiations and names are still pure, vast possibilities over which the artist could range freely and creatively. Its structural characteristic was: *not yet—but surely some day when the time is ripe.* Far from ever having been lost and from being recoverable only through mediation, the state of grace was man's secret and inalienable possession. Christianism and society had unfortunately poisoned the purity of that reality by introducing the concept of sin or the tyranny of tradition and convention, thus forcing man to retrace his steps in order to find himself again. Actually, the world was not sinful, but holy: God and man were made of the same stuff (Sievers, 43-44). Innocence, virginal primitiveness represented a state not to be recovered by first overcoming the conflict between good and evil, by renunciation or resurrection; it was to be found in a layer of consciousness available at all times to those who had the courage to reach down into their own depths (*Br. Muzot*, 140-144). It was in every individual as childhood, where good and evil did not exist even as memory; it was in everyone as yearning, not for a utopian future as in the case of the Romantics, but as a yearning inward as for the first day of creation; it was everywhere for the taking: in the simple gestures of nature, in things and plants, in children, girls, women, plain folk, and in the dead. It is remarkable how consistently Rilke steers clear of all other worldly complications, indeed of every world foreign to himself. The world which he sought to realize was immanent in him, where everything—life and death, distraction and concentration, division and wholeness, temptation and innocence—was equally at home, equally within reach and possible control.

What Rilke bemoaned with growing concern was that man, unwilling to face whatever was mysterious, elusive, inexplicable, therefore dangerous, had, in his overbearing pride, pushed it away from himself into a world all its own, foreign and basically hostile. He had done so with God, with death, and with sex. He had done so in the hope of being better able to cope with them, if not on equal terms, at least by levelling them out, by ridiculing them or treating them superciliously or cynically. In reality, so Rilke thought, man was only fooling himself: God, death and sex were ineradicably embedded in the life of every individual, and went on ripening unknown. "God is the oldest work of Art," he wrote in the *Florentine Journal*. "He is poorly preserved, and many parts have in the course of time been somewhat restored. But, of course, it has become part of civilization that one should be able to talk about Him and that one should have seen what is left of the original" (*JF*, 55). In matters of sex Rilke rejected as vicious and undignified all notions of puritanism or compunction. The lascivious as well as the frivolous amounted to a profanation, for which religion and society were responsible. Just as artistic creation was purely a matter of the individual, so were God, death, and sex. As soon as society or institutionalized religion became mixed up with them, their meaning was distorted. Even the difference between the sexes and the resulting illusion of communion in love, were regarded by Rilke as incidental, as likely to be misunderstood and to destroy the state of innocence. Marriage was convention, but so, too, was extra-marital love, every one of its gestures, even separation. Only the individual, in his undiluted solitude, was able to be unconventional (*Br. Dichter*, 31-34, 37-39).

Strictly speaking, there is no denying that there is truth in all this. Society, even when it consists of not more than two people, cannot get along without convention. Any individual act done publicly becomes the object of interpretation, possibly of talk, and is therefore subject to classification and distortion from its original meaning. To that extent it is a temptation for the individual to conform to his reputation or fame and to become a lie unto himself. Nevertheless, it would be wrong to infer that Rilke ever became an advocate of anarchism. What he envisaged was an order, however illusory, in which each stood watch over the completest freedom of the other and in which the artist played an eminently responsible role.

There are some amazing statements in regard to these matters in the *Letters to a Young Poet*. "Loving is basically nothing in the nature of that which we call losing oneself in, surrendering to, or uniting with another person . . . it is a noble occasion for the individual to ripen, to become something in himself, to become world, to become world for himself for the sake of someone else" (*Br. Dichter*, 37-38).

". . . perhaps the sexes are more related than one thinks, and the whole renovation of the world will perhaps consist in this: that man and girl, freed from all false sentiment and false pleasures, will not seek each other as opposites but as brother and sister, as neighbors, and will come together as *human beings*, in order to bear in common the weight of sex which is laid upon them, to bear it simply, earnestly, and patiently" (*Br. Dichter*, 26, 41). Rilke wrote this two or two and a half years after he was married, and what he had in mind had nothing to do with the "free love" or the androgynous ideal of the Romantics, nor with the "emancipation of the flesh" of the Young Germans. What was back of these strange ratiocinations was nothing more nor less than the concern of the artist for pure receptivity, for the undiminished beauty of the new beginning, for the glorious and creative state of grace on the basis of phallic innocence.

Against this background the often recurring motif of "temptation" can be understood in its true perspective. The monk of the *Book of Hours* confesses again and again having lost himself in strange pursuits and having had to build himself up again "with the broken bits of his shame" (*AW*, I,57). In *The Temptation*, inspired by a Cézanne painting, a whole pack of hounding and yelping demons torment the flesh and the soul of the saint with voluptuous embraces, until his Angel drives them all back into his interior. To drive them out, as Christ had done with the devils, would not do. They must remain within, in order that the saint may distil the not yet clarified God out of the putrid fever (*NG*, 148-149). How well this interpretation fits Rilke's experience of art as he conceived it, with the temptations corresponding to all the inner "monsters" and to the long periods of distraction. These were only valleys alternating with the peaks and belonged with the latter to the general landscape. In fact, the peaks cannot exist without the valleys. Rodin used to say that around cathedrals the air seemed to become agitated and tormented by their greatness and purity, so that there was always a bad, penetrating wind circulating about their counterforts (*Br. 1902-06*, 295). And the pope, so Rilke suggests in a French poem of *Vergers*, simply cannot avoid attracting the devil, by the mere law of contrast (*GFS*, 20). With Rilke the same law of contrast would operate, but in reverse; it was the "storms" of the *Elegies*, still more or less open at both ends, which called forth the compact *Sonnets* rising like a high tree in the ear: "O hoher Baum im Ohr" (*Son.*I, 1). Rejected are only those whose lives are without peaks altogether, and those who despair in moments of depression, like Christ in the poem *The Garden of Olives* (*AW* I,167-168). But the saints, like the artists, are able to distil their God out of corruption and putrefaction, just as in Baudelaire's poem *Une Charogne* the sky witnesses the superb carcass of a carrion, with legs spread apart and stretched upward, open and unfold like a flower. It all was part of Rilke's understanding of art as a peremptory mission to cope with the whole reality of existence, including its monsters and its terrors.

Rilke's concern with this poem by Baudelaire is illuminating. In one of his famous letters to his wife about Cézanne he expresses the opinion that "without this poem the whole trend to objective 'saying,' which we now believe to recognize in Cézanne, could not have taken place: that poem had to be there first, in all its inexorability. First, artistic vision had to conquer itself to the point of seeing true reality also in that which is terrible and repulsive." Arbitrary discrimination, "a single refusal at one time or another" on the part of the artist "casts him out of the state of grace, makes him thoroughly sinful" (*Br.* I,207). Like Saint-Julien-l'Hospitalier in Flaubert's tale the artist must be prepared to join the saint in his determination to lie beside the leper and to share with him the warmth of his body and of his heart. Rilke is greatly moved at the thought that Cézanne knew Baudelaire's poem by heart and recited it word for word in his last years. Sainthood begins when one has gone to such limits of "self-conquest." Those who, like Rilke's Malte, have stopped short of those limits will be able to *see* in Heaven "the Virgin Mary, a few saints and little prophets, King Saul, and Charles the Bold, but of Hokusai and Leonardo, of Li-Tai-Pe and Villon, of Verhaeren, Rodin, and Cézanne—and above all of God they will only be able to *hear*" (*Br.* I,208).

It is easy to see that the kind of self-conquest which Rilke has in mind is that of the artist in his "artistic vision," no more, no less. There is no shadow of a hint that the artist should act out of Christian charity, like Saint-Julien-l'Hospitalier. That aspect of sainthood is completely ignored (see above, p. 64). What Rilke admired so in Cézanne was precisely his "objectivity which avoids all meddling in strange beings." No inkling of the artist giving away the least bit of himself to another. Cézanne's hands, like those of Verlaine, were so full of his work that they were empty for others. "Je ne donne rien aux pauvres," says Verlaine in *Mon Testament*, "parce que je suis un pauvre moi-même" (*Br.* I,206). The hierarchy of saints in Rilke's Heaven speaks volumes. Moreover, Rilke was quite in sympathy with Malte's dislike of the last lines of Baudelaire's otherwise admired poem. In them the "memento mori" is too clearly expressed and the Aristotelian distinction between form and matter, between spirit and body is too reminiscent of Christian dualism. Here, so Rilke thought, Baudelaire had strayed off from the domain of art where no such division could be tolerated (*AW* II,66).

At the core of all these Rilkean attitudes there was, it seems to me, an intense desire to come to terms with the recalcitrant elements of outside reality. This was his poetic way of facing the very old problem of how the gap between object and subject can be bridged. Rilke was in no way concerned with the philosophical angle of the problem. Philosophy as a strict discipline of thought was not his business, and he knew it (*Br. Muzot,* 322). The bridge which he needed had to be of the nature of an image and a symbol not only acceptable to reason but gratifying to his poetic as well as existential consciousness. For if anything is characteristic of Rilke it is this: that his body and his soul demanded to be equally engaged in his creative work, in harmonious unity. Sickness of the body was a baffling and entirely incomprehensible phenomenon to him. He knew all the time that as far as he was concerned there existed "an old hostility between human life and greatest work" (*AW* I,219), but that was his way of experiencing the antithesis of subject and object which he wanted to overcome. In order to do so, outside reality and the functions of his body had to yield somehow to the transfiguring catalysis by art. Rilke's poetic motifs and symbols were intended to be existentially confirmed. If that were not so, it would be difficult to appreciate many of his letters since the guidance and promptings which he had to offer were deeply colored by his experience of the nature and function of art. Between his letters and his poetry there is no basic difference of substance and meaning, only one of form and symbolization. Rudolf Kassner sees between Rilke's poetry and his letters the same relationship as that between a garment and its lining (Kassner, *Erinnerung,* 305).

Kassner goes so far as to say that Rilke strove to overcome not only life but art itself through art (*Das Inselschiff,* 125). If the contradictions of life and art could be harmonized through creative magic, it might be possible again to live and die, simply, in pure obedience to cosmic law, like the animal or the plant. As early as 1899 Rilke published in *Ver Sacrum* an essay *On Art* in which he calls art "a mode of being." By that he meant not a circumspect "control and containment for the sake of a definite aim," but rather "a blind wisdom." Evidently "this mode of being has something naïve and instinctive," and resembles the state of unconsciousness, of childhood. "Childhood is the realm of great justice and deep love. No thing is more important than another in the hands of the child. It plays with a gold brooch or with a white meadow flower, and when it tires it drops both and forgets that they seemed equally resplendent in the light of its joy" (*VPN*, 47). In that state, which is that of creation and, so Rilke feels, ought to be transferable to life, all ambiguities are resolved; subject and object are one. Similar views are expressed more than a decade later in the *Letters to a Young Poet*, and in 1922 Rilke advises a youth who had confided in him to "strive guilelessly" (*Br.* II,349). To a blind person who had sent him manuscripts for appraisal in the hope that his blindness would elicit special consideration Rilke explains: "Your bodily defect rightly remains the unmovable center from which all perspectives and movements of experience and soul are to be measured. But once this arrangement is granted and acknowledged, your quiet efforts should aim at enduring this suffering increasingly without any specific name. In your artistic endeavors that would be reflected through the absence of any trace of the infinite limitation which induces you to expect infinite consideration in your creative performance. Art can only proceed from a purely anonymous center. But even for your life (regardless of what else it may produce) such an achievement seems to me the decisive one; it alone would constitute the core of your resignation" (*Br.* II,189). No clearer illustration is needed of Rilke's desire to solve the puzzles of life through art and, beyond that, to emerge on the other side of art in a new kind of existence.

More interesting still is Rilke's growing conviction that the work of art itself is, in the last analysis, irrelevant to art (*Br.* II,132; *Br. Muzot*, 132). Even here, in this most intimate and vital sphere of his being, the thing resulting from his creative activity reveals itself as something that needs to be reckoned with existentially. Like the Magician "He calls it. It startles and stands. What stands? The other, all that he is not becomes being." The work of art, once achieved, is a thing which even its author has to face: "And the whole thing turns a swiftly wrought face, that is more, toward you." It reveals elements and powers of which the artist himself was not aware (*AW* I,390). Like the gold which is melted and shaped into the mounting for a precious stone: it plunges "its claws with metallic hate" into the flesh of the goldsmith (*AW* I,391). If the artist is not watchful his work becomes his master and tyrant. Besides, together with the other things it becomes part of outside reality, subject to endless misinterpretation by the public. Like fame, it makes it more difficult for the author to remain himself; it becomes a danger to his freedom, to the freedom for a new, virginal beginning. It ought not to be the intention of the poet or artist that his work be read or admired, and Rilke goes to great lengths explaining, almost apologizing for, the autonomous existence of the work of art. Already the *Florentine Journal* contains this exclamation: "The deuce!—people will say—don't have your books printed nor your works of art exhibited if they are not made for us!—But [the poet answers] we must exteriorize our past in works and thus put an end to it. They are completed only when they are no longer part of ourselves, when they have been translated into your language, that is, when the book is book and the painting is painting as you understand it. From that moment there is no more bridge between them and us; they are behind us and we cannot rule over them" (*JF*, 58). "Art goes from one solitary one to another, passing over the people's heads" (*JF*, 53).

What is more important is the creative moment and everything else that leads up to it. The poet must be his own mouth and ear at the same time, like those stone masks from whose orifice clear water flows unceasingly and confides to them the secrets of the earth, of the living and the dead. Nothing but a marble basin, "an ear of the earth," receives in its hollow the liquid murmur: the Earth's mouth speaks through these fountains into her own ear. A jug held between the two only interrupts Earth's revelation to herself (*Son.* II, 15). That a poem or a work of art issues forth is an immense relief and gratification, but it must not be the poet's justification or intention. Therefore, "it would be presumptuous to expect of a work of art that it be of any help to others. But the fact that the human tension which a work of art carries in itself without applying it outward—the fact that its inner intensity, without becoming extensive, could produce by its mere presence the illusion that it was meant as ambition, expectation, courting—as wooing and transporting love, as a stirring appeal or as a calling: that is the good conscience of the work of Art (not its mission)—and all this mutual deceit of it and forlorn man is identical with all those sacerdotal deceits with which from time immemorial the Divine has been fostered" (*Br.Frau*, 7f).

Because of this remarkable intertexture of art and existence Rilke can never be accused of pure "aestheticism." As Rudolf Kassner points out "there may be in Rilke's life as well as in his work much that can be called ornament, arabesque, play, but nothing was cliché. He was a poet and a personality even when he only washed his hands. . . . That which many might consider 'aestheticism' in his work was not lack of greatness, but rather a want of the cliché of greatness. Or: his real greatness was his unity of form and content" (*Das Inselschiff*, 125).

The antagonism of life and art is the chief topic of a letter to Countess Sizzo in which Rilke takes issue with Richard Dehmel's views on these matters. Dehmel had accused Rilke of not putting his art directly in the service of the time and society in which he lived, of not being militantly social-minded. Rilke comments on this as follows (*Br.Sizzo*, 17-18):

"Dehmel's wish to see the poet placed in the midst of life . . . probably arose chiefly from his dislike, from his horror of desk literati, in which dislike he agreed so wholeheartedly, for example, with his friend Detlev von Liliencron (and after all, with whom not?); but at bottom there was a mistake somewhere in this, a lack of thoroughness of thought and observation. Is it so sure that around a desk, to which someone might retire, there is no life at all? Is it true that fate, existence, nothingness, and all the distressing, menacing forces of life do not extend as far as that so-called escapist at his desk? What makes his work weak, untrue, superfluous, or laughable, is not the place at which he finds himself but the fact that at this place (which might represent as vital a center as any other place in the world) he develops the habit of looking away from life, which presses and surges about him there, too—the fact that he no longer notices any life whatsoever, but only the paper and the ink-spot on his finger: it is that which makes this—eminently German—

type so hopeless and repugnant. But why fight him—is it not enough to ignore him?"

34. ART AND SAINTHOOD

◇◇◇

Nun aber, weiss ich, dass diese Arbeit [des Dichters] genau
so bestritten ist wie das Heiligsein. . . .

(*AW* II,159)

But now I know that this work [of the poet] is exactly
as controversial as is sainthood. . . .

◇◇◇

In the light of what has been said, it is not unreasonable to inquire into Rilke's existential relationship to his symbols, including that of monkhood and sainthood. With artists who are able to keep their art and their life more distinctly apart, such inquiries might be idle; with Rilke they become imperative. Besides, his interest in sainthood was so insistent that it compels our attention. The saints of his Catholic childhood were succeeded by those of the Italian painters and of the Russian icons. His frequent visits to churches and monasteries, with their statues, tombstones and painted windows, kept his interest alive, and at various times he read books on the lives and legends of saints, notably one by the Spaniard Ribadaneira. In the course of 1911 he even translated laboriously about a dozen chapters of St. Augustine's *Confessiones* (Zinn, 220). The names of St. Augustine, St. Francis of Assisi, St. Theresa of Avila, and others often occur in his letters, and in a number of poems he tries to capture essential modes of being of individual saints in order to find in them a confirmation of, or a challenge to, his own paradoxes. To Benvenuta he confessed in February 1914 that the saint had always been of the greatest concern to him and that he had longed to become like him (*Br. Benvenuta*, 33f). Moreover, Rilke had many and prolonged conversations with Rudolf Kassner, whose work shows that the problem of sainthood occupied his mind greatly.

There are poems in which the experience of the saint is depicted as very similar to that of the artist. In one of the *New Poems* St. Sebastian lets the arrows penetrate his body with such apparent unconcern that he only smiles faintly, until he realizes mournfully and scornfully that the perpetrators of his martyrdom are destroying a beautiful thing, his body (*NG*, 47). This sort of serene detachment which comes from an inner, indestructible core of innocence and unity is not different from that which Rilke demanded of the artist and of himself. In another poem, entitled *From the Life of a Saint*, all the horrors of loneliness which assail the saint serve only to prepare him for the moment when, happy at last, he can lay himself into his own hands "like the one and whole creature" (*NG*, 168). What else is this than the familiar motif of oneness and wholeness as the *sine qua non* of creation and true living? In the *First Elegy* the poet exhorts himself to listen to the inner voice "as only the saints have listened, when the mighty call raised them up from the earth, while they knelt on impossibly, and took no heed—and thus they learned to hear" (*AW* I,247). When Rilke wrote from Ronda, Spain, that in attempting to understand the human being he could not help skipping over man until he found the saint, he gave as a reason that only in the latter could he see realized that intensity of duration, that absolute integrality which the artist needs and craves (*Br.* I,428).

However, in the same letter he also confesses that perhaps the saint is no longer so exemplary and significant for us as he used to be in certain periods of the past. Because, he explains, "maybe we are more interested in finding out what such a deployment of effort would achieve, if instead of being directed toward God it were unnoticeably distributed among concerns in the present world where it might perform equally great, if less conspicuous, things" (*AW* I,428-429). We shall see that it was especially in Spain, where Rilke stayed in the winter of 1912-13, that the saint lost much of his prestige in favor of the hero (see below, p. 279). Obviously the above quotation hints at characteristics of sainthood for which the poet had no room in his symbols and which are nonetheless vital and essential. They draw a sharp line between the artist, even the most genuinely inspired one, and the saint. Since Rilke had cast aside his inherited God, he was obviously in search of some substitute that might occupy the empty space. "Everybody wears mourning when he leaves the deathbed of the God of his childhood," he wrote in his *Florentine Journal* (*JF*, 55). A personal God, existing not only *in* His creation but also beside and above it, more particularly a God who could lay down the law to man in accordance with His Supreme Will and who, if need be, might expect the sacrifice of one's own genius—such a God Rilke instinctively rejected. And even a pantheistic God—if that is what his God might be called—would have to borrow His power from the poet, if the latter were to submit to Him in humility and obedience. With reference to the better parts of his *Stories of God* Rilke writes that if the Angel should deign to grant him similar great work in the future he would be willing to sacrifice everything in order to be so graced; but he adds that he himself would be the creator of that Angel (*Br. 1902-06*, 90-91). Evidently art is compatible with that kind of allegiance, but true monkhood or sainthood is not. Even the mystical saints, those women who, as Rilke puts it, used Christ "as a bedfellow, as a sweet surrogate of masculinity, as the loveliest paramour that was available, at last still available" (*Br.* I,245)—even they came by their felicity only through a basic abdication of their personal selves. In the true mystical experience the saint seeks happiness by relinquishing his identity to the point of utter anonymity, but in so doing he surrenders to another being. At the basis of true mysticism there is always the assumption of dualism between finite man and infinite God.

Mysticism was the more offensive to Rilke as it was a tendency to which he was prone and which had a blurring effect on image and symbol. The only way in which he could avoid its dangers was through the form-giving magic of his word. He disapproved of those for whom the love of God is nothing but "a secret, deadly sweet love of chaos; who love the gods only for the sake of the twilight of the gods" (Mason, *Lebenshaltung*, 43). His yearning for anonymity, for humility and poverty, his eulogy of St. Francis of Assisi as the saint who became diffused in the things of nature and in the hearts of women, were expressions of his desire for primitiveness and virginity as the necessary basis of creativity. For the mystic, anonymity or loss of identity in God is a final gain; for Rilke it was a means, a new starting point of creative lordship fundamentally akin to that of God himself. It is true, notwithstanding a statement to the contrary of October 21, 1924, that Rilke read the work of mystical writers, notably those of Meister Eckhart, Mechthild of

Magdeburg, and Suso. But what he has to say in this connection in two unpublished letters of 1905 and 1913, respectively, is revealing. He points out that he had been Eckhart's disciple and herald long before he knew him, but that somewhere he grew beyond him, namely in those places where the German mystic's statements and conceptions seemed to imply finality. Wherever Eckhart appeared as a "flowing stream," descending in broad falls toward God and "issuing with its wide delta of Trinity into Eternity," Rilke felt intimately related to him. To clarify his position he singles out with especial approval two Eckhart sermons in which the identity of origin of God and man is emphasized (Sievers, 29); in this sense the poet is entitled to say without fear of presumption or pride: "I seize the plastic day. Nothing was yet complete until it was caught in my glance; all that moved stood still" (*AW* I,9).

Rilke knew exactly where art ends and sainthood begins. He knew, too, that he himself would never "spread the good odor of sanctity" (*Br. MTT*, 245). Here and there this awareness even takes the form of a vague sense of guilt against which he must defend himself. Repeatedly in the *Book of Hours* the monk apologizes for appearing haughty and overweening. Rilke's infallible instinct guided him when he reduced Christ to a mere road-marker, religion to a mere direction of the heart, God to an endlessly growing and metamorphic force—when he denied true love all concrete object or aim, when he by-passed wilful man and lavished his love on "patient, obedient" things, when he kept waiting for some sort of female gnome who would look after all his needs without making any claim on his heart. Marianne Alcoforado was no saint *because*, scorned by an unworthy lover, she had learned to let her love go into the "open" and no longer expected fulfilment in any object, be it human or divine. "To love" safeguards freedom and leaves the heart wide open for possibility; "to be loved" throws a weight of responsibility on the heart and imprisons it. When Rilke occasionally says that the saint is the only person who knows how to love, his mind dwells with undisguised partiality on the circumstance that the saint's love does not attach itself exclusively to any one person. He conveniently overlooks the fact that such love tends toward a distinct superior reality: God.

There is a strange entry in Rilke's Spanish diary, dated Epiphany 1913, which has a distinct bearing on this whole matter (*Br. 1907-14,*

286-287). It is annexed to a letter to Lou, and although the third person is used, Rilke intimates clearly enough that he himself is meant. Conscious of his achievements so far, with on the credit side the *Book of Hours*, the *Book of Images*, the *Notebook of Malte Laurids Brigge*, the *New Poems* and several *Elegies*, he records with deep satisfaction that he has realized in a high degree the spirit of Franciscan poverty and anonymity:

"His inner experience was already outside, stood in the convinced things with which children play, and vanished in them. Or it was saved in the strange look of a woman who went by, at any rate it lingered there at its own risk. But also the dogs ran about with it, worried and looked backward for fear that it might again be taken away from them. When, however, he stepped in front of the almond tree which was in bloom, he was startled to find it there so completely outside of him, completely transfused, completely occupied, completely detached from him and himself not precisely enough opposite, too turbid even to mirror this his own being. Had he become a saint, he would have extracted a cheerful freedom from this condition, the utterly irrevocable joy of poverty; for that is perhaps how Saint Francis lay dissolved and absorbed, and the whole world was the sweet flavor of his being. He himself, on the contrary, had not peeled himself clean, had torn himself out and given away pieces of rind, had even (as children do with dolls) often clung to an imaginary mouth and smacked his lips, and the morsel had remained there. And so he now was like dregs and obnoxious—however much sweetness might have gathered in him."

In other words, whereas the saint had surrendered to the point of vanishing in the things of the world until they had become a limpid mirror of his whole being, the poet had given away pieces which he had torn out of himself and which remained there, unassimilated, still plainly recognizable as parts of himself. Those were precisely the pieces by virtue of which the "patient" and "obedient" things remained under the dominion of the poet, and which in the last analysis kept the latter infinitely removed from the clear image of the saint. It is such pieces, too, which keep staring at us from the *New Poems* and give them their subjective connotations in spite of their otherwise distinct objectivity. It is as if in the presence of the blossoming almond tree Rilke, the creative artist, became instinctively envious, and insisted on taking an active part in its blooming growth.

External reality, that which was other than himself, the "thou," was a perpetual problem and, often enough, an obstacle for Rilke. For man Fate meant "to be opposite, nothing but that, for ever to be face to face" (*Eighth Elegy*). Rilke was so expansive that he must either be swallowed up by the "other thing" or swallow it up. At times he creates the impression of seeking to achieve the former, but in reality his whole effort went in the other direction. That is where the artist differs from the ordinary human being as well as from the hero of action, and whence springs that "old hostility between life and great work." Somehow the artist must achieve a state of mind from which the "opposite," as the cause of involvement and distraction, is absent. In this sense his function is to be "without fate," that is to say, without entanglements or attachments (*AW* II,348). Carried to its last consequences that means terrifying solitude, where only "the wind full of cosmic space tugs at your face" (*AW* I,245), where you wait in a theatre in which the lights have gone out and "emptiness is wafted from the stage with chill, grey air." Yet you wait (*AW* I,256-257). "In my way of perceiving things," Rilke writes, "there is something that consumes them, without leaving a trace; with my feeling I pick it up, as it were, not only out of the book but out of my own knowledge, it enters into my blood, there it mixes with God knows what, and risks being all but lost" (*Br.* I,372). But at the right moment the poet exercises his magical power and "He calls it. It startles and stands" (*AW* I,390). Unlike that of the mystic, Rilke's attitude is firmly embedded in a will to form, that is, to overcome, if not to conquer, a will to mastery, if not to power. As Heidegger puts it, over Rilke's poetry lies the shadow of a mild sort of Nietzschean metaphysics (Heidegger, 264). In a sense, this can be said of all art and artists, indeed of all life, but in the case of a poet who keeps insisting on patience and humility it sounds paradoxical.

If we remember that Rilke himself was an extreme representative of ambivalence we can appreciate both his elegiac and his accusing words in regard to the world of man. But when it comes to the saint, who sacrifices his whole being to a supreme God, Rilke's attitude tends to turn into grudging resentment of both God and saint. In

his essay *On a Young Poet* written in 1913 he asks with anxious
concern what would happen to the human heart, if outside, "somewhere in the world, there should come to exist certainty, ultimate
certainty. How the heart would at once lose its whole tension built
up over thousands of years. . . . For, truly, even the greatness of the
gods depends on their distress, namely on this: that, irrespective of
the buildings which we may keep for them, they are nowhere secure except in our hearts" (*AW* II,294). Conspicuously annoyed at
the thought of a God who asserts His distinct reality and superiority,
he may indulge in such a sally as this: "I now feel an unspeakable
pleasure in sparing Him—in not troubling Him when I am deeply
stirred. *Qu'il se repose. C'est assez encombrant d'avoir fait le monde.*
It would be a courtesy on the part of this world to pass God over
in silence, at least for a while" (Salis, 62). His *Florentine Journal*
of 1898 contained this quip: "It is a frequently observed characteristic of incompetent people that they let themselves be sustained and
guided by their parents as long as possible. So long as a God of this
kind exists all of us are mere minors. He must die, for we want to
become fathers ourselves. But He *is* dead; it's the old story of Kara
Mustapha: the viziers must keep his death a secret, in order that the
Janizaries shall not revolt but keep on fighting" (*JF*, 54). Rilke's
jealousy of God as the Supreme Creator is as real as that which the
monk of the *Book of Hours* attributes to Michelangelo: "Only God
remains far above his will: and so he loves Him with his high hate
for His inaccessibility" (*AW* I,25). "The poet alone," he feels, "has
unified the world" (*SG*, 119). Unlike faith, "religion has no opposite" (*Br. Muzot*, 79).

35. FATALISM AND SACRIFICE

◇◇

> Warum muss einer gehn und fremde Dinge
> so auf sich nehmen. . . .
>
> *(AW* I,350)
>
> Why must one go out and
> take strange things upon himself. . . .

◇◇

RILKE's concern with fate was as ambiguous as his attitude to life and art. He sometimes professes a sort of *amor fati*, but when he does so, fate is given a meaning which safeguards his own lordship. Far from destroying his personal freedom, it confirms it in a singular way. "A thinking fate," he writes in May 1922, "a fate that knows of us . . . indeed, one would often like to be strengthened and confirmed by such; but would it not be at once a fate looking at us from outside, observing us, a fate which would prevent us from being alone? The fact that we are embedded and dwell in a 'blind fate' is in a sense the condition for a view of our own, for our own seeing innocence" *(Br. Muzot,* 153). That kind of fate does not enter man from without but stems from within. From this point of view "we have no reason to distrust our world, for it is not against us. If it has horrors, they are *our* horrors, if it has abysses, these belong to us, if there are dangers we must try to love them" *(Br. Dichter,* 47). But referring to Maurice de Guérin, whose *Le Centaure* he translated, Rilke writes with reference to the other kind of fate, namely that which confronts us from without: "Perhaps the poet is meant to exist outside of all fate and becomes ambiguous, imprecise, insecure, whenever he engages himself. Whereas the hero becomes true only in fate, the poet becomes falsified in it; the one maintains himself in tradition, the other in indiscretion" *(AW* II,348). If only the poet could always share the mode of being of the laurel, the symbol of his art. All it has to cope with is its slightly darker green compared with that of its surroundings, and, at the rim of each leaf, the gentle waves which are like the smile of a breeze. But, being human, the poet is forced to participate in things human, condemned to the indiscretion of yearning for fate while at the same time avoiding it *(Ninth Elegy).* The hero plays at leap-frog with the vicissitudes and dangers of life. Impatience is the law of his being, as it is the fig tree's law to skip quickly over the blossoming stage and to leap into fruit. He cares not to last: his resolutely ripened death is his predestined glory (*AW* I,246). The poet envies his nimble-footed dash through sojourns of love to towering heights (*AW* I,265).

In the fall of 1910 Rudolf Kassner was in Paris at the same time as Rilke and was writing his *Elemente der menschlichen Grösse* (*Elements of Human Greatness*). Every day they spent long hours together until late into the evening. One night, on returning to his hotel, Kassner wrote in his notebook this reflection which his conversation with Rilke had prompted: "From creative empathy to greatness there is only one way: the sacrifice" (*Das Inselschiff* 120-121).[1] Briefly, Kassner saw the difference between Christian and

---

[1] This sentence is one of Kassner's "Sentences of the Yogi," the first installment of which appeared in the *Neue Rundschau*, vol. 22 (1911), 92-93. The exact wording was: "Who wants to proceed from 'Innigkeit' [innerness] to greatness must sacrifice himself" (*DuV*, vol. 40 [1939], 122). Of course, Rilke quoted from memory, but the form in which he remembered Kassner's words is symptomatic. While the Yogi's authentic formula clearly demands the sacrifice of *oneself*, Rilke's version is couched in less directly and personally committing terms: it merely speaks of "sacrifice," without specifying its kind or nature.

For Kassner the supreme pattern of the sacrifice in the post-Socratic world is that of Christ, which in its negative aspect means renunciation, in its positive aspect, love. It is the "peripeteia," the turning and pivotal event by which the dualism of "inner" and "outer," which was more or less irrelevant and ineffective in the pre-Socratic era but acquired prominence later, becomes once more nullified. The result was that while the Greek god Dionysos could still enter into such intimate communion with poetry that he could function as God's mouthpiece in Greek tragedy, no such compact was thinkable between the highly conscious modern poet and Christ. For the modern poet the only means of objectivizing the world and himself is the word, for Christ it was the sacrifice, since in Him the Word itself had become Flesh.

But Rilke not only misunderstood what Kassner meant by "sacrifice," he also misinterpreted the meaning of "Innigkeit" (*Rudolf Kassner*, 123-125, 195). It is a word whose peculiar connotations are difficult to render into English in any kind of context. In view of the gulf which actually separated Rilke's universe of experience and thought from that of his friend, it is not surprising that the latter's ideas acquired a Rilkean twist as they passed over into the poet's mental and creative mould. I believe that by and large the two men talked past each other and only attracted each other like two poles without ever meeting on truly common ground. Kassner was the active, the male pole, Rilke the more passive and feminine one whose tendency it was to surrender, to listen without reservation and thus to "empty" himself. When during the war, at Munich, Kassner read extracts from his *Zahl und Gesicht* to a gathering of friends among whom was Rilke, he found that of all his listeners the latter assented with the most highly sublimated feeling, with a conscious devotion so intense that he was reminded of the poet's over-strained efforts to do "work of the eyes," to "gaze, kneeling," as in the days of the *New Poems*. According to Kassner, kneeling is the appropriate posture for contemplation with closed eyes, not for gazing. But Rilke was so inordinately conscious

ancient man in that the former was supposed to love his enemy, the latter not. For the Christian, therefore, the domain of possible guilt was immensely enlarged, indeed it became limitless, the only alternative being self-sacrifice. The ancients were great because they were not introvert (with them introversion of the individual entailed *hybris*, madness and tragedy); their measure and that of the stars were the same. Their harmony was original, not the synthetic product of compromise after division. Their solitude was not in eccentricity, it was the solitude of the planets. Self-sacrifice was meaningless to them, they knew no pathos, no sentimentality, no "creative empathy." Greatness in the Christian world could be achieved only through guilt or through the self-sacrifice of the saint.

Apparently Rilke was much interested in Kassner's work and its analysis of human greatness, for, when in the summer of 1911 his friend's book was being prepared for publication, he asked the

---

and persistent in his seeing and looking that he ended by sitting in front of an empty stage, "watching himself see himself" as it were (*Rudolf Kassner*, 113).

At any rate, in the sentence of the Yogi I have interpreted Rilke's understanding of "Innigkeit" as "creative empathy," while in another context (see below, p. 222) I have translated it by "simple inner harmony" (of the gnat). Rilke's use of the word in the Yogi context is, I believe, well covered by "empathy," meaning "an affective identification with another," which in his case was eminently creative.

There are some chronologically related statements by Rilke which clearly point in the direction of the meaning suggested by my translation. On February 18, 1914, he wrote to Benvenuta: "And then, you see, there was the ugly. I could not remain standing in front of it in my art, for it was not my business to be opposite the things but: inside them. That is precisely why I had the 'Innigkeit' [empathy], in order that I be in the ugly also. It was not given me to lie abed with the leper, I lacked the love to do so; leprosy would not have been converted underneath me into its happy contrary. But I had to enter into it wholly, down to the spot where leprosy's innocence was, where it still had childhood; there I had to gather all my strength and be forceful and urgent, and talk leprosy out of its consciousness of being ugly ['creative' empathy]" (*So lass*, 60-61). And at the end of one of the *Late Poems* entitled *Pond in the Woods*, written immediately before, and as a sort of prelude to, his programmatic poem *Turning* of June 20, 1914, he wrote this: "For this is my nature in relation to the world: that things existing outside of me enter joyfully into me from afar, as if answering the call of a soft noise":

> Denn dies ist mein Wesen zur Welt:
> dass sich draussen Erscheinung
> wie auf ein stilles Geräusch hin
> [in mich innen] weither in mich hineinfreut.

On the same page on which these lines are written Rilke further noted: "That this habit of mine of looking away from out of me, which uses me up and empties me, be now replaced by a loving concern for my own inner fullness." ("Dass dieses leerzehrende Aus mir hinausschaun abgelöst werde durch ein liebevolles Bemühtsein um die innere Fülle." *DuV*, vol. 40 [1939] 122ff.) Rilke's self-denying attempts at "objective" poetry at the time of the *New Poems* had left him empty and chilled. Hence his decision from now on to seek his own "inner fullness," his "inner girl."

publisher to let him read an advance copy of it (*Br. 1907-14*, 141). Several letters written at this time show Rilke deeply stirred not only by its contents but also by the above sentence which he had penned from memory in his notebook. Kassner reports that Rilke wrote to him: "This sentence I have copied for myself. It, too, is somehow, for and against me" (*Das Inselschiff*, 121). On June 16, 1911 Rilke wrote further from Paris: "As for me I still have not achieved the turning which my life must take in order to be again productive or, at any rate, good. Once, in Cairo, I wrote this aphorism of yours in my notebook: 'The road from creative empathy to greatness goes through the sacrifice.' (I quote from memory, do not know whether literally correct)—I suppose that is it, but how?" (*Br. 1907-14*, 141-142). And in a significant letter to Benvenuta he wrote on February 17, 1914, that Kassner's sentence had struck him with such incisive force that it almost seemed like a dagger secretly aimed at his very heart (*Br. Benvenuta*, 97).

We must remember that the conversation between Kassner and Rilke took place about half a year after the manuscript of the *Notebook of Malte Laurids Brigge* had been completed, and that as a result of this arduous work our poet felt as if he had spent himself and would never again be able to write anything worthwhile. It was in this mood that Kassner's maxim impressed him as having especial relevance for him. Less than a year later, in the above-mentioned letter of June 16, 1911, he admitted that the "turning" which would usher in a new period of productivity had not yet come, and that his unreadiness for sacrifice must have had something to do with it. "But how?" he wonders. Rilke was in or near Cairo in February and March of 1911. He had just visited Luxor and Karnak where he had been deeply moved by the monumentality of the temples with their columns and pylons. Besides the entry in his notebook referred to above there is further evidence of his concern with sacrifice in those days. In one of the *Posthumous Poems of Count C. W.*, written some nine years later in November 1920, he recalls the grandiose gateways and columns of those ancient ruins, and he marvels "that such standing could be part of the same existence as that in which we [modern Christians] keep dying." He complains of having lost his youthful freshness of apprehension and of being able to visualize the Egyptian world of space and magic only theoretically, by withdrawing hermit-like from ordinary life. Nevertheless, the reliefs on these immense structures had taught him that it was the sacrifice which gave meaning and measure to their immensity. Unlike ours, the sacrificial offerings of the ancient Egyptians were so pervasively spread over their whole lives that their gods were in a permanent state of appeasement, like nursed babes, so that the mere "gesture" of offering sufficed to keep them stilled. No need any more of actually cutting the flowers of the papyrus and of stringing them into garlands; the symbolic movement of rounding one's hands around them was enough. When we, on the other hand, proceed to make offerings to our God we insist on doing so on special occasions, by means of actions which are mere interruptions of our otherwise selfish pursuits. Our "Sunday rises, and the long weeks know him not" (*AW* I,354-357).[2]

Meanwhile, in January 1912, the first two *Elegies* and a few fragments came about, not as the fruit of systematic labor in the manner of the Malte *Notebook* and the *New Poems*, but "inspirationally" in a manner similar to that of the *Book of Hours*. At the beginning of 1914 he became involved in the ill-fated correspondence with Benvenuta, followed by their meeting in Berlin and a sobering trip to various cities of Germany, Austria, and Switzerland, to Paris, Duino, and Venice. By May the whole attachment had ended and Rilke, profoundly disillusioned, returned to his solitude in Paris. During a stopover in Assisi he was amazed at the chasm which separated him from the *poverello*, who no longer had any hold on him, whose poverty, palpable as a stone, was just as hard (*Br.* I,495). "I was numb and hard as a stone," he wrote a month afterward from Paris, "and I continue in that mineralogical state; for which reason I have been fully engaged in sleeping, the most stone-like occupation" (*Br. MTT*, 384). However, Kassner's sentence about the sacrifice evidently kept haunting his mind, for on June 20, 1914 he used it as a motto for a poem, written that morning, which he at once sent to

---

[2] On May 28, 1924, at Muzot, Rilke remembered that a few days later Katharina Kippenberg would celebrate her birthday. In his garden there were at that time no flowers which he could send her, because they would not be able to stand the journey to Leipzig. And so he decided not to pick them, but to offer them in the same manner in which, according to the reliefs of Karnak, the Egyptians used to dedicate their flowers to their gods: by putting his hands quietly and intently around the living, growing stems in the garden. This gesture would direct the fragrance of the blooms as a blessing toward his distinguished friend (*Br. Kippenberg*, 537). Whether Rilke actually performed this ritual gesture or not, the mere suggestion of it illustrates again how closely his artistic experience was embedded in the context of real life.

Lou with this comment: "Lou dear, here is a curious poem . . . which I am sending you because I instinctively called it *Turning* [*AW* I,321-323]—because it represents that kind of change which surely must come if I am to live" (*Br.* I,506).

We have already quoted the relevant portions of this poem in another connection (see above, p. 157). Evidently Rilke meant Kassner's motto to have some bearing on its contents. We may even assume that this bearing was twofold: "for and against me." During the "Rodin period" Rilke had done "eye-work" to the images in him, and he had done so, "intensely wanting, imploring deep down in his look," that is, at the cost of something dearer. His work had been wanting in warmth and love and had, therefore, left him without further inspiration. Out of many maidens he had distilled "the one inner maiden," whom, however, he had not yet learned to love.

It would seem, then, that Rilke felt that he had sacrificed something precious, namely warm, inspiring love, and was, therefore, threatened with sterility. But that was not the kind of sacrifice meant by Kassner who was fully aware of Rilke's life and work up to the time of their conversations in Paris. On the other hand, the love which Rilke resolved to practise from June 1914 on was love of his "inner maiden gained out of a thousand maidens." In other words, he was determined to stop loving actual women otherwise than for the purpose of confirming his "inner maiden." His recent experience with Benvenuta had taught him that, even though the immediate effects of this lesson were to last only a few months. Rilke's poem evidently suggests two kinds of sacrifice: one, inadequate, which consists in giving up warm inspiration in favor of sculptural, cool objectivity, another, which consists in giving up "eye-work" in favor of a new inspirational love strictly reserved to the "inner maiden." Judging by the tenor of the poem in conjunction with his comment to Lou, Rilke seems to have thought that both his manners of creation involved a real sacrifice, but that the kind demanded by his love of the "inner maiden" was the one which Kassner had in mind and would pave the way to greatness. Kassner's sententious reflection could, therefore, have meaning both "for and against" Rilke. That this was Rilke's understanding is confirmed by the definition of sacrifice which he gave to Benvenuta even before he had met her in person. "What is sacrifice?" he asks. "It seems to me that it is nothing else than the boundless resolve, subject to no limitation whatsoever, to be ready for one's own purest, innermost possibility" (*Br. Ben-venuta*, 97).

However, that was not at all what Kassner meant. In his essay of 1927 in memory of Rilke he has this to say: "He [Rilke] did not want the sacrifice, or rather: he did want the sacrifice of the Old Testament (the fruits of the field, a lamb, or what other things are dear to man), but not that of the New Testament. He did not want us to gain the measure of ourselves and of others through the sacrifice from the start. Perhaps because he felt that one had to be God if one were to avoid being simply arrogant. . . . No, he did not understand and comprehend the Kingdom of the Son . . ." (*Das Inselschiff*, 121). Kassner, who had a good chance to form a first-hand opinion of Rilke's attitudes, insists upon this peculiar distinction between the Kingdom of the Father and that of the Son. He apparently had found it originally in the Upanishads. As far as the problem under discussion is concerned, the difference seems to be that the Father, as Supreme Lord and last resort, chooses the kind of sacrifice He wants—a supremacy of free decision which certainly appealed to Rilke. A corollary seems to be that the Father always enjoys the enviable privilege of new and fresh creation, independent of any sort of mediation. The dialectics inherent in the Father's sovereignty over His created Kingdom is of a nature which leaves Him unaffected by all undesired arbitrariness and autonomy on the part of the created world. It is neither arrogance nor robbery on His part when He claims himself to be the measure of all things and all relations. The Son, on the other hand, must, like Christ on the Mount of Olives, pray to the Father: "O My Father, if this cup may not pass away from me, except I drink it, Thy Will be done." That Rilke rejected this kind of sacrificial self-denial has become abundantly clear: "for Angels shun the ones so praying" (*AW* I,167). The free sacrifice of one's own freedom, the readiness to sacrifice one's own genius, that was a horrible thing, not to be contemplated.

No doubt, many will be inclined to agree with Rilke. Nevertheless it all depends upon the point of view, whether monkhood and sainthood are monstrosities or a sublime expression of true freedom. Moreover, we will do well to pause before applauding Rilke's view, and to remember that what he denied God he claimed for himself, and that he called art "a movement contrary to Nature, a reversal of one's forces." "For beauty is nothing but the beginning of terror"

(*AW* I,245). The "terrible, insensate will to art" (*Letters to Merline*, 48), that is, his own creative demon, was Rilke's supreme law; upon its altar he was resigned to sacrifice everything, including loyal and binding love, both in his own joy and that of the beloved.

Rudolf Kassner was not far off the mark when he identified Rilke's Kingdom as that of the Father. Rilke is known to have read the Bible with great eagerness all his life. Judging by the marks he made in the copy he owned, it was above all the Old Testament, more particularly the Psalter, that attracted him (Sievers, 9). In the Psalms he underlined chiefly those passages which characterize man's life as a struggle for God. Following Psalm 50: 9-13, which he underlined, and opposite Psalm 51: 1ff, he wrote in the margin: "God accepts nothing." Some of the prayers which the Psalmist utters in these verses are these: "For thou desirest not sacrifice. . . . I will take no bullock out of thy house, nor he-goats out of thy fields. For every beast of the forest *is* mine, and the cattle upon a thousand hills. . . . Will I eat the flesh of bulls, or drink the blood of goats?" To Rilke these words obviously meant that the sacrifice was senseless, since it implied that man considered things his property, whereas in reality all things were only and always God's. In that sense the words of the Psalter suited Rilke's artistic instinct perfectly. Writing about the *Imitation of Christ* by Thomas à Kempis he joyfully subscribed to Rodin's statement that substituting the word "Art" for "God" would take away nothing from the truth and wisdom of the book (*Br.* II,192-193). If in the *Book of Pilgrimage* the monk-poet calls God his son, his heir, he does not consider this a blasphemy; for he wants to lavish on his Son-God all his love, for which he knows he will not get any love in return. Even though the father is like "a wilted leaf which one places in old books seldom read," what does it matter? Is not the son *his* son? And is not that son "all that the father was and, in addition, all that the father failed to become"? (*AW* I,60-61). What does that mean, if not that the son is father in an eminent and cumulative sense?

Rilke often insisted that he had never felt the slightest desire to mortify his body in order to bring about the creative state of grace. As has already been pointed out, what he needed above all was a perfect understanding between soul and body. He does not "belong to those who are able to achieve an increase of spiritual life by utilizing a failure of the body. . . . My body has too frequently cooperated in creating the riches of my soul" (Salis, 128-129). Rilke could only create from a state of concentration so absolute that all consciousness of dualism was temporarily obliterated. He himself was torn by such dualisms as that between self and the outside world, self and God, body and soul, art and existence. Often they became the very object of his poetry, but they could enter into his poems only in moments of creation in which the inharmonious and painful contradictions had ceased. Somehow their disruptive conflicts had to be overpowered in one unifying thrust in order that they could emerge subdued and transfigured in the plastic form of his poem. Rilke was by no means able to achieve this harmony at all times or in respect of every refractory element of his experience. Some of these elements of conflict simply resisted sublimation and, despite all he could do, kept threatening his spiritual balance. Thus he found heroic words of understanding and acceptance when interpreting bodily suffering in others but was lost and helpless when sickness destroyed the equilibrium of his own creative faculties.

Moreover, even his most glorious successes invariably developed flaws when the rapture of the moment was over. The God of the *Book of Hours*, sung with such sweetness of melody and wealth of imagery, dropped more and more out of sight as His warm nearness proved increasingly deceptive while His presence and power kept lurking uncannily in obscure corners. Similarly, the Orpheus of the *Sonnets*, whose vast nature had sprung from both the domains of life and of death, whose praise extended to mouldering kings, who reached dishes with fruits of praise far into the gates of the dead (*Son.* I,7), lost his charm and appeal in the hours of the poet's approaching death (*Br. MTT*, 955-956).

Yet Rilke was right when he wrote: "In one poem that I succeed in making there is far more reality than in any relationship or attachment that I may experience. When I create, I am true, and I should like to base my whole life upon that truth, upon that infinite simplicity and joy which is sometimes given me" (*Br. 1902-06*, 115). In moments of detached reflection he sometimes found rational formulae for this state in which opposites are resolved. "In lovers and in saints," he says, "renunciation and fulfilment become at bottom identical" (*Br. Muzot*, 142). The experience of the purely possible or even impossible is still felt as a positive increment of inner reality and possession. "Absence" can contribute in a real sense to the joys of presence

(*AW* I,384, 403). The human spirit and soul are spread over a pyrami-
dal area of consciousness and subconsciousness: at its top occur the
actions and decisions of our practical everyday life, while in its lowest
and broadest strata are embedded those realities of earthly existence
to which time and space as well as all other mutually exclusive contrasts are irrelevant (*Br. Muzot*, 291-292).

36. THE KINGDOM OF THE FATHER

Künstler sein heisst: nicht rechnen und
zählen; reifen wie der Baum.

(*Br.* I,47)

To be an artist means: not to calculate
nor to count: to ripen like the tree.

IN SEVERAL other matters Kassner's views serve to elucidate those of
Rilke, although the latter seems to have had some difficulty in understanding them or, at any rate, in accepting them and recognizing
their applicability to himself. An admirer of Kierkegaard, Kassner
saw the destiny of man and the solution of his problems as lying
outside the confines of art. But, having made extensive studies of
human physiognomy and character, both European and Asiatic, he
was able to unravel complexities which Rilke had deeply experienced.

According to Kassner the history of mankind has moved from a
predominating consciousness of space to one of time, from a sense
of architecture to a sense of music. In early times the concept of
evolution, of linear progression *ad infinitum*, was still inarticulate;
instead, there prevailed a feeling of metamorphosis, of interchange-
ability of all things because of their basic identity within a closed,
finite universe. Evolution stresses steady differentiation of individuals, types and species; metamorphosis emphasizes the identity of basic
substance of which only the forms change in a self-contained movement. In such a metamorphic world the consciousness of individuality as something essentially incommunicable and autonomous was
still dormant and ineffective. Everything was magic: name, image,
and thing were interchangeable, quantity and quality, subject and

object, the dead and the living were not yet incompatible opposites. The architecture of ancient Egypt was primarily spatial, reflecting a timeless world. All surplus vitality found containment in massive monuments defying the centuries, instead of describing flighty curves in the air and spending itself in speed (*Son.* II,22). Greek sculpture was already more conscious of time and movement, while the highest degree of mobility was expressed in the Baroque of modern times. The Old Testament, too, was still full of magical immediacy, with the relationship between God and the world chiefly one between God and a chosen people in their predestined land, rather than between God and the individual. The sacrifice of animals and of the fruits of the land was a symbol of tribal allegiance, not the expression of atonement or surrender on the part of the isolated heart. With the growing consciousness of time and individuality the sense of basic wholeness, of the magical circle of things and events, became all but obliterated. The process had already begun in the pre-Christian era and is prominently reflected in the personality and dialectics of Socrates. When Christ appeared on the scene, individualism had reached a critical stage, with its keener awareness of sin and personal guilt, of transitoriness and death, of this life and the life beyond. Western civilization is characterized by its progressive sense of historicity and hence of relativism. The significance of the Absolute has been proportionately weakened. In Asia and, to a lesser degree, in Russia the meaning of time is overshadowed by that of space, and the attitude toward the individual as well as toward death is vastly different from that in the West. On his travels through India Hermann Keyserling was struck by the relatively insignificant role which individuality plays in the consciousness of the Hindus in contrast with the emphasis which we Westerners give it (Keyserling, I,671). The impact of Occidental historism and individualism upon the Asiatic and Russian minds has caused profound upheavals in the souls of the people and is strangely reflected in their writings (Kassner, *Zahl*, passim).

There is an episode in Malte's *Notebook* which illustrates the effects of that impact in a striking way and, characteristically, it is placed in St. Petersburg, the city from which Occidentalism has ranged most widely over Russia. Nikolaj Kusmitch had one day the idea of counting the time which he could still expect to live, some fifty years. Dividing these years into days, then into minutes and seconds he arrived at a figure which was larger than he had ever seen and which made him dizzy. For a moment he experienced the fear, characteristic of rich people, that someone less wealthy might rob him of part of his capital. But most of the time he felt elated at the thought of his huge possession. In a whim of self-duplication he found his "poor self" admonishing his "rich self" not to become overbearing on account of his riches. "Don't forget that wealth is not everything, that there are poor, yet quite respectable people; there are even impoverished noblemen and generals' daughters who walk the streets offering something for sale."

Nikolaj went on living as usual, pausing only on Sundays to straighten out his accounts. But soon he became alarmed at the rate at which he had been drawing upon his capital, and he made up his mind to be more economical. He decided to get up earlier in the morning, to wash less frequently, to drink his tea standing and to race to his office in order to arrive there much too early. He felt that he had been cheated by his other, his calculating self when he exchanged his years for small cash. And so he demanded his remaining time back in large bills: four of ten years each and one of five. The rest he was prepared to forego and to let the devil have it. But his other self did not respond to his request, and time-rich Nikolaj was left with his tens of thousands of slippery seconds in his hands. He could only console himself with the reflection that he did not know anything about numbers anyway, and that after all they were no more than a state institution for the sake of order. "Nobody had ever seen a number except on paper. It was impossible that one should ever meet a Seven or a Twenty-five at a social gathering." For the rest, the thorny matter of time was the same for everybody, even though they might not realize it. Nevertheless the incubus could not be shaken off easily. Nikolaj Kusmitch became more and more aware of flowing time, until he literally saw all those innumerable little seconds running by, uniformly alike, but quickly, quickly. He became sensitive even to the revolving movement of the earth under his feet, until he had a sensation of seasickness and reeled in his room as on a ship's deck, and was afraid of using a street-car (*AW* II,145-151).

This curious episode probably owes its origin to Rilke's conversations with Kassner who admits that ever since childhood he had wondered why he never found a number instead of a pebble beside the road (Kassner, *Erinnerung*, 144). Even the name of Kusmitch occurs in one of Kassner's dialogues entitled *The Leper* (1914) where Feodor Kusmitch figures as the murderer of Czar Paul I. Moreover, in this dialogue Czar Alexander I, Paul's son, tormented by thoughts of complicity, takes upon himself the murderer's guilt and leads a life of solitude and penance (Kassner, *Chimäre*, 47). We are reminded of the *Fourth Elegy* where in the concluding paragraph Rilke contrasts the murderer's understanding of death as a terminal event with the child's timeless relation to death in life. As to the story of Nikolaj Kusmitch in Malte's *Notebook*, it evidently bears the stamp of Rilkean caricature. It illustrates with manifest exaggeration the growing time-consciousness and the passion for reflection characteristic of Western civilization, of which Rilke himself was an eminent exponent. In Russia, he thought, these features were far less pronounced and when they did acquire prominence in individuals their effect was pernicious. His meeting with Tolstoy in 1899 caused Rilke to reflect retrospectively in 1913 that all that which is truly valid "is unconcerned with time and radiates through it, leaving it behind once and for all." And Dostoyevsky interpreted time "as an entirely provisional symbol of things external" (Buddeberg, 153).

Kassner argued that Christ's sacrifice on the Cross signified that qualitatively the life and the death of each individual contained their whole essence and that nothing was added to them by the fact that millions might live and die. Life and death cannot be counted. Numbers have become mere formalized devices which can reveal nothing of the quality of the things themselves. Quantity and quality have become irremediably divorced from one another. Several other strange passages in the Malte *Notebook* are better understood with such considerations in mind, for example that in which Malte in his little room in Paris asks in a mood of despair: "Is it possible that we know nothing of the girls who yet live? Is it possible that we say 'the women,' 'the children,' 'the boys,' and do not suspect (with all our education do not suspect), that these words lost their plural long ago and are only uncountable singulars?" (*AW* II,24). Of all the attempts made—so Kassner thinks—to recover the sense of value and greatness by a reconquest of the Absolute and Eternal, only that which Christ has taught us is valid and effective. The "Christian" sacrifice alone is capable of uniting again the worlds which we have separated.

In the Orient and, to some extent in Russia, the idea of sainthood is different from ours. With us asceticism is predicated upon a depreciation of the body and of life on this earth in favor of the soul and of the life beyond; in the East it is not in the same sense and measure a requisite of sainthood (Kassner, *Erinnerung*, 262-272). Neither the Buddhist monk nor the Hindu Yogi seek to achieve spiritual knowledge and perfection through mortification of the body. Hermann Keyserling suggests that in the Orient the slogan of sainthood is negative and passive: do not do to others what you do not want done to yourself—whereas in the West it is aggressive and activistic: do to others what you would like to have done to yourself (Keyserling, I, 51-52, 140). In this respect, as in many others, the piety of the Russian is remarkably similar to that of the Hindu (Keyserling, I,229). However, by and large it is quite obvious that when Rilke stigmatized the West he had in mind an extreme version of it, a sort of caricature, whereas Russia, the object of his praise, appeared to him an ideal world in which Western dualisms were not effective. Rilke was not unaware of his bias. "Have I wronged," he asks in a poem of June 1914, only a day or so before he wrote his poem *Turning*, "have I wronged that which I have wrested from reality, heedless of how I would apprehend it, and have I imprisoned in my serried heart the things accustomed to bigness?" (*SG*, 22-23). On the other hand, in defense of his imperturbable attitude even to the ugly and morbid he writes: "One must not interfere with my surrender even where it is too absolute, even where it is untenable. Believe me, in order that the world be complete it is necessary that now and then somebody be on hand who carries his devotion to the point of imprudence" (*Br.* II,12). And in view of his *Sonnets* it cannot be denied that his "tree of ecstasy" bore resplendent fruit. It must be admitted, too, that putting things in sharp relief upward or downward, "putting it on thick" one way or another, helps bring out the middle, that middle which Rilke glorifies in a number of poems.

The West and the East became for Rilke symbols of two equally fundamental characteristics of himself and of man in general: the yearning for endless speed and progression, and a craving for immanent movement in a finite world. Rilke, who was born on the fringes of West and East, experienced both with equal intensity but somehow regarded Occidentalism as an aberration that could and should have been avoided. Genetically and culturally he himself was a victim of all the paradoxes of the Christian West; his creative spirit sought refuge in a less historically conscious world in which these paradoxes could be ignored. And if they could be ignored, what use was there of Christ and His sacrifice, which seems to proclaim that between life and death there is a deep chasm, both in time and in kind? In a spatial, ahistorical world, where metamorphic transformation takes the place of evolutionary change, life and death are mutually complementary, mere aspects of the same identical thing. What use is there of original sin, or, for that matter, of sin at all, and of redemption from sin—and therefore of self-sacrifice? Moreover if it is true that the East and the West represent two complementary modes of being equally inherent in human nature, and if we consider that never before in history have the two become so acutely aware of each other as today, may we not see in this a reason among others for the growing interest in a poet whose manner of experience seems to point in the direction of mutual understanding and reconciliation?

Many of Rilke's odd manners of experiencing are tied up with the intense desire of the artist for wholeness in the midst of a time-ridden world. As long as his fancy can bend the linear flow into a circle, with each moment being at the same time beginning and end, it is only a matter of finding the fitting symbol for it, and the magical world becomes inner reality. But when external circumstances, such as the war, suddenly cause a violent break of continuity, Rilke's creative powers are shattered and he is like a ship without a rudder. And that applies to the man as well as to the artist. No wonder that he envies the animal, whose eyes open into unbroken space, ignorant of death and past. The more complete the ignorance, the greater the envy. For in this respect there is hierarchy in the animal kingdom. Those born in a womb are not entirely free of a dim "remembrance that what we long for is that from which we were severed and which once was warm and near. What now is distance was then pure breath." These beasts instinctively "suspect that even man is none too securely at home in his construed world." The birds, on the other hand, hatched out in a nest, seem more independent of the force of gravity which is like memory. Still, their nest is a sort of womb borrowed, as it were, from the earth, and their flight in the open spaces does not completely rid them of the weight of their earthy origin. And how dismayed is the bat, which is winged like the birds and forced to fly with the memory of the womb in her. "As though afraid of itself it zigzags through the air like a crack through a cup. Thus the trail of the bat tears through the porcelain paleness of the evening." Of all the animals, that which comes nearest to enjoying a life unfractured by severance at birth, is the gnat. This small creature always remains in the womb which bore it: its womb and the world in which it lives are one. "The gnat ever hops within, even when it mates: for the womb is all." Hence its simple, inner harmony (*Eighth Elegy*).

However, Rilke's praise of the gnat is not all envy. Somehow he also sees in the uterine origin of man an example of how on a different level poetic creation must come about. For in the measure in which outside events and realities are excluded from the processes of pregnancy, man in his pre-natal existence becomes himself world. That is precisely what the artist must become again: world, inner cosmic world, whole and round, unwedged by external, accidental reality.

PART VII
ELEGY AND ORPHEUS

◇◇◇

Aber ein Turm war gross, nicht wahr? O Engel, er war es,—
gross, auch noch neben dir?

(Seventh Elegy)

But a tower was great, or was it not? Oh Angel, it was—
great, even beside you?

◇◇◇

37. LIVING IS DYING

◇◇

Vous ne pouviez vous comprendre sans restriction
aucune, car vous êtes le poète de la vie—de la vie
belle, terrible, joyeuse, tragique . . . mais toujours
de la vie—et lui était le poète de la mort! . . .

(Br.MTT, 962)

You could not understand each other unreservedly
because you are the poet of life—of beautiful,
terrible, joyous, tragic life . . . at any rate of
life—whereas he [Rilke] was the poet of death! . . .
(Princess Marie von Thurn und Taxis
to Hugo von Hofmannsthal)

◇◇

COMPARED to the complexities of the human world the physical universe is simple. We not only know that the sun will rise every morning and set every evening; we can calculate to the minute the time
at which it will do so every day of the year. Where this certitude
exists there is no room for fear. But which seed will fructify and
when, which of us will die tomorrow, who can tell? This incer-
titude makes our expectancy the more tense and fearful the more
certain we are that life continues to be born and that die we must.
But the unpredictability in things human extends infinitely further.
We can wilfully interfere with germination and growth; we can
murder or commit suicide if we wish. According to the Bible, death
first entered into the world through fratricidal murder. Inanimate
things are fearlessly embedded in the harmonious play of natural
forces, but man can disturb these forces with wanton indiscretion
and create insecurity. The bird sings its pure song in candid response
to instinct, while man can shroud his joy in silence and disguise his
indifference in song. His cry is torn by inner contradiction, thus
driving a wedge into guileless Nature.

When God created the world he stressed the word "Life" and
spoke "Death" softly (*AW* I,12). Death was there, to be sure, but
as the natural complement of life it caused no fear. Man did not
stare at it in a conscious return upon himself, he did not stride to-

ward it, horror-stricken, as toward an abyss. Inasmuch as he carried it in him, it was already behind while yet before. His gaze did not bounce back from an impenetrable wall behind which there is darkness, but went freely into the open like that of the animal (*Eighth Elegy*). When death is immediately near, man may still share this animal's gaze and see death no more. Nature is law everywhere, free man lives by his wits and is chance in every fold of his being. Law makes secure; within its purview death agrees with life no less than does birth. Chance is wayward; it divorces birth from death and isolates life between them, infinitely brittle and subject to a fate which it seeks, yet shuns.

Rilke's suspicion of man's freedom as a source of arbitrariness and cunning is only apparently in contradiction with his demand for undiluted autonomy. It rather makes this demand all the more urgent since man's arbitrariness threatens to thwart the intentions and aspirations of the artist. Art, as Rilke understands it, is obedience to law in all its gravity, intuitively achieved but freely willed. Of this paradoxical necessity of combining a conscious, intensely free will with blind, intuitive surrender Rilke was already aware at the time of his *Florentine Journal*: "I am now much more conscious during all these sensations and shall, therefore, be more naïve in my creative moments" (*JF*, 37). "We [moderns in contrast with the artists of the early Renaissance] are no longer naïve, but must command ourselves to become primitive, in order that we may begin again with those who were so in their hearts" (*JF*, 80). When in the *Fourth Elegy* the distressed poet sits before the stage of puppets with their bodies of rags, their wires, and their blank faces, he is determined to remain there, alone, even after the lights are out and nothing but grey air spreads coldly from the stage—and to wait and gaze until, to counterpoise his gaze, an Angel is compelled to appear and to pull the puppets upward.

"Falling" is more in keeping with great creative art than "flying," humility more than conceit (*AW* I,280). In the roots lies the strength of life, and the roots feed on what has died and is buried. It is the artist who must realize the truth that living is dying, that death is only an intense movement of life and that neither life nor death must be desecrated by wilful escape into an imaginary Beyond. The salvation of humanity cannot come from the womb of one that gives birth to a God but must issue from the artist of the future who shall erect his life into an espalier in order that he may bring forth deified Death, gloriously ripened in the warm climate of a Southern exposure (*AW* I,93). The artist is he who returns Death to its rightful owner: to Life. Rilke's concern with death was anything but aesthetic flirting or romantic flight. In a sense, of course, it was flight, but its motive was, besides fear, a strong desire to face squarely and unflinchingly life on this earth which he had no inclination to leave or to ignore. To him it was a most realistic attempt to conquer death through art instead of through religious faith, and to give back to life its full value. If existentially the attempt failed in crucial moments, that failure detracts nothing from the authenticity of Rilke's attitude and its artistic expression.

The truth is that Rilke's elemental and nightmarish fear of death constituted a never flagging challenge to his vital instinct and to his creative demon. We can follow the progress of his toilsome travail from early childhood, when his fancy was still haunted by the imagery of Catholic symbolism, to the final screneness of the Orphic myth in the *Sonnets*. In his diaries and letters as well as in his poems he is constantly and laboriously at work devising formulae and symbols by means of which he hopes not only to tame and domesticate death but to harness its tremendous power for the furtherance of his creative aims. At Viareggio, in 1898, he sees the somber Brother of Mercy, his head covered by a cowl with openings only for the eyes, standing in the midst of a luxuriantly fragrant garden: Death in the warm, congenial atmosphere of abundance and life (*JF*, 93-98). In *The White Princess*, which owes its origin to the Viareggio experience, a messenger describes to the Princess the ghastly horrors of death with which an outbreak of the plague has visited the surrounding country (*FG*, 131-132). "You have never seen how Death comes and goes, entirely as if he were at home in your house; yet he is not *our* death but a foreign one, hailing from some thoroughly debauched city; no death in God's pay." But the Princess, whose eyes have erred dreamily toward the sea, reflects:

"You see, thus Death is in Life. The two are as intertwined as the threads which run through a tapestry, and to one who passes by there emerges a picture. When someone dies, not that alone is death. Death is when someone lives and does not know it. Death is when someone cannot make up his mind to die. Much is death, you cannot bury it. Sorrow and joy are no more than colors to the stranger who looks at us. That is why it is so important that we should find him who really sees and gathers us completely in his look, saying simply: 'I see this and that,' while others only guess or lie. At every moment there is dying in us and birth, and we are as unmindful of either as Nature, which outlasts both, indifferent and without mourning."

This early passage contains the essence of Rilke's bitter-sweet fruit of death. Deep down in the core of our being we recoil from death with terrified aversion, and our imagination is at all times ready with phantoms to give substance to our fear. Rilke was never able to rid himself entirely of these hideous phantoms. They stalk through his work like ghosts, now appallingly palpable, now pervasively invisible. The *Book of Poverty and Death*, the *Notebook*, the *Elegies* are full of them in one form or another, and in the *New Poems* they lurk in countless crannies. Of all potentially hostile realities death was the most formidable. Its inescapabilities could not be denied, yet had to be subdued. If ever creative magic was needed, it was here. Traditional religious as well as current secular approaches were of no help, the former because of their metaphysical presumptions, the latter because of their shallow sophistry. They were either "guesses or lies." Both left life and death in separate compartments, and between them only a one-way channel. If the sinister power of death was to be put again into the service of life, the artist alone was able and duty-bound to do so. He alone could see us as we really are and "gather us completely, saying simply: I see this and that."

In this as in all other matters of objective reality the only way open to the artist was to immunize death's otherness and strangeness by luring it into the intimacy of his own being. In this "inner space," cosmic by its absence of boundaries between life and death, between past, present, and future, it could come and go in endless metamorphoses, side by side with the "inner girl" and all the other "singulars" distilled out of countless "plurals." As long as that inner universe of domesticated demons could be given truth and reality, no danger could come from the hard facts of life, from wasteful duties and obligations. But when all is said and done, every poetic symbol, however gratifying otherwise, leaves behind a residue of reality which has resisted full assimilation. Not only does the naked fact of death remain untouched in its core by artistic sublimation, but the more fitting and adequate the sublimating symbol, the more subtly it will reveal the artist's anguished fear. Just as the misery of the poor, the despair of the unrequited lover, the suffering of the abandoned wife or child, and every other kind of existential ill is in reality brought out more sharply by the artist's "redeeming" symbols. Nikolaj Kusmitch ends by avoiding all movement and lying down day and night, reciting only soothing verses in the hope of eliminating from his consciousness the flux of time (*AW* II,150). Is not thereby the whole perplexing problem of transitoriness put into sharper relief, unsolved?

38. DEATH, CONCENTRATED OR DILUTED?

⟨◇◇◇⟩

> O Herr, gib jedem seinen eignen Tod.
> (*Stundenbuch*)

> Oh Lord, give each his own death.

⟨◇◇◇⟩

ALL of Rilke's interpretations of death have this in common: that they place it in the midst of life. With reference to the undivided wholeness of the two halves of the moon, death is called the invisible side of life. Or it is put on the same level as all other privative experiences of everyday life, such as losses, departures, separations. All these inner happenings are modes of death and you cannot bury them. As life goes on, we cannot help dying every minute. In the *Requiem* on the death of a young friend of Clara's (November 1900) the poet reflects: "Life is only a part . . . of what? Life is only a tone . . . wherein? . . . Your Death was already old when your life began; and so He attacked it in order that it should not survive Him" (*BB*, 164, 168). In the *Book of Images* Death sits behind the Knight's armor and waits impatiently for the coat-of-mail to be pierced, so that He may stretch and spread out in comfort (*BB*, 11). "Death holds us all in His hands. He is no stranger, for our blood is His home." The poet cannot believe that Death is unjust, though many slander Him (*BB*, 64). In the final poem of the same book "we belong to Death in the very midst of our laughter" (*BB*, 169).

Death so conceived as part and parcel of life appears now as a seed, slowly growing and ripening into mellow fruit, now as a diluted essence which permeates invisibly our whole being and the whole universe. The seed and fruit symbol was especially elaborated during the *Book of Hours* and the "Malte" periods. In connection with it the distinction was made between our own authentic death ("der eigne Tod"), and the unauthentic, counterfeit death ("der uneigne Tod") which has become so common in our modern, urbanized society (*AW* I,92ff). The latter owes its loss of authenticity to the influence of mass behavior and interpretation, to the levelling-out processes of institutionalized medicine and religion, which have reduced true, individual death to a mere *exitus lethalis* that belongs to a diagnosed disease, or to a fragrance of flowers and of incense in a Gothic chapel. Death is more and more deprived of the opportunity to open up into a fruit that tastes of the person in whom it grew, such as the one of Count Brigge in Malte's *Notebook* (*AW* II,14-17). Too often the fruit of death is picked unripe and green, stunted and dwarfed by a society which hates uniqueness and distinction. Yet this same society, by expelling death as some degenerative process out of all domains of life, by passing it over in silence whenever possible, has actually increased our death-consciousness a thousandfold in a most shameful manner. Death means for the believing Christian either Heaven or Hell, for the secularized unbeliever something akin to sheer nothingness. In the child, before the grown-ups have forced it "to turn and see things that are formed behind it, not the open space" (*Eighth Elegy*), that consciousness is still undeveloped. A child's death is still as plain and unquestioned a part of its young life as an ordinary piece of "grey bread that hardens," or as "the core of a ripe apple that is held in its round mouth" (*Fourth Elegy*). We, the "enlightened" grown-ups, always look into a world of aims and limiting objects, never into pure space, into "a nowhere that yet is not nothing" (*Eighth Elegy*).

The most notorious form of the seed-fruit symbol is that which is found in the *Book of Poverty and Death*. The poet fancies the highest aim of man's endeavors to be this: to fertilize death's seed in life's womb and to nurture it lovingly to full fruition and glorious birth (*AW* I,94-96). Society has so prostituted the sexual function that motherhood is often forced to yield to whoredom, that procreation is sickened, and only a wizened embryo is prematurely born in painful labor. The world has become sterile through the frivolous distortion of values, and death itself has become unviable like the product of a miscarriage (*AW* I,94). We have become so accustomed to embellishing death with trivial make-up that civilization has turned the undertaker's parlor into a beauty shop where dead girls are groomed as for an evening party; we have already emasculated death by converting life into a milliner's domain where "Madame Lamort" turns out, wholesale, "cheap winter hats of fate" adorned with the "restless paths of the earth" as with "ribbons, frills, flowers, cockades, and artificial fruits" (*Fifth Elegy*). It is necessary that birth be given again to a vigorous death, a death which man is prepared to recognize as his, and which every artist is called upon to presage and foreshadow. For death is the highest instance of life which forces our smooth cleverness back to "the spot where we yet failed to master the trick and fell from each other like ill-suited beasts attempting to mate" (*Fifth Elegy*).

The artist-monk of the *Book of Hours*, and Rilke himself at the time when he created his pseudonym, knew that mankind was neither ready for such strangely deep experiences nor great enough to give them gratifying form. He felt that the ultimate bearer of that great Death would be assailed and persecuted, like the grave-digger in his early Worpswede sketch (1899) who had transformed the village cemetery—even the unused part which had hitherto been covered with wild growth—into a garden with colorful and fragrant flowers, until the two parts could hardly be distinguished from one another and at times an old mother could be seen praying at a spot where there was no grave. Although the villagers kept aloof and left the strange gardener to his solitary task (with the exception of young Gita, the mayor's daughter, who visited him daily in defiance of her parents), they tacitly appreciated his work, since it helped them bear the weight of death more lightly. But when the plague began to ravage their village, the beautiful garden lost all its power and charm and appeared to them as a wicked challenge to Death in all His frightful hideousness, for which their mysterious grave-digger was responsible. If, in their attempt to stone him they left him unhurt, killing only Gita, it was because their murderous intention aroused Death to all the greater fury, thus causing devastating confusion in their ranks. They kept dying in large numbers; black Sicco and his cronies went on throwing disfigured corpses over

the wall of the cemetery, until the stranger, exasperated by their unreadiness to experience death as "a friendly invention of the earth"
(*AW* I,275), smashed Sicco's head with his spade and went off,
nobody knows whither (*Br. Frühzeit*, 212-219). Nevertheless, the
Rilkean monk also knew, even at that early stage, that death, authentically experienced, is the hidden source and goal of all our
longing for the Eternal and the Absolute. And "we need eternity,"
Rilke wrote in his *Florentine Journal*, "for it alone gives amplitude
to our gestures, and yet we know that our time is strictly limited.
Therefore, we must create the Infinite within these limits, since
we no longer believe in Immensity" (*JF*, 79). Hence, death is the
fruit about which everything revolves. "For its sake maidens grow
up and go forth like a tree out of a lute, and boys yearn for man-
hood. For its sake the things seen by the artist become timeless
and remain long after they have faded away—and all those who
have formed and built have become world for the sake of this fruit"
(*AW* I,93). Its kinship with procreation and sexuality is emphasized
by its relationship to rapture in love: the consciousness of time is
obliterated. Death, like love, throws upon all transitory things a
shadow which gives them deeper meaning and converts them into
atoms of eternity. "Be out of time, only one day, and you will see
how much eternity is in you" (*JF*, 87).

Rilke's image of authentic death, of a fruit that ripens within us
with a unique flavor of our own, was directed against the equalizing
tendencies of modern society. Rudolf Kassner considered it the
corollary of a false premise; according to him it was either an artificial device or a truism: "even the smelliest gypsy-woman dies her
own death" (*Rudolf Kassner*, 207). Rilke himself used it more spar-
ingly in his later poetry. It was a direct, though odd, offshoot of his
extreme demand for freedom, the freedom not only to live but to die
in accordance with each individual's self. It caused him some embarrassment when he had to account for those unavoidably accidental or violent deaths from external causes. Even before he had
found the name for it in Jens Peter Jacobsen he prophesied in the
Florentine Journal: "The day will come when fate will strike no one
before he has become fruit. The days of harvest will come" (*JF*, 82).
In one form or another he clung to it to the end of his life, even
when his own turn to die had come. He notoriously refused to see
in death a mere biological occurrence accounted for by defined patho-

logical disturbances. Death remained for him a unique and ineffable experience, a singular mystery. He forbade his doctor ever to mention any of the medical rubrications that might range his death among a mass of others (*Br.MTT*, 955).

It is important to realize that the ripening of death as Rilke understands it is just as conscious-unconscious as the ripening of God. It is the result of an inner transformation which strengthens life, not of morose reflection which saps energy and robs life of its fullness. The Christian *Memento mori* concentrates our attention on a life beyond; Rilke insists on mixing death with life as a leavening and intensifying ingredient. The kind of thought and talk about death standardized by Western tradition is precisely what Rilke considered the cause of man's loss of naïve, pure existence. It erects a wall right across the horizon of man's vision. Instead of making free it imprisons. We, men, alone see it. "The free beast has its death always behind it, and before it God, and when it walks, it goes into eternity, as fountains do" (*Eighth Elegy*). Death must be so diluted in the vital sap that, living, we live in death without seeing it. Instead of dying "in Christ," which means dying in the hope of coming back to life through the resurrection of the body, we must die "in Eurydice" (*Son*.II, 13), which means accepting death as the other side of life, a return from which would be a puerile denial of its laws. To be dead *in Eurydice* means a habitual state by which death is disposed of in advance, by which all departures and separations are anticipated and left behind even before they occur. "Keep ahead of all farewell" (*Son*.II, 13). The idea of a Last Judgment, when in frantic search of their bodies the dead impatiently answer the call of the Angels' trumpets and, naked, thirst for the weird gratification of all the lusts of their frustrated lives before the final sentence is passed, that idea is a horrible invention of man, avid for ever new morsels of a meaningless life. In his early poem *The Last Judgment* Rilke fervently begs God never to let such a horror come about (*BB*, 80-86). And in the later poem of 1913 entitled *The Resurrection of Lazarus*, Christ, infinitely saddened by the people's clamoring for a miracle, reluctantly proceeds to do violence to peaceful Nature. In every fibre of His being anger swells at the thought of the trivial distinction which humans make between the dead and the living. Slowly and heavily He raises His hand shaped like a claw, and in a hoarse voice He commands: Lift the stone! And something rises, bent and crooked, which once again a vague and indistinct life takes back as a supernumerary bargain (*AW* I,345-346).

The notion of a "diluted" death such as that exemplified by the *poverello* of Assisi, did not become definitely associated with the name of Orpheus until late in Rilke's life, although such an association is vaguely foreshadowed in 1907.[1] Speaking about various Rodin sculptures among which there was one representing Orpheus, the poet says: "And I already feel how the name melts in my mouth, how all these figures are nothing but the poet, the same poet, called Orpheus, when in a formidable sweep his arm goes over all things to the chords [of his lyre]" (*Rodin*, 86). This passage may be considered a remote forerunner of the *Fifth Sonnet*: "Erect no monument. Let only the roses bloom each year for His sake. For it is Orpheus. His metamorphosis in this and in that. We need not trouble about other names. Once and for all it's Orpheus when there is song. Coming he goes and going he comes." But in the poem of 1904, entitled *Orpheus, Eurydice, Hermes*, the Greek mythological figure is still the representative of restless, impatient man, whose unchecked curiosity causes him to forfeit all that he had gained through the charm of his musical art. Eurydice, his wife, on the other hand, was in her young death like a fruit full of sweetness and darkness, intangible like a budding maiden. Her sex was closed like a young flower toward evening. She was as flowing as loose hair, her abandon was like the fallen rain, and she was distributed like abundant food. She was already root (*AW* I,199-202). Likewise in the poem *Alceste* of 1907, it is the man, Admetus, who begs for every last crumb of life, while the woman, for whom life is nothing but a chain of farewells, offers it calmly and smilingly in the place of his (*AW* I,202-205).[2] These women are in the eyes of Rilke akin to the things: like them they are self-contained, demanding and ex-

---

[1] Rilke became acquainted with the various aspects of the Orpheus legend through reading Ovid's *Metamorphoses*, a book which evoked a world of magic and "transformation" so wonderfully suited to his ripening dreams (Zinn, 219). He is reported to have used a French translation by M. Cabaret-Dupaty (Paris), in which he underlined a number of passages, especially the one referring to Narcissus: "Heu, frustra dilecte puer!" (Ovid, *Metamorphoses*, Book III, 500.) Merline added appropriate drawings illustrating the main themes, such as that of Narcissus (Simenauer, 739f).

[2] For the relationship of Rilke's *Alkestis* to Greek mythology see Zinn, 201-210.

pecting nothing from outside, referring themselves to nothing that is not in them. And so is God, and so must the artist be.

Rilke's "dilution" of death was an aesthetic device designed to perform the realistic function of taking the sting out of death "undiluted." The symbol of a diluted death would probably never have been invented, had not the naked fact of death been so overwhelmingly distressing. In this respect our poet undoubtedly felt related to Tolstoy, of whom he wrote in an important letter of November 8, 1915 (*Br.* II,58):

"His enormous experience of Nature . . . enabled him in a remarkable way to think and write from within the whole, out of a feeling of life so permeated with the most diluted death, that the latter was present everywhere like a spice in the strong taste of life —but precisely for that reason this man could be frightened so profoundly, so desperately, when he realized that somewhere there was plain death, the flask filled with the thick substance of death, or that cup with the broken handle and the senseless inscription *Faith, Love, and Hope* out of which someone was forced to drink the bitterness of undiluted death. . . . His relationship to death was no doubt to the end for him an enormously pervasive fear, a fugue of fear, a huge edifice, a tower of fear with corridors and stairs and railingless projections and chasms on all sides. . . ."

The next day Rilke wrote his remarkable poem *Death* in which the same symbols recur, that of the flask full of thick bluish poison and that of the cup with the cracked handle and the ludicrous inscription. In order to prevail over that horrible death Rilke had to call vividly back to his mind the falling stars which he had witnessed from a bridge at Toledo, Spain, in the winter of 1912-13, and which had taught him the contrasting lesson: "to stand" (*AW* I,360).[3] And nowhere is the bitter-sweet taste of death more poignantly praised than in the *Tenth Elegy*, in which one of the older Plaints leads a dead youth "through the broad domain of the Plaints and shows him the columns of the temples or the ruins of those castles from which Plaint-Princes once ruled wisely over the land. She shows him the weeping trees and fields of flowering melancholy (the liv-

---

[3] Kassner is of the opinion that in this poem Rilke's treatment of death is trifling and shallow, that the poet immodestly exhibits himself with a showy naked death as a bare-shouldered woman does with her low-necked dress (*Rudolf Kassner*, 207).

ing know them only as soft foliage); she shows him the animals of mourning, grazing. . . . Once," she comments, "we were a great race. Our forefathers exploited mines in the big mountains; among men you sometimes find a polished stone of ancient sorrow. . . . Yes, that came from there. Once we were rich."

39. REQUIEM FOR PAULA

Komm her ins Kerzenlicht. Ich bin nicht bang,
die Toten anzuschauen.

(AW I,214)

Come here, into the candle's light. I'm not afraid
to look upon the dead.

IN TWO poems of some length, the *Requiem* for Paula Modersohn-Becker and that for Wolf Graf von Kalckreuth, both written in the fall of 1908, Rilke has denounced with manifest feelings of personal involvement the lamentable reality of "unauthentic" death. These requiems put into sharp relief the relationship of death to Rilke's art and the peculiar responsibilities of the artist in regard to life and work. They also show clearly that dying one's own death means in the first place living one's own life. With his innate tendency to surrender, Rilke needed just that: to be true to himself in the face of all manner of enticement or dread interfering with his work.

Paula was a painter of real genius, the blond friend of Clara Westhoff. To the glorification of her maidenhood Rilke's Worpswede diary winds fragrant wreaths of mystifying sentiments. During the months which Rilke spent among the painters of Worpswede prior to his marriage he was fascinated as much by the peculiar charm of Paula as by the more conventionally solid virtues of her friend Clara, the sculptress and former pupil of Rodin. Indeed, on reading Rilke's diary of the period one cannot escape the feeling that Paula appeared to him as the more intriguing and piquant young woman. On the other hand, Paula's own letters and diary suggest quite clearly that, while she appreciated some of Rilke's poems and readings, she was far more attracted by Otto Modersohn, one of the painters of the Worpswede colony to whom she became engaged in the spring of 1901. As far as Rilke was concerned, according to his own confessions his main object in marrying had been to find some sort of shelter for his unstable mental and bodily condition, the more so since Lou's psychological ascendancy had proved too enslaving a burden. We can understand, therefore, that in his memory Paula became associated with ambiguous feelings of frustration and self-consciousness. On Paula's part there undoubtedly developed some jealousy of Rilke who had robbed her of a good friend while Rilke held a secret grudge against Otto for having won the favor of Clara's lovable friend. Paula's experiment with matrimony lasted a few years longer than Rilke's, but in February 1906 she, too, left her husband in order to devote herself once more completely to her art. In Paris, where she stayed after the separation, Rilke had established his headquarters a few years earlier, and the two met from time to time. Although the external circumstances which accompanied the break-up of their respective homes were different, its basic significance seems to have been the same, namely the incompatibility of matrimonial responsibilities with their work. But unlike Rilke, Paula returned to her partner at the end of the year. She became a mother on November 21, 1907, and died shortly afterward. "What a pity!" were her last words (Modersohn-Becker, 243).

Rilke's *Requiem* leaves no doubt that he could never forgive Paula for yielding to her husband's pleas that she return. An unmistakable note of rancor runs through the poem, not only against Otto but against Paula as well. It was caused no doubt in part by Rilke's genuine conviction that art and worldliness do not mix, but in no small measure also by a sense of guilt and a desire for self-vindication. Perhaps other, unidentified, motives contributed their share to a complex relationship from which to this day the veil has not been lifted. To Paula's brother, who had sent him a copy of her diary, Rilke admitted in 1913 that her death had shaken him more than any other death; "perhaps a few other circumstances helped to produce this effect" but the main reason was because "of the immeasurable loveliness of her heart" (*Br.* I,441). And Katharina Kippenberg quotes Rilke as saying sadly: "She is the only dead friend who troubles me" (Kippenberg, 44), a sentiment which forms the prelude of the poem. In the last analysis, of course, all these Rilkean motifs are rooted in his demonic desire for untrammeled independence and freedom in the pursuit of his art. Like the Prodigal Son in Malte's *Notebook* Rilke became morbidly afraid of being loved, lest such love impute to him wishful modes of being which he repudiated. The Prodigal Son of the New Testament returned home, repentant; Rilke's returned and stayed, only to use the affection of his family as a welcome screen behind which his own freedom could be all the more secure (*AW* II,211-218). Conversely Rilke was terribly afraid of being pursued by the phantoms of death lest they impose upon him a mode of life which would have paralyzed his creative faculties. Yet he returned to these very same monsters and used them in the erection of a tower of solitary freedom.

When Rilke himself got married he could still cherish the illusion for a while that in spite of his pecuniary uncertainties marriage was a necessity for him. "In my bachelor's room," he wrote on January 8, 1902, "my world, which had so few connections with temporal life, was unprotected and exposed to all winds; it needed for its deployment a quiet home of its own under the broad skies of solitude. Besides, I had read in Michelet that life with two was simpler and cheaper than the existence of the single person, which is the object of deceit and abuse on all sides—and I naïvely believed the child Michelet" (*Br. Frühzeit*, 141).[4] But already a few months earlier he had made this more revealing confession: "For the rest, I am of the opinion that 'marriage' as such does not deserve the emphasis which convention has given it. Nobody thinks of expecting a single person to be 'happy'—but no sooner does he get married than surprise is expressed if he is not 'happy'" (*Br. Frühzeit*, 107). Paula, too, had apparently drifted into marriage, but had later made the fateful mistake of returning, not in the same spirit as Rilke's Prodigal Son but in the erroneous belief that motherhood and art could exist side by side. For this she paid with her death. In the spring of 1898, in Tuscany, Rilke had written in his diary: "A woman who is an artist must cease to create when she has become a mother. She has put her goal outside of herself and can continue to *live* [italics mine] art in the deepest sense" (*JF*, 135). But, paradoxically, with regard to Clara's simultaneous motherhood and artistic aims Rilke's qualms, if he had any, were not so categorical. One may interpret statements in this connection in the early days of their married life as partly

[4] Rilke had read that in Jules Michelet's *L'Amour*.

self-deceptive; nevertheless, their tone of assurance is remarkable: "For the woman the child is, in my conviction, a fulfilment and a deliverance from all strangeness and uncertainty: it is spiritually, too, a sign of maturity; and I am deeply convinced that the woman-artist who has had and still has a child whom she loves is, in the same measure as the mature man, able to reach all the heights of art which the latter can reach under similar conditions, that is, if he is an artist" (*Br. Frühzeit*, 188-189). Later Rilke returned to his original view that art and womanhood do not mix well—all of which seems to indicate that his ideas were not the result of impersonal considerations but the natural flowering of empirical experiences and needs; they were subject to change with the circumstances. If that is kept in mind, together with the fact that with him life tended to be absorbed in art, we may be forgiven for describing them as rationalizations.

In the *Requiem* he blames Paula for having betrayed her creative genius to a world where "saps will have their way" (*AW* I,214)—a sin all the more deplorable as she had given abundant proof of her ability to transform all things into enduring inner substance, of mirroring them out of her own being back into it as timeless and out of all desire's reach. Instead of continuing to "transmute every sap into a strong existence that mounts and circles, blindly and in equipoise" (*AW* I,214), she let herself be lured back into the world of time—"and time is long. And time drifts on, and time piles up, and time is like a recurrence of a long illness" (*AW* I,215). The poet would like to cling to the memory of her creative days, when, as in one of her self-portraits, she stood naked before the mirror and entered into it, leaving nothing but her large gaze in front of it saying not: that is me, but: that is. So uninquisitive, so unpossessive, so truly poor was that gaze that it desired even herself no longer: "a holy gaze" (*AW* I,213). But now, alas, her restless curiosity keeps her from being at peace even in death. Somehow the poet is haunted by the fear that she may roam about accusing him of not returning also to the world of natural relations and obligations, trying to lure him, too, back to it. "Oh, do not rob me of that which I am slowly learning. I am right and you are wrong, if you are moved by a homesick longing" (*AW* I,211). It is Rilke's own sense of doubt and guilt which utters this beseeching cry of protest. "Do not come back," he begs, "if you can bear it, be dead among the dead. The dead are occupied. But help me in a way that won't distract you, as the most distant sometimes helps me: within" (*AW* I,219).

Rilke's *Requiem* for Paula is a stirring document of self-defense in which the poet at bay counters accusation with accusation. The two princes are at war in the poem because they have discovered that they woo the same maiden: art, which is life. If Paula has surrendered to a borrowed death, if she has insisted on breaking bits of herself out of the law that was hers, if she has "dug out of the night-warm earth of her heart the still green seed from which her death was to grow" (*AW* I,215), her own death germane to her own life, to be sure, that was a shame, but it was her business and involved no commitment for Rilke. She chose the "little death" (*AW* I,28, 92), of which the poet, guided by his instinct of self-preservation, refused to believe that it ought to remain a cause of anguish. "I am still living," says the monk of the *Book of Hours*, "I have time to build: my blood is red longer than the roses" (*AW* I,28). And if the poet accuses, not Otto Modersohn personally but all men in him, more bitterly than he chides Paula, it is because he sees in man (and incidentally in the male within himself) the chief culprit and danger. Man's spurious love causes untold suffering and is built "upon prescription like a habit, and claims as a right that which he unjustly usurps" (*AW* I,217). Woman, on the other hand (and by that Rilke also implies his own receptive femininity), is naturally obedient to the earth and its laws of life and death, but needs protection against the encroachment by man.

40. REQUIEM FOR WOLF

Was hast du nicht gewartet . . . ?
(*AW* I,222)
Why did you not wait . . . ?

THE other *Requiem* was written in memory of a young poet and translator of Verlaine and Baudelaire, Wolf Graf von Kalckreuth, who at the beginning of his military career had committed suicide.

Rilke had never met him in person but had had friendly relations with his family. Here again we have an artist, a young man this time, who dies an unauthentic death. Paula's death had stirred up in Rilke emotions in defense of his own determination to remain free from outside attachments. We have diagnosed these emotions as an affirmation of a mode of life, not as an expression of romantic flirtation with death. This positive aspect of Rilke's relation to death comes out still more distinctly in his *Requiem* for Wolf. For here he resents not only the wrong way of dying but the arbitrary will to die. Paula died reluctantly, her sigh of grief in the face of death seemed to be that of the artist who is forced to leave so much beautiful work undone. Wolf, on the other hand, with that impatience characteristic of man, had voluntarily cut short a life full of creative possibility. Paula was accused of surrendering to the trivial demands of the world; Wolf was charged with not having surrendered with enough patience and endurance to the promptings of the "Holy Spirit." It can be seen that the two requiems complement each other as the two poles of one and the same Rilkean fear: that of losing himself in the wrong kind of surrender, and that of not persisting in the right kind to the glorious end. To one pole corresponds Rilke's need of unqualified concentration and self-assertion, even to the point of ruthless sophistry; to the other, his demand for unquestioning humility and obedience, for utter anonymity and self-obliteration. On one hand the pride of the artist, on the other the submissive faith of the saint. Here the wide-open responsiveness of the puppet to the will of an outside moving agent, there the narcissistic, self-mirroring containment of the Angel. If these two, the Angel and the puppet, could act as one, if the pride and rich fullness of the artist could be wedded to the humility and anonymous poverty of the saint, then would "come together what we ever separate by our existence" (*Fourth Elegy*), then the emptiness of our surrendering will would swell with the proud riches of our self-manifestation. It is the dream of a world of magic in which the circle is squared and the square circled with equal ease, through the conjuring power of the word.

It is noteworthy that in the *Requiem* for Wolf there is no such rancorous spite as in that for Paula. On the contrary, Rilke's feeling seems to be one of sympathetic understanding as much as of regret. In fact it almost sounds like an apology when at the end of the poem he says: "But it is petty to think what was not. Besides there is in these comparisons a semblance of reproach which does not touch you. That which takes place has such an edge on that which we think, that we can never overtake it and experience how it actually looked. Be not ashamed when the dead brush by you, the other dead, those who persevered to the end. (What does it mean, the end?) Exchange looks with them, calmly, as is the custom, and fear not that our mourning weighs upon you strangely, otherwise you will shock them. The great words from the days when events were still transparent are not for us. Who speaks of conquest? Endurance is all" (*AW* I,225). In part, this condoning attitude may be explained by the nature of the case: Rilke did not know Wolf personally whereas he had come very close to Paula, and he did not wish to hurt the feelings of the young officer's survivors. But that does not tell the whole story. In spite of his many periods of depression Rilke never seriously contemplated committing suicide. To be sure, in Vally Rhonfeld's reminiscences, which she allowed to be published after Rilke's death, the vindictive old lady asserts that her young wooer in Prague sometimes threatened to take his life when she spoke of breaking off their amorous relations (Hirschfeld, 716). Similarly after the second Russian trip Lou warned her neurotic friend that his mental condition might have fatal consequences. But in neither instance was there any real cause for concern; Rilke's will to live was far too strong, in fact so strong that the enticements of the world could be effectively challenged only by his unconquerable creative demon.

On the other hand, in Paula's return to her husband Rilke sensed a reproach to himself for not returning to his wife and daughter. That such reproaches were made to him, and that he was very sensitive to them, is beyond question. In July and August 1903, shortly after he had returned from Paris, he spent a few weeks with his wife in Worpswede at the house of Heinrich Vogeler and with Clara and Ruth at Oberneuland at the house of Clara's parents. In his freshly resumed confessions to Lou he admitted that Paris had made him "denser," that there were "fewer pores" in him, "fewer intermediate spaces which fill and swell when foreign matter intrudes" (*Br. Lou*, 70). But that progress in regard to himself and his work had been achieved at the cost of a corresponding deterioration of his human relations: "... nobody can find support in me: my little daughter has to be with strangers, and my young wife, who has her own work, is dependent on others who look after her professional devel-opment, and I myself can nowhere be useful and earn nothing. And although those who are nearest to me and whom it concerns, do not reproach me, nevertheless the reproach is there and the house in which I have just lived [H. Vogeler's] is completely full of it" (*Br. Lou*, 71). "I, too," he writes a little later, "do not want to divorce art from life; I know that somehow and somewhere they are of one mind. But I am a bungler of life" (*Br. Lou*, 100-101). Less than a year before Paula's death Lou Andreas-Salomé, in a letter to Clara, had accused Rilke of having made an irresponsible choice between his duties by evading those which were most natural and lay closest to him. "If Lou knew," Rilke explains from Capri to his wife, "how many letters I write to myself in thought. Long letters with similar arguments. I know them all. I know their faces, into which I have stared for hours at a time, I know how they come toward me, nearer and nearer, straight and blindly . . . but my nearest and most natural duties have always, ever since my boyhood, been these here, on whose side I keep trying to stand, and if I have sometimes wanted to as-sume others, they were not meant to be a new task in addition to the first one, which was big enough by itself, but because I thought that I would find a support, a help, something which in my shaky homelessness would constitute a firm, unmovable point, a lasting reality" (*Br.* I,148). To an acquaintance at Soglio, Rilke is reported to have confessed in 1919: "I, too, was married once upon a time—but things didn't turn out well" (*Br. Nölke*, 163).

There is still another reason for the poet's greater indulgence to-ward Wolf. Rilke knew Paula's latest and best work, though for a time he seemed to underestimate her genius. His statement of Oc-tober 1924 that he knew little of Paula's ripest work either at that time or in 1906 when he last saw her must be taken with a grain of salt (*Br. Muzot*, 322). His *Requiem* belies it, and it looks very much like another mystifying expression of his resentment against her. Paula had learned the secret of great art, which according to Rilke consisted in the complete abnegation of personal desire, the total immersion of the artist's will and soul in his created work. It was an unforgivable sin against the "Holy Ghost" to have violated that secret. Consecrated to the terrible Angel of Solitude she be-longed to Him for life. With Wolf it was different: he was only on the threshold of art, of which he had caught a glimpse without recognizing it because of inexperience. He did not fully realize yet that "beauty is nothing but the beginning of terror," and that if we only endure it, though barely, "it serenely disdains to destroy us." Had he known that, he would have found the patience to wait. "Why did you not wait until the burden becomes quite unbearable: that is the moment when it turns and is so heavy because it is true. You see, perhaps that was your next moment: perhaps it was just arranging the wreath in its hair in front of your door when you closed it with a bang. Oh that bang, how it travels through the universe, when somewhere from the heavy and sharp draft of impatience something that is open is suddenly slammed and shut" (*AW* I,222). Paula knew authentic death from its spurious counterfeit, yet she chose the latter. Wolf did not distinguish one from the other and picked the wrong one by mistake. Paula had come out of the mirror, into which she had entered so fully that artist and image were one. Sitting up in childbed she had taken herself out of its image and was now completely before it, looking at it as she combed her hair and put her jewels around her neck, saying: that is me, instead of: that is. Wolf had not yet learned how to close the gap between subject and object. Like so many of his fellow poets he still *talked about* his feelings instead of *forming* them; he still merely *described* his anguish, instead of transforming it into the word "as the carver of a cathedral doggedly transforms his self into the unperturbed stone" (*AW* I,224-225). We have witnessed it time and again: Rilke writhed under his griping dualism and split consciousness, which only Orphic art could erase: "He would more expertly bend the wand who by instinct knew the willow's roots" (*Son.* I, 6). Paula had learned to do so; to have undone it was a betrayal of her only duty, and was fatal—as it would have been for Rilke. Wolf was overcome by darkness on the way; his self-destructive deed was regrettable, but understandable. Rilke had reason to fear Paula's relapse as a ghost threatening his own gains; he felt fairly immune from Wolf's immature violence.[5]

[5] A little more than a year and a half before Rilke wrote the *Requiem* for Wolf he commented on the suicide of another young poet, Walter Calé, interpreting it likewise as an expression of impatience and too much haste (*Br. 1906-07*, 201-202).

◇◇◇

Jetzt wird in 559 Betten gestorben. Natürlich
fabrikmässig. Bei so enormer Produktion ist
der einzelne Tod nicht so gut ausgeführt, aber
darauf kommt es auch nicht an. Die Masse macht es.

(AW II,11)

Now there's dying in 559 beds. Of course,
the deaths are factory-made. With such a huge
production the individual deaths are not so
carefully finished, but that's not what matters.
It's the mass that counts.

◇◇◇

It was in Paris that Rilke was concerned with death in its ugliest
forms, trying desperately to discover some hidden sweetness in it.
All the negative elements of his own existence became magnified
as he saw them reflected in the faces of haggard women, of girls
cheated out of youth and love, of starving students, of beggars and
cripples, of sick people driving in taxicabs at a few pennies an hour
to wholesale death in the hospitals. The mouldy odor of all the
secretions of poverty—of its births, its lusts and its deaths—well-
nigh smothered him at the sight of a demolished tenement (*AW*
II,42-45). To be strictly exact, the thick daubs of this picture belong
to the poet's pseudonym, Malte. But all we have to do is to step
back and look at it from some distance, and the Rilkean physiognomy appears true to life. His letters of the period, in fact his whole
work, substantiate it. After all, what else could be expected of such
a hypersensitive soul as we have found Rilke to be. Married scarcely
over a year, unaccustomed yet to the unexpected taste of fatherhood
and of a home of his own, he had been forced by economic difficulties to leave wife and child on the heath of Worpswede or in the
care of relatives. Alone, with only the burning flame of poetic aspiration in his heart, he was compelled to live frugally in a poorly fur-
nished room, walled in among neighbors whose mysterious coming
and going echoed faintly in his solitude. And outside, the hum of the
city, hard and heavy with the weight of human suffering borne by
a light-hearted race. It is true, a few miles away there was Rodin,

and closer by there were the Jardin du Luxembourg, the Jardin des Plantes, Notre Dame and the Louvre. But these belong in another chapter. Paris meant for Rilke both the hope of fulfilment of his artistic dreams and the descent into the depths of human woe and death.

In the Malte *Notebook* death, together with all infirmities of flesh and soul, is in the crucible for purification. But the partly purified product is no longer associated with Malte. It appears in the lonely, self-contained things of the *New Poems,* only to be thrown back into the alembic of the *Elegies* and to emerge crystalline and transparent in the *Sonnets.* In his Malte-moods Rilke fingered human misery and death in all their sinuous folds with that same passion for form which moved Rodin in his search for the *modelé.* By itself the *Notebook* is only the negative cast: it must be read with that understanding.

Malte revels in the ghastliest manifestations of human wretchedness with a determination that has every symptom of mad morbidity, and yet he is conscious of the fact that with all his dread he is "like one who stands on the threshold of something great" (*AW* II,49). As far as Rilke himself is concerned it all is like a mud bath designed to bring health and strength. The death of Malte's grandfather, Christoph Detlev Brigge, is something that engulfs with fierce voracity all that used to come under the equally autocratic sway of the chamberlain's robust personality (*AW* II,14-17). It would be a childish simplification if we classified this death as the biological outcome of dropsy, just as Rilke on his deathbed would have repudiated the suggestion that the meaning of his own death could be exhaustively diagnosed as leukemia. Similarly the life of Malte's father was so perforated with the fear of death that he carried in his briefcase the story of King Christian IV who, three hours before dying, asked his doctor: "Oh doctor, doctor, what is your name?" and answered his own question with the clear voice of agony: "Death, Death" (*AW* II,140). No wonder that the father's will contained a clause ordering his doctor to pierce his heart in order to make quite sure that he would not be buried alive. And Malte, his son, insisted upon being present at the awful operation (*AW* II,135-136). And when Malte's dog died, its hard, strange look accused its master of having allowed death to come (*AW* II,141-142). Also the attitude of the living toward death is a matter of insistent curiosity on the part of both Malte and Rilke. Malte's grandmother Margaret was so possessed with self-asserting vitality that she resented all rivalry and looked upon life and death as a competitive sport in which she was always to come out on top. She even could not bear the indiscretion of her own daughter who was bold enough to die before her (*AW* II,108). Malte remembers a fat girl dying suddenly in a streetcar in Naples. In a frantic effort to scare death away, the mother disarranged her daughter's clothes, poured something into her mouth, shook her body shouting her name and finally slapped her face (*AW* II,141). Such is our obstinacy in refusing to grant death its turn to live.

In the prose of Malte's *Notebook* a great variety of deaths and of fears are microscopically scrutinized and elaborately worked out, in keeping with Rilke's will to defeat death by facing it and giving it form. His poetry is filled with the same things, the difference being that here the details have been filtered and the substance mitigated by the more abridged and purified symbol. All the resources of his rich fancy are called upon to pry into the kind of existence and of consciousness that may prevail on the other, the invisible side of life. Especially the lovers and those who died young are frequently interrogated, because they, more than others, disclose the distinctive features of the landscape of death in relation to that of life. They both "hold the door of the grave open," the former by their total abandon in love, the latter by their incompleteness and innocence in youth, so that we who experience them "keep the half, which is life, fresh and open to the other half, which is like an open wound" (*Br.Muzot*, 377). Also the death of the poet is revealing, and so is that of dear ones. In the *Elegies* even the human blood is probed for traces of death, left there by an endless chain of ancestors (*Third Elegy*). Rilke's whole antiquarian curiosity, far from being an expression of historical interest, springs from his desire to experience death as a constituent part of the total landscape of human existence. Ancestral portraits have a peculiar fascination for him for that reason. Likewise Malte's historical reminiscences in the *Notebook* must neither be examined nor interpreted with a desire for sober historical perspectives, they are mainly vocables of the poet's anxieties (*Br.Muzot*, 359).

This kind of gestation of inner experiences and poetical motifs, accompanied by recurrent throes and intermittent births, goes on all the time during Rilke's life. If we consider the *Duino Elegies* and the *Sonnets to Orpheus* the highest achievement of his poetical career, there is reason to credit him with the glorious accomplishment which in the *Book of Poverty and Death* he had prophesied for the artist of the future, namely that of giving birth to a great and beautiful death. When Rilke completed the *Elegies* in February 1922 he had at first neither the intention of writing the *Sonnets* nor any inkling that they were on their way. For the continuation of the *Elegies* themselves he had waited and prayed in anxious suspense. Only a few days before the storm broke loose again at Muzot after ten years of waiting he complained of not being able to bring about the happy turn and of being reduced to practise more patience (*Br.Muzot*, 109). The *Elegies* are less a birth than the pains of a birth extending over a decade. Hence their inner restlessness and fermenting turbidity. In contrast with the Angel, whose symbolic meaning, wrested from repeated crises dating back to childhood, had undergone a profound change, the Orpheus of the *Sonnets* appeared as by magic, thrown ashore like Venus in all his finished splendor.

Rilke had happened to notice in a shop window in Switzerland a little engraving of Orpheus with the lyre, and "in a flash the *Sonnets* had grouped themselves around this figure which had given them their name and had merged with the girl who had died young and with the monument erected to her memory" (Kippenberg, 327-328). The girl was Wera Ouckama Knoop, whose mother, shortly before the new flow of *Elegies* began, had sent Rilke a journal of her daughter's long and fatal illness. Wera was "a lovely child who began with dancing and excited wonder in all those who saw her." One day, out of a blue sky, she declared to her mother that "she neither could nor would dance any longer . . . (that was toward the end of her childhood), her body underwent a peculiar change and became, without losing its beautiful oriental outline, strangely heavy and massive . . . (which was already the beginning of the mysterious glandular disease that was to entail death so quickly). . . . During the time still left to her Wera pursued music, finally she only sketched—as if dancing which was denied her kept issuing from her more and more gently, more and more discreetly. . . ." (*Br.Sizzo*, 42-43).

By this time Orpheus had come to mean for Rilke not only the man who, by the power of his art, had visited the underworld and liberated Eurydice, his wife, but the demi-god who, like Dionysos, was torn to pieces by the maenads and scattered through the universe, where his song henceforth emanated from all things (*Son*.I, 26). He had become the symbol of the all-pervasive creative power of nature and art, the personification of Death diluted in life. These two external stimuli, Wera and Orpheus, precipitated the *Sonnets* in the very midst of the *Elegies*. In a real sense the *Sonnets* are the sweet fruit of the elegiac throes. They, not the *Elegies*, were the secret goal, hidden even to himself, of Rilke's life-long labor. He admitted that they were "perhaps the most mysterious dictate which he had ever endured" and that, "at a time when he had readied himself for another great work" (*Br.Muzot*, 205). Even to him their meaning revealed itself only gradually, as he read them aloud to himself or to others. In the *Elegies* the painful gestation is in its last stages, accompanied by anticipations of the approaching Messiah and by vistas of the Promised Land. They are still tempest-tossed, agitated by inner tensions, roily from the muddy sediments. In the *Sonnets* we are in the timeless land of magic, where the dead rub shoulders with the living, where music in the ear is transformed into temples and trees, where initiation into art is inseparable from feasting on poppy-seeds with the dead. Here, "to sing is to be" (*Son*.I, 13), and art has at last triumphed over death.

The magic formula by which this remarkable new world arises out of time into inner reality is *Transformation*: "Let change be thy aim. Oh, be in love with the flame where a thing fades out of sight resplendent with change" (*Son*.II, 12). Relentlessly Rilke endeavored to grind down all that confronted him as present, past, or future, until it became volatile essence that could be breathed in and out in soothing rhythm. In the *Elegies* these attempts have reached their climax; all the resources of his creative genius, tested in numerous victories and retreats, are gathered in a supreme productive effort. The whole lot of monsters and demons which at one time or another he had tackled singly with less concentration of power, come in for a final reckoning. And each of the recalcitrant elements issues, chastened and freed, out of the *Elegies* into the *Sonnets*.

The essence of Rilke's formula can be described as a transformation of everything external that is subject to physical laws and time, hence to transitoriness and death, into inner substance which partakes of the feeling of subjective and personal identity. The multiple object is sucked into the one subject; it loses thereby its weight, but only after that weight has been endured until it is no longer felt. The subject is essentially the artist, who is able to carry out this metamorphosis of the objective world into subjective reality without at the same time destroying or diminishing the former. The uncertainties and ambiguities of human existence remain, but, lured into the magic circle of the artist's soul-space, they lose their time-eaten brittleness and become the points of intersection where eternity and time, subject and object, meet. Inasmuch as the subject is also an object, it is perishable, and dependent on all the laws of time and causality. As creative subject, however, it is timeless; its death is not of the ugly variety which means cessation and discontinuity; it is metamorphosis within experienced cosmic identity and hence safeguards continuity: "that which is gone is not past; it is metamorphosed" (*Gedichte 1906-26*, 301; *Son*.I, 19).

We have already noted that Rilke had not only read St. Augustine's *Confessions* but actually translated parts of them in 1911. In that year he presented his "dear mama" with a German copy of "that splendid book in remembrance of the hour spent together discussing its contents." A short poem accompanying the gift reveals that their conversation had dealt with Augustine's reflections on Time and Eternity (*Gedichte, 1906-26*, 328). St. Augustine was as much concerned with this problem as Rilke. For the Christian saint Eternity was, of course, a transcendental reality whose nature could be divined, if not understood. His aim was to delineate a mode of experience in which the mystery of Creation could be analogously revealed. The aim of Rilke was to circumvent all transcendental implications and to endow his own poetic symbols with enduring meaning in the midst of a fleeting existence and a changing world. Both men agreed, however, that in order to achieve their aims the experience of time must somehow be transmuted into an experience of space by spreading it out extensively within the subject's consciousness. To that end Rilke devised his Inner Cosmic Space, where all real women were metamorphosed into the one Madonna Lisa and all counting became irrelevant. Augustine situated the trinity of temporal phases into the human mind: the past in the form of memory, the present in the form of momentary consideration, and the future in the form of expectation (*St. Augustine*, I,189-212, passim). Conceived thus they are three potentially active phases of the same extensively present mind, a conception which somewhat corresponds at the empirical (ontic) level to Heidegger's notion of the three "ecstasies" on the "horizon" of time.

In the *Elegies* hostile reality still stalks with all its keen-edged distinctions, its dualisms and contradictions. There are still the horrors of death, the betrayals and usurpations in love, the elusiveness of time. Growth is too slow or too fast, the greed for acquisition and the conceit of possession are rife. Life is still honeycombed with departures and separations, with nightmares and fears, with endless dislocations and incompatibilities. These are less broadly unfolded here than in the *Notebook*, less meteorically scattered than in the *Book of Hours*, but in their abridged and condensed symbols their effect is, if anything, more incisive. Even what Rilke in former moods used to contrast favorably with man, now shows rifts that tend to accentuate the feeling of distress. The animal's open look has become melancholy and suspicious (*AW* I,271), the longed-for nights are gently disappointing or darkly menacing (*AW* I,245), the springs do not fulfil their promises (*AW* I,246). Beauty vanishes like dew from the grass in the morning, and lovers, who promised each other eternity from their embraces, are forever encountering failure (*AW* I,249-250). The hope of the mother and the girl, who think they can capture and arrest the boy's roving desires, comes to naught as they realize that his dreams throw him back through the darkness of his blood into primeval passions (*AW* I,252). The doll and the puppet heedlessly expose their contents of sawdust, and the child, that constellation of artless truth, loses its glow as it begins to reflect and to long for growth (*AW* I,257-258). And the oiled smoothness of modern acrobatic efficiency has been achieved only by dint of a ruthless will and drill which have congealed the smile of the child and quashed the dawning love of the maiden (*AW* I,261). Worst of all, the things, those glorified emblems of law and wholeness, though signally destined to outlast us, vanish more and more, as in our thirst for deeds and mastery we violate their innocence (*AW* I,268).

The *Elegies* are the expression of Rilke's existential crisis at its height, and that crisis is dominated by the fear of death. Everything that conceivably promised a measure of permanence and stability has proved only slightly less ephemeral than we. The few things that remain are hopelessly out of reach. The saint, perhaps, hears the voice of God, but we, though we listen as intently as he, could not hear it and live. Only the drafty breath of the uninterrupted message from the silence of death reaches our ears (*AW* I,247). The Angel, so obediently shielding in childhood, so graciously helpful in the days of Tobias, has become so aloof that if He stepped from behind the stars but one step, our heart would break from the force of its startled beat (*AW* I,249). The hero's veins have been bent in a manner apart by the gardener, Death; his exit is a pretext for his being, it is his ultimate birth, achievable only by few. The love of abandoned women, the only love that is great because deprived of fulfilment, is sterile, since Nature, in bringing it forth, each time exhausts herself and takes it back into her womb (*AW* I,246).

42. TRANSFORMATION

. . . und diese, von Hingang
lebenden Dinge. . . .
wollen, wir sollen sie ganz im unsichtbaren
Herzen verwandeln.
(*Ninth Elegy*)

. . . and these things
whose existence means fading. . . .
expect us to transmute them wholly in our
invisible hearts.

PRECISELY because in the *Elegies* the dead end seems to be reached, the turn of the road comes into sight. It is one of Rilke's most reassuring convictions that enduring to the utmost brings about ineffable relief. Enduring precludes impatience as well as calculated effort. Impatience was the fatal error of Wolf von Kalckreuth; both it and calculating effort are the pitfalls of modern civilization, whose efficiency is the result of technical acrobatic skill so that "pure want has been converted into empty profusion" (*Fifth Elegy*). True endurance requires humility which in turn demands openness and freedom for death. This unexpected turn is eminently Rilkean:

from death, which he fears, he borrows his highest affirmation of life. But since his unbendable instinct for survival as an artist has forced him to reject all current meaning and fear of death, he must give death a new form and meaning. It is at this point that Orpheus, the Rilkean Messiah, appears and that the *Sonnets* are born: out of the alluvial soil on the fringe of the land of the mourning Plaints (*Tenth Elegy*). "Only in the realm of Praise is the Plaint free to travel, the nymph of the spring of tears" (*Son.*I, 8).

After all the fallacies of the currently construed life have failed, two unmistakable realities remain: the intangible expanse of death and the visible earth in all its transitory appearance. Neither must be reasoned away or dreamt out of existence. There were times when one was readily convertible into the other by visible means, because the boundaries were not sharply defined. The Egyptian Sphinx, the columns and pylons of Karnak are lasting monuments of their people's magical communion with their dead. And the Gothic cathedrals, too, continue to testify to a creative faith which, earth- and stone-bound, arrested movement and time in gestures held in eternal equipoise. These Rilke holds up proudly to the Angel as incontrovertible proof of man's fundamental timelessness (*AW* I,269). Also the Greeks were able to find a narrow strip of pure humanity between the rocks and the stream, because they used their magic wand which was "Restraint." On the Attic stelae "love and farewell are laid lightly on the shoulders, as though they were made of a stuff other than ours. Their hands rest without pressure, although strength rises in their torsos." It is true that their own hearts outweighed them no less than ours outweigh us, but in images that soothe and in the bodies of gods they could watch them grow in self-control. Beyond that they did not search, because in their mastery of themselves they caught the eternal in the flux of time (*AW* I,251).

But those times are gone. We, moderns, even impute to the dead our own impatience, our inquisitiveness, our homesick desires. The spirit of our age "creates vast stores of power, formless like the tense impulse which it draws from all things. . . . Our life goes by in transformations, and ever fainter become the things outside. Where once there was a durable house, we throw an imaginary picture across the horizon of our consciousness and store it complete in our brain. Temples, those products of man's prodigal heart, we know no more. Where a thing survives that once issued out of kneeling prayer and service, it already ranges itself among the invisible things of knowledge. Many have ceased to notice it, though without the benefit that would come from erecting it inwardly, with pillars and statues, greater!" (*AW* I,268)

This, then, is Rilke's ultimate diagnosis of himself and of modern man: "We forget so easily what the laughing neighbor does not confirm, or grudges us. We want to lift it up high in order that it be seen, when in truth the most visible joy is not revealed until we transform it, invisible, in us. Nowhere is world, my love, but within." The monuments, cathedrals and temples which more innocent peoples could hew out of themselves into solid granite or stone, we must build within ourselves out of our experiences of relationships and change (*AW* I,267-268). This involves two things: we must accept the realities of life on this earth; with "our tongue that lies between our teeth as our heart lies between the blows of the hammer" (*AW* I,274) we must praise them—This represents the most realistic and engaging feature of Rilke's wisdom—But we must also realize the changed meaning of outside reality: since "the things which we can experience fade more and more away, displaced by action without contour and form" (*AW* I,274), we must draw them into ourselves and give them inner life and form, invisible but enduring. This represents a distinctly artistic feature whose validity is highly questionable where the hard facts of life are concerned. Even Katharina Kippenberg woefully remarked in February 1925: "To form within oneself a new Earth is difficult" (*Br. Kippenberg*, 560). And granted that it can be done, what measure of help would it provide?

It is in the *Seventh* and *Ninth Elegies* that Rilke's determination to praise is most clearly formulated. These *Elegies* come nearest in thought and in mood to the *Sonnets* and confirm what we have observed all along, that Rilke's anxieties as well as his remedies are in the first place those of the artist and only then, in a derivative way, of the human being. The *Ninth Elegy* begins by asking why it is that the artist can exist as artist and must at the same time cope with things human, "avoiding fate, yet seeking it." The answer is: certainly not because there is such a thing as happiness, "that hasty fore part of an imminent loss"; nor because of a natural curiosity on the part of the artist, or a desire to test his heart: such motives may be purely artistic and need not involve fateful engagement. The real reason is because "to be on this earth is much," and precisely "because all the things of this earth, transient themselves and strangely concerning us, apparently need and use us, who are the most transient of all. . . . This: once to have lived here, once only to have been of this earth, seems not revocable" (*AW* I,273). But how can there be any security and duration in that, when it is a foregone conclusion that we must leave all things behind and that there is no Beyond? Here Rilke becomes very emphatic, in order to make quite sure that he will not be caught abandoning this earth in favor of empty speculation which defies plastic expression. Supra-terrestrial matters belong in the sphere of the Angel, not on man's earth. There is no use praising to the Angel a world for which we have no appropriate words and which He knows better than we. No, we must remain with our things, because they need us. More than ever do they expect us to unlock their imprisoned beauty; only thus can we save them and ourselves from oblivion and obliteration. How? By "saying" them, but by saying them so lovingly and understandingly that our word reveals their humble truth—and truth is eternal. Perhaps we need not single out for special distinction the things of art such as "the column, the tower of a cathedral," though with them we may astound the Angel more; but the ordinary familiar things may do: "the house, the bridge, the fountain, the gate, the jug, the fruit-tree, the window," provided that we fill them with our enraptured feeling. Even our mourning and sorrow may find shelter and form in a thing, die into it and emerge as a song (*AW* I,274-275).

It seems, therefore, to the poet that the mysterious will of the Earth is this: that we transform its visible, transient things into invisible things of the heart. "Earth," the poet exclaims, "is it not this you want: to rise invisible in us?—Is it not your dream, to be invisible once?—Earth! Invisible! What is your urgent command, if not transformation? Earth, dear Earth, I will. . . . Ineffably I am yours, from the beginning of time. You have always been right, and your holy invention is the friendly death" (*AW* I,275). There we have it: death as a holy device caught in the magic net, without the help of Christian faith, without Mediator or Redeemer, by the mere virtue of the poetic word, of which Orpheus can now be the sole custodian and dispenser. A last visit through the Land of the Plaints in the *Tenth Elegy*, and the poet's mourning rises as pure Song and Praise in the *Sonnets*.

Gesang ist Dasein.
(*Son.*II, 3)

To sing is to be.

THE *Sonnets* are, in my judgment, the most exquisitely beautiful part of Rilke's work, the fruit in which all the sweetness of his ripened genius is gathered. Enough of the elegiac mood is left to give them a rich, luxuriant depth without diminishing their resplendent lucidity. Rilke's whole work may be pictured as a weather map on which countless arrows indicate currents, cross-currents and counter-currents, the total drift of which, however, moves unmistakably toward a final pattern in which all the opposing forces seem to circle in immanent harmony. His drift toward Orphic experience and expression is constant: as it progresses slowly it finds frequent temporary fulfilments but culminates in the *Sonnets*, "that tree of ecstasy" (*Son.*II, 18).

In order to appreciate these *Sonnets*, we must realize that here we are in a world of magic and metamorphosis, in which the passing from time into space, from music into plastic reality is an easy occurrence. In the presence of the quietly firm earth we must be able to experience that we are flowing; in the presence of running water we must feel that we partake of timeless being, and all the while we must know that one is a function and condition of the other (*Son.*II, 29). Between the arts as between the sensations there is only imperceptible space, easily bridged. On seeing the gracefully significant movements of a dancer, we must be able to live the southern landscape which they evoke and feel the warmth radiating from them; we must taste the astringent sweetness of the orange, drowning in itself yet struggling against its sweetness (*Son.*I, 15). We must understand that these miracles are performed through the poet's word and symbol, that Orpheus is the poet, and the poet is Rilke.

All this is possible only if the density of objects and bodies is enormously loosened and lightened, so that their being is opened up and readily penetrable. Every thread of reality exists only as part of the whole, but without it the whole is no longer whole either. The important feature of such a world is its self-contained identity within which tensions and relations not only move from one thing to another but circle completely through them all. It includes the living on the earth and the dead in it, whence they continue to feed the roots of life. Its space is its time; between the two the inter-penetration is such that we must conceive of space as temporal and of time as spatial. Soon after Katharina Kippenberg became ac-quainted with the *Sonnets* she finely commented: "Here, it seems to me, something is formed which often comes from very far, some-thing essential that emanates out of the Egyptian experience. . . ." (*Br.Kippenberg*, 455). Time seems to be embedded and contained in space, which latter is finite, yet without identifiable beginning or end, therefore, in a sense timeless. It is a world of relations rather than of opaque things, but it is evident that relationship in a meta-morphic world is something different from what it is in the causal universe. In the latter it is an abstraction quite distinct from the things, in the former it is the things themselves in their basic mutual pervasiveness. The metamorphic artist is continually standing in the central gate which opens in every direction into the whole; he is neither here nor there, but infinitely capable of being anywhere and everywhere. His reality is possibility. Like the *Buddha in His Glory* of the *New Poems* he is "the middle of all middles, the kernel of all kernels" (*NG*, 255). He is the *Voice of the Poor One* whom the Angel escorts through the streets and who confesses: "What I see, attains not to what I have always known" (*AW* I,395).

When Rilke insists that we must learn to experience "pure rela-tion" instead of ownership and possession, it is that kind of meta-morphic relationship which he has in mind (*Son.*I, 12; II, 13). "Be-ing, we must at the same time know the conditions of non-exist-ence." No use counting any more: number is abolished (*Son.*II, 13). No need of erecting monuments in stone commemorating the past or the dead; "only let the roses bloom each year for his sake. . . . Once and for all, it's Orpheus when there's song" (*Son.*I, 5). "Is he of this earth? No, out of both realms his wide nature has grown. . . . He mingles the features of the dead in all that we see" (*Son.*I, 6).

If the metamorphic age is past it does not mean that it cannot be regained. The Russians did not seem to Rilke to have quite lost the sense of primitive wholeness, and in 1912-13 he found in Spain a people and a land where "Heaven and Earth" were still one (*Br.* I,401). The moments of Rilke's lamentations in February 1922 were also moments of unconquerable faith. "For how deep is still embedded in us the day of the Athenians, and the Egyptian God or Bird." Childhood is still there, and "the wombs of justly giving mothers": their creativity can be kindled and "future rivers can be born again, irrespective of the quickset hedges which fence them in." "The secret bounds with which Evil surrounds even those who remain still and do nothing" can be wiped out again, as can also the boundaries of death and those of the sexes (*AW* I,372). To the child in us they are as unknown as is the distinction "between the quality of whiteness and the white of the dress" (*AW* I,374). "Even now, existence is full of magic; in a hundred spots there is still origin. A play of pure forces which nobody touches who does not kneel and admire" (*Son.*II, 10).

In fact modern civilization is unwittingly creating conditions favorable to a renewed realization of metamorphic consciousness. Again and again Fate has destroyed the gods whom we planned in bold sketches: "only in furnaces the former fires keep burning" (*Son.*I, 24). Nevertheless, "all the playful fountains of the Villa d'Este are meant for us, too, we are the heirs of these praised gardens. . . . Not one of the gods be allowed to perish. We need them all and each" (*AW* I,373). Perhaps the curves of our flights and those who trace them are not in vain, though they remain only as thought (*Son.*II, 22). We must not undo what we have proudly achieved. Rather must we learn to act out of motives other than vainglorious ostentation or calculated gain. Our boyish pride must learn to experience the growing machine as a symbol of pure, aimless movement, whence abundant gain will then come, unexpected (*Son.*I, 23). The pace of time must be taken as trivial in what always remains (*Son.*II, 27). In our frenzy of action "our strength is going like that of swimmers" (*Son.*I, 24), but our very breathing is "an invisible poem," if we but knew it. Breathing is "pure exchange of world-space with intimate being . . . stored space. . . . How many of these places in space have always been in me? Many a wind is like my son. Do you know me, air, still full of places that were once mine? You, who once were smooth bark, are now round volume and leaf of my word" (*Son.*II, 1).

We must stop seeking fulfilment of our more and more impossible wishes; rather must we praise every beauty unknown and inaccessible, realizing that privation cannot exist when we have resolved to *be* (*Son*.II, 21). We must be "dead in Eurydice" in order to outlast all winters even before they come (*Son*.II, 13). The grief of the *Elegies* must be drawn into the magical sphere of our praise, even such a "guilty" thing as loving a woman and then leaving her, which Rilke so pathetically frowns upon elsewhere. Here, in the *Sonnets*, he jubilantly confirms as a natural right what elsewhere was usurpation, and no longer must the lonely woman put the blame for her lot on the ruthlessness of man: "Oh affectionate ones, step now and then into the breath which does not mean you, let it branch off at the fork of your cheeks; quivering it unites again behind you" (*Son*.I, 4). Indeed, here is a remarkable formula of a master-magician for whom already early in youth sensuality was "a joy-bearing torch which we hold laughingly, behind all transparences of our being" (see above, p. 27), and who in the meantime has learned how to make his words rustle above the heads of women and lull them to sleep (*FG*, 3). Don Juan could hardly be a better "hunter of images" in his desire to transform loving women into Heloïses (*AW* I,185) and to give them "the inspired curve that marks them for divine uses forever" (*Letters to Merline*, 46). It is easy to see how nicely all this fits in the pattern of Rilkean art and experience such as we have seen it unfold out of the seeds of his childhood. All the motifs which we have encountered have come to cluster about the Angel of the *Elegies* and the Orpheus of the *Sonnets*.

In conclusion, in order to characterize once more the delicate and fragile essence of Rilke's magical world when measured with the hard facts of life, we must draw attention to a *Sonnet* (I,11) in which he glorifies the apparent union of the steed, "that lump of pride made of earth," and its rider "who drives and contains it and whom it carries." In their harmonious oneness they are almost as exemplary as a constellation. It is true that on second thought this harmony proves less deep than appearance suggests: it only exists in so far, and as long as, their common journey lasts. After that, "the table and the pasture namelessly separate them" and reveal their stellar union to be illusory. But what of it? "Let us rejoice for a while," the poet sings, "in believing the symbolic figure. That is enough."

PART VIII
ANGELS

◇◇

. . . und will jede [Stelle meines grossen zukünftigen Buches] zu einem Engel machen und mich von ihm überwinden lassen und ihn zwingen, dass er mich beuge, obwohl ich ihn gemacht habe. . . .
(Letter to Clara, April 24, 1903)

. . . and I shall make every [part of my great future book] into an Angel and let myself be conquered by Him and force Him to bend me, although it will be I who shall have made Him. . . .

◇◇

44. THE GUARDIAN ANGEL
TURNS TERRIBLE

◇◇◇

Seit mich mein Engel nicht mehr bewacht,
kann er frei seine Flügel entfalten,

(FG)

Since my Angel no longer guards me
He is free to spread His wings.

◇◇◇

IT IS usually assumed that the Angel of the *Elegies* has little in
common with the Guardian Angel of childhood, but in fact there
is direct filiation between them. Of course, all Christian connotations
were soon dissociated from the concept, but the superhuman element remained. Moreover, some of the Christian features concerning the Angel's priority in the scheme of creation and their hier-
archic order are to be found even in the *Elegies*. Rilke maintained
that the Angel of his late work bore greater resemblance to Islamic
than to Christian tradition, but if that is so it is no more than a
coincidence. Rilke was not in the habit of adapting his symbols to
foreign patterns unless the essential implications of these symbols
had first crystallized out of inner experience. It is always his experienced relationship to outside reality that is involved, not the reality
as such.

The *Book of Images* contains a poem in which the meaning of the
Guardian Angel is well described: he was the nameless "bird whose
wings came when he [the child] woke up in the night and cried,"
in whose shadow he went to sleep and who somehow supplied the
food of all dreams. When nightmares made the boy fear that his
sleep was like death, it was the Angel who lifted him up from the
darkness of his heart and "hoisted him on all towers like scarlet flags
and draperies." It was the Angel "who talked of miracles as of common knowledge, of human beings as of melodies, and of roses as of
flaming occurrences that took place in His look" (*BB*, 25-26). To the
child the Angel was like a mother who changed the phantoms of the
night into harmless things, who was at his beck and call in all moments of uncertainty and fear. The age of childhood was like the

Old Testament, when Rafael could appear as a friendly guide to To-bias, the youth (*AW* I,249). But when Rilke wrote the *Book of Images* he and his Angel had already parted ways. The latter was already the "stern angel of ebony, the giant unconcerned" (*FG*, 26). Restive, the emancipated youth questioned both the presumed power and the loving interest of the Angel, whose overwhelming presence had concealed from him the unfinished God of his growing creative consciousness.

However, if the Guardian Angel kept haunting Rilke's memory only as a vague relic from the lost age of innocence, the reality of Angels in general remained. But instead of being an intimate part of the poet's existence their heaven was now divorced from the earth of the poet (*FG*, 20-21). Angel and Earth had become mutually exclusive, Rilke had to face them separately though neither had lost its power over him. It is characteristic of his whole development that as time went on he identified himself more and more with the Earth and left the Angel to His sphere, not because the latter became less important but because His nature became increasingly associated with all that is existentially overpowering and undaunted. Here, then, we have Rilke standing between Angel and Earth, wrestling with both, in a sense conquering the Earth and conquered by the Angel. In the background, in dim outline, intentionally passed over in growing silence, an indistinct God whose unaccountable power increases in proportion as the "future" God of the *Book of Hours* becomes problematical.

We have already observed that Rilke's Earth was primarily all that is not man as the ambiguous exponent of time-consciousness and unpredictable arbitrariness. In so far as our poet succeeded in reducing to relative impotence all unmanageable forces of existence they entered, purified and tamed, into the orbit of his Orphic art, and the poet could rejoice for a while "in the stellar union." But in so far as "rider and steed" were constantly threatened by the incompatibility of "table and pasture" (*Son.*I, 11), the Angel loomed as the forbidding custodian of a beauty which is "the beginning of terror, which we barely endure and admire so because it serenely disdains to destroy us" (*AW* I,245). Far from being the friend and brother of Orpheus, the Angel is his rival and continually challenges his rule. It is true, in order to enter into the sphere of art and praise, it is necessary to pass through the Land of the Plaints (*Tenth Elegy*).

Orpheus can be experienced only if the inexorability of the Angel has been endured, though the latter's power, temporarily side-tracked, remains. With Orpheus, the poet "comes and goes" through all mutually exclusive realms, but he despairs of ever crossing the threshold of the Angel's domain: envious and proud he refuses to woo Him, yet woos Him with professed humility by holding up to Him the "lasting" achievements of creative man (*Second, Seventh,* and *Ninth Elegies*).

Rilke eventually threw all the intractable ingredients of his and man's existential ills into the lap of the Angel who alone proved able to absorb and, hence, to ignore them. He needed a symbol which would provide a shelter for all the negative aspects of life and in which these would be transformed into positive attributes which were denied him. The Angel remained at all times Rilke's own creation, the formula which covered all that he neither was nor could be but longed to be, provided he could at the same time remain human. By thus enclosing the impossible in a symbolic shrine he was able to use it as an inspirational bait as circumstances suggested. He needed the Terrible, the Unattainable, and called it Angel. Orpheus is the symbol of Rilke's triumph in art, the Angel that of his inescapable anxieties and of his failures in life. In a sense, Orpheus is an escape from, as well as a triumph over, the terrors of the Angel. If the Angel is to be interpreted as a symbol of creative inspiration it can only be in the sense in which the impossible still constitutes an eternal incentive. Its actual realization would mean the complete neutralization of human anxiety, therefore of the very stimulus which Rilke needed. Against such a possibility Rilke, the artist, had to defend himself with the same ambiguous determination with which he yearned existentially to achieve it. There is Promethean resignation and daring in the concluding words of the *Seventh Elegy*: "Think not that I woo you, Angel. Even if I did, you would not come. My call is filled with the movement of a flowing stream; against such a strong current you cannot reach me. Like an outstretched arm is my call. And its hand, open at the end and ready to grasp, remains open before you, wide open, as a warning and as a defense, you Unattainable one."

This relationship of Rilke to the Angel at the time of the *Elegies* was the upshot of long growth. In the years of the *Florentine Journal* and of the *Book of Monkish Life,* when in the first flush of adolescent emancipation the household gods were dismissed with nostalgic agnosticism, when the Guardian Angel was sent back to the skies where Angels belong, Rilke could still deem it simple and easy to plant the seed of a future God in the Russian Earth. In the *Book of Hours* the Angels are disposed of as representatives of Western reason and dispensers of time-knowledge. They are relegated to the periphery of the earth's life where, together with their worshippers in the cities, they make a lot of noise at the seamy fringe of the Tree: God. They come very near attracting to their side Lucifer, "the Prince in the Land of Light and the shining God of Time" (*AW* I,39). And if in the *Book of Pilgrimage* the monk is impressed by the fact that even the Renaissance Angels no longer fly but sit about God like "ruins of birds" (*AW* I,69), it is further evidence of the ease with which the young poet flung to the winds a pretentious being that had proved so ineffective in the face of his awakening genius. But while in all this the Angels are treated with scarcely concealed superciliousness and boastful humility, they are at the same time associated with some distressing symptoms of man's existence: with his conceit, his thirst for distraction, his lack of concentration, his feeling of transitoriness and, hence, his masking of death. As yet the Angels do not appear as terrible but rather as pitiful. In his youthful enthusiasm, blessed with the first waves of inspiration and enfranchised by Lou's psychological reasonings, our poet looks down upon them. He has not yet come to real grips with the hard core of factual life which will prove so difficult to endure and to reconcile with art. As time goes on the Angel will reveal Himself better able than the poet to carry the burden imposed upon him. He will be capable of containing all that emanates from Him, while the poet "breathes his soul away whose warmth loses its fragrance from blaze to blaze" (*AW* I,249). In proportion as the truth dawns upon Rilke that his recurrent inspirational successes as well as his more systematic endeavors still leave him exposed as ever to fate, the Angel will loom larger in enviable aloofness and inaccessibility.

In keeping with Rilke's overlapping manner of experience, something of the later "Terrible Angel" is already foreshadowed in the *Book of Monkish Life*. God commands the monk to write that Cruelty, the privilege of kings, be the *Angel* before Love, and that without it God would have no bridge into Time. With Love alone man would be timeless, like God himself. The Angel of Cruelty injects the element of precariousness, thereby subjecting man to fate (*AW* I,41). Also in a poem of January 1901, under the impact of one of those storms which sweep "through forests and through time," the Angel appears as the symbol of eternity and of enormously excelling power. "To be conquered by Him," who even disdains to combat us, means "to wax great in defeat" (*AW* I,146-147).

In the years of *Malte* and the *New Poems* the weight of solitude in Paris nearly broke Rilke's spirit, and the stone world of Rodin eventually sent chills through his intensely eager soul. After scarcely more than six months in the French capital, he shook off its yoke and fled to the warmer climate of Tuscany. He resented the numerous tunnels through which he had to pass on his way to Viareggio: "It feels as if the weight of the whole mountain lay on you . . . the weight of the rocks, the ores and the springs, and on top of them the heavy, heavy snow and the cold sky above. . . ." (*Br. 1902-06*, 69-70). The *Book of Poverty and Death*, written in that mood, begins with these moaning words: "Perhaps I am going through mountains inside hard arteries, alone like an ore . . . everything has become nearness and all nearness has become stone" (*AW* I,89). And back in Germany Rilke confessed to Lou that he had suffered in Paris from the overwhelming greatness of Rodin's example, which he could not match because his own art did not provide him with comparable means: "The fact that I cannot [like Rodin] create corporeal things caused a pain in my very body, and that dread, too (whose content and substance consisted in the close proximity of something too hard, too stony, too big), sprang from the incompatibility of [our] two worlds of art" (*Br.Lou*, 95). It is only natural that these features should pass over to the Angel, who becomes decidedly unfeeling and impervious. Forswearing every sort of obligation, He is concerned exclusively with that which goes on within Him. To His light hands you cannot entrust any of your burden, "unless He should come during the night to test and seize you in order to break you out of the very form of your being and create you anew" (*NG*, 49). In a letter of December 17, 1906, Rilke tried to assuage his wife's loneliness in separation: "Have not the Angels imposed this burden upon us before, with that deep, unerring inexorability which belongs to Angels?" (*Br.* I,151) And in regard to the *New Poems*, which arose out of a determination not to shrink from hard realities for the sake of lyrical effusiveness, Rilke felt that "there can be nothing so forbidding and denying but that the multiple action of artistic mastery could leave it with a great positive balance as something affirmative, something determined to be: as an Angel" (*Br.* I,263). Rilke created his Angel, each time, in accordance with his needs, as a repository in which he could enshrine and turn into their opposite all his anxieties. His Angel is Janus-faced: on one side open to receive the poet's residual horrors, on the other hermetically closed. Sublimated, these horrors keep circling in perfect peace but narcissistic sterility. Something of our being is in the Angel, but "in His whirling existence He takes no notice of it" (*AW* I,250). This process of infusion was never to cease; if Rilke had been able to receive back his perplexities completely solved, it would have been the end of his art. He needed an Angel who was no sooner mastered than He showed up again at the next turn for a new encounter (*Br.* I,306). All the time the Angel could serve as a sort of ideal judge and prompter, whose code of law, however, was binding only with Rilke's own signature.

That is also the meaning of the accusing Angel in the *Requiem* for Paula Modersohn-Becker (*AW* I,217). Here the Angel castigates man's "selfish" behavior toward woman and Paula's evasion of her one and only duty. "If somewhere deep in me there arises a yet unknown remnant of childhood, perhaps the purest feature of my once having been a child: I will not know it. Without looking, I will make an Angel out of it and I will thrust Him into the first rank of crying Angels who remember God." The Angel is being made to carry the burden of Rilke's own matrimonial dilemma and somehow to homologate his own shortcoming in love. And strangely enough, this Angel is made of the purest features of the poet's one time childhood: the age of innocence itself is called upon to become the recriminating Angel, "blindly, without looking." Of course, the purity of childhood would add strength and weight to the accusation in the eyes of God; above all it would eliminate all suspicion of personal bias. But it is not easily compatible with the kind of denunciation entertained in the *Requiem*. Not only might the child in Rilke fail to see the wrong done by Paula but it might even make him understand and forgive. And to do so would come dangerously near to admitting that Paula and Otto were after all not so guilty when they united again to found a family. But where would that

leave Rilke in his relation to Clara? No, the authority of pure childhood had to be invoked, stoically, with eyes turned away, in order
that the appearance of unprejudiced judgment be quite unequivocal.
Did all this bring Rilke, the man and the artist, nearer to a solution
of his problems? Were the demons of his childhood thereby exor-
cised, his art sanctified and his mode of life vindicated? How deep
the sting of guilt must have sat in Rilke's flesh, and how he needed
an Angel on whom he could take it out.

45. THE DUINO ANGEL

> . . . Und dennoch, weh mir,
> ansing ich euch, fast tödliche Vögel der Seele.
>> (*Second Elegy*)
> . . . And yet, woe to me,
> do I hymn you, well-nigh deadly birds of the soul.

IT IS little wonder that in January 1912, some three years after Rilke
wrote his *Requiem* for Paula, the woeful cry should rend the storm-
beaten air at Duino: "Who, if I cried, would hear me from the orders of the Angels? And assuming that one of them should suddenly
raise me to His heart: I would perish by His stronger being" (*AW*
I,245). The Angel is no more help than man, beast, or thing; and
as to love, that greatest breeder of illusions, where are its promised
guarantees? Only when a loving woman is denied enduring reci-
procity can she, in her loneliness, become a guiding star. "Don't
you know it *yet*?" the poet asks her. "Fling the void which you
hold in your arms into the air which we breathe; perhaps the birds
will experience the thinner air with their more intimate flight."
Rilke knew very well that in the eyes of his wife Clara such exalted
views were a poor substitute for responsible family life; he knew
that she, an artist like himself, was left with the task of bringing up
their common child and could hardly be expected to appreciate the
inexorability of her husband's Either-Or, and of his finespun envy
and glorification of that other abandoned woman: Gaspara Stampa
(see below, p. 324). It was certainly no oversight on the part of Rilke

that Clara was for a considerable time excluded from the number of the privileged few who were allowed to read the first *Elegies* which arose at Duino in 1912 (*Br.MTT*, 298).

Besides the lonely women there are those among the dead who died young and who, too, can help us, though they themselves may find it hard to get used to their unfamiliar mode of being. They have died for our sake, because we need them dead, because their death makes it possible for us to be, and for art to be great (*AW* I,248). Obviously, here Rilke is in the throes of giving birth to Orpheus, though for the time being the Angel alone seems capable of ignoring the dividing line between life and death. "Angels (so people say) often do not know whether they are among the living or the dead. The eternal stream tears through both realms, all ages, and outweighs them in both" (*AW* I,248). But alas, the Angel is a "well-nigh deadly bird" (*AW* I,243) and "who, if I cried, would hear me from the orders of the Angels?" To Lou Rilke wrote on March 1, 1912, little more than a month after completion of the *First Elegy*: "The body sometimes abuses the soul which in the animals is at rest and is secure only in the Angel" (*Br.* I,372). Naturally so, for the Angel is bodiless, a state which Rilke had no desire to share. What he seems to crave is something that would be both at the same time: pure Angel and plain body, Angel and doll (*AW* I,257): an impossibility at the human level. The mixture of the two, in which the angelic potentialities continually escape through a time-riddled body as through a sieve, and in which on the other hand the body is falsely padded with eternal illusion instead of with unadulterated sawdust, such a mixture is a hybrid which offers to both the Angel and the body in us nothing but a heap of frustrations. Yet, that appears to be the only arrangement in which art and the artist can and must exist, a truth which will command Rilke's attention with increasing force. When it will have sunk in deep enough, the poet will be resigned to dedicate himself to the Earth made invisible within him. Out of this "invisible Earth" of the *Elegies* will rise Orpheus, the only "spirit that can unite us," although alas only because "we truly live in symbolic figures" (*Son.*I, 12).

However, in 1912 Rilke had not yet come to that clear realization. In spite of all frustrations he still nourished the vague hope that existence and art, as he understood them, might be brought to terms.

To put it differently, although he was relentlessly being driven into a cul-de-sac he was still not irredeemably convinced that he could not remain human and at the same time partake of the Angel's self-sufficient autonomy. By unloading bit by bit his human shortcomings on the Angel who was to overcome them, he had evolved a symbol of enviable but terrifying power, the possibilities of which still had to be explored and tested. That, I think, is the meaning of a passage in the *Second Elegy* in which the poet summons the Angels for questioning. "Who are you?" he asks them bluntly, as if he were determined to get at the bottom of it all. And the answer, which brings to mind the rich, lapidary imagery of a Catholic litany, is highly symptomatic. It leaves no doubt as to the Angels' superhuman nature, although they are creatures of God. In this connection we cannot fail to remember Rilke's often expressed views on the nature of God: a mere direction of the heart, an unfinished, a future God, for the creation and realization of whom the artist has a special mission. How can we evade the inference that the Angels, too, are the artist's creatures? But as such they are beings of instantly achieved success ("Frühe Geglückte"), not subject to struggle and growth. They are "the spoiled sons of creation," since they are able at the outset to confound all fears of man, even though the latter, in the person of the artist, be their creator. They are "the summits and high ridges shining in the morning glow over all creation," unlike their creator, the artist, who must shun the vicissitudes of fate in the valley, yet seek them. They are "the pollen of blossoming godhead": in the bloom of His growth God produces the Angels as the pollen that is to fructify the world in which the artist lives. And since the real function of the artist is to give birth to a great death for whose sake "all things seen become lasting and timeless" (*AW* I,93) the Angels serve as fertilizing agents in the production of that glorified death-fruit which is the warrant of timelessness in the newly experienced world of things. The Angels are furthermore "links of light," articulated knowledge in contrast to the dense dumbness of the doll which is nothing but body. Rilke was always greatly impressed by persons capable of achieving balance and equipoise through superior rational or psychological insight. Lou was such a person, and to Rudolf Kassner, whose *Elements of Human Greatness* he had just read, he wrote: "You manage to find more and more certainties for yourself, and surely you are better able to enter into pure relation with the great things than any of us" (*Br.* I,309). Still greater was his awe and admiration when he met persons whose un-erring self-assurance was achieved by heroic discipline in the pursuit of their art, as was the case with Rodin, Cézanne, and Paul Valéry. If the Angels could prevail, they would sweep all darkness from the world of man, but unfortunately (or shall we say fortunately?) they do not prevail. At any rate, they are "pathways" through which the artist must pass if he is to achieve the glory of praise; they are "steps" which, like the hero's sojourns of love in the later *Sixth Elegy*, lead to "thrones" above all lovers' heartbeats, from where lordly choice is available over a boundless range. The Angels convert Rilke's disquieting awareness of time into "spaces of being," an angelic function which will become increasingly prominent. More-over, to Rilke, who craved a mode of being capable of controlling and directing his effusive tendencies, the Angels are protective "shields made of rapture." In them the fear of losing himself in-appropriately becomes assuaged, and "tumultuous storms" are sub-dued to "enraptured feeling," the kind of feeling which unexpectedly came over the poet at Duino in 1912 and which, after the cold "work of the eyes" under the stewardship of Rodin, he had been waiting for with growing anxiety. "Do now heart-work with the images in you, the imprisoned ones," will be his slogan two and a half years later (*AW* I,322).

It may be observed that all these attributes which apply to Angels plurally still betray on the surface a certain kinship with inherited religious patterns. But Rilke becomes more emphatically heterodox when he considers the Angel singly. Here he plainly ascribes to Him features more usually associated with God, the kind of God the artist presumes to be. The reason why the Angel can perform His superior functions in the scheme of creation is because He is a *mirror*. All the things He means and is capable of doing are nothing but the sum total of His immanent essence from which all intention of communication and all desire are absent. Indifferent and self-con-tained, Rilke's Angel radiates His beautiful being and reflects it back into His own countenance in an endless circle of pure space (*AW* I,249). He can surrender totally, without fear of isolation and soli-tude, without having to face any opposite "that turns a swiftly wrought face which is more than he toward him" (*AW* I,390). The Angel is a mirage of Rilke's constantly renewed making, a mirage which can become reality only in a magical world in which the name and the attributes of the Angel are exchanged for those of Orpheus.

When he wrote the first *Elegies* in January 1912 Rilke knew that he must find his way back from "objective" poetry to warm, vivifying inspiration. But how could he do so without falling back into the kind of consuming adolescent outpouring which, in effect, had landed him in the abyss of the Malte moods? Above all, how could he find his way to a love that would fill the soul to the bursting point, yet leave it free from existential bonds and disappointments? The answer, as we now know, will be that all living women must eventually be transformed into the one Madonna Lisa, and all the living girls into the one inner girl, and all the passing things of this world into Inner Cosmic Space. All the raptures of love must be absorbed by the consuming rapture of creative art. In view of this Rilkean line of development it is clear that the *Second Elegy* can be properly understood only if we keep in mind that for him creative art was of the same nature and intensity as sexual experience. "But you," he asks the lovers, "who swell in the rapture of the other until, overwhelmed, he or she beseeches you: no more . . . I ask *you* about us. I know, you touch each other with such blissful delight, because the caress lingers, because the spot which you, affectionate ones, cover does not vanish; because underneath it you sense pure duration. Thus you promise each other almost eternity from your embrace." (*AW* I,250). When in the winter of 1913 Princess Marie was translating the *Second Elegy* into Italian, Rilke was dissatisfied with her rendering of this passage. Proud of having found a valid expression for such tactile intimacies, he insisted that nothing of the plastic quality be lost through a paraphrase (*Br.MTT*, 334-335). Further evidence of this complication of art with sex in the genesis of the *Elegies* is the fact that the beginning of the *Third Elegy* also arose at this time: "It is one thing to sing the loved ones. Another, alas, to sing that hidden, guilty Flood-God of the blood. . . . Oh the Neptune of Blood, oh his terrible trident, oh the dark storm of his breast from the conch shell!" No wonder that the restraint of the ancient Greeks is longingly evoked, although it is no longer within our grasp because we who have taken to flight and speed can no longer soothe our impetuous hearts by embodying them in gods (*AW* I,251). Now that we are able to survey Rilke's whole work we know that the tormenting problem will be resolved only when he will be re-signed to the belief in the illusory "stellar union of rider and steed" (*Son*.I, 11). For the time being he himself was still groping for the happy formula, although its anticipated outline is discernible at many points. The beginning lines of the *Tenth Elegy*, which also originated at Duino in 1912, leave no doubt that the Orphic future is in sight in spite of the forbidding Angel: "Let me some day, at the end of grim understanding, sing exulting praise to assenting Angels! Let none of my heart's clear-ringing hammers refuse to strike because of soft, doubtful or snapping chords!" And in the *First Elegy* we find the equally revealing passage: "Is the legend in vain which reports that once, in the mourning for Linos, earliest groping music broke through into barren existence?"

Just as in 1922 the *Sonnets to Orpheus* arose as a sort of by-product of the *Elegies*, there also came about an unexpected flow of poems entitled *The Life of Mary* while Rilke was writing his first *Elegies* in 1912 (*AW* I,229-241). To Countess Sizzo he commented in 1922 that "in the details and arrangement of this sequence of images much does not originate from my invention." He mentions paintings by Titian and Tintoretto as models, and the *Painters' Primer of Mount Athos* as well as the *Kiewski Paterik* as sources. Moreover he points out that even the general tone of the poems, though authenti-cally his own, belongs to an outgrown past. Art, so he argues, must come out of life, not out of already existing art, unless the poet adds a substantial amount of his experience to the work. This he claims not to be the case in *The Life of Mary*, at least not for the most part (*Br.Sizzo*, 11-12; *Br.MTT*, 700).[1]

[1] There seems to have existed some confusion in Rilke's mind in regard to the origin of *The Life of Mary*, for in a letter of October 21, 1924, to H. Pongs he declares that these poems owed their birth to mere external circumstances. During his early days in Westerwede he had occasionally written poems about Mary in Vogeler's guestbook; later he had heard that Vogeler intended to publish these early poems and to illustrate them with drawings. "In order to prevent that," Rilke writes, "and in order at least to supply him with better and more coherent texts, should he still want to carry out his intention (which he did not), I wrote in a few days, consciously retracing my moods, these (with the exception of one or two) insignificant poems . . ." (*Br.Muzot*, 333). I think, however, that the contradiction is not as great as it looks: the "external circumstances" merely functioned as the occasion for the otherwise unexpected emergence of the poems. Interesting de-tails concerning Rilke's indebtedness to the *Painters' Primer of Mount Athos* as well as concerning the Greek motto to his *Life of Mary* are given by Ernst Zinn (Zinn, 215-217). By a misinterpretation, Rilke seems to have understood that motto to mean "Having space within oneself," which would correspond to his "Inner

In so far as the moods expressed in them are still clad in Catholic symbolism, these poems represent, of course, a return to past days. It may also be granted that from the point of view of technique and form these poems do not measure up to Rilke's best achievements (Belmore, 203ff). But apart from that, many will find it difficult to go all the way with Rilke in his depreciating comment. At any rate, the meaning of the Angel in one of the poems entitled *Annunciation* is entirely different from that which we have encountered in the earlier poem of the same title (see above, p. 135). In this earlier one the Angel was nostalgic and envious of Mary who, in turn, was insensitive to the light shed by Him; in the later one He is terrible, even for Mary. And the reason is interesting: her innocence and purity are not disturbed by His apparition as such but by the fact that His youthful look meets hers with such complete mutual penetration that the outside world is emptied and voided. And that is beautiful but terrible. It is beautiful because only through such radical interpenetration of the seeing and the seen, of subject and object, is birth given to great things; it is terrible because it involves complete severance from the "tree on the hillside, or yesterday's road, or the pampered faith of a habit that was fond of us" (*AW* I,231). Such was the paradox of Rilke's Angel and of his art: he must intensely woo them but fear to attain them, because they are hostile to all that is humanly dear. Truly, a tragic dilemma, between whose horns there is only room for the belief "in the symbolic figure." At the end of the common journey "the table and the pasture separate rider and steed."

Cosmic Space."

In the *Life of Mary*, as in the *Sonnets to Orpheus*, we have a striking manifestation of Rilke's split-level experience and two-edged manner of creation. In January 1912 at Duino, in the midst of resurgent inspiration, the "sculptural" manner of the Paris years asserted itself with belated strength and gave rise to the Marian cycle, whose form had, therefore, lost some of its authenticity. Since in this case it was the old which encroached upon the new, Rilke felt that he must apologize. In February 1922 at Muzot the protracted anguish of gestation found a sudden release in the *Sonnets*. It was the unexpected new which supplanted the old. Hence his feeling of liberation and joyful approval.

46. SPANISH ANGEL AND HERO

◇◇◇

Ich halte sie für die Angreifer *par excellence*.
(Letter, March 15, 1913; *Br. 1907-14*)

I take them [the Angels] to be the aggressors
par excellence.

◇◇◇

AFTER the great creative days at Duino Rilke slumped back into a state of restlessness, with the tantalizing Angel overhead who gradually had come to consist of a host of domesticated demons. For the next decade his life may be described as a continuous wrestling with that Angel for the completion of, and liberation through, the *Elegies*. At first he put his hope in a contemplated visit to Spain, the land in which he confidently expected to find a stimulating virtue similar to that of Russia. As early as 1900 his attention had been drawn to the Iberian peninsula by a book, illustrated with drawings, by the Dutch painter Joseph Israels (*Br.Frühzeit*, 85). Soon afterward, in 1902, he made the acquaintance of the Spanish painter Ignacio Zuloaga, some of whose paintings he had already admired in German museums. In a limited way Zuloaga played the same role in regard to Spain which Lou Andreas-Salomé had played in regard to Russia: through him Spain became a living reality full of promise, the more so as in his studio in Paris Rilke found several El Grecos. And when in 1907 the poet had the good fortune of finding El Greco's *Toledo* in a Paris exhibition, he felt that that city, rising along a slope on the banks of the Tajo "toward its cathedral and, still higher, toward its fortress, square and massive," would be a congenial place for his dreams. In El Greco's painting a thunderstorm has suddenly caused a ragged light to tear the earth open and to show "here and there pale-green meadows like patches of insomnia" (*Br. 1907-14*, 58). On October 2, 1912, Rilke admitted to his publisher Kippenberg that El Greco was for him one of the greatest events of the last two or three years (*Br.Verleger*, 179). Moreover several of his acquaintances—among whom Rodin, Princess Marie von Thurn und Taxis, Kassner—had visited Spain and had talked to him about the land, its cities and people. In the fall of 1912 Rilke took part in spiritist experiments at the Duino estate of Princess Marie, whose son Pascha was a medium and who herself was a member of the Society of Psychical Research. In the course of these sessions, in which a woman ghost allegedly from Toledo answered questions put by Rilke, reference was repeatedly made to that city, to its stars, its skies, and its Angels (*Br.MTT*, 902-914). Very soon afterward Rilke was on his way to Spain, with the intention of spending the whole winter in Toledo.[2]

The impression which Toledo made on him was perhaps as profound as that which Moscow had made a dozen years earlier, the differences reflecting his development since. Moscow can be called the city of Rilke's "future" but realizable God, Toledo that of his acutely present but deterring Angel. They have some features in common: space, and a prophetic, Old Testament grandeur (*Br. 1907-14*, 255-262, 266). But the Russian space was that of the endless steppes with kurghans vanishing in the darkening distance; the Spanish space is that of a sky without perspective, of a light so sharp that things and men are like constellations without the benefit of soft transitions. Later Rilke saw a great similarity between the landscape of Spain and those of Provence and of Muzot, whose sky was "most indescribable (almost rainless)" (*Br.Muzot*, 8). The God of the *Book of Hours* was in the roots and meant the Earth, the Spanish Angel is Light and means the Stars. The Russian God is warm, the Angel is cold, incapable of tender sympathy. There is a decidedly intellectual quality to the Angel, which both the early God and the later Orpheus lack. The reason is that the Angel has become the epitome of Rilke's negative, ambiguous features turned into their positive and unequivocal opposites. He is a symbol of creativity only in this privative, or antithetical, sense and, therefore, belongs naturally in the *Elegies*; with both the Russian God and Orpheus Rilke felt warmly related, almost to the point of identity. In so far as the God of the *Book of Hours* was remote, he is akin to the Angel of the *Elegies*, in so far as he was brotherly and near, he is related to Orpheus. In the *Book of Hours* these two antithetical aspects were still one in God; in the *Elegies* and *Sonnets* they are mutually exclusive and distinct.

After all, Rilke had passed through the Rodin world which had

[2] An interesting article by Gabriel Marcel on Rilke's concern with occult manifestations can be found in Silvaire-Vigée, 136 ff.

taught him that each thing had its own ambiance and contour; and the effect of this had been disjunctive. Besides, he was emotionally much farther removed from childhood and warm religious feeling, both of which are unifying. His stay in Spain is notorious for his sharp anti-Christian utterings. We have already quoted one of his virulent thrusts in this direction originating from Ronda on December 17, 1912 (see above, p. 61f). Two days later he wrote to Lou that he was reading a book by Fabre d'Olivet, a French writer whose Hebrew studies had lead to the conclusion that "the books of Moses in their original text mean something entirely different from what either the Greek or the Latin translations contain" (*Br. 1907-14*, 281). Rilke's ignorance of Biblical exegesis was appalling.

Strange as it may seem, through Rodin Rilke had learned to concentrate, but by practising that concentration with studied and penetrating effect in regard to large numbers of isolated things he had in a sense scattered his energies and jeopardized the warm embrace of the whole. He had done "eye-work" which, though animated with a kind of glow borrowed from the object, was nevertheless impersonally analytic; now he needed to do "heart-work," which unites, but this time it was not to gravitate about a vague God or related religious symbols. Already Malte complained that in his toilsome labor in the search of God he had come very near losing sight of God (*AW* II,216). As to the Angel, He is no doubt the visible pivot of the *Elegies*, but His function is catalytic, in the nature of a challenge. As is evident from many scattered statements, Rilke knew that some day the Angel's yoke would have to be broken, but when and how, he could not foresee. Twice in letters from Spain he quotes a passage from St. Angela da Foligno's *Instructions* (13th century), which shows that the new revelation could come only from a completely new orientation of the heart: "If all the wise men and all the saints of paradise showered me with their consolations and their promises, and God Himself with His gifts—if He did not change *me*, if He did not start deep within me a new operation, the wise men, the saints, and God would inflame beyond all expression my despair, my rage, my sadness, my grief, and my inner darkness" (*Br. 1907-14*, 271-272, 277). It goes without saying that the inner change which Rilke expected was different from that intended by the Spanish saint.

Spain is a sort of dividing line also in the sense that Rilke's concern with the saint underwent a decided shift in favor of the hero, an areligious type. The saint is a Russian ideal, the hero an Occidental one. Characteristic of the saint is that he lets himself glide gently into God; the hero suggests a steep ascending movement by which the stages are skipped as is the case with the fig tree that leaps into fruit. There is something aggressive about the hero, as there is about the Spanish Angel. Only a few months after leaving Spain Rilke wrote from Paris: "It is incompatible with the passionate nature of the Angels to be mere lookers-on; they surpass us in action exactly in the same measure as God is more acting above them; I take them to be the aggressors *par excellence*" (*Br. 1907-14,* 291). This means that in order to confront and master the Angel, the poet, too, will need an increasing amount of daring. Rilke's Spanish Angel is a descendant of the early "stern angel of ebony" who was defiantly told: "There's one greater than Thou: Thy shadow" (*FG,* 16). Something of that shadow was already in the young poet himself. The saint does not use men and things for the attainment of a great terrestrial destiny: the hero, on the other hand, is related to the genius: his very nature demands that he "race through sojourns of love and climb to fulfilment over many hearts that beat for his sake" (*AW* I,265).

The shift from the saint to the hero was associated with Rilke's increasingly keen experience of conflict between the demands of life and those of art. Especially in Paris, after abandoning his newly established home on the heath, it became clear to the bewildered young husband and father that in order to survive as an artist he must be determined to practise a well-defined ruthlessness toward everything not conducive to art. Again and again he points out in his letters that Rodin was a shining example of such uncompromising single-mindedness. "His daily life and the people who are part of it lie there like an empty river-bed through which he no longer flows; but there is nothing sad about that: for nearby one hears the great rush and the powerful course of the river which has resisted being divided into two branches. . . ." (*Br.* I,58). Rilke quotes Rodin as saying: "Il est mieux d'être seul. Peut-être avoir une femme—parce qu'il faut avoir une femme" (*Br. 1906-07,* 36). However enviable a creature woman may be in some respects, she is a necessary evil for the artist and ought not to be allowed to interfere with his work. One must "look neither to the right nor to the left . . . ," Rilke continues. "One must choose and decide: either this or that. Either happiness or art. . . . All great men have let their lives be overgrown like an old roadway and have put everything into their art. Their lives are like atrophied organs which they no longer need. . . ." (*Br. 1906-07*, 36-37). And after Rodin it was Cézanne who became a sort of heroic type and example. "Perhaps he [Cézanne] did go to his father's funeral; he loved his mother, too, but when she was buried he was not there. He was 'sur le motif,' as he called it" (*Br. 1906-07*, 366).

On reading Emerson, Rilke seems to have been impressed as early as 1898 by the terse sentence in *Considerations by the Way*: "The hero is he who is immovably centered" (Mason, *Münchhausen*, 21; *DuV*, 122). He used this sentence in 1902 as a motto for his monograph on Rodin, who at that time seemed to him such a heroic type. Later, as is well known, he changed his mind (*Br. 1907-14*, 158). Before his experience of Paris, Rilke was not in such great need of a symbol like the "terrible Angel" with the resulting necessity of heroism in facing Him. The Russian monk was endowed with "humility" and a semblance of sainthood, and that was thought to be good enough protection against the temptations and hazards of the world. And even in Paris, that "place of damnation," an Angel could still help Rilke understand "the sufferings of the damned" (*Br. 1907-14*, 335-336). The heroism of Rodin and, a little later, that of Cézanne, both of whom seemed "immovably centered," was at that time still deemed within reach of the poet, because it was a purely artistic category. In the *Requiem* for Wolf Kalckreuth of 1908 Rilke expressed the view that the poet ought to be able to transform himself "into the word, as the carver of the cathedral doggedly converts himself into the unperturbed stone" (*AW* I,225) and thus to contend successfully with the Angel. Heroism did not yet imply the total and unproblematic engagement of existential tasks with the unquestioned assurance of conquest and victory. On the other hand, we have already noted that later, in 1911, the hero appears to Rilke as something which the artist can never be, namely the typical extrovert, the Homeric type, whose very nature it is to "become true," that is, to become himself, by engaging the forces of the outside world, human as well as cosmic. The poet, so Rilke now thought, seems doomed to remain without fate or, whenever worldly interests do overwhelm him, to become untrue and divided

(*AW* II, 348; see above, p. 207). In this respect a distinction must be made even between the poet and the sculptor, the latter being better able to be entirely in his work because it is made of tangible, solid matter. He is in a better position to ignore the temptations which come from outside. The poet's medium of expression is infinitely more volatile and leaves him more exposed "on the crests of his heart" (*AW* I,334).

Rodin, the man who had, at least on the surface, succeeded in subordinating all exigencies of the day to his work, the man with a core as hard as the stuff which he sculptured—Rodin was a sort of Angel of Terror whom Rilke, the lyrical, sensitive poet could only woo without being understood. Like the Angel of the Meridian in the cathedral of Chartres he seemed heedless of "our hours gliding from his full sun-dial on which the day's total sum stands in deep equilibrium, as if all hours were rich and ripe." "Angel of stone," the poet asks, "what do you know of our being?" (*NG*, 32) But in 1906 Rodin, like the Archangel, had chased Rilke from the Paradise; and when at last, after years of erring and seeking, the poet was blessed with the first *Elegies* at Duino, the "grace" proved niggardly and short-lived. The necessity to brace himself, more alone than ever, in defiance of the Angel, became inescapable; and in Spain he hoped to find the proper climate to do so. Hence the feature of heroic steepness, of ruthless contrasts, associated with it. In order to make a city like Toledo possible he felt that "a saint and a lion must have worked together" (*Br. 1907-14*, 267).

While these features found their clear poetic articulation only at the time of the Spanish experience, they had emerged gradually, especially during the Paris years. No wonder, therefore, that already in the *First Elegy*, the hero appears as a type of man superior to the ordinary mortal, as a man for whom death "is only a pretext for being: his final birth" (*AW* I,246). And there is something of both hero and genius in the loving youth of the *Third Elegy*, which was begun at Duino but completed in 1913 in Paris. "He loved his inner self, the wilderness of his inner life, that primal forest within him . . . he followed his own roots into tremendous origin, where his small birth had already been outlived. Loving, he descended into the older blood, into the ravines, where the Terrible lay, still sated with the ancestors." And the Terrible smiled at him, because "he was in love with it." Just as the hero's lordly choice began in the mother's womb, the smiling Terrible was already "dissolved in the liquid which makes the embryo light." With all its deep symbolism of the dark forces of love and sex, the *Third Elegy*, too, is above all a vindication of the artist's right to be loved without having to love in return, except by way of "passing sojourns." Into the womb in which he was born "countless girls have precipitated themselves from the brink of their hearts, future victims of the son" (*AW* I,265).

Like all other Rilkean motifs, that of the hero, such as it crystallized in and immediately after Spain, was subject to further amplification. Already in two sonnets of November 1913 the abrupt and violent steepness of the Spanish type is made to bend and curve until he becomes part and parcel of the circling stream of "the whole." "Besides the hero," the poet says, "there is yet the circle. . . . Where is a thing that knows not of the other?" We men, who insist so earnestly on classification and order, who are so much at home in all that comes to an end and perishes, we are perhaps incapable of experiencing at one and the same time "the part and the counterpart," the resplendently heroic and the timidly yielding. Only women seem to reveal by the expression of their faces that they know how to blend the two (*SG*, 40).

Rilke was aware of the significance of Spain as a compensating counterpart of Russia. Edmond Jaloux quotes him as remarking that he liked the feeling of the circle that closes. By that he expressed his gratification at finding that a new experience which appeared like an increment of knowledge was in reality a mere confirmation of what he had intuitively known a long time. Without suspecting its name, he had already experienced the city of Ronda years earlier in Russia while perusing the travel journal of a former young nobleman (*Rec.* 14). Toledo was a city of "Heaven and Earth, in the same measure present for the eyes of the dead, of the living and of the Angels" (*Br. 1907-14*, 258). A boundless measure of nuances in Russia, a landscape with sharply identified stars in the clear sky of Spain —these were complementary symbols of Rilke's yearnings. And the two were not to be thought of as easily reconcilable by inventive wit or clever humor. While in Ronda, Rilke read Cervantes in German translation and was irritated by his "childish" *Don Quijote*. He found that from an artistic point of view the book had "no limits at all, except perhaps the kind which a clever and fanciful costumery might have in reality—and even these are frivolously and vastly overstepped" (*Br. 1907-14*, 275). But, then, where would Rilke's grandiose struggle with the Angel be, if it could be lightly dismissed as a fight against windmills?

The *Sixth Elegy*, the heroic one, originated in Ronda although it was not completed until 1922 in Muzot. The hero spurns the humble endurance of the saint and rejoices in racing along "in advance of his own smile" (*AW* I,265). This elegy documents a conscious accentuation of Rilke's aggressive determination which, via the *Elegies* in general, will find its crowning in the *Sonnets to Orpheus*. In this sense the *Sonnets* are a lyrical document of defiance born out of grim, heroic resignation, the artist's defiance of the deaf Angel as the self-centered transformer of existential anxieties. They are, moreover, a defiance of the sculptor's world of stone by the fluid word of the poet and its "tree of movement" (*AW* I,310), a proud victory of the metamorphic Orpheus over the contained glow of the Apollo of the *New Poems*, who, after all, had much in common with the Angel of the Meridian. Such a defiance and victory implied heroism, the only kind of heroism which Rilke eventually claimed for himself. It never entered his mind to distinguish himself by genuine heroic exploits, except perhaps as a whimsical dream in the days of his military training at St. Pölten. He frankly admits this in a note which he sent to Lou in October 1925. Acknowledging his enormous estrangement from natural human relations, he felt that precisely thereby he had gained a certain freedom toward people. Of course, the latter could not suspect "that (unlike the hero) he had not achieved his kind of conquest by sharing their bonds or by breathing the heavy air of their hearts, but by living in another world whose spaciousness was so ill suited to human concerns, that his fellowmen would have no other name for it than 'the void'" (*Br.Muzot*, 351-352). With reference to the war, Rilke wrote on October 10, 1915: "Is there nobody who can prevent and stop it? Why are there not two, three, five, ten people who stand together and shout on the market places: Enough! and are shot and will at least have given their lives for crying that it is enough. How many withhold that cry—or don't they? If I am mistaken, and if there are not many who could cry thus, then I do not understand human beings and am not one and have nothing in common with them" (*Br.* I,49). If Rilke ever craved heroism of action, it was in terms of action of the soul which guaranteed "lordly freedom of choice." If Samson smashed columns "it was when he broke forth from his mother's womb into the narrower world where he continued to choose and to succeed" (*AW* I,265). All other types of active heroism Rilke left to others as a matter of course.

47. IMPASSE

◇◇◇

Ausgesetzt auf den Bergen des Herzens.
(*AW* I,334)
Exposed on the crests of the heart.

◇◇◇

SPAIN did not nearly fulfil all of Rilke's hopes. The climate as well as his general feeling of malaise forced him to return to Paris early in 1913, much sooner than he had planned. How intensely he had hoped and prayed for the great poem worthy of the stars can be gathered from the first poem of his *Spanish Trilogy* of January 1913 (*Gedichte, 1906-26*, 103f). He had seen many El Grecos in Toledo but their effect had been less overwhelming, cushioned as it was by their home surroundings (*Br. 1907-14*, 261). There was one painting, however, which he often visited, namely the *Assumption of Mary* in the church of San Vicente: the Angel rises out of the flowers and in His ascent carries off the Virgin Mother. "Bow toward us with your grace, strengthen us as with wine," Rilke prays to her, "for of understanding there is no question" (*Gebser*, 32-33). In another poem, entitled *To the Angel* and written in Ronda, the poet expresses his terrifying loneliness, a familiar note of his *Elegies*. "Angel," he asks, "do I lament? do I complain? But how would the plaint be mine? Alas, I howl, with two pieces of wood do I rattle, and I do not mean to be heard. . . . Shine! Shine! Make me better known among the stars, for I fade away" (*AW* I,348).

In the days of Munich and Schmargendorf, Lou Andreas-Salomé had helped young Rilke straighten out his obscure inner happenings; now he was left alone face to face with his Angel. "If we only cling together, the Angel and I, and you from afar," he wrote to Lou in October 1913 (*Br. 1907-14*, 317). But a few months later he admitted to Princess Marie that the Angel had forsaken him; and without the helpful Angel of former years he found "no plausible and noble meaning" to his distress (*Br.MTT*, 344). "Good Lord . . ." he writes in December 1914, "how uncanny are life and death if one does not all the time see both in one and scarcely distinguishes one from the other. But to do that is precisely the privilege of the Angel, not ours, except in rare moments achieved in labor and pain" (*Br.MTT*, 346). In October 1915, shortly after he wrote the *Fourth Elegy*, he complained from Munich that the task confronting him now was no longer to create a world seen from the point of view of man, but seen in the Angel. In his youth, so he comments, the outside world cast an immediate spell over him, a spell which was capable of transporting completely his deeply engaged heart. Later, influenced by Rodin and Cézanne, he became so absorbed in the search for objectivity, that only very rarely did a thing speak to him with spontaneous generosity without demanding at the same time that he produce it and endow it with the same significance and equivalence he had given to other things. And that tendency reached its climax in Spain, "because there the outside thing itself: the tower, the mountain, the bridge, possessed from the first the unparalleled, unsurpassable intensity of inner equivalence, by means of which one might have been able to represent it. Appearance and vision met, as it were, everywhere in the object; in each was exposed a whole inner world, as if an Angel, embracing space, were blind and gazed into Himself." But in order to create a world of things thus seen in the Angel, "how protected and how contained one would have to be!" (*Br.* II,51)

In this interesting statement Rilke singles out three stages in his relative position to life and the Angel. In his early work, including the *Book of Hours*, reality seemed to be surmountable by the mere transport of the heart. Obviously Rilke considered himself at that time a rather undiscriminating instrument of overpowering inspiration. "Tree, beast, and the year's season" were magical revelations of his inner self; appearance and vision were still in a state of primal oneness. They met in the subject rather than in the object. God, the Thing and authentic Death covered everything, and they were obedient to the poet as the poet was obedient to them. Their hidden strangeness and potential ugliness had not yet detached themselves as isolated features requiring a special symbol. Subjective feeling got the better of them with remarkable ease, and the Angel was relegated to the sphere of light, far away from the roots which are God. He was a mere decorative contrast.

In the *New Poems* and in Malte's *Notebook*, features such as transitoriness, aridity of soul, distraction, loneliness, death, deficiency in love, sexual demons show up more threateningly, and slowly begin to call for an enshrining symbol. The Angel begins to absorb them with increasing insistence, though not yet with such jealous possessiveness as to preclude the possibility of mastering them through daring confrontation. The things of outside reality can still be equated with disciplined and controlled yearnings. The Angel is not yet the exclusive authority in deciding what is and what is not within man's reach. The discriminatingly active poet has a vision which is directed toward the object, an inner equivalence capable of bringing it to full realization of itself. The result was the subjective-objective quality of Rilke's studies from nature as represented by the *New Poems*. The object, from the point of view of man, was dependent on and had a claim on the poet's vision, with which it was to merge in a sort of mutually operative osmosis. The Angel who absorbed that reality was distinctly self-centered and hard to reach, but the poet still felt equal to the task of penetrating His core.

In Spain that objective tendency reached its climax. By dint of practising unbiassed justice toward the object, the poet had made the latter so self-revealing that it could no longer gain anything from an equation with his inner vision. Especially in its negative, repelling aspects, complex reality became defiantly unruly, except in so far as it could be contained and set off in a unifying symbol of ultimate inaccessibility, the Spanish Angel—and that meant, existentially, no mastery at all. This Angel was blind and wanted nothing from the poet. So thoroughly and so consistently had Rilke subordinated his vision to the object that the latter had become emancipated and, like the Angel, merely gazed inward. Angel and poet had come to be at extreme poles and the two could not meet. Repelled by the untoward Angel who alone could defeat all that is wayward and refractory, the poet was to be pushed into a world of magic, where not the Angel but Orpheus ruled. This world, akin to that of his early years, differed from it in several important respects: admittedly its validity was limited by the artist's power to give a measure of reality to his own devised symbols and, owing to the poet's mature genius, everything had acquired a fluid and luminous plasticity. The Angel, with His terrific superiority, could only be faced with heroic defiance or with plaintive yearning. "How protected and how contained one would have to be" oneself, if the world of things were thus to be "seen in the Angel," and no longer "from the point of view of man!"

We have repeatedly suggested that Rilke knew, with progressive clarity, that the hidden meaning of his jerkingly growing *Elegies* was that of being a mere scaffolding for the *Sonnets* yet to come. What he wrote from Paris on December 27, 1913, with reference to the French poet Léon Deubel (1879-1921) described the situation very well and was dictated by his desire to set off his own lamentations from those of the French poet (*Br. 1907-14, 336-338*):

"In the end, in this strange profession [of the poet] there prevails the *bénédiction* [i.e. the grace of inspiration]; it simply gets the upper hand, everybody must admit that. That is why, when somebody wants to make the *misère (cette misère revêche qui s'entête)* a constructive ingredient of the poet's existence while at the same time denouncing it reproachfully, something emerges that is arbitrarily distorted and no longer true (in our eyes). We simply *do not know*, what misery destroys and what it builds up in the heart. In no case is it constructive, it is at most the scaffold covered with rags, behind which, as time goes on, the definitive stones find their suitable places in judicious order. But, of course, one must let it be taken down when it is no longer needed, instead of attaching final significance to the boards and planks with the posters and proclamations which have gradually filled the bare space. . . . As a poet one must not make a mistress out of one's *détresse*, but put all affliction and joy into one's work, and one's life must be so marked by these that one refuses to experience either elsewhere."

The effect of the Spanish experience on Rilke's work was deep and lasting. Besides the main part of the *Sixth Elegy*, the beginning lines of the *Ninth* and a number of very characteristic poems date from Spain or arose out of its atmosphere. In general the distinguishing features are a sharpening of the contrasts of darkness and light, a consequently greater isolation and loneliness, an increasingly elegiac note of frustration, a more pronounced secularization of religious motifs, an emphatic shift toward perspectiveless stellar space, a more decided repudiation of human bonds and, by way of compensation, an enormously heightened craving for warm womanly affection. Moreover, the atomizing effect of his "objective" endeavors carried in its wake a keen desire to rediscover the link with magic childhood. There is much of El Greco's passionate expressionism in it all. From the moment he left Spain to the confining years of the war Rilke wandered erratically from place to place, changing his sojourns almost a score of times.[3] His health was precarious, his mind and soul agitated, his correspondence with Lou became lively. There was a serious deterioration in his relationship to Clara, which in the fall of 1913 almost resulted in divorce (*Br.MTT,* 329, 332; Albert-Lasard, 55). In Paris he was much occupied with Marthe, the poor factory girl who lived with a savage Russian sculptor and whom Rilke fathered with a strange affection (*Gedichte, 1906-26,* 525-527). After a hectic trip through Germany from end to end, he found Paris so heavy and unbearable that he escaped for a short while into the province, to Rouen. "A whole cathedral would be necessary to drown the noise that is in me" (*Br.Lou,* 315). In a quiet street of Rouen the eyes of a passing woman so moved him that he could hardly see anything or collect himself afterward. "I am frightened when I think how I have been living away from myself, as if incessantly standing in front of a telescope, endowing every approaching woman with a felicity, the felicity of my onetime loneliest hours." With bitter melancholy he remembers the years of the *New Poems* when he was able to feel like the desireless Stranger who was ready to forego all nights of love for his nights of roving freedom (*NG,* 231). Now he was once more nothing but desire, and all had to be done over.

It is not surprising that to the post-Spanish years belong a number of poems in which Rilke seeks refuge from his own divided self and his barrenness of soul. He seeks comfort in the cosmic spaciousness of Night (*Gedichte an die Nacht*), he implores the Angel for help

[3] Here are the chief stations in Rilke's peregrinations from the time he left Spain at the end of February 1913 to the outbreak of the war in August 1914: Paris, Bad Rippoldsau (Black Forest), Göttingen (with Lou), Leipzig, Weimar, Heiligendamm (on the Baltic), Berlin, Munich, Dresden, Riesengebirge (in the company of Lou), Paris, Berlin (where he joined Benvenuta, then with her to:) Munich via Zürich to Paris, Duino, Venice; then, alone, back to Paris, via Assisi and Milan; then again Leipzig, and finally Munich.

and yearns for some new passion that would overwhelm him like music, yet trembles at the thought of it. "Easily does the god persuade himself to embrace. The fragrance of a smile would drive him into the dismayed womb" (*Gedichte, 1906-26*, 550). Even before leaving Spain he complained of having lost all power of concentration: "Pearls roll away. Alas, did one of the strings break? But of what use is it if I string them together again: I lack you, strong clasp that would lock it, my love . . . only you do I desire. Must not the split in the pavement, when, wretched, it feels the urge to grow grass: must it not want the whole Spring? Lo, the Spring of the Earth" (*AW* I,323). And later: "Overwhelm me, music, with rhythmic wrath" (*AW* I,324)—"Is grief, as soon as the ploughshare, incisively placed, reaches down to a new layer, is grief not good? . . . How much suffering is to be endured? When was there time to experience the other, the lighter feeling?" (*AW* I,368f) There are poems in which all the charms of incipient love come to life again, but with the constellation of fate overhead. "Behind the guiltless trees, old Fate slowly forms its speechless face," though for the time being it remains aloof, "imponderous in its heavenly gait, an airy figure" (*AW* I,325). Rilke's empty heart demanded with unrestrained aspiration to be filled to overflowing. "You are a great, a very great poet, Serafico," Princess Marie wrote to him in March 1913, "and you know it quite well. You are in love (no arguing!), you are in love, persistently in love (with whom, where, and how does not matter). You have a small studio in Paris—and it is March, the whole wonderful spring knocks at your door. Let it enter, Serafico, call it in at once!" And commenting further, the Princess adds: "But Rilke always wanted the extraordinary also and above all in love. . . ." No wonder that the letters of the Portuguese nun fascinated him at this time: "What a reckless splendor," he writes, "but how frightful [it is] to excite love, what a conflagration, what a calamity, what a ruin. Of course, to be consumed oneself, assuming that one be capable of it, that would be something worth living and dying for" (*Br.MTT*, 69, 70).

But when in early January 1914, instead of thrilling inspiration the vague outline of an enthusiastic woman appeared on the horizon in the person of Benvenuta, he intuitively knew that he had already lost his love "in advance." On his trip from Paris to Berlin, where he was to meet her for the first time, he confided to "the intimacy of his notebook" that, having left the light sphere of his own feelings, he would now have to bear the weight of close proximity and "daily sadness" (*Gedichte, 1906-26,* 554). Soon after the Benvenuta comet had passed he characterized the condition of his soul in a letter of June 8, 1914:

"Dear Lou, here I am again, after a long, broad and heavy time, a time spent without strength and reverence but which I have tortured to its conclusion until it has died (in doing which I shall not easily find an equal). . . . [I am] forced this time to realize that nobody can help me, nobody, though he came with the most legitimate and immediate claims of the heart and proved himself worthy up to the stars: though he endured me, no matter how clumsy and helpless I might prove to be, and persevered in a pure, undeviating direction toward me, regardless of whether I broke his love darts ten times with the turbid and thick waters of my underground world. . . . What has ended in my utter misery began with many, many letters—light, beautiful letters which issued like cataracts out of my heart; I can scarcely remember ever having written such letters."

A poem, written a month or so later, reveals in a different way the dangerous effect of Rilke's failure to reestablish inner balance. At the time he was licking his wounds in Paris and, from the depths of disillusionment, in a wanton effort to forget he throws a wild party of roses for himself, revels in thousands of sprawling rose-petals spread out or curled within their own folds in numerous bowls. During the long and cold winter, and in the whirl of his quest for love and fullness of the heart, he had all but lost the feeling and the fragrant memory of the rose, so that now his convalescent soul plunges recklessly into a riot of blooms in a mood of rapturous exultation: "Night of roses, night of many, many brilliant roses, clear night of roses, sleep of a thousand rosy eyelids, radiant sleep of roses, I am your sleeper: bright sleeper of your fragrances, deep sleeper of your cool intimacies" (*Gedichte 1906-26,* 556).[4] De-

___

[4] It is not without reason that I place this poem in the context of the Benvenuta experience. The poem was written in July 1914, and it appears that on July 14 Rilke reviewed and closed the whole incident. For on that date he made a small bundle of all the letters which he had received from Benvenuta, sealed it, and wrote on it: "Property of Mrs. Magda von Hattingberg (Benvenuta), sealed July 14, 1914" (*Br.*

spite its diaphanous and triumphant lightness this poem acqu
a somber and disquieting background when we confront it
those famous lines which Rilke later willed to become the epi..,
on his grave: "Rose, o pure contradiction, desire to be nobody's sleep
under so many eyelids" (*AW* I,405).

There is little doubt that the tragi-comic Benvenuta episode gave
abundant food to the *Elegies* and dealt a severe blow to the poet's
hope for early liberation in Orphic praise. He had hoped, through a
normal relationship of love, to achieve a healthy and balanced attitude toward the human world as well as toward his own body or,
as he puts it, to acquire a proper sense of "all distances" (*Br.Lou*,
349). He was much worried by the fascination which worldly distractions had for him; they constantly threatened to break down
barriers and to wipe out all consciousness of distance between himself and the world. In Rome he had once observed a little anemone
which had remained so intensely and widely open during the day
that it was unable to close at night and "it was awful to see it in the
dark meadow . . . breathe in the superabundant night with its calyx
furiously agape" (*Son*.II, 5). Comparing himself to that little flower
he found that because of the unchecked intensity of his ardor in
love he, too, had failed to put order into his inner confusion and was
worse off than ever. He had allowed relationships to intrude between himself and his body which only served to incite the latter
and which "probably shared their general turbidity with his usual
relationship in matters of the body" (*Br.Lou*, 350). The upshot was

---

Benvenuta, 7). It seems inconceivable that he should have sorted these letters and
checked their chronological order without dwelling once more here and there on
their contents, and without reviving the moods which they had generated and the
moments of trembling anticipation which had preceded the communion with his
beloved idol. I use the word "communion" deliberately, because in one of his last
written messages Rilke himself used the same kind of language and evoked the same
kind of images with which a Catholic child prepares itself for its First Holy Communion (*Br. Benvenuta*, 145). Their meeting took place in Berlin on February 26
and only a few days before, on February 17, Benvenuta had written: "Oh, roses! I
have always had the greatest longing to see roses in silver bowls (not to own them,
my longing has by no means ventured that far), many, many. You know, they have
them in Florence, I have never seen any like them, with their strange intimate red
and with a fragrance unlike that found elsewhere. Also the familiar bright ones
called 'La France' . . . and the 'Snow-Queen' . . . and the 'Sultan of Sansibar,' dark
red, intoxicatingly fragrant" (*Br. Benvenuta*, 88). To which Rilke replied, among
other things: ". . . is not all this that I write you your flowers; not one among them
that does not owe its life to you, Heart-Sun; and how many more do you call and
call forth, for which my earth is not big enough, you Shining Voice" (*Br. Benvenuta*, 118).

that he could count only on that hidden and innermost core of his creative vitality which, while indestructible, was condemned to live in constant fear of privation as "in a state of siege" and could erupt only in intervals of faith and confidence, in the form of "fragments of elegy" or of "a beginning line" of poetry. Rilke was to experience the same distressing symptoms of frustration at Berg am Irchel, Switzerland, in the winter of 1920-21 as the result of his entanglement with Merline, although on this occasion he was perhaps more successful in preventing their relationship from interfering so devastatingly with his work, or, at any rate, in giving to the loving woman "the inspired curve" which marked her "for divine uses for ever" (*Letters to Merline*, 46). That the Benvenuta affair had caused far deeper disturbances is shown by the poem *Plaint* of July 1914: "To whom shall you complain, my heart? Ever more solitary your path winds among incomprehensible people. Perhaps even more in vain since it keeps its direction, the direction of the future, the lost one.—Formerly, did you complain? What was it? One fallen berry of exultation, an unripe one. But now my whole tree of jubilation breaks, my slow-growing tree of jubilation breaks in the storm. Most beautiful tree in my invisible landscape, which used to make me better known to the Angels, the invisible ones" (*AW* I,334). Indeed, a moving document, showing clearly that the poet's longed-for jubilation in Orpheus would be some day his singular way of impressing the Angel and was, therefore, his secret goal.

PART IX

DOLLS

◇◇

Und schon spaltet sie an, im Rückgrat, des Willens
Gerte, dass sie gegabelt, ein zweifelnder Ast am
Judas-Baume der Auswahl wachsend verholze.

(AW I,333)

Already the switch of our will starts on our backs
its two-pronged growth and thickens into a wooden
fork, a dubious branch on the Judas-tree of choice.

◇◇

48. ANNUSHKA'S DOLL

Ich habe noch eine ganz grosse Puppe.
(Br.Frühzeit, 228)

I have yet another doll, a very big one.

RILKE's elegiac creativeness in the years following his visit to Spain culminated in the *Fourth Elegy* which was written in Munich on November 22 and 23 of 1915, a year and a quarter after the outbreak of the First World War and not long before he was to be enlisted in the Austrian army. This elegy, together with many other poems gravitating about it, shows clearly that childhood was much on the poet's mind; it contains some of the most mystifying passages with a distinctly biographical tenor, and seems to link, in however wide a sweep, the two basic childhood experiences: that of the doll, and that of the Angel. In order to understand this and much of what happens in the poet's later struggles, it is necessary that we retrace our steps and delve into the recondite layers of childhood and early adolescence, in the hope of discovering some of the "items" that add up to the "lyrical sums."

Like childhood itself, the Angel and the doll are ambivalent—symbols of sheltered happiness and frightful loneliness. In the early years of yet undeveloped consciousness Rilke actually experienced the full wholeness of life, in intimate companionship with both Angel and doll. Toward the former his attitude was confidently receptive, toward the latter it was more creatively bestowing. From both he could expect, and for a while, received, unquestioned response. But with the child's awakening reflectiveness and growing independence they lost their magic: the Angel's help proved imaginary and ineffective; the doll became incapable of inspired understanding. The primitive state of innocence and charm remained only in the form of vague memory, of melancholy yearning. Its loss was the pivotal event of Rilke's life, the secret source of his elegies and, by ricochet, of his praise of terrestrial existence. Both loss and residual memory were necessary for the flowering of his art, and his awareness of that fact impelled him to keep the effectiveness of both undiminished all his life.

The early distinguishing features of doll and Angel were never obscured: the Angel remained knowing and active, endowed with the power to communicate, which power, however, He became increasingly loath to use; the doll remained passive and dumb, submissive and eventually too unimaginative even to receive. Each in its own way became a challenge, and since they belong to two opposite categories of experience their differences cannot be resolved at the existential level. A solution becomes possible only when existence is somehow sublimated, and with Rilke sublimation could be attempted only through art. At that level the Angel and the doll will drop out of sight behind the pervasive symbol of Orpheus.

There is still another difference between the two: the reality of the Angel, like that of God, is backed by religious tradition and is fundamentally spiritual. It, therefore, retains considerable independence even after the belief in Him has vanished. Because of that measure of autonomy He is more capable of inspiring awe and fear, if He is to go on playing a part in grown-up consciousness. The doll, on the other hand, is entirely dependent on the creativeness of the growing child; its reality is at the mercy of the child's faith, lacking which there remain only rags, fillings, and an impassive look. It is not sustained by any circumscribed belief; toward it Rilke could be condescendingly superior without qualms while the Angel could become "terrible" and inaccessible.

There are also important differences between the doll and the puppet, although Rilke does not always draw the line sharply. In German the same word may be used for both and, after all, they are both dolls. However, unlike the individual doll the puppet implies a stage, a drama, and spectators; it is caught in a complicated web of relationships with the puppeteer, with the other puppets, with the spectators, and even of the latter with the wire-puller. The doll exists in the one simple relationship to the child, a warm intimate relationship in which the child is the active agent. Whatever the doll may give in return is in reality the child's invention, but in spite of its one-sidedness the imaginative contribution is flawless and full. By virtue of its creative magic the child has breathed a soul into the doll body, and the two have become inextricably one. But since reflection tends to disrupt that unity, a helpless young life is gradually confronted with a strange world and the memory of a lost wholeness. As Rilke points out in his *Notes on Dolls*, the doll soul, which is now without a body, is real enough and goes on living in the hearts of men, but, without a tangible outline, roams about, ethereal and elusive. In its vagueness it is subject to gradual neglect and eventually to utter disregard and staleness. That entails a feeling of frustration and loss in the grown-up who may try to compensate himself with more corporeal forms of reality. In so doing he may think himself safe in a world of solid substance, but in reality he has unwittingly become a puppet among other puppets with a hidden puppeteer overhead. Meanwhile the doll soul in him keeps the memory of original fullness alive and shows up every now and then the worthlessness of the body of rags as well as the unreality of the puppet-show on the human stage.

Unlike his friend Kassner, Rilke felt that the puppet had imagination whereas the doll had none. For Kassner imagination is tied up with the ability to recognize one's own image in the mirror, and of that the puppet is as incapable as the doll (Kassner, *Melancholia*, 145). Rilke's experience was that the doll in its utter unresponsiveness and silence caused man for the first time in his life to face empty space and to feel its horror. While the puppet could produce the same effect, it was, however, capable of evoking a world full of life and action (*AW* II,278-279). Moreover, although the movements and expression of the puppets are on the whole synchronized with the spoken word from above, it sometimes happens that they reveal an unexpectedly distinct personality which was not intended.

On November 8, 1899, shortly after completing the *Book of Monkish Life* and before writing the *Stories of God*, Rilke wrote a gruesome story entitled *Mrs. Blaha's Maid* which conceals important autobiographical facts behind an obscure symbolism (*Br.Frühzeit*, 222-229). Mrs. Blaha hailed from a poor, marshy region of Bohemia and was married to a small railroad employee in the city. Every summer she returned to her native village and on one of these visits decided to ask the daughter of an acquaintance to accompany her to the city and to do housework for her. In this way the girl would enjoy the advantages of the city and have a chance to learn something. What she might learn, Mrs. Blaha would have been at a loss to say. When the acquaintance mentioned the proposal to her husband, the latter asked after some hesitation: "But does the lady know that Anna is with child?" "Blockhead," replied the wife, "you don't want to suggest that we tell her. . . !"

Annushka went to the city where she spent most of her time alone in her mistress's kitchen. There were no children, and both Mrs. Blaha and her husband worked out. Every morning the organ-grinder would come and play in the courtyard, and Anna would lean out of the window and listen with such intent joy that she felt like dancing until she became dizzy and scared. She would, then, start walking through the whole dark tenement and sometimes land in the smoke-filled tavern downstairs where someone was singing in his first drunkenness. On such trips she would always meet children who for some reason or other expected her to tell them interesting stories. When they followed her into the kitchen, Annushka sat down near the stove, covered her blank face with her hands and said: "Let me think." But she thought so long that the children became frightened and ran away, so that the poor maid burst into tears and felt lonely and homesick. It was hard to say what she was homesick for, perhaps a little bit for the beatings she used to get at home, but mostly for something indefinite that once was or that maybe she had only dreamed. Slowly vague memories welled up: first something red, very red, and then many people. And then a loud ringing bell, and a king, and a peasant, and a tower. And the peasant said: "My dear King . . ." and the king answered: "Yes, I know." Of course, why should a king not know all that a peasant may have to say?

One night, around Christmas, Mrs. Blaha went shopping and took her maid along. In a brightly-lit store window the poor girl suddenly saw her memory: the king, the peasant, the tower. She could scarcely suppress her joy, but for fear of betraying herself she quickly looked away and stuck close to the side of her mistress who had not even noticed the puppets in the window.

Shortly afterward, on her free Sunday, Anna did not return home at night. A man whom she had seen before in the tavern had persuaded her to go with him she knew not where. Back in the kitchen on Monday morning she found everything much colder and greyer than it used to be, and on that day she broke a soup dish, for which she was rudely scolded, but her escapade with the strange man remained unnoticed. Before New Year she spent three more nights out and after that no more. Every day she locked herself in the apartment and sometimes did not even go to the window when the organ-grinder came.

One Sunday morning, when the dreary winter had yielded to a hesitating spring, Annushka gave birth to a child, completely unexpectedly although she had felt heavy and swollen for weeks. Without visible emotion she looked at the child who began to cry just as Mrs. Blaha called and a bed next door creaked. Annushka grabbed her blue apron, tied the strings around the baby's neck, and put the entire blue bundle in the bottom of her trunk. She then went about her morning duties as if nothing had happened.

A few days later, when she was again alone, she counted her earnings, locked the doors, and opened the trunk. She laid the blue bundle on the kitchen table and measured the dead body from head to foot, after which she put it back in the trunk and went to the store where she had seen the puppets. She was disappointed to find that the king and the peasant and the tower were a good deal smaller than her "big doll," but she bought them just the same, especially since there were other puppets as well: a princess, with round red dots on her cheeks, an old man like a Santa Claus with a cross on his chest and a long beard, and two or three other less beautiful and less significant ones. In addition there was a stage, with a curtain that went up and down, so that alternately a garden appeared and disappeared behind it.

Annushka's homesickness had vanished. She set up the stage in the kitchen and, as behooves a stage manager, went behind to operate it. Every once in a while, when the curtain was up, she stepped forward in order to look at the beautiful garden with its high trees, and every vestige of greyness disappeared. Again she would go behind the curtain, put a few dolls into position and have them say things of her own invention, but without ever spinning out a real play. At most there was the odd dialogue, and now and then two dolls would bow to each other with a scared expression. Or the two together would bow to the old man, who was unable to reciprocate because he was made of solid wood. He merely managed to fall to the ground, out of gratitude.

When the children heard about Annushka's theatre, they flocked to her kitchen at dusk, at first distrustfully, then quite naturally, and watched intently the beautiful dolls who always said the same things. One day Annushka, her cheeks hot with excitement, announced: "I have still another doll, a very big one." This aroused great curiosity among the children, but Annushka seemed to forget all about it and kept putting all the dolls in the garden, except those that were unable to stand by themselves. These she placed against the wall, and among them was a harlequin whom the children had never noticed before. Meanwhile they clamored to see the big doll, if only once for a short moment.

Annushka went to her trunk, leaving the children and the puppets alone in the dark and general silence which made them look strangely alike. After a while it seemed as if the wide open eyes of the harlequin anticipated something terrible, and the children were overcome with such fear that they all, without exception, fled. When Annushka returned with her big, blue doll, the kitchen had become quite dark and empty, but though her hands trembled she was not afraid. Calmly smiling she went to the stage, kicked it down with her feet and smashed all the little pieces of wood that represented the garden. Then, in the now completely dark kitchen, she split the heads of all the dolls, including that of the big blue one.

49. CHILDHOOD MONSTERS

◇◇◇

> Ich habe um meine Kindheit gebeten, und sie ist
> wiedergekommen, und ich fühle, dass sie immer
> noch so schwer ist wie damals und dass es nichts
> genützt hat, älter zu werden.
>
> (Malte's *Notebook, AW* II,59)
>
> I have wanted my childhood back, and it has come
> again, and I feel that it still is as heavy as it
> used to be and that I have gained nothing by growing
> older.

◇◇◇

LIKE some of the other early sketches which we have mentioned the Annushka story has puzzled most Rilke scholars who either ignore it as an insignificant freak or interpret it as an expression of Rilke's secret liking of the gruesome. The fact is that we have here a remarkable document of his peculiar kind of psychoanalysis through art. Literally scores of threads could be shown to issue from the dark background of early experience and to converge into the pattern of this story, although some speculation may be un-avoidable in regard to details. In the first place there is the sharp contrast between the grey, narrow world of family and bourgeois environment symbolized by the kitchen—and the bright, promising world of love and art, symbolized by the garden and the stage. Mrs. Blaha as well as her city belong in the sphere of the kitchen, the organ-grinder and the Christmas atmosphere with its puppets and illumined shop windows pertain to that mood of "longing which makes the great poets." Annushka's adventures of the night are ob-scure offshoots of that mood, which in his monograph on Rodin Rilke calls the "depravities and lusts against nature" (*Rodin*, 38; see above, p. 177). Like Annushka, Rilke had left his home and gone into the great world, to Munich, Florence, Berlin and Moscow, where he could learn something, however indefinite that something might be. Like Annushka, too, Rilke was yet infinitely lonely and homesick, perhaps for the endless frustrations at home and at the military academies, but mostly for something vague that once was or that maybe he had only dreamed. *Ewald Tragy* describes these para-doxical longings with bitter humor (*ET*, passim). Nor were the nightly escapades lacking, either at Linz or at Prague (Hirschfeld, 715, 720). Moreover, Rilke was pregnant with something he had con-ceived in the dark moments of his awakening, and this he kept a secret for fear that its revelation might shock all those who had been near to him. His father had expressed grave doubts as to his eccentric ideas and his determination to become a poet; his relatives had dis-missed him with a shrug of the shoulders; only his mother in her vanity was willing to let him go and give birth to something unique and great. In Rilke's story Annushka is by no means stupid; intellect is irrelevant here—what counts is the blind instinctive force which drives her and which she does not understand, exactly as was the case with the poet himself.

What was it that Rilke bore in him and that he was so anxious not to betray? The answer to that question may be found in *Ewald Tragy*. In a fit of angry revolt Ewald tells his aunt: "I am my own lawmaker and king, nobody is above me, not even God . . . there is nobody, there never was anybody like me. . . ." (*ET*, 26). No sooner had he said that than he wept, not because he was sorry for having been rude and overbearing, but because such outbursts only served to betray his secret. In a sketch of the same date as the Annushka story

Rilke lets a young bastard who is to become a cardinal and then pope make a similar utterance. The youth was a poor student but a great lover of falcon hunting. When his teacher who—Rilke ironically adds—did not know much about hunting, asked him what he would do if the falcon should one day not come back, the fiery pupil replied with great excitement: "Then, then . . . then I shall grow within me the feeling of wings" (*Br.Frühzeit*, 219-220). What Rilke was pregnant with was a new God, a God after his own image and of his own making. It is not difficult to imagine that he must have picked up the seed at a time when his disappointment with the old God had reached a climax, and that happened at St. Pölten when his morbid religious mysticism made place for a profound grudge against a God who showered his enemies with glory and abandoned his fervently praying servant like a forgotten wallflower to solitude and misery (*Br.Muzot*, 309). Yet we know how ardently young Rilke wanted to excel and shine, but for that he needed another God, not a deaf and dumb doll but a responsive puppet whose wires he alone could pull. Only by such a God could he have himself knighted and crowned king or ordained a monk. One has only to read the poems of *Dreamcrowned* and *Advent* to realize out of what resplendently solitary pride the humility of the future Russian monk was made.

That the memory of St. Pölten kept haunting Rilke's mind in those days is evidenced by the fact that he was seriously thinking of writing a military novel in which those years of suffering would find form. And it is interesting to read in his diary why he did not write that novel. So many other things kept crowding his fancy and what did it matter which came first? After all, the subject matter is no longer of importance in a work of art. What matters is the sentiment, which is like a curtain stretched out in front of actions. The latter we may choose at will and we may use them to make whole dramas for the sole purpose of making us conscious of, and richer by, a single new sentiment (*Br.Frühzeit*, 205-206). Isn't that what Annushka sought to do with the puppets and her stage? Moreover, Rilke found it impossible to give adequate form to a situation in which crowds, such as that of the cadets of St. Pölten, were involved. The individual is always at bottom a child, but in the multitude he becomes a nondescript force of stupid cruelty. Rilke not only hated masses but had an instinctive grudge against the "third person." In his *Notebook* Malte considers it a sign of unimaginative thinking that dramatists always need the "triangle" in which a third actor is used as a cheap means of starting and complicating that which goes on in the souls of individuals (*AW* II,22). No wonder that Rilke could never be a dramatist: he was unable to create a world in which personalities fight out their conflicts in an autonomous universe of multiple forces (*BTK*, 164-165). Little wonder, too, that An-nushka does not make her puppets spin out a real drama, but at most a kind of dialogue, something in the nature of the strophe and antis-trophe of the ancient chorus. Later, in February 1914, Rilke wrote to Benvenuta that in Munich he had bought three puppets for his daughter Ruth in the hope that his friend Regina Ulmann would write a play for them, for—so he admits—he himself was not able to invent one (*So lass*, 50). It is true that up to a point Rilke was able to write objective poetry—so-called—in his *New Poems*, where each time he faced one single thing. But even in regard to this type of poetry he had to confess in Spain that he had not "peeled himself clean, had torn himself out and given away pieces of rind, had even (as children do with dolls) often clung to an imaginary mouth and smacked his lips, and the morsel had remained there" (*Br. 1907-14*, 286). At any rate, it was easier for Rilke to adapt and attune forces to each other when only two were involved and he was one of them, so that adequate osmosis could ensue; any third agent was a nuisance, an outside observer, a joker, a judge, or a harlequin with a grin. Rudolf Kassner would say that in the Kingdom of the Father, which was Rilke's, there is no drama, only a dialogue which is a disguised monologue (*BTK*, 167ff; *Das Inselschiff*, 120).

We need not speculate on what Annushka's vague memory of something red and of loud ringing bells is supposed to symbolize; as to her peasant, her king, and her tower, these are easily recogniz-able in Rilke's work as symbols of essential creative prerequisites: earth-bound simplicity, royal sovereignty, even to the point of cru-elty, and proud solitude. It is amazing with what sureness of instinct Rilke was able to size himself up and with what striking brevity he could cast his whole being into a few cryptically suggestive names.

The embryo with which Rilke had felt "heavy and swollen" was that of the God of the *Book of Monkish Life* to whom he had just given birth unexpectedly in a sort of somnambular inspiration. We have already observed that the religious climate in which this embryonic God had grown was that which prevailed "immediately following the military school, or rather already during that period," when Rilke admittedly "began to indulge ruthlessly in that relationship with God which it would be impossible to define confessionally" (*Br.Muzot*, 309). How was he going to let that God see the light of day without offending? He was still financially dependent on his father, whom he loved, and on his relatives, most of whom he despised; emotionally he was still, in spite of everything, caught in that vast web of childhood attachments and adolescent dreams. Did he not want to prove to all his scoffing and unbelieving acquaintances and relatives that he was a genius capable of bringing forth a masterpiece? That his relatives were alarmed by whatever evidence of his new state of mind had reached their ears after his departure from Prague, may be gathered from a short notice which he sent from Berlin to his Aunt Gabriele on December 30, 1897: "No quarrel shall embitter our days. We wish to hurt nobody and to cast no God from His throne. Not even when we preach our new Faith 'Beauty.' So be it in the coming year of grace '98 and thenceforth forever and ever." This note is signed "René-Rainer, in old gratitude and sincerity," which subtly underlines the fact that Lou was closely associated with his new faith (*Br. 1892-1904*, 52; see above, p. 88). It was also during these years of growing pains that he kept insisting on the necessity of lying, "sometimes upward, sometimes downward" (*ET*, 25). Even in his late French poems of the *Carnet de Poche* he calls the lie "a weapon of the adolescent . . . the friend of childhood"; in fact, the "brooding adolescent" is the personification of the "naïve lie" who has "sisters so great and so pure that the centuries use up all their resources trying to measure their greatness and purity." The lie is like "the fragrance of calyxes which indistinct governesses had embroidered on pillows. . . ." (*GFS*, 96-97). And is not Rilke's Prodigal Son, after his return home, the personification of a methodical lie? The whole complex of pseudonymity has its source in Rilke's years of emancipation, and it suggested itself all the more forcefully as his embryonic God was in a considerable measure made of phallic substance: witness the erotic quality of some of the *Book of Hours* poems; witness also his lifelong emphasis on the close relationship between art and sex. All doubts in regard to this matter are quickly dispelled if one reads attentively the recently published correspondence of Lou and Rilke.

Just as Annushka cast only a quick glance at the window with the puppets, Rilke, too, was careful at this time not to betray what was brewing in him. For five years he kept the *Book of Monkish Life* from the world (with the single exception of Lou), just as Annushka hid her baby at the bottom of her trunk. It is true that one reason was, as we have pointed out, that he did not consider his mood as having found final articulation (see above p. 148); but another was undoubtedly that he was not yet ready to show himself as he was. Of this there is abundant evidence in the scattered entries of his diary as well as in *Ewald Tragy*. And that explains, it seems to me, the peculiar shyness and roundabout way with which he tells his *Stories of God*, not to the children directly for whom they are intended, but to the lame Ewald or to a woman. When he does tell some to a socially orthodox teacher, his shyness takes the form of subtle irony or satire (*GG*, 160ff). The *Stories of God* are honeycombed with hieroglyphic pseudonymity, permeated with deeper meanings wrapped in dense symbolism. Their symbolism is indeed in great need of a thorough and unbiassed investigation. Rilke's play at hide and seek obviously irked his friend Paula. In her letter of the late fall of 1901 in which she accused Clara of neglecting her, and Rilke of violating his wife's personality (see above p. 56), she addressed the poet in these words: "I thank you very much, dear friend, for your beautiful book. And please, please, please, do not give us any riddles to solve. My husband and I are two simple people, we find it so difficult to guess, and afterwards our heads and our hearts ache" (Modersohn-Becker, 166). The "beautiful book" referred to was probably the *Stories of God*, the first version of which appeared in 1900 and the second in 1901. Rilke had known a long time that he was a stranger among men and that his real self, if it were known, would shock them out of their wits (*Br.Frühzeit*, 249-250; (see above, pp. 59, 108). On the other hand, for one who had withdrawn into the desert to presume that he could come back and teach his fellowmen was one of those all too common errors which he proudly sought to avoid (*Br.Frühzeit*, 254-258).

But we must return to Annushka's puppets. Needless to say, the death of her strangled baby is to be understood symbolically. For Annushka it was as alive as the other dolls who could bow and carry on a dialogue. Indeed it was more truly alive since it mysteriously came out of her body as the ripe fruit of a deep personal experience. Besides, the God of the *Book of Hours* had a strange likeness to Great, Authentic Death, which only the artist of the future would be able to bring to final fruition. Rilke considered himself a forerunner of that artist and felt duty-bound to prepare his path by attempting again and again to create such a conveniently metamorphic God. This whole line of thought and associated images certainly needed some careful sugaring before they could safely be offered to the public for swallowing. Rilke himself was by no means wedded to them for life, but for the time being they functioned as answers to his creative anxieties. His great poetic genius needed no psychoanalyst.

That these intimate problems, so gruesomely secreted in the symbolism of the Annushka story, were very much on Rilke's mind, is abundantly evident in his writings of the day: in *Ewald Tragy*, in his diaries, and in his *Florentine Journal*—all of which were not written for publication; in his *Book of Hours*, which was published at a later date; and in his circumspect *Stories of God* which appeared in 1900 but, like Annushka's stories and puppet-show, were cautiously addressed to children, that is, to a select type of people who were supposed to have a natural feeling for such strange realities (*Br.* II,215). But even the children could not help sensing something horrible in Annushka's mysterious behavior, and the unexpected grin of a hitherto unnoticed harlequin acted like a distorting and disfiguring mirror of the ghastly spectacle and drove them away horrorstricken. Expressions of intransigence and revolt such as *The Apostle* and others remained safely hidden until after Rilke's death. We know from Lou's recent book of reminiscences that the poet not only withheld the *Book of Monkish Life* from publication, but that he destroyed a number of "prayers" to which the sensual substance clung too conspicuously (Lou, *Lebens.*, 175-176; see above, p. 127). And in his diary of the period there are entries which testify to moments of almost nihilistic despair (*Br.Frühzeit*, 404-407). When Annushka found the kitchen quite dark and empty at the very moment she was about to put her own child amongst the puppets in the bright, fragrant garden, she suddenly realized the hopeless discrepancy between life and art. In so far as her last act of vandalism and self-torturing "masochism" reflects a mood and a sentiment, it is descriptive of young Rilke. Later, he will learn to face even that kind of frightful situation without flinching, but not until he had distilled the Angel of the *Elegies* out of his existential and creative fears (*AW* I,257). When the Annushka sketch was penned in 1899, Rilke had let his Guardian Angel go and play in the tree tops although he saw to it that he could pull Him back at any time like the squirrel he used to hold on a long leash. Meanwhile the Angel could not be of much use, whereas the doll, with its nursery associations, kept haunting him with all the more fascination. In the *Fourth Elegy* the feeling of emptiness is at last outweighed by the presence of an Angel in whom all the horrors of life have been turned into strength. Although it was a forbidding strength, Rilke had evolved a symbol for it and that in itself was a matter of creative pride.

50. THE PUPPET THEATRE

Die Marionetten können traurig sein wie die Frauen
alter flandrischer Meister in einer Beweinung: gebogen
von Gram, und ihre Frohheit steigt in ihnen wie in den
Seligen auf dem jüngsten Gericht des Angelico.
                                                (*BTK*, 181-182)
The puppets can be sad like the dirgeful women
on the paintings of old Flemish Masters: bent
by grief, and their happiness can mount to Heaven like
that of the blessed ones in Angelico's *Last Judgment*.

SOMEWHERE in Rilke's nature there was a focal spot which made him be a child all his life and from which he was able to see deep into the dark beauties of "that vast forest which was childhood" (*Br.* I,466). But that spot was overgrown with a bewildering thicket of ambivalences: he himself could see through the open spaces but the child outside was not always able to find the image of its soul behind the impenetrable hedge. Rilke would have liked to enjoy the confidence of children, but paradoxically he was clumsy and ill at ease in their company (Kippenberg, 59; *MTT*, 21f). "I know nothing of children," he writes on December 16, 1902, "I don't know how to behave with them, I am awkward and embarrassed, and their world remains closed for me" (*Br. 1892-1904*, 285). Even his own cousin Egon, the boy with the immobile eye, who died very young and whose friendship Rilke, like his pseudonym Malte, wooed in vain—even Egon Rilke remained indifferent to his advances (*AW* II,104). In the *Fourth Elegy* we find him at the side of the poet in front of the dark and empty stage when all the others have left, but in the end he, too, goes away and leaves him utterly alone. In 1915, when Rilke's secret had long become publicly available through the *Book of Hours*, the *New Poems*, and above all Malte's *Notebook*, all these early experiences welled up again from the remote past, as if the poet were instinctively driven back to them in order that he might justify his behavior in the Angel's and in his own eyes. That these attempts at self-vindication were closely related to his desire to win the approval and confirmation of his family and early acquaintances at home is shown clearly in his *Fourth Elegy*. "Am I not right?" he insistently asks his deceased father and all those who used to love him. Whether many people realized at the time the widely ramified autobiographical implications of Rilke's work is beside the point; the fact is that he himself was profoundly aware of them, and remained so all his life.

Annushka's puppets are divided into two categories; those who are flexible and, hence, capable of responsive movement and life, and those who are made of solid wood, unbendable and unable to stand up by themselves. These are put against the wall and excluded from the play; they represent all that Rilke despised as orthodox and staunchly bourgeois. Lacking flexibility and ability to change they have to be propped by something else. Among them is the old man with the beard and the cross, evidently the effigy of the old, inherited God. How deep Rilke's grudge against Him was at this time is revealed by the role He is made to play: He has become stiff and wooden, He is excluded from the life of all but the narrow-minded and unemancipated, and if it happens that He is bowed to by two of the other puppets He is so overcome with gratitude that He falls over.

It is interesting to note that the first significant document on dolls which Rilke allowed to be printed was his essay of 1914, and we shall see that those who could read between the lines were struck at once by the weird underground experience out of which it had grown. It is true that there are a few minor references to dolls here and there, but they are purely descriptive, not symbolic. The most interesting one occurs in an essay on Maeterlinck's theatre which appeared in a Hamburg weekly at the beginning of 1901, a little more than a year after Rilke had confided the Annushka story to his diary. What makes this reference worth quoting is its obvious relationship to the poem *Marionettentheater* of July 20, 1907. "The doll has only once face," young Rilke writes, "and its expression is definite and final. There are horrified dolls and pious ones and simple ones. Each has only one feeling on its face, but this it has wholly, in its highest degree. Besides, each has at its disposal a flectional body. Its movements are not many, and they do not take place in its wrists or shoulder joints but are rather concentrated in a few oblong areas of the figure. There they are executed with zeal and with emphasis, and they are widely conspicuous. The puppets can be sad like the dirgeful women of old Flemish masters, bent by grief; and happiness rises in them as it rises in the blessed ones in Angelico's *Last Judgment*. And I believe that both feelings cannot be expressed more greatly, more simply, more intelligibly" (*BTK*, 181-182). It will be seen that the similarity of descriptive detail found here and in the *Marionettentheater* is striking and the first part of the poem, which contains the raw material of the original experience, could very well have been written as early as 1901. In reality, however, we have here another example of a potential poetic motif which remained dormant in Rilke's memory until it became pregnant with symbolic significance much later, in the fall of 1906. During his visit to Flanders, shortly after he had been dismissed by Rodin, he was reminded of his earlier association of the puppets with Flemish women as well as with the Flemish-French Maeterlinck. Even the memory of Angelico's *Last Judgment* seems to have crept into the symbolism of the poem.

At any rate, when the *New Poems* were to be published Rilke decided after some hesitation to withhold the *Marionettentheater*, for a reason which he could not explain (*Br. 1906-07*, 299, 305). It is likely that he had some misgivings as to its composition and form, but in the light of what we have learned we may reasonably assume that here, too, qualms of a more intimate nature played their part. Until the very last Rilke was keenly aware of the disconcerting gap between the effect which the ripe and noble symbols of his poetry had on the naïve reader and the down-to-earth reality in which they were embedded. He often warned eager correspondents not to confuse these two entirely different things. Ariel, too, that lovable pure creature in Shakespeare's *Tempest*, was in the service of "the foul witch Sycorax" before he became the airy ministering spirit of the wise and noble magician Prospero. Rilke's works may be compared to water-lilies waving their pure whiteness on the surface of a pond but reaching with a slimy stem into a muddy bottom. The question may be asked: why not be content with admiring the flowers without evoking the ugly image of the stem? True, not everybody can see the ugly beside the beautiful without the latter suffering from the juxtaposition. But while Rilke sometimes proclaimed that the work of art was *sui generis* and, therefore, resented all prying into its authorship and origins, he insisted with far more genuine authenticity upon the Beautiful being only the beginning of Terror. As Maritain states, "creative innocence is in no way moral innocence. . . . Thus it can be that a great poet can be corrupt, while his creative intuition never is. . . . Time, so Shelley puts it, will wash away all the sins of the poet in the eyes of those who receive from him the pure gift of a more profound discovery in the experience of beauty and the human soul" (Maritain, 374ff).

The symbolism of the *Marionettentheater* was inspired by a penitential procession which Rilke had witnessed in Furnes, West Flanders, in the summer of 1906. Unusually large statues representing penitent saints are carried through the streets by townspeople in the garb of penance. These religious demonstrations are always associated with a *Kermis* or fair enlivened by amusement and merriment. The Flemish are a sensuous people with a strong taste for pranks and thick laughter. Among the spectators there prevails a mixture of devotional curiosity and festive hilariousness, and it is difficult for them to resist the temptation to poke fun at the grotesque figures and at the angular movements of their bearers. These movements are a bit wooden and disjointed, unlike the oiled smoothness of the saltimbanques whom Rilke had watched with interest in the streets of Paris (*Fifth Elegy*; *Br.* II,575-576). Such processions date from the Middle Ages when people were still naïve believers whose conception of a defined God was, in Rilke's opinion, an illusion born out of fear of the unknown. Rilke was struck by the incongruity of a medieval faith clumsily displayed against the background of a modern spirit of jocose secularism. The whole thing reminded him of a puppet show in which not only the jointless statues were the puppets but their bearers as well. They did not seem aware of having been betrayed by their faith into becoming encaged prisoners of a misconceived God. Their voices were not theirs, but those of their imagined bondage; their faces seemed as uniform as their common belief, "plain, urgent and ideal," like those of children. It is against this background that we must try to understand Rilke's poem, a rough translation of which must be attempted for the sake of our analysis (*Gedichte, 1906-26,* 452ff).[1]

PUPPET THEATRE

Behind bars, like beasts,
they pile up their doings,
their voice is not theirs,
but in response they swing
their arms and swords
unusually and widely,
(inventive utilizers
of that which happens to shriek).

They have no joints
and hang a bit obliquely
and woodenly in the system of wires,
but they are very able
to kill or to dance
or even in general
to bow and do more.

They do not use memory;
they make themselves conscious
of nothing, and of their inner selves
they use only their breast,

---

[1] Rilke's symbolism of the doll and the puppet is sometimes brought into relationship with Kleist's essay "Über das Marionettentheater" (Mason, *Lebenshaltung,* 85; Kurt Bergel, "Rilke's *Fourth Elegy* and Kleist's Essay 'Über das Marionettentheater,'" *Modern Language Notes,* vol. 60 [February 1945], 73-78). While Rilke was much impressed by Kleist's work, especially in 1913-14 about the time of his *Notes on Dolls,* I am inclined to think that he was mainly so because Kleist's ideas seemed to coincide with his own in some important respects. Rilke's symbolism was the fruit of his own experience and creative activity. I should not be surprised if his conversations with Kassner were found to be more important in this connection than his acquaintance with Kleist's work.

sometimes to strike it
as if they smashed it to bits.
(they know, such behavior
is unequivocal and generally used).

Their big faces
are once and for all:
not like ours: plainer,
urgent and ideal;
open as on awakening
from the depths of a dream.
Naturally, that causes laughter
outside in the pit,
from where those on the benches
see
how the puppets hurt
and frighten each other and die in bundles
from the effect of their farces.

If someone should understand it otherwise
and sit and not laugh;
their only play would vanish
and they would enact their Last Judgment.
They would pull at their strings
and drag before the small wings
the hands from above, the hands,
the ever hidden, uncovered
ugly hands in red:
and they would rush out through all doors
and climb over the walls
and strike the hands dead.

    This poem does not give a mere realistic picture of a puppet show: in such a picture the revolt against the "hands in red" on the part of the dolls turned human would make no sense. We are obviously in the presence of symbolism which calls for interpretation. There are the puppets and their "only" play, there is the laughing audience and, in its midst, the imagined lonely observer who does not laugh, there are the hands in red and the revolt against them; a Last Judgment is mentioned, and all the time the poet observes the whole. What can it all mean? Whatever the answer, it must take into close account the whole context of Rilkean experience and thought.

The puppets themselves reveal two facets which Rilke puts into sharp relief in each of the four stanzas that constitute the first part of the poem. On one hand they seem entirely unaware of the leading actor overhead and, since they do not reflect upon themselves, the unauthenticity of their part in the drama remains hidden to them. That sort of naïveness begets contagious conviction which in turn makes for unusual and ample gestures. To that extent the puppets are entirely at one with themselves and their surroundings, they have the "open look" of the animal and the unperturbed frankness of the child; they are "full" in the sense of the *Fourth Elegy*. Their changeless expression, "once and for all," lacks the vacillating and unreliable mobility of the self-conscious human being torn by doubt. But they also lack the refined moderation of movement which is the result of discipline, self-control, and drill. They are still in a state of pure possibility, "like awkwardly matched animals that fall off from each other trying to mate" (*AW* I,261-262); and that makes their movements a bit wooden and jointless. All these are features which, as we know, Rilke admired but had lost, of which he had a vague memory and latent sense, but which he could no longer effectively reclaim. Later, in the *Fourth Elegy* he will find himself sitting "before the curtain of his heart" watching the happenings which pile up behind and which he realizes not to be his but those of some blind agent above. In the poem under consideration the assumption still seems to be that this agent is not blind but knowing and cruel. And that is precisely what he resented and what the puppets, too, resent when they find out. We have seen that Rilke later came to believe in a blind fate because that gave him a sense of greater personal freedom (see above, p. 207). For the time being, however, with the wound caused by his loss of Rodin's confidence bleeding in his heart, he had not yet found a satisfactory formula for his experience of fate; he was in an iconoclastic mood, like his puppets behind the bars of their little stage.

But there is another facet to the puppets in the poem: they do seem to have some instinctive awareness of an audience; they know that beating their breasts with great force is a widely used practice, likely to be unequivocal and impressive. Although they do not realize that their voice is not theirs, they are inventive enough to make good use of what they happen to hear, and there are a lot of noises in the world. And they seem to respond cheerfully to being watched and applauded. Somehow they like to mirror themselves in their audience, not knowing that the reflected image is superficial and deceptive. We are reminded of Malte with his mask and costume before the mirror, enjoying the reflection of his theatrical poses and gestures, or of the children amused by Annushka's dolls, until the harlequin's grin appeared and destroyed the illusion. Kassner, the rationally disciplined thinker, could logically deny the puppet all imagination, but Rilke, the poet, more at home in the world of symbolism, found it natural to impute to it some of his inventive imagination. To him the difference between the unresponsive doll of early childhood and the puppet was real.

It is interesting to note what sort of activities Rilke singles out as coming within the range of the puppet's performance. They can swing their arms and swords unusually and widely; they are very able to kill or to dance; they can bow and do other things of a similar nature; they can beat their breasts with conspicuous exaggeration; and they can hurt and frighten each other until they die in bundles. It is not difficult to recognize in these gestures those of the common run of people who are actors in life without knowing it, who can very well dance or kill while unctuously beating their breasts, of all those who live unauthentic lives and die unauthentic deaths. And all this, because they have blocked their open look with the obstructing wall of an audience, of an outside world, by means of a lopsided consciousness. If that wall could be ignored or broken through, their eyes could again range over the open space.

In order to define the role played by the audience in the pit, Rilke sets off their function in a separate line of the poem: they *see*, that is, as far as they know they face the spectacle without being in it. But though looking on, they, too, are in a sense part of the show; while they may know that there is a puppeteer, that knowledge is temporarily ineffective and is not the cause of their laughter. Besides, the puppeteer is thought to be concerned only with the puppets, not with the audience. What makes them laugh so naturally and irresistibly is the puppets' big, changeless faces, so different from "ours," that is, from those of all of us, including Rilke, in so far as we ourselves are engaged in the drama of life. We have become so opinionated that we laugh at the naïve behavior of the child in the nursery, as well as of the child in us. It is impossible not to be reminded of Rilke's controversy with Carl Hauptmann at Worpswede, in which he professed the view that the essence of the world's voice was laughter. We know what that universal laughter had done to solitary Rilke at the military academy and on various occasions in later life (see above, p. 123). It must also be remembered that Rilke himself was keenly aware of the peculiar psychological complex of the actor, whose very existence demands that he impersonate others, at the risk of forfeiting his own authentic self (Rehm, *Rilke*, 353ff). It was that sort of penetration into the other person or thing which he had been induced to attempt in his *New Poems* under the aegis of Rodin, and it looks very much as if at the time of his *Marionettentheater* he already instinctively rebelled against such an unreal mode of being.

As to the lone spectator who sits and does not laugh, that is the artist who alone is able to say: "I see this and that, while the others only guess or lie" (*FG*, 132). And the effect of his ominous silence is the same as that of the joker in the mirror: it makes the puppets see that it is not they who act but that they "are acted" by someone above. Suddenly realizing that they have been cheated out of their most precious possession, namely their inner childhood, by their awakened consciousness of the hidden phantom with "hands in red," they are stricken with horror, with a horror all the more intense as that phantom evidently uses the audience, too, as an instrument and as a victim of its hideous contrivances. In their wrath and fury they drag the "uncovered, ugly hands" down on the stage and call them to account in a Last Judgment of their own. Their play, which they thought so interesting and varied, has revealed itself monotonously the same and has come to naught; what is left is a dark empty stage and a grey waft of air congealing the horrified audience. It seems, therefore, that in the end the effect of the imaginative puppet and that of the stupid doll were the same in this respect: they both caused Rilke to experience the horror of the void. In fact, the puppet show, being admittedly an artistic performance, proves even more nihilistic in its effects than the doll, since it exposes with appalling force the vulnerability of all art, including that of Rilke himself.

Finally "the hands in red" are those of a hidden God who had been taken for granted as a provident one. According to the *Stories of God* man was created by an absent-minded God whose hands worked independently while His eyes were directed to the earth where things had begun to stir. It then happened that in his impatience for freedom man slipped out of the kneading hands before he was completed, so that God was not even able to see what His creature looked like. In order to find it out He had His right hand (Christ) cut off, and He sent it down to the earth in order that it observe humanity and report to Him. Meanwhile God's bleeding arm covered the whole earth with blood and He almost died as a result of it. Realizing that He had made a mistake He promptly called His right hand back, but to this day He does not know what man looks like. The only ones who can tell Him are the children and—so Rilke adds with great caution and reserve—"those who paint, who write poems and who build" (*GG*, 13). Moreover, keeping in mind that for Rilke there existed a close kinship between God and Death, we may refer to one of the *New Poems* entitled *Experience of Death* which he wrote on the island of Capri not very long after his trip to Furnes (*NG*, 64; Schnack, 12). In it Death wears a tragic mask which conceals His true face from us so that we really have no reason for showing Him either admiration and love or hatred. In this disguise Death plays the leading role in the world of men, and so long as we are avid for applause and anxious to please, He keeps playing with us, although our applause is not meant for Him. But every now and then something happens in the show, the effects of which the masked actor neither intended nor foresaw. When someone dear to us dies we suddenly see beyond the deceptive stage and catch a glimpse of the true reality behind. While those to whom that happens must continue to make "eternal gestures" and to recite what they have learned, their experience of death enables them to play life more authentically, without any thought of success or applause.

From all this we may conclude that by 1907 Rilke's grudge against the conventional God had increased rather than weakened in intensity. Even the "near" God of the *Book of Hours* was no longer effectively real and a satisfactory substitute was not at hand. Rilke had few qualms about dethroning Christ and robbing the Madonnas and the Saints of their nimbus, but his treatment of God, which always remained closely linked with his nebulous memory of childhood, was exceedingly ambiguous, vacillating and, on the whole, discreet. In a poem of September 1923 entitled *Imaginary Career of Life* Rilke retraced in great strides the circle of his life. First, a boundless childhood, aimless and without frustration. Then, all of a sudden, "fright, barrier, school, drudgery and precipitous descent into temptation and loss." Then, "pride," challenge and triumphant revenge! And finally, alone, in the light, cold atmosphere of vast space. But here, in the depths of achieved erect stature, a pause, a longing for the beginning, for the old. And that was the moment when "God burst forth from His ambush" (*Br.Muzot*, 217-218). There came to prevail "an indescribable discretion" between Rilke and God (*Br.Muzot*, 196). Meanwhile he was overcome again and again by anguish and a ghastly dread of annihilation, until he found a measure of relief by unloading them on the Angel and taking refuge in Orpheus. The God "in ambush" produced in him a growing feeling of uncertainty and fear and, hence, a general reluctance to face Him outright in his own name; instead, he used all sorts of pseudonyms and sought devious approaches via the Angel, Death, or Orpheus. The apocalyptic horror which causes the puppets at the end of their drama to kill the hands in red, is the same kind of horror which in the *Fourth Elegy* Rilke faces stoically in the expectation that, if he waits long enough, something redeeming must happen.

   Some time during 1913, in the arid days of disillusionment caused by Spain, Rilke read Shakespeare's *Tempest*, obviously in Schlegel's translation. It must have made a deep impression on him for it inspired a poem *The Spirit Ariel* which he wrote soon afterward. And no wonder, since here was Prospero, a former Duke of Milan, who after being betrayed by a deceitful brother had withdrawn to a lonely island far away from the world of men. In this blessed solitude he finds himself possessed with powers which enable him to unlock as by magic Nature's creative secrets. These are now at his disposal in the person of Ariel whom he has freed from abject service with the same unexpected suddenness "with which a youth tears himself away from all conventions and petty considerations." But Ariel, the creative spirit, will not serve forever! His vast home is the universe and he is impatient to vanish in it, diffused and anonymous. Prospero must coax him, remind him of what he has done for him and reiterate the promise that he will set him free as soon as a last set of magical feats has been accomplished. In his post-Spanish mood Rilke imagines Prospero almost relishing as a sweet temptation the prospect of letting Ariel go and of returning to the world of hazard and dependence. The old magician consoles himself with the thought that once he was privileged to have the airy spirit at his beck and call and that, though now poor, weak, and aging, he will continue to breathe in Ariel's invisible fragrance. And like Shakespeare's play Rilke's poem ends with an epilogue, which he puts between parentheses. "(Have I already let it go [i.e. the elemental creative spirit]? Now that this man has become a duke again he frightens me. How he gently pulls the wire through his head and hangs himself among the other puppets and begs the play from now on to be kind to him. . . . What an epilogue to once achieved lordship. To undo, to stand naked with nothing but one's own strength: 'which is most faint')" (*AW* I,352-353). Unlike Shakespeare's epilogue, which is addressed to the audience, that of Rilke, for whom the audience is notoriously irrelevant, is addressed to himself. Moreover, the more realistic Shakespeare let his Prospero return to the world of men where he properly belonged, or, as Rilke sarcastically puts it, where he could gently pull the wire through his head again and hang himself up among the other puppets, in the hope that from now on the play would be kind to him. Rilke himself, who had so passionately accused Paula Modersohn of doing just that, only toyed with the idea as with a bitter-sweet temptation but in the end shied away from it as from a poor "epilogue to once achieved lordship." Depending on his mood, Rilke could use the doll or the puppet now as the symbol of enviable "openness" and creative innocence, now as that of hopeless futility and fatalism in a world of stupid convention and chance.

◇◇

Die Puppe hat das grausig Realistische . . . und
am Effekt erhitzt sich das Blut. . . .

(Br.Lou, 377)

The doll has that horribly realistic appearance . . .
and its effect is to excite our blood. . . .

◇◇

RILKE's *Notes on Dolls*, an essay in masterly prose, was prompted
by a collection of unusual dolls of which he saw colored reproductions in Paris and which belonged to an eccentric woman of the
avant-garde, Lotte Pritzel. Rilke saw her quite often later in Munich. Her wax dolls were characterized by a high degree of sophistication; they were stylized to the point of bloodlessness, in dancing or
supine positions of intellectual suggestiveness (*LPP*, 14ff). Their
existence, so Rilke comments, was entirely divorced from childhood
whose joys and sorrows they had outgrown; they had started a life
of their own, completely made of unreality (*AW* II,274-284; *SW*,
43-50).

Rilke wonders whether in the end such is the destiny of all childhood dolls and whether, therefore, all the fuss made over them is not
the result of a shameful fraud on their part. This leads him to scrutinize his own relationship to them in the light of his later disillusionment. Initiated into the first nameless intimacies of early nursery life, they were dragged into spindle beds as promising bedfellows or, cuddled in "the heavy folds of sickness" they became implicated in the dreams of feverish nights. And what did they contribute to that fullness of imagined companionship? Exactly nothing.

With cutting resentment Rilke contrasts their impotent limpness
with the warm and grateful helpfulness of other things of daily
usage. These may become outwardly worn, but in sharing their
melancholy mortality with man they glow with tenderness and
delicate beauty. To be sure, the child needed such impassive things
which could do nothing but put up with all its whims. In its relation with the grown-ups the child could confidently surrender to

their superior knowledge, lose itself in them; but with the doll it was forced to assert itself because there was nothing to surrender to. The stupid doll forced the child, as it were, to split itself into part and counterpart, if the overwhelming world outside was to be kept from engulfing it. It became a kind of test tube in which the child watched the bubbling and coloring of all the mysteries of its own young life, although even that function was of the child's invention. Had the doll had the least bit of imagination it would have found a way of using its unresponsive silence as a means of inspiring awe and achieving fame, as was the case with the Christian God and the Ancients' Fate.

At a time when everybody else seemed anxious to give soothing answers the doll's blank stare confronted Rilke for the first time with "the feeling of hollowness, that heart-pause, in which one would perish if the whole gently enduring Nature did not carry one over abysses like a lifeless thing. Are we not strange creatures, who let ourselves go and invest our first love where it has no chance of being repaid, with the result that our lingering taste of that most spontaneous affection becomes permeated with the bitter knowledge that it was in vain? Who knows whether in later life many a one does not derive from such memories the suspicion that he is incapable of being loved? Whether in some of us the doll does not continue heinously at work so that we keep hankering after some vague gratification simply because we rebel against the discontentedness with which the doll has spoiled our nature?"

It is obvious that the reason why the doll comes in for such a severe treatment is because the boy, having been brought up as a girl, was hopelessly torn in opposite directions from the beginning. Details of the analysis make it clear that the doll which Rilke had in mind was a female one. His false girlish relationship to her could not for long arouse his imagination to creative activity and his boyish affection for her was doomed to still greater sterility. When he writes about the rocking-horse, his spirit of adventure is kindled to flaming enthusiasm, and even the head of a Punch, indestructible in his ugliness, is able to produce a feeling of positive significance. Here Rilke is at home in an appropriate world and the illusion of valid vitality is at least supported by his sex. Not so with the doll which can convince neither the boy nor the girl in him.

Rilke, as has already been pointed out, often accused himself of being cruel and inconsiderate in his human relations and for this he blamed his early association with dolls. In its uncouth affection the child handles the doll roughly, sometimes taking sadistic enjoyment in tearing her fingers out of joint, and that cruelty is carried over into later life (*So lass*, 36-37). The essay on dolls had been written at the end of January or the beginning of February 1914, just about the time his correspondence with Benvenuta had begun; it was published in a monthly in March of the same year. When Rilke read it to Benvenuta a little later at Duino, she at once sensed the perverse implications of this uncanny autopsy of the most innocent joys, and she did not hide her feelings from him (Hattingberg, 202-208). Back in Paris, disillusioned and sick unto death, Rilke asked Lou in a letter of June 9, 1914, what she thought of it. Unfortunately Lou's first reply is lost but on June 20 the poet commented as follows: "But is it not frightful that one should unconsciously write such things and deal with one's innermost realities under the pretext of doll memories, and immediately afterward put one's pen down in order to chew the ghastly cud again, endlessly and as never before, until every morning one's mouth is dry from the rags with which . . . one has been filled up into one's throat?" (*Br*. I,506-507) Together with this comment Rilke also sent Lou his poem *Turning* with the Kassner motto "The way from creative empathy to greatness goes through the sacrifice," which Lou brought into direct relationship with the Benvenuta experience (see above, p. 212). To her this experience appeared basically as the effect of a frustrated body that insisted on more than mere artistic "eye-work." Rilke's body— so she thought—had sensed the need for "a turning" long before his mind had become aware of it with the result that it had thrown him into the arms of a woman "who saw herself in his eyes as in mirrors" (*Br.Lou*, 344-346), instead of wedding his spirit to the one "inner girl never yet loved." We have already noted the restlessness in which Rilke found himself after his stay in Spain, and in which his body was as deeply involved as his spirit. He and Lou had taken a trip to the Riesengebirge in October 1913 during which their conversation had dwelled a great deal on the problem of sex in the modern world. Apparently Rilke had planned to write a cycle of *Phallic Hymns*, in connection with which Lou remarked that compared to the complex and meaningful articulation of the other parts of the body the phallus stands out as a uniquely stupid part. It concentrates an indescribable totality on such a small space that the latter is experienced as something radically "other," almost as a mere symbol. For us moderns, who use matter only as the basis and "lowest step" toward the spiritual, sex has become "a contradiction, something strangely undifferentiated, yet fateful—something half-way between a giggle and a dismayed shudder" (*Br.Lou*, 329-330, 601).

Later, in a letter of June 27, 1914, Lou refers again to that uncanny experience in which we are for the first time confronted with our body as with the inert, sluggish counterpart of our selves. Organic though it is, it nevertheless has the effect of something inorganic, almost hostile and makes a persistent claim on us, an illegitimate claim perhaps, but an irresistible one. The conscious emergence of our body as the most immediate and inescapable "thou" with which we have to cope was in Lou's opinion basically related to our first encounter with the weird otherness of the doll (*Br.Lou*, 346-348). When in September 1914 Rilke sent her a copy of the *Five Songs* in which the War God is at first enthusiastically hymned, then sadly accused, Lou was again reminded of the doll. She had read in the newspapers that a chauvinistic populace had vented its "patriotic" feelings by placing a puppet in enemy's uniform in the path of an oncoming train. We give our children dolls —so Lou felt—not merely for play's sake but in order that they may learn to assert themselves in a strange and possibly hostile world. Unfortunately children learn so thoroughly that even when they grow up they will use the horribly realistic features of the doll to gratify their passions vicariously upon it. The doll becomes a dreadful ghost demanding hideous sacrifices. Truly the keen-eyed Freudian Lou was able to interpret the meaning of Rilke's dolls in all their obscure ramifications, and her comments were by no means mere elucubrations of her brain. Rilke, too, made the world of man responsible for the wretched existence of those aging, wizened girls who walk the streets of Paris, with whom Life played as with dolls and "whose arms it kept stretching out spring after spring until they became loose in the shoulder joints" (*AW* II,181). In conclusion we may add that as early as April 3, 1903, Rilke had written to Ellen Key: "I believe my mother played with me as with a doll" (*Br. 1892-1904*, 332). No wonder that he explained his inability to assume the responsibilities of love by the fact that he could not love his mother.

52. THE DOLL, THE ANGEL'S PLAYTHING?

Engel und Puppe: dann ist endlich Schauspiel.
(Fourth Elegy)

Angel and doll: then at last there is drama.

RETURNING to the *Fourth Elegy* we are surprised to see the Angel appear suddenly as a sort of ideal complement to the puppet (*AW* I,257). Nowhere in the three documents discussed in the preceding chapters is any reference made to the Angel, although He was as genuine a part of childhood as the doll. But in the child's consciousness as well as in man's memory they are kept strictly apart: the soul of the Angel resists being breathed into a body of sawdust. Even the picture or the statue of an Angel could not be played with in the same way as the doll or some other toy. At the outset the Angel had wings and could fly from heaven to earth and from earth to heaven; He could lift the child from the depths of nightmares back among the familiar things of the day, or above them to rapturous heights, but He could not be used as a warm bedfellow or share the burning fever of restless nights. Later, the "stern Angel of ebony" still remained a reality of potential power. Moreover, the doll-soul could kindle mature creative imagination only after it had been dissociated from the rags, and even then only by virtue of imaginative functions which belong not to the doll but to the puppet.

In the letter of January 23, 1912, in which Rilke confesses having "no window on men," he singles out two types of people capable of making him appreciate things human, namely those who died young and still more the woman in love (*Br.* I,345-347). The reasons which he gives are that they appear to him "with the unproblematical distinctness of the puppet (which is outward surface designed to express conviction), and that they are closed types beyond which you cannot go, so that you could write the natural history of their soul." The soul of the dead youth and that of the woman in love are open to immense possibility and are for ever left in that "happy" state, the one by death, the other by privation. They can no longer become involved in the ambiguities of life so that their petrified physiognomies are "once and for all" like the face of the puppet, and in that outward appearance they suggest unequivocal conviction. A diagnosis such as this shows clearly that Rilke's odd concern for these two types of people was dictated at least as much by his search for poetic symbols as by genuine human sympathy. He was sitting "before the curtain of his heart" and the drama behind it was to make him more conscious of, and richer by, sentiments for which we have seen him grope all his life, namely those of aimless innocence and of unfettered freedom. And by no means is it pure chance that in this connection an affinity is felt to exist between the loving woman and the puppet.

The woman whom Rilke had especially in mind was Marianne Alcoforado, the Portuguese nun who had been betrayed by her French lover de Chamilly. Her case "is so wonderfully pure," Rilke writes, "because she does not project the flow of her sentiment into the imaginary but leads its genial quality back into herself with infinite strength; merely enduring it, doing nothing else. . . . Her rare tactfulness deemed it repugnant to apply to God something which was not at the outset meant for Him and which Count de Chamilly could scorn" (*Br.* I,347). It is appropriate to observe that this latter aspect, too, was part of the sentiment by which Rilke became the richer through Marianne's experience. But Marianne not only failed by a slim margin to become a saint, she might even have become an Angel, had she not only not let her sentiment flow into God but had she also allowed God to thrust it back into her.

We have here an interesting clue as to how Rilke differentiated between the puppet, the saint, and the Angel. The puppet is, by its very nature of pure outwardness and face, unaware of the puppeteer; if it ever became aware of him it would cease to be a puppet and become a meaningless object. In its relation to the audience it has an "open" look and, hence, is unequivocal and convincing. The saint is aware of God, the puppeteer, but far from destroying him this awareness causes him to flow into God as into a safe harbor. He also faces the world, is even tempted by it but makes constant efforts to look away. To that extent he lacks the "open" look, shares the ambiguities of man, and is neither quite unequivocal nor convincing. The Angel is conscious of God but does not flow into Him because God Himself throws him completely back into himself. By the explicit sanction and will of God the Angel's essence is to be self-contained; to such a being the audience, that is, the world of man, is entirely irrelevant, as if non-existing. Hence the Angel is unequivocal, no doubt, but in His narcissistic "selfishness," forbidding and unconvincing. Finally, in this whole context it must not be forgotten that in the light of Rilke's conviction God is not a true reality, but is in the making, and His maker is the poet. If Marianne had not brought the flow of her sentiment back into herself but allowed it to drift into God, she would merely have fooled herself. In a letter to Eva Cassirer of January 2, 1914, Rilke points out that in his opinion even the saint does not at bottom believe in God's effective help (Mason, *Münchhausen*, 21). Elsewhere in his *Memory in Verhaeren*, which provided the thoughts for his fictitious *Workman's Letter* of 1922, he writes: "How wonderful, Verhaeren, that God does not make Himself more clear; how He would overtake us and make everything [that we do] meaningless" (Mason, *Münchhausen*, 73; *AW* II,408).

In short, both doll and puppet were in constant danger of revealing themselves as frauds and, since Rilke had "no window on men," the result was the yawning abyss—were it not for the Angel. But the self-centered Angel meant solitary containment and total indifference to the "world" which lay as a vast beckoning expanse between the mutually exclusive precincts of the puppet's absolute naïveness and the Angel's absolute consciousness. In this "world" outwardness and engagement prevail, but without naïve innocence; again and again Rilke yielded to its enticements, widely, shrewdly, and evasively, shunning such bonds as interfered with his work, but on the whole with a feeling of frustration and guilt. If Rilke had been able to take the ambiguities, obligations, and anxieties of life for what they are, namely realities which must be assumed and affirmed courageously together with all the rest, if he had not been inclined to draw the blood out of them first and to encapsulate them in an uncommunicable Angel, or to volatilize them into metamorphic movement and pure symbolism, we would have neither his *Elegies*, nor his *Sonnets* and would be the poorer to that extent. But let us not make the mistake of giving to these beautiful poems existential meanings which they cannot have. Plain, unconscious outwardness and undiluted inward consciousness cannot be made to function simultaneously in the world of time and space. It is true that in the *Fourth Elegy* such a fantastic possibility is envisaged inasmuch as the Angel is literally forced by the poet's silent persistence to take hold of the puppet, draw it into His immanent movement and play with it. But Rilke instinctively knew that such a performance could not by any stretch of the imagination be thought of as taking place in our midst: if at all, it was to be imagined *above us*, and that remains fiction, whichever way we look at it. The only act of life in which that fiction can be given any semblance of reality (outside of mysticism) is that particular kind of artistic creation in which time and space are temporarily obliterated and a magical world is evoked. This shows again how insensibly Rilke's Angel had to give way to Orpheus, how the *Sonnets* had to issue out of the *Elegies*. Rilke felt very keenly that some such transformation of the complexities of life into an expression of wholeness had to be attempted, if the centrifugal forces of modern civilization were to be checked; but it is obvious that his own desperate solution drove a deep wedge between him and his environment. No wonder that he was frightfully anxious to be sanctioned by his father who, he suspected, did not even approve of him in death; just as in the *Requiem* for Paula he insisted with deep concern that he was right, not she.

One cannot escape the conclusion that in spite of his emphatic self-dedication to the Earth Rilke was far less realistic than Goethe who admonished himself through the mouth of the Goddess of Truth: "You see how wise, how necessary it was to unveil to you only a little at a time! Hardly are you safe from the coarsest illusions, hardly are you master of your first waywardness of childhood, than you think yourself a superman, than you neglect to fulfil man's duty! How are you so different from others? Know yourself and live in peace with the world!" Granting that twentieth-century Rilke had to cope with a degree of social complexity and cultural deterioration unknown a century earlier, he not only lacked Goethe's firm grasp of empirical reality but shied away from it with intuitive fear of committing himself. There was a time, in 1908, when Rilke took Goethe severely to task for not having responded generously to Bettina Brentano's exuberant veneration expressed in her letters. "I wish I could have been the one to answer her letters; that would have become an ascension into Heaven, without blushing, in full sight of everybody. . . . How we would have loved each other, face to face" (*Br. 1907-14,* 45-46). Less than four years later he did indeed attempt such an ascension with Benvenuta, only to fall back on the ground with broken wings. No wonder that immediately afterward he envied Goethe to whom even in youth "life's actual yield became at once the measure of what he could assimilate and of what Fortune might offer him." Young Goethe laid his hand on "nothing that was not suited to him and made the right use of everything suitable" (*Br. Lou*, 351). Of Rilke it may be said that in the beginning was the word, the beautiful, liberating Rilkean word; the more universally-engaged Goethe, on the other hand, insisted on appropriate active participation in the affairs of men: "In the beginning was the Deed" (*Faust*).

Between November 1915, the time of the *Fourth Elegy*, and February 1922 Rilke was unable at any time to gather all his creative forces for the successful completion of the *Elegies*. In the winter of 1920-21, in the lonely castle of Berg am Irchel, he came very near reaching his goal, but the uncertainty of tenure of this cherished retreat and the emotional agitation caused by his concern for Merline kept his mind in a state of division. It has been suggested that the strange poems of the fictitious Count C. W. arose as a poor substitute and that Rilke's peculiar reluctance to acknowledge them as his was due to that circumstance (Bassermann, 355). Be that as it may, the thick sediment of childhood in these poems reveals Rilke's secret hope that childhood might be the link with which his broken sense of continuity could be restored. This is confirmed by the large number of poems of the preceding years, all gravitating somehow around the *Fourth Elegy*, in which childhood is a recurring theme. A few days before this elegy came into being Rilke was inspired by Dürer's *Apocalypse* and composed a poem in which the Lord bids John to write, with both hands, words of utter destruction, rejecting all temporal concerns of man. Only in the child is the Son of God willing to pause and to allow the diffuse worldly roar to collect in His shell-like ear. "Lo, in this narrow creature, placed apart, will I organize the tumult of my worlds" (*Gedichte, 1906-26*, 570-573). A similar apocalyptic mood, though more bacchanal and personally colored, prevails in the *Ode to Bellman* written a few months earlier. Its recklessness reminds us of Annushka's destructive madness or of the puppets' revolt against the "ugly hands in red."[2] Again, the *Requiem*

[2] The *Ode to Bellman* was written against the background of the war which by now was threatening to engage Rilke in a military way. Bellman was a Swedish

on the Death of a Boy, dated November 13, 1915, is literally permeated with the mysteries of childhood and the happy condition of
early death (*Gedichte, 1906-26*, 121-125). It is true that Rilke's short
stay in Paris in the latter part of October 1920, a few weeks before he
went to live at Berg am Irchel, also helped him recover his lost
sense of continuity. But it is significant that during that visit he
did not seek to renew personal contact with old friends and acquaintances but only with the city, as the scene of his anguish in
the years of the Malte experience. And that anguish was basically a
symptom of his desperate need to come to terms with obscure childhood obsessions. It was not Paris but childhood, that innermost personal possession, which constituted the connecting link in the broken
chain of past and future.

As to the *Fourth Elegy* itself, it expresses the melancholy feeling
that we have irremediably lost the yardstick with which to measure
the child's universe: "Who shows a child first as it stands? Who
places it in its constellation and puts the measure of distance in its
hand?" (*AW* I,258). It is more than a coincidence that in December 1920 at Berg am Irchel Rilke penned a fragmentary poem which
reads very much like a comment and paraphrase of this obscure passage. At the very beginning of this fragment stand the lines: "That
childhood was, let not that nameless trust of Heaven be snatched
from you by fate."[3] And the poet goes on to exalt childhood as an
ineffable gift of Heaven, although he realizes that it, too, is exposed to
countless dangers, less protected even than the grown-ups since it is
not aware of the threat. The mother's solicitude strengthens the
child's feeling of security based on ignorance, but how deceptive her
protection in reality is! The moment of anguish and doubt comes

---

writer, composer and singer of popular tavern songs, some of which Rilke had
heard performed at Munich in the early fall of 1915. One of these songs, which
seems to have made a particularly deep impression on Rilke, is addressed to a
versatile but consumptive musician and suggests a macabre scene in which wine
and sex are wedded to sickness and death (Bellman, 57f). In some of his songs
Bellman parodies the Epistles of St. Paul. Hendrik van Loon has translated and illustrated a selection of them in *The Last of the Troubadours* (Simon and Schuster,
New York, 1939), in which book the original accompaniments for the lute are reset
for the piano by Grace Castagnetta.
[3] In *AW* I this fragment is dated "Winter 1913-14," which would mean that it
was written either in Paris or somewhere in Germany. That dating would have
been plausible enough since Rilke was obsessed with childhood at that time. However, according to the recent and more authentic volume of poems from 1906 to
1926 it originated in Berg am Irchel in December 1920.

unexpectedly, and treacherously grows the fork of ambivalence "on the Judas-tree of choice," invading even the child's innocent play with the doll. The generous feeling imputed without envy to the body of rags is received back by the child in a movement of fancied reciprocation which serves only to underline the child's self-duplication and frightful loneliness. "Vastness of the play," the poet exclaims, "when fertile and confident Nature used to apply her happy invention to spending herself even among remotest descendants, far beyond grand-children" (*AW* I,333). Indeed, in the child's consciousness the doll could pass painlessly and in easy metamorphoses through a hundred deaths, be at the same time mother, child, and grandchild. The enormous expanse of feeling created between child and doll was as vast as the space between stars; it made the child lonely and remote like a constellation. We grown-ups have become utterly incapable of penetrating through the atmosphere which separates us from childhood. "Oh doll, remotest figure—just as the stars are reared into worlds by the effects of distance and space, so you convert the child into a constellation." In this enviable state the child remains inaccessible until it outgrows its firmament, until the "nameless rupture" takes place—when, "filled with half the [child's] existence, it [the doll] no longer complies, but disowns and refuses to know. Stares with a gaze of refusal, lies prone, unknowing: not even a thing any more . . . see, how the things are ashamed for its sake . . ." (*AW* I,334).

It would seem, therefore, that it took Rilke this long agonizing period from Duino 1912 to Muzot 1922 to outgrow the terrible Angel in a desperately continued tug of war, and to enter, transfigured, into the ethereal realm of Orpheus. Already in some of the later *Elegies* his dedication to the Earth, his determined will to transform the visible things and man's achievements of the past into invisible inner possession with which he might impress the Angel, were expressions of the poet's enthusiastic resolve to escape from the elegy into Orphic praise. He labored and moaned to get over the hurdle of the *Elegies* just as years ago he had toiled to complete Malte's *Notebook*: "I cannot go any further until I get through him [Malte], he lies in my way" (*Br. 1907-14*, 50). On the day before the *Sonnets* came about he wondered: "Oh when, oh when, oh when will there be enough of wailing and of saying?" (*Gedichte, 1906-26*, 147).

There exists a remarkable parallelism between this period, pivoting on childhood and the *Fourth Elegy*, and the period of adolescent awakening. Just as in his adolescence Rilke had cut himself loose from under the protective wings of the Guardian Angel, he now emancipates himself from the Terrible Angel. It is by no means an expression of humility when in the *Seventh Elegy* the poet exclaims: "Wooing no longer, not wooing, grown-up voice, be the nature of thy cry." In plain language he means to say that from now on the inaccessible Angel is to be left to His own sphere in order that the poet may gain complete freedom from the potential threat of anxieties transformed and embodied by the Angel. As far as Rilke is concerned he is going to build his own invisible world in which he can sing his pure and undisturbed praise. It is true that the *Eighth Elegy* constitutes a check to that trend, but it is to be observed that, though written in 1922, its mood and symbolism go back to the winter of 1912-13 in Spain. After returning to Paris, Rilke read Lou's *Three Letters to a Boy* which contained ideas similar to those of the *Eighth Elegy* concerning the "small creature, the gnat" whose womb was the world in which it lived; and in a letter of February 20, 1914, he comments at some length on this enviable manner of unfractured existence (*Br.* I,489-490; Kassner, *Erinnerung*, 317). It is also a fact that the *Tenth Elegy* conjures up once more the vast dominion of the Plaints, but only as a clarification and final confirmation of an earlier vista of future praise, expressed in the opening lines which date from January, 1912: "Let me some day, at the end of grim understanding sing exulting praise to assenting Angels" (*AW* I,276). In 1922 the time had come when the Angels could be made to assent.

From the point of view of cyclical composition Rilke achieved a distinct artistic effect by embedding the lamentations of the *Eighth Elegy* in the optimism of the *Seventh* and *Ninth*: his Orpheus issues everywhere out of the Angel. Equally effective in this sense is the position of the Land of the Plaints at the end of the cycle, as the gateway through which the God of Praise must break forth, and here again the phallic implications are unmistakable. Indeed, in the *Tenth Elegy* the land where "children play and lovers embrace each other— away from the road, in the poor grass where dogs follow their instincts"—that land of "true reality" is situated immediately on the other side of the planks which separate it from the booths of the fairgrounds where grown-ups are watching "how the money multiplies, anatomically; the very sex organ of money is shown and everything else, the whole process, not for entertainment's sake only but because it educates and stimulates fertility" (*AW* I,277). We are reminded of the *Book of Poverty and Death* where God is to "build a beautiful womb" for the artist of the future "whose shame shall be erected in a blond grove of young hair" (*AW* I,94; see above, p. 168).

In the *Fourth Elegy* the poet imagines himself sitting "before the curtain of his heart," and the spectacle which he sees when the curtain rises is a review of what has taken place on the stage of his life. Since that stage is the heart, we must expect events of inner quality and significance rather than external incidents. The first and most pervasive of these events is characterized as "leave-taking." To Rilke that was easy to understand, for his life was riddled with it in an endless variety of ways: the loss of childhood, of the Guardian Angel and the dolls, of his inherited God, Madonnas and saints, the forced departure from home for the military school, the voluntary farewell to his family and to Prague, the separation from wife and child, at first necessitated by circumstances, later willingly perpetuated, the countless severances from love and other human bonds throughout life. The second event is the garden, slightly shaky and unreliable, well-known to Rilke, too, the kind of garden which Annushka loved because it made her forget the grey kitchen but which she later destroyed because it had proved incapable of receiving the big blue doll, the fruit of her body; it meant the dream-garden of Rilke's early poetry which helped him ignore all narrowmindedness of his environment in Prague and elsewhere; it was the symbol of later illusory attempts to solve existential anxieties through art. Then comes "the dancer," the actor who pretends to gambol through life with social smoothness and assumed mimicry, like Wilhelm von Scholz in Munich, like Rilke himself at Linz and in all intervals of life in which he displayed his polished elusiveness in a shallow world. That sort of existence, of "acting" for the entertainment of oneself and others, he often labelled a fraud, the hidden core of which was drabness and kitchen-greyness; its mask was half full and half empty. It is significant that here, too, Rilke passes over all expressions of sincere human endeavor outside of art, because they appeared to him vitiated by self-consciousness and self-deceit. Under those circumstances there only remained art unspoiled, the puppet with the "open" look and a face "once and for all." As long as this lasted, it created the sensation of fullness, but when it faded away with the return of the grin in the mirror, there was nothing left but darkness. It was some such grim outcome that Rilke's father had vaguely feared for his son when the latter had decided to become a poet. Yet Rilke remained obdurate and faced the darkness many times, sometimes for long periods, until finally he created his Angel of the *Elegies*. Unfortunately this Angel had taken on characteristics wholly incompatible with the puppets' naïveness, thus emphasizing the conflict all the more sharply and necessitating the search for a new level of enlightened illusion: that presided over by Orpheus.

Of course, there is nothing to prevent one from interpreting more ideally and in terms of more universal significance the complex relationship of Angel and doll, Angel and Orpheus, Elegy and Praise. But the basic autobiographical implications are so unequivocal that losing sight of them entails the risk of twisting the poet's intentions beyond recognition.

Late in 1925 Rilke was asked by his Polish translator von Hulewicz for some elucidation of his *Elegies*. "Am I the person," he answered, "who can give the right explanation? The *Elegies* reach infinitely beyond me" (*Br.Muzot*, 371). Nevertheless, he then proceeds to explain, obviously realizing that whatever he may have to say will be in the nature of a *post factum* analysis. Indeed, his comment is a sort of rationalization, made almost three years after the *Elegies* were completed, that is, when the throes were long past and a more abstract interpretation could be attempted. But such retrospective formulations tend to falsify, both because they make use of a different context and because perspectives have shifted. Of the Angel Rilke writes: "The Angel of the *Elegies* is that creature in whom the transformation of the visible into the invisible, which we carry out, appears already completed. For the Angel of the *Elegies* all towers and palaces gone by are still extant, *because* they have long been invisible, and the existing towers and bridges of our days are already invisible, *although* still materially enduring (for us). The Angel of the *Elegies* is that being which warrants our granting a higher rank to the real in the invisible—hence 'terrible' for us, since we, His lovers and transformers, still cling to the visible" (*Br.Muzot*, 376). Now, the *Elegies* themselves contain nothing that would indicate that the Angel ever had performed the function of transforming visible palaces and towers and bridges into invisible ones. In him they were invisible from the start. It is the privilege of the poet to do the transforming;

it is the poet who thereby hopes to impress the Angel in His self-centered aloofness. The Angel's superiority came from His ability to immunize existential anxieties and to abolish or ignore the hostility between them and creative work. For the poet himself that remained an ideal beyond reach, so that he had to content himself with achieving sovereignty in an illusory Orphic sphere. If later Rilke endowed the Angel in an eminent degree with a function which belonged in a less perfect manner to the poet, that was the effect of retrospective abstraction.

53. DREAMCROWNED AGAIN

Es ist ein Spiegel, was sie hält. Siehst du:
sie zeigt dem Einhorn sein Bild—.
(Malte's *Notebook, AW* II,114)

What she holds in her hand is a mirror.
You see: she shows the Unicorn its image—.

THE question may be asked: what validity for himself and for us is there in Rilke's construed and strangely solitary world? That it provided him with a shield against the inner and outer ambiguities of existence which he felt so keenly, of that there is no doubt. But plenty of evidence is at hand to show that it did so only up to a point. Not only was he at times confronted with circumstances which left him utterly helpless and adrift, not only was naked Death with its old-fashioned Beyond incessantly lurking behind the armor which he had put on, but even the God of his childhood was never completely forgotten, not to mention the mystery of "grace" to which he repeatedly referred with awe as to a pure gift.

In this connection I quote a confession which reveals Rilke's own doubts as to the ultimate validity of his Orphic formulae, even for himself. It was made on August 22, 1915, in reply to a letter from Ellen Delp, the adopted daughter of the Salomé's, when the first World War was about one year old (*Br. 1914-21*, 75-76). Rilke was in Munich at the time and was engaged in planning all sorts of things, but "with a remarkable lack of confidence" (*Br.* II,48). Soon afterward his pessimism proved justified, for on November 14 he was found fit to bear arms in the *Landsturm*. On January 4, 1916, he was actually incorporated into the Austrian army; what he had dreaded for a long time was now inescapable reality. In her letter to him Ellen Delp had apparently dwelled upon the feelings that had been aroused in her at the sight of some birds, which, attracted by the glare of a lighthouse, found death in the very light they had sought. Rilke admits that what happened to these birds was quite in conformity with the laws of life, and undoubtedly in more normal circumstances he would have found glorifying words in approval of those laws. (Compare his *Sonnet to Orpheus* II,11 about the birds of the Karst.) But now it was different. Caught in anxieties of a most personal and imminent nature he saw the more terrifying aspects of "the other side of life." He found that the fate of these birds was due to "a misunderstanding of the senses [which] causes raptures and deaths merely because there is a thing [the lighthouse] which belongs to the world of man, which in the familiar world of the birds would not occur, ought not to occur, something from their point of view preposterous—a kind of music. The reason why that thing destroys them is because it exists not for them (very much as a ghost would kill us)." And then Rilke proceeds to compare the light-house with God and the birds with mankind, including himself:

"The most horrible thing for me is this, that in our innermost immanences we, too, do not at all become true through realities which are true, but through things which do not belong to us, which are for us nothing but incomprehensible exaggerations of a force that is, as it were, in us only in the form of a question mark and devours us with the power of its overwhelming answer. But of course I know, if you go deep enough, the divine is thinkable only as outside of us, as some such thing as a lighthouse in a space that exceeds ours. And so it would seem that we are faced with the necessity of waiting for the greatest, the utmost of all misunderstandings of which we are capable, in order to perish, jubilantly, in that flame which is the least intelligible and the most fatal: in no less a one. Is that life?"

Katharina Kippenberg quotes Rilke as having said once: "Art is superfluous," and she interprets the despondent mood out of which this confession arose, as meaning that art cannot heal wounds nor take the bitterness out of death. It does not quiet despair, it does not feed the hungry, it does not clothe those who freeze (Kippenberg, 237). Toward the end of his life the "raw material" of suffering caused Rilke to complain to Erika Mitterer that his heart-space was unable to absorb his anguish and that his mental measure was unfit to fathom it. "I who set out to say 'yea' to both life and death, am now stunned by the struggle which is called sickness" (*Br.Mitterer*, 54). But whatever true measure of comfort Rilke may have found in his own world, for the ordinary mortal who must still cope with the situations of the day and, in so doing, "go through the kitchen into the dwelling," (*AW* I,256), his voice in the wilderness can never have the same authentic ring as that of Christ in the Sermon on the Mount. On entering with an open heart into the sanctuary of Rilke's poetry, we can let the fragrance of childhood envelop us and for a while believe with him in the unicorn, that "pure animal which never did exist" and yet, "scarcely in need of being, gently reared its head" in the heart-space of men. "They nourished it not with corn but with the mere possibility that it be. And that gave such strength to the animal that its brow put forth a horn. A single horn. White, it went to a maiden—and was in her silver-mirror and in her" (*Son*.II, 4). Apart from that, it must be left to each one to decide for himself what encouragement he can find in Rilke over and beyond the joy that comes from things beautiful and conducive to thought.

Perhaps we may use the picture of one of his *New Poems* as a simile and compare the edifice of his creation to one of those cathedrals which can be seen in French provincial towns and which his poem depicts (*NG*, 33-34). Quietly it stands in the old folds of its counterforts amidst small houses and shops huddled at its feet, where men and women and children, in constant search of happiness, carry the burden of their days from cradle to grave, and where sweat is traded for pleasures and gold. So close to them stands the cathedral that they scarcely know it is there, though at night, when the shops are closed, they raise their ears and listen upward. For in the foundations of that towering structure there are also hidden throes, and in its rising stones are strength and inspiration; its portals are full of sighs, and everywhere is love like wine and bread. And in its tower, truncated as by renunciation, there is death.

A COMPLETE bibliography of Rilke's published works and of the entire Rilke literature up to 1951 can be found in Walter Ritzer, *Rainer Maria Rilke Bibliographie* (Vienna: O. Kerry, 1951). In addition, 227 titles of translations, articles, and books in English are listed in Richard von Mises, *Rilke in English. A Tentative Bibliography* (Cambridge, Mass.: The Cosmos Press, 1947). In the following list RMR preceding a title indicates that the work is by Rilke.

Albert-Lasard: Lou Albert-Lasard, *Wege mit Rilke*. Frankfurt a.M.: S. Fischer, 1952.

Angelloz: J. F. Angelloz, *Rainer Maria Rilke: L'évolution spirituelle du poète*. Paris: Paul Hartmann, 1936.

AW I, II: RMR, *Ausgewählte Werke*. I, Gedichte; II, Prosa und Übertragungen. Hrsg. vom Rilke-Archiv in Weimar in Verbindung mit Ruth Sieber-Rilke und Carl Sieber durch Ernst Zinn. Insel Verlag, 1950.

Barney: Natalie Clifford Barney, *Aventures de l'esprit*. Paris: Emile-Paul Frères, 1929.

Bassermann: Dieter Bassermann, *Der späte Rilke*. München: Leibniz Verlag, bisher R. Oldenbourg Verlag, 1947.

Bellman: Carl Michael Bellman, *Fredmans Episteln*. Translated from the Swedish by Felix Niedner. Jena: Eugen Diederichs Verlag, 1909.

Belmore: Herbert W. Belmore, *Rilke's Craftsmanship, An Analysis of His Poetic Style*. Oxford: Blackwell, 1954.

Berdyaev: Nicolas Berdyaev, *The Russian Idea*. London: Geoffrey Bles, The Centenary Press, 1947.

Berger: Kurt Berger, *Rainer Maria Rilkes frühe Lyrik. Entwicklungsgeschichtliche Analyse der dichterischen Form*. Marburg a.L.: N.G. Elwert'sche Verlagsbuchhandlung, G. Braun, 1931.

BB: RMR, *Das Buch der Bilder*. Leipzig: Insel, 1935.

Br. I, II: RMR, *Briefe*. I, 1897-1914; II, 1914-1926. Wiesbaden: Insel, 1950.

Br. 1892-1904: RMR, *Briefe aus den Jahren 1892-1904*. Leipzig: Insel, 1939.

Br. 1902-06: RMR, *Briefe aus den Jahren 1902-1906*. Leipzig: Insel, 1930.

Br. 1906-07: RMR, *Briefe aus den Jahren 1906-1907*. Leipzig: Insel, 1930.

Br. 1907-14: RMR, *Briefe aus den Jahren 1907-1914*. Leipzig: Insel, 1939.

Br. 1914-21: RMR, *Briefe aus den Jahren 1914-1921*. Leipzig: Insel, 1938.

Br. Benvenuta: RMR, *Briefwechsel mit Benvenuta*. Hrsg. von Magda von Hattingberg. Esslingen: Bechtle Verlag, 1954.

Br. Dichter: RMR, *Briefe an einen jungen Dichter*. Leipzig: Insel, 1929.

Br. Frau: RMR, *Briefe an eine junge Frau*. Leipzig: Insel-Bücherei No. 409, 1946.

Br. Frühzeit: RMR, *Briefe und Tagebücher aus der Frühzeit, 1899-1902*. Hrsg. von Ruth Sieber-Rilke und Carl Sieber. Leipzig: Insel, 1933.

Br. Kippenberg: *Rainer Maria Rilke—Katharina Kippenberg Briefwechsel*. Wiesbaden: Insel, 1954.

Br. Lou: *Rainer Maria Rilke—Lou Andreas-Salomé Briefwechsel*. Hrsg. von Ernst Pfeiffer. Zürich: Niehans; Wiesbaden: Insel, 1952.

Br. Mitterer: RMR, *Briefwechsel in Gedichten mit Erika Mitterer, 1924-1926*. Wiesbaden: Insel, 1950.

Br. MTT: *Rainer Maria Rilke und Marie von Thurn und Taxis, Briefwechsel*. I, pp. 1-490; II, pp. 492-1034. Zürich: Niehans & Rokitansky; Wiesbaden: Insel, 1951.

Br. Muzot: RMR, *Briefe aus Muzot, 1921-1926*. Leipzig: Insel, 1937.

Br. Nölke: RMR, *Die Briefe an Frau Gudi Nölke*. Wiesbaden: Insel, 1953.

Br. Reisegefährtin: *Briefe an eine Reisegefährtin, Eine Begegnung mit Rilke*. Geschildert von Ulrich Keyn. Wien: Alfred Ibach Verlag, 1947.

Br. Sizzo: RMR, *Die Briefe an die Gräfin Sizzo, 1921-1926*. Leipzig: Insel, 1940.

Br. Verleger: RMR, *Briefe an seinen Verleger, 1906-1926*. Neue erw. Ausg. I, II. Wiesbaden: Insel, 1949.

Br. von Oe: RMR, *Briefe an Baronesse von Oestéren*. New York: Verlag der Johannespresse, 1945.

Brutzer: Sophie Brutzer, *Rilkes Russische Reisen*. Stallupönen (Prusse Orientale): Verlag Klutke, 1934.

BTK: RMR, *Bücher. Theater. Kunst*. Hrsg. Richard von Mises. Vienna: Jahoda und Siegel, 1934.

Buddeberg: Else Buddeberg, *Kunst und Existenz im Spätwerk Rilkes. Eine Darstellung nach seinen Briefen*. Karlsruhe: Stahlberg, 1948.

BVP 1896: RMR, *Briefe, Verse und Prosa aus dem Jahre 1896*. New York: Johannespresse, 1946.

CW: RMR, *Aus dem Nachlass des Grafen C. W. Ein Gedichtkreis*. Wiesbaden: Insel, 1950.

Das Inselschiff: *Das Inselschiff. Dem Gedächtnis Rainer Maria Rilkes*. April 1927, VIII,2. Leipzig: Insel.

DE: RMR, *Duineser Elegien*. (Quotations in this book from the *Duino*

Elegies are taken from *AW* I; references in the text to the *Elegies* are by number.)

Demetz: Peter Demetz, *René Rilkes Prager Jahre*. Düsseldorf: Diederichs, 1953.

Dostoyevsky, A.: Aimée Dostoyevsky, *Fyodor Dostoyevsky: A Study*. London: William Heinemann, 1921.

DuV: *Dichtung und Volkstum. Zeitschrift für Literaturgeschichte*. Hrsg. von Hans Naumann und Hermann Pongs. Weimar, 1934-1945. (Except where otherwise noted, references are to volume 40, 1939.)

EG: RMR, *Erste Gedichte*. New York: Frederick Ungar, n.d.

ESF: RMR, *Erzählungen und Skizzen aus der Frühzeit*. Leipzig: Insel, 1928.

ET: RMR, *Ewald Tragy*. New York: Johannespresse, 1944.

FG: RMR, *Die Frühen Gedichte*. New York: Frederick Ungar, n.d.

Gebser: Hans Gebser, *Rilke und Spanien*. Zürich-New York: Verlag Oprecht, 1940.

Gedichte 1906-26: RMR, *Gedichte 1906 bis 1926*. Hrsg. vom Rilke-Archiv in Verbindung mit Ruth Sieber-Rilke. Wiesbaden: Insel, 1953.

GFS: RMR, *Gedichte in französischer Sprache*. Gesamt-Ausgabe. Wiesbaden; Insel, 1949.

GG: RMR, *Geschichten vom lieben Gott*. 6 Aufl. Leipzig: Insel, 1918.

Gitermann: Valentin Gitermann, *Geschichte Russlands*. 3 Bde. Hamburg: Europäische Verlag Anstalt, 1949.

Hattingberg: Magda von Graedener-Hattingberg, *Rilke und Benvenuta. Ein Buch des Dankes*. Wien: Wilhelm Andermann Verlag, 1943.

Hausmann: Ulrich Hausmann, *Die Apollosonnette Rilkes und ihre plastischen Vorbilder*. Berlin: Verlag Gebr. Mann, 1947.

Heidegger: Martin Heidegger, *Holzwege*. Frankfurt a.M.: Vittorio Klostermann, 1950.

Heller: Erich Heller, *The Disinherited Mind*. Cambridge, Eng.: Bowes and Bowes, 1952.

Hirschfeld: C. Hirschfeld, "Rilke-Erinnerungen Valéry von David-Rhonfelds." In *Die Horen. Monatshefte für Kunst und Dichtung*. Hrsg. von Hanns Martin Elster, Wilhelm von Scholze. V. Jahrg. Heft VIII, 1928-29, pp. 714-721. Berlin: Horen Verlag.

Holthusen: Hans Egon Holthusen, *Der unbehauste Mensch*. München: R. Piper & Co. Verlag, 1952.

JF: RMR, *Journal Florentin de R. M. Rilke*. Traduction de Maurice Betz, avec des illustrations de J. Despierre. Paris: Emile-Paul Frères, 1946.

Kassner, *Chimäre*: Rudolf Kassner, *Die Chimäre. Der Aussätzige*. Leipzig: Insel, 1914.

Kassner, *Elemente*: Rudolf Kassner, *Elemente der menschlichen Grösse*. Leipzig: Insel, 1911.

Kassner, *Erinnerung*: Rudolf Kassner, *Buch der Erinnerung*. Leipzig: Insel, 1938.

Kassner, *Melancholia*: Rudolf Kassner, *Melancholia. Eine Trilogie des Geistes*. 2 Aufl. Leipzig: Insel, 1915.

Kassner, *Zahl*: Rudolf Kassner, *Zahl und Gesicht*. Leipzig: Insel, 1919.

Key: Ellen Key, *Seelen und Werke*. Berlin: S. Fischer, 1911.

Keyserling: Graf Hermann Keyserling, *Das Reisetagebuch eines Philosophen*. 2 Bde. Darmstadt: O. Reichle, 1919.

Kierkegaard, *Gegenwart*: Søren Kierkegaard, *Kritik der Gegenwart*. Übers. von Theodor Haecker. Basel: Hess-Verlag, 1946.

Kierkegaard, *Werke*: Søren Kierkegaard, *Gesammelte Werke*. Übers. von Wolfgang Pfeiderer und Christoph Schrempf. I: *Entweder-Oder*. Hrsg. von Victor Eremita. Jena: Eugen Diederichs Verlag, n.d.

Kippenberg: Katharina Kippenberg, *Rainer Maria Rilke. Ein Beitrag*. 4. Ausg. Zürich: Niehans & Rokitansky, 1948.

Letters 1892-1910: *Letters of Rainer Maria Rilke,* Vol. I, 1892-1910. Tr. Jane Bannard Greene and M. D. Herter Norton. New York: W. W. Norton, 1945.

Letters to Merline: RMR, *Letters to Merline, 1919-1922*. Tr. Violet M. Macdonald. Introduction by J. B. Leishman. London: Methuen & Co., 1951.

Lou, *Lebens.*: Lou Andreas-Salomé, *Lebensrückblick. Grundriss einiger Lebenserinnerungen*. Zürich: Niehans; Wiesbaden: Insel, 1951.

Lou, *Rilke*: Lou Andreas-Salomé, *Rainer Maria Rilke*. Leipzig: Insel, 1928.

LPP: RMR, *Lotte Pritzel. Puppen*. München: Hyperionverlag, 1921.

Magdalena: *Die Liebe der Magdalena*. Ein französischer Sermon gezogen durch den Abbé Joseph Bonnet aus dem Manuskript Q I 14 der Kaiserlichen Bibliothek zu St. Petersburg. Übertragen durch Rainer Maria Rilke. Leipzig: Insel, 1921.

Maritain: Jacques Maritain, *Creative Intuition in Art and Poetry*. Bollingen series XXXV. New York: Pantheon Books, 1953.

Mason, *Lebenshaltung*: Eudo C. Mason. *Lebenshaltung und Symbolik bei Rainer Maria Rilke*. Weimar: Verlag H. Böhlaus Nachf., 1939.

Mason, *Münchhausen*: Eudo C. Mason, *Der Zopf des Münchhausen. Eine Skizze im Hinblick auf Rilke*. Einsiedeln: Johannes Verlag, 1949.

Mead: Margaret Mead, *Male and Female: A Study of the Sexes in a Changing World*. New York: William Morrow, 1949.

Modersohn-Becker: *Briefe und Tagebuchblätter von Paula Modersohn-Becker.* Hrsg. und biographisch eingeführt von S. D. Gallwitz. München: K. Wolff, 1925.

Mövius: Ruth Mövius, *Rainer Maria Rilkes Stundenbuch. Entstehung und Gehalt.* Leipzig: Insel, 1937.

MTT: Fürstin Marie von Thurn und Taxis-Hohenlohe, *Erinnerungen an Rainer Maria Rilke.* 3. Aufl. München-Berlin: R. Oldenbourg, 1937.

NG: RMR, *Neue Gedichte.* Leipzig: Insel, 1935.

Ockel: Gerhard Ockel, *Die Heilung des kranken Mönches. Betrachtungen über ein Gedicht aus Rainer Maria Rilkes Stundenbuch.* Berlin: Falken-Verlag E. Sieber, 1949.

Phia: Phia Rilke, *Ephemeriden.* Neu hrsg. und mit einem Essay versehen von Wolfgang Schneditz. 1. Aufl. Graz: Verlag Jos. A. Kienreich, 1949.

Réau: Louis Réau, L'Art Russe. I: *Des Origines à Pierre le Grand*; II: *De Pierre le Grand à Nos Jours.* Sous le patronage de l'Institut d'Etudes Slaves de Paris, 1921, 1922.

Rec.: "Reconnaissance à Rilke." In *Les Cahiers du Mois,* 23-24. Paris, 1926.

Rehm, *Kierkegaard*: Walter Rehm, *Kierkegaard und der Verführer.* München: Verlag Hermann Rinn, 1949.

Rehm, *Rilke*: Walter Rehm, *Rilke und die Duse.* Freiburg-München: Karl Alber, n.d.

Rilke et Merline: *Rainer Maria Rilke et Merline. Correspondance 1920-1926.* Ed par Dieter Bassermann. Zürich: Max Niehans, 1954.

Rilke-Gide: *Rainer Maria Rilke—André Gide, Correspondance 1909-1926.* Introduction et Commentaires par Renée Lang. Paris: Corréa, 1952.

Rodin: RMR, *Auguste Rodin.* Leipzig: Insel, 1934.

Rudolf Kassner: *Rudolf Kassner zum achtzigsten Geburtstag.* Hrsg. von A. Cl. Kensik und D. Bodmer. Gedenkbuch. Winterthur, Switzerland: Eugen Rentsch Verlag, 1953.

St. Augustine: *Basic Writings of St. Augustine.* 2 vols. Edited with an introduction and notes by Whitney J. Oates. New York: Random House, 1948.

Salis: J. R. von Salis, *Rainer Maria Rilkes Schweizer Jahre* 2. Aufl. Frauenfeld-Leipzig: Huber & Co., 1938.

Schmidt-Pauli: Elisabeth von Schmidt-Pauli, *Rainer Maria Rilke. Ein Gedenkbuch.* Basel: Benno Schwabe Verlag, 1940.

Schnack: Ingeborg Schnack, *Rainer Maria Rilkes Erinnerungen an Marburg und das hessische Land.* Marburg: N. G. Elwert Verlag, n.d.

SG: RMR, *Späte Gedichte*. Leipzig: Insel, 1934.

Sieber: Carl Sieber, *René Rilke. Die Jugend Rainer Maria Rilkes*. Leipzig: Insel, 1932.

Sievers: Marianne Sievers, *Die biblischen Motive in der Dichtung Rainer Maria Rilkes*. Berlin: Verlag Dr. Emil Ebering, 1938.

Silvaire-Vigée: *Rainer Maria Rilke*. Translations and Essays Collected by André Silvaire and Claude Vigée. Paris: Librairie des Lettres, 1952.

Simenauer: Erich Simenauer, *Rainer Maria Rilke: Legende und Mythos*. Bern: Haupt, 1953.

So lass: RMR, . . . *so lass ich mich zu träumen gehen*. Letters to Benvenuta, with a foreword by Rudolf von Jouanne. Gmunden-Bad Ischl: Buchhandlung und Verlag J. Mader, 1949.

Son. I, II: (This abbreviation refers to the two parts of the *Sonnets to Orpheus*. In each part the sonnets are numbered.)

Stundenbuch: RMR, *Das Stundenbuch*. (References in the text to *Das Stundenbuch* are from *AW* I.)

SW: RMR, *Selected Works*. Volume I, Prose. Translated by G. Craig Houston, with an introduction by J. B. Leishman. London: The Hogarth Press, 1954. (This work contains the "Essay on Dolls.")

Trakl: Georg Trakl, *Nachlass und Biographie*. Ed. Wolfgang Schneditz. Salzburg: Otto Müller Verlag, 1949.

VPN: RMR, *Verse und Prosa aus dem Nachlass*. Leipzig: Elfte Jahresgabe der Gesellschaft der Freunde der Deutschen Bücherei, 1929.

Wydenbruck: Nora Wydenbruck, *Rilke, Man and Poet: A Biographical Study*. London: John Lehmann, 1949.

Zinn: Ernst Zinn, "Rainer Maria Rilke und die Antike." In *Antike und Abendland. Beiträge zum Verständnis der Griechen und Römer und ihres Nachlebens*. Hrsg. von Bruno Snell. Bd. III, pp. 201-251. Hamburg, 1948.

BIBLIOGRAPHY

*Selected English Translations
from the Work of Rainer Maria Rilke*

Correspondence in Verse with Erika Mitterer. German text with an English translation by N. B. Cruickshank. Introduction by J. B. Leishman. London: The Hogarth Press, 1953.

Duineser Elegien. Elegies from the Castle of Duino. Translated by V. Sackville-West. London: The Hogarth Press, 1931.

Duineser Elegien. The Elegies of Duino. Translated by Nora Wydenbruck. Vienna: Amandus, 1948.

Duino Elegies. The German text, with an English Translation, Introduction, and Commentary by J. B. Leishman and Stephen Spender. London: The Hogarth Press, 1939.

Fifty Selected Poems. With English translations by C. F. MacIntyre. Berkeley: University of California Press, 1940.

Five Pieces of Prose. Translated by Carl Niemeyer. Cummington, Mass.: Cummington Press, 1947. (This work contains the "Essay on Dolls.")

From the Remains of Count C. W. Translation and Introduction by J. B. Leishman. London: The Hogarth Press, 1952.

The Journal of My Other Self. Translated by M. D. Herter Norton and John Linton. New York: W. W. Norton & Co., 1930.

Later Poems. Translated, with an Introduction and Commentary by J. B. Leishman. London: The Hogarth Press, 1938.

Letters to Benvenuta. Translated by Heinz Norden, with a Foreword by Louis Untermeyer. London: The Hogarth Press, 1953.

Letters to Frau Gudi Nölke during His Life in Switzerland. Edited, with an Epilogue and Notes by Paul Obermüller. Translated from the German by Violet M. Macdonald. London: The Hogarth Press, 1955.

Letters to a Young Poet. Translated by M. D. Herter Norton. New York: W. W. Norton & Co., 1934.

Letters to Merline, 1919-1922. Translated by Violet M. Macdonald. Introduction by J. B. Leishman. London: Methuen & Co., 1951.

The Life of the Virgin Mary. Translated, with an Introduction and

Notes by C. F. MacIntyre. Berkeley and Los Angeles: University of California Press, 1947.

The Notebook of Malte Laurids Brigge. Translated by John Linton. London: The Hogarth Press, 1930.

Poems. Translated by J. B. Leishman. Published by Leonard and Virginia Woolf. London: The Hogarth Press, 1934.

Poems. Translated by Jesse Lemont. New York: Columbia University Press, 1943.

Poems from The Book of Hours. "Das Stundenbuch." Translated by Babette Deutsch. Norfolk, Conn.: New Directions, 1941.

Requiem and Other Poems. Translated, with an Introduction by J. B. Leishman. London: The Hogarth Press, 1935.

Rodin. Translated by Jesse Lemont and Hans Trausil. New York: Fine Editions Press, 1945.

Selected Letters, 1902-1926. Translated by R. F. C. Hull. London: Macmillan & Co., 1946.

Selected Poems. Translated by J. B. Leishman. London: The Hogarth Press, 1941.

Selected Poems. Translated by Ruth Spiers. Cairo: The Anglo-Egyptian Bookshop, n.d. (about 1943).

Sonnets to Orpheus. The German text, with an English Translation, Introduction, and Notes by J. B. Leishman. London: The Hogarth Press, 1936.

Sonnets to Orpheus. Translated by M. D. Herter Norton. New York: W. W. Norton & Co., 1942.

Sonnets to Orpheus. Duino Elegies. Translated by Jesse Lemont. New York: Fine Editions Press, 1945.

Stories of God. Translated by M. D. Herter Norton and Nora Purtscher-Wydenbruck. New York: W. W. Norton & Co., 1932.

The Tale of the Love and Death of Cornet Christopher Rilke. Translated by M. D. Herter Norton. New York: W. W. Norton & Co., 1932.

Thirty-One Poems by Rainer Maria Rilke in English Versions, with an Introduction by Ludwig Lewisohn. New York: B. Ackermann, 1946.

Translations from the Poetry of Rainer Maria Rilke. By M. D. Herter Norton. New York: W. W. Norton & Co., 1938.

Wartime Letters, 1914-1921. Translated by M. D. Herter Norton. New York: W. W. Norton & Co., 1940.

Works in English on Rilke

Bowra, C. M. *The Heritage of Symbolism.* New York and London: The Macmillan Co., 1943, pp. 56-97.

Butler, E. M. *Rainer Maria Rilke.* Cambridge, Eng.: Cambridge University Press, 1946.

Daniel-Rops, Henry. *Where Angels Pass.* Translated from the French by E. Craufurd. London: Cassell and Co., 1950.

Hartman, Geoffrey H. *The Unmediated Vision: An Interpretation of Wordsworth, Hopkins, Rilke, and Valéry.* New Haven: Yale University Press, 1954, pp. 69-97.

Hattingberg, Magda von. *Rilke and Benvenuta: A Book of Thanks.* Translated by Cyrus Brooks. London: William Heinemann, 1942.

Heerikhuizen, F. W. *Rainer Maria Rilke: His Life and Work.* Translated from the Dutch by F. G. Reiner and A. Cliff. London: Routledge and Kegan Paul, 1951.

Holthusen, Hans Egon. *Rainer Maria Rilke: A Study of His Later Poetry.* Translated by J. B. Stern. Cambridge, Eng.: Bowes & Bowes, 1952.

Mason, Eudo C. *Rilke's Apotheosis: A Survey of Representative Recent Publications on the Work of R. M. Rilke.* Oxford: Oxford University Press, 1938.

Olivero, F. *Rainer Maria Rilke: A Study in Poetry and Mysticism.* Translated from the Italian. Cambridge, Eng.: W. Heffer & Sons, 1931.

Rose, W. *Rainer Maria Rilke: Aspects of His Mind and Poetry.* Edited by William Rose and G. Craig Houston, with an Introduction by Stefan Zweig. London: Sidgwick & Jackson, 1938.

Salinger, Herman. *An Index to the Poems of Rainer Maria Rilke.* Madison: University of Wisconsin Press, 1942.

Wydenbruck, Nora. *Rilke, Man and Poet: A Biographical Study.* London: John Lehmann, 1949.

(A separate index of Rilke's works follows the main index)

POEMS AND WORKS BY RILKE
Titles (in italics) or first lines